Sugar Snips & Asparagus Tips

Woman's Auxiliary, Infant Welfare Society of Chicago

A special thank you to the members of the Woman's Auxiliary of the Infant Welfare Society of Chicago and the Chicago celebrities, who generously shared their favorite recipes, and to the food consultants, who enhanced the cookbook with their culinary knowledge.

For additional copies, use the order forms at the back of the book or write:

Sugar Snips & Asparagus Tips
2751 North Clybourn
Chicago, IL 60614
(312) 929-7720

Library of Congress
Catalog Card Number
91-073756

ISBN 0-9630199-0-2 $22.95

Printed in United States of America
American Printers & Lithographers, Inc.

Designer
Kathleen Sullivan Kaska

Published by
Woman's Auxiliary
Infant Welfare Society of Chicago

*I*n 1911, The Chicago Milk Commission joined with the Children's Hospital Society to combat the city's spiraling infant mortality rate. The new organization was named the Infant Welfare Society of Chicago and its mission was to provide well baby care and to instruct mothers how to feed and care for their infants.

One of the individuals dedicated to Infant Welfare's mission was my uncle, Philip D. Armour. As President of Infant Welfare from 1929 to 1948 and a business man, he believed not only in the organization's ability to reduce mental and physical suffering but also in its economic significance to Chicago in terms of human lives and potential. He realized that prevention and early treatment made sound fiscal sense.

Today, the Infant Welfare Society operates pediatric, dental and gynecological clinics and a Home Based Visiting Program at the Philip D. Armour Child and Family Center in Chicago. The services continue to expand every year as does the demand for high quality, preventive and affordable health care. I am proud to continue my family's history of involvement with Infant Welfare by supporting this cookbook which will help fund the increased operating expenses from the organization's most recent plans for expansion.

Vernon Armour

TABLE OF CONTENTS

Publishing Information

Designer
Kathleen Sullivan Kaska
Burson-Marsteller/Chicago

Photographer
Laurie Rubin Photography
Chicago, Illinois

Consultants:

Cheese
Tommy Verboncouer, Vice President Sales
Superfresh, Dairy Service for Fine Restaurants
Glen Ellyn, Illinois

Produce
Sue Ashton-Becker, Executive Chef Dominick's
Finer Foods, Inc.
Northlake, Illinois

Wine
Anthony Terlato
Paterno Imports
Chicago, Illinois

Printer
American Printers & Lithographers, Inc.
Chicago, Illinois

Typesetting
Gail Kernes
Dona Kight
Chicago, Illinois

Color Separations
L. A. Filmco, Inc.
Burbank, California

Binding
Nicholstone Book Bindery
Nashville, Tennessee

Warehouse & Office
W. E. O'Neil Construction Co.
Chicago, Illinois

Special Acknowledgements
Daniel A. Kaczmarek

Kathleen Sullivan Kaska

Land O'Frost
Lansing, Illinois

Marshall Fields

William E. O'Neil, II

The Quaker Oats Company

Laurie Rubin

Whitman Corporation Foundation
Chicago, Illinois

Chairmen and Committee Members

Chairman Vivian J. Kaczmarek
Design Kathleen Sullivan Kaska
Computer Editor Barbara Westover
Recipes Linda Celesia
Celebrity Recipes Nanci John McKeon
Testing Barbara Buikema
Food Editors Nancy Eichler, Rosalind V. Hodgkins
Line Editor Judi Thomas
Marketing Nancy Davis, Madeleine McMullan
Pre-Publication Sales Susan Perkins, Peg Deaton
Retail Sales Susan Strachan
Wholesale Sales Cynthia Reasor Swinson
Special Sales Sylvia Allen Kinney
Promotion Lynn Cloud, Fran Ferrazzano,
    Diane Jacobson, Minnie Sandstedt
Distribution Laurie Wiesemann, Joan Conway
Secretary Nancy Petkunas
Corresponding Secretary Ruth McElwain
Treasurer Alison Deniston

Auxiliary President Suzanne Murin
Auxiliary Coordinator Leslie Wells Holling

Committee Members

Barbara Benezra	Syndee Link
Joan Blackburn	Jeanine Parkhurst Lopez
Bev Brand	Suzanne Maviano
Paula Brennan	Linda Meierdierks
Mel Brown	Ginny Munson
Linda Bussey	Denise O'Leary
Mary Lou Cesca	Janet O'Neil
Nancy Dee	Char Pankros
Ann Devine	Grace Ann Parkhurst
Rosemary Dignan	Barbara Purdy
Gloria Duarte	Joann Raber
Jane Elsner	Charlotte Shestokas
Lucille Facchini	Mary Jane Scheel
Nancy Gmitro	Nicolene Shields
Diane Gruber	Vera Smith
Judy Herman	Mary Ann Stitak
June Hocter	Penny Van Horn
Mary Ann Howie	Karen Victor
Antje Kalov	

"No one is denied care

because of inability to pay."

*T*he mission of the Infant Welfare Society of Chicago is to provide for the healthy physical and mental development of disadvantaged children in order to give them a foundation for a future productive and wholesome life. This commitment thrives after eighty years of serving indigent children and women.

In addition to pediatric, gynecological, dental and social work programs, we operate a Teen Clinic to meet the increasing needs of adolescent boys and girls for medical care, health information and psychological counseling. Other services include laboratory screening and testing, pediatric cardiology, vision and hearing screening, nutrition counseling and a learning-through-play program.

The Woman's Auxiliary, composed of 34 Centers and a membership of more than 1,200 volunteers, provides regular volunteer and financial support to the Infant Welfare Society. The Auxiliary has conceived and managed many projects that greatly benefit Infant Welfare's patients, including a food pantry, thrift shop, sewing classes, children's field trips, and Christmas Stockings to name a few.

The dedication of the Woman's Auxiliary to Infant Welfare's mission is demonstrated by their competence and creativity in this fine cookbook. Sugar Snips & Asparagus Tips represents the collective efforts of the Auxiliary to support Infant Welfare's commitment to a child's healthy development.

APPETIZERS

Cold Appetizers

Antipasto Terrine 21
Asparagus Canapés 22
Avocado Caviar Pie 24
Chutney Party Pinwheels 22
Eggs Paté 22
Goat Cheese Pancakes 25
Greek Cucumbers with Yogurt 25
Marinated Dilled Shrimp in
    Cabbage "Mum" 24
Marinated Mushrooms and
    Artichokes with Mozzarella 23
Mousse of Bay Scallops 23
Roasted Red Peppers
    and Scamorza Cheese 21
Salmon Tartare Pie
    with Cucumber Sauce 27
Sesame Asparagus 31

Cold Spreads

Chicken Liver Paté 34
Herb Cheese Spread 35
Mushroom Nut Paté 35
Salmon Paté 34
Shrimp Paste 33

Cold Dips

Salsa Verde 37
Spicy Salsa 36
Tuna Tapenade 37
Vegetable Spinach Dip 38
Water Chestnut Dip 37

Hot Appetizers

Artichoke Cream Ramekins
    with Rich Tomato Sauce 26
Artichoke Puff Pastry 28
Clam Fritters 25
Clams Casino 26
Cocktail Meatballs
    with Green Olives 28
Crostini Con Broccoli Italiano 27
Lamb Shish Kebab 33
Molletes 31
Mushroom Palmiers 30
Mustard-Ham Bites 29
Phyllo Spinach Diamonds 32
Sesame Chicken Wings 29
Shrimp in Beer 33
Skillet Sombrero Pie 30
Taco Tartlets 36
Tiropita (Baked Cheese Pie) 31

Hot Dips

Bread Pot Fondue 38
Chiles Rellenos Casserole 32
Simply Elegant Artichokes 32

Hot Spreads

Baked Pecan Brie 36
Vegetable Brie 35

Snips & Tips

Cheese 243
Crudités for Dipping 237
Fruit 241

A N T I P A S T O   T E R R I N E

2 8-ounce packages cream cheese
¼ cup freshly grated Parmesan
    cheese
2 cloves garlic, minced
1½ teaspoons chopped fresh basil
½ teaspoon good quality olive oil
½ cup chopped toasted almonds
6 thin slices provolone cheese
8 thin slices mozzarella cheese
6 slices prosciutto

In food processor work bowl, mix cream cheese, Parmesan cheese, garlic, basil, salt and pepper. Refrigerate for 6 to 12 hours.

Oil bottom and sides of an 8x4-inch loaf pan; line with wax paper or plastic wrap that has also been brushed with oil.

Bring cream cheese mixture to room temperature. Reserve ½ cup of mixture for later use.

Place 2 to 3 slices of provolone cheese to cover bottom of loaf pan; spread ⅓ cup cream cheese mixture over provolone. Next arrange ¼ cup almonds on cream cheese. Spread additional 3 tablespoons of cream cheese carefully over almonds. Place 4 slices of mozzarella as next layer. Again carefully cover with 3 tablespoons of cream cheese. The next layer is 2 to 3 slices of prosciutto; spread with 2 tablespoons cream cheese.

Repeat layers; ending with prosciutto. Do not top with cream cheese! Cover and refrigerate loaf for at least 12 hours. Bring terrine and ½ cup of reserved cream cheese mixture to room temperature before serving. Lift the terrine out of loaf pan and remove wax paper. Frost loaf with the reserve cream cheese.

Thinly slice and serve with Italian bread, crackers or cocktail rye bread.

R O A S T E D   R E D   P E P P E R S   A N D
S C A M O R Z A   C H E E S E

12 red bell peppers
1 pound fresh scamorza cheese,
    sliced
¼ cup olive oil
1 clove garlic, peeled and chopped
¼ cup chopped Italian parsley

Preheat oven to 425°.

Place whole bell peppers on baking sheet.

Bake for 1½ hours. Peel, core and seed peppers; drain all liquid.

Slice peppers and arrange on a platter with alternating slices of scamorza cheese. Add chopped garlic to the olive oil and drizzle over the pepper/cheese arrangement. Sprinkle with chopped parsley. Serve with thin slices of Italian bread.

4 to 6 servings

ASPARAGUS CANAPÉS

1 loaf very thin sliced white bread
1 8-ounce package cream cheese,
    softened
1 4-ounce package bleu cheese
1 tablespoon mayonnaise
1 egg, beaten
20 fresh asparagus spears,
    steamed until crisp tender
1 cup butter, melted

Trim crust from bread and roll flat. In food processor work bowl, process cheeses, mayonnaise and egg until smooth. Spread on bread. Place an asparagus spear on bread. Roll up jelly roll fashion, dip in butter and wrap in plastic wrap. Freeze. Cut frozen rolls into thirds. Refreeze.

Preheat oven to 400°. Place rolls on cookie sheet. Bake for 15 minutes.

CHUTNEY PARTY PINWHEELS

2 8-ounce packages Neufchâtel
    cheese, softened
4 ounces cheddar cheese or
    English Cheshire, shredded
2 scallions, minced
1 tablespoon curry powder
½ cup diced celery
¼ teaspoon salt
4 tablespoons dry sherry
4 12-inch tortillas
Chutney, chopped

In a bowl, combine Neufchâtel, cheddar cheese, scallions, curry, celery, salt and sherry. Mix well. Spread even layer on tortillas. Top with a thin layer of chutney. Roll up jelly roll fashion and wrap tightly in plastic wrap. Chill at least 2 hours.

When ready to serve cut off ends and cut rolls into 1-inch slices.

36 servings

EGGS PATÉ

6 hard cooked eggs
1 12-ounce can paté de foie gras
2 tablespoons mayonnaise

Cut eggs in half lengthwise. Scoop out the yolks and set aside. Fill whites with paté. Arrange on serving plate. Cover each egg with 1 teaspoon mayonnaise. Put yolks through a sieve and sprinkle over eggs.

4 servings

MARINATED MUSHROOMS AND ARTICHOKES WITH MOZZARELLA

Vinaigrette Marinade:
1 cup safflower or corn oil
¼ cup tarragon vinegar or wine
vinegar
¼ cup fresh lemon juice
¼ teaspoon dry mustard
1 clove garlic, minced
1 green onion, chopped
1 teaspoon salt-free seasoning
2 tablespoons chopped fresh tarragon
½ teaspoon oregano
2 leaves chopped fresh basil
1 tablespoon chopped fresh parsley
8 ounces to 1 pound fresh mushroom
caps, wiped
1 package frozen artichoke hearts,
cooked
1 small jar pimiento
Mozzarella cheese substitute

Garnish:
Green onions, chopped

Vinaigrette Marinade: Several days in advance, whisk in a small bowl the oil, vinegar, lemon juice, dry mustard, garlic, onion, salt-free seasoning, tarragon, oregano, basil and parsley until well mixed.

Variation: Substitute 2 teaspoons dried tarragon and 1 teaspoon dried parsley for fresh herbs.

Marinate fresh mushroom caps, artichoke hearts and pimiento in marinade overnight in the refrigerator. Flavors ripen the longer marinated.

Before serving, toss with cubed mozzarella cheese substitute, sprinkle with salt-free seasoning and additional chopped green onions.

MOUSSE OF BAY SCALLOPS

1½ to 2 pounds scallops,
rinsed and dried
2 cups whipping cream
Salt and freshly ground pepper
Whole basil leaves

Preheat oven to 325°.

Line bottom of small soufflé dish with whole fresh basil leaves.

In food processor work bowl, process scallops; add whipping cream, season with salt and pepper; puree until smooth. Pour into prepared mold. Place mold in a water bath.

Bake for 15 minutes, or until knife, inserted in center, comes out clean.

MARINATED DILLED SHRIMP
IN CABBAGE "MUM"

Marinade:
⅔ cup extra virgin olive oil
¼ cup white or red wine vinegar
¼ cup Dijon mustard
1 clove garlic, pressed or very
*   finely chopped*
2 tablespoons chopped fresh dill
2 teaspoons finely minced
*   fresh ginger*
2 tablespoons chopped shallots
½ teaspoon sugar
Salt and freshly ground pepper

1½ pounds shrimp, cooked, peeled
*   and deveined*
1 head red or green cabbage

Marinade: Whisk olive oil, vinegar, mustard, garlic, dill, ginger, shallots, sugar, salt and pepper in small bowl. Add shrimp to mixture and marinate at least 24 hours in refrigerator. Mix a few times. This can be done up to 2 days in advance.

Cabbage "Mum": Trim stem end of cabbage, so cabbage will sit flat. Make intersecting cuts, through the top center of cabbage, ¾ of the way down the head of cabbage, until you cannot cut anymore. Immerse cabbage in ice water in non-metallic container. Cover and refrigerate overnight.

When ready to use, remove cabbage from water, drain and position on serving tray. Place shrimp on long skewers and stick into cabbage "mum".

AVOCADO CAVIAR PIE

5 ripe avocados, peeled and mashed
*   not pureed*
2 tablespoons fresh lemon juice
½ teaspoon unflavored gelatin
6 eggs, hard boiled and coarsely
*   chopped*
3 tablespoons melted butter
1 8-ounce package cream cheese,
*   softened*
1 cup chopped scallions
2 tablespoons red pepper sauce
1 14-ounce can red lumpfish caviar,
*   drained in fine sieve for 2 hours*
1 24-ounce container sour cream
1 7-ounce black lumpfish caviar,
*   drained in fine sieve for 2 hours*

Lightly oil an 8-inch diameter springform pan.

First Layer: Dissolve gelatin in lemon juice and mix thoroughly with avocados. Spread mixture in bottom of prepared pan. Chill for 1 hour.

Second Layer: Drizzle melted butter over chopped eggs and toss gently. Cover avocado layer with eggs. Melted butter sets egg layer. Chill 1 hour.

Third Layer: Combine cream cheese, scallions and red pepper sauce and gently spread over egg layer. Chill 1 hour.

Fourth Layer: Spread red caviar over cream cheese. Chill 1 hour.

Fifth Layer: Spread sour cream over red caviar.
Pie can be made up to this point 1 day in advance.
Before serving, gently slide a knife around the edges of pan to loosen and carefully unmold. Spread black caviar on top of pie leaving border around edges to show sour cream. Apply black caviar last to avoid staining.

Garnish with lemon twists around pie. Serve on pumpernickel or rye cocktail rounds.

50 servings for hors d'oeuvres

TZATZIKI (GREEK CUCUMBERS WITH YOGURT)

1 pint plain low-fat yogurt
2 small cloves garlic, finely minced
2 tablespoons good quality olive oil
Lemon juice to taste
Salt and freshly ground pepper
2 cucumbers, peeled, seeded and
    finely chopped
Loaf of Greek bread, cut in
    small pieces

Line a bowl with cheesecloth; spoon yogurt onto cheesecloth. Tie to form a bag and allow the yogurt to drain into a bowl. Refrigerate 2 hours.

Remove cheesecloth; place drained yogurt in mixing bowl. Add garlic, olive oil, lemon juice, salt and pepper to taste, mixing well. Add cucumbers.

Serve with bread.

Variation: Italian bread may be substituted for Greek bread.

6 servings

GOAT CHEESE PANCAKES

6 eggs
1¼ cups all-purpose flour
½ teaspoon sugar
3 tablespoons sour cream
7 ounces goat cheese
2 tablespoon butter, divided

Garnish:
Smoked salmon, sour cream
    and golden caviar

Whip eggs gently; add flour and sugar. Add sour cream and crumble goat cheese into mixture. Add 1 tablespoon melted butter and stir gently. If batter is too thick, add sour cream. If batter is too thin, add flour.

In a large skillet, melt 1 tablespoon butter over medium heat. Pour pancake mix into 3-inch circles and cook.

Garnish with thinly sliced smoked salmon, sour cream and golden caviar.

10 servings

CLAM FRITTERS

1 cup all-purpose flour
¼ teaspoon salt
⅛ teaspoon freshly ground pepper
2 eggs, beaten
¼ cup milk
¼ cup clam juice
1 teaspoon vegetable oil
1 dozen clams, cleaned and chopped
Oil for frying

Sift flour, salt and pepper into a large bowl. Add eggs, milk and clam juice, mix until smooth. Add oil and clams.

Drop by tablespoons in deep hot oil and fry about 5 minutes turning once or until browned. Drain on paper towels. Serve immediately. Do not freeze.

ARTICHOKE CREAM RAMEKINS
WITH RICH TOMATO SAUCE

Rich Tomato Sauce:
1 medium onion, chopped
2 tablespoons olive oil
2 28-ounce cans Italian plum
*   tomatoes with juice*
2 cloves garlic, minced

Artichoke Ramekins:
2 10-ounce packages frozen
*   artichoke hearts*
2 tablespoons fresh lemon juice
4 eggs
1 cup whipping cream
½ cup freshly grated Parmesan
*   cheese*

Rich Tomato Sauce: In a large saucepan, cook onion in olive oil until soft and golden. Puree tomatoes in blender and add to onion and oil. Add garlic, stir and simmer gently, uncovered, until thickened, about 2 hours.

Artichoke Ramekins: Preheat oven to 325°. Butter 8²/₃-cup ramekins.

Cook artichoke hearts according to package directions, adding lemon juice during cooking. Drain, coarsely chop and divided among ramekins.

Combine eggs, cream and cheese in blender or food processor. Process until smooth. Pour over chopped artichoke hearts, ¾ full. Place ramekins in a large roasting pan. Fill roasting pan halfway to two-thirds from top of ramekins with hot water.

Bake 35 to 40 minutes until set. Cool slightly; unmold on plates and top with warm Rich Tomato Sauce.

8 ramekins

CLAMS CASINO

1 18 to 20-ounce can minced clams,
*   drained (save liquid)*
1 cup butter, divided
1 cup coarse flavored bread crumbs
2 8-ounce cans water chestnuts,
*   finely chopped*
4 ounces chipped ham (chopped) or
*   ½ pound bacon, crumbled*
Salt and freshly ground pepper
Paprika

Preheat oven to 350°.

Drain clams, reserving half the liquid. Set aside ¼ cup melted butter. Mix remaining ¾ cup melted butter, minced clams, bread crumbs, water chestnuts and chipped ham or bacon. Add salt and pepper to taste. Let stand 5 minutes.

Divide mixture among 4 individual serving shells. Drizzle with remaining ¼ cup melted butter.

Bake for 15 to 25 minutes.

Hint: If frozen before baking, let stand at room temperature for 2 hours before placing in oven.

SALMON TARTARE PIE WITH CUCUMBER SAUCE

2 pounds fresh salmon, center cut
2 large bunches fresh dill, chopped
1/4 cup kosher salt
1/4 cup sugar
2 tablespoons freshly ground pepper

Cucumber Sauce:
1/3 cucumber, seeded, grated
   and drained
2 teaspoons minced onion
1/4 cup mayonnaise
1 cup sour cream (may substitute
   1/2 cup plain, nonfat yogurt)
2 tablespoons white wine vinegar
2 tablespoons minced fresh parsley

Place 1/2 salmon skin-side down in a deep glass baking dish. Spread dill and spices on salmon; top with remaining salmon slice. Cover and weigh evenly. Refrigerate 48 to 72 hours. Turn and baste every 12 hours.

Cucumber Sauce: In a small bowl, mix cucumber, onion, mayonnaise, sour cream, vinegar, and parsley. Cover and refrigerate. Serve cold.

When ready to serve, scrape seasonings off salmon and pat dry. Either slice thinly and serve with lemon or dice salmon small and serve in dish with toast points for hors d'oeuvres. Accompany with Cucumber Sauce.

CROSTINI CON BROCCOLI ITALIANO

1 pound fresh broccoli
1 to 2 cloves garlic
1/2 teaspoon fresh lemon juice
2 teaspoons salt-free seasoning
1 tablespoon dry red wine vinegar
Freshly ground pepper, to taste
3 to 4 tablespoons olive oil
French bread rounds, toasted

Garnish:
Walnut halves

Steam broccoli and cook until tender. Drain and pat dry.
In food processor work bowl, add broccoli, garlic, lemon juice, salt-free seasoning and vinegar. Process until smooth, stopping machine and scraping bowl occasionally. With machine running, pour 3 to 4 tablespoons olive oil through the feed tube in a slow steady stream and continue mixing until as smooth as possible, scraping down sides of work bowl, as necessary. Blend in pepper. (Puree can be prepared up to one day ahead and refrigerated.)
Use pastry bag with star point or spread on bread rounds. Garnish with walnut halves.

COCKTAIL MEATBALLS WITH GREEN OLIVES

18 to 20 pimiento stuffed large
    green olives
1 pound ground lean beef
¼ cup water
2 tablespoons butter
½ 10-ounce package frozen chopped
    spinach, cooked, drained
Light vegetable oil
2 eggs
¼ cup bread crumbs
2 tablespoons grated Romano cheese
Fresh parsley, chopped
Salt and freshly ground pepper
Flour
1 egg, beaten, plus 1 tablespoon
    water
Fine bread crumbs

Remove pimiento from green olives and reserve. Soak olives in water to remove salt; change water several times. Begin at open end of olive and cut olive in a spiral fashion; set aside.

In a large skillet, melt butter; add water. Brown beef in skillet until dry; add cooked spinach. Remove from heat and allow mixture to cool.

Preheat light oil in deep fryer or heavy saucepan to 375°.

Chop reserved pimiento, add with 2 eggs, bread crumbs, cheese, and parsley to beef mixture. Blend well and add salt and pepper to taste.

Form appetizer-size meatballs and wind with spiral cut olives. Roll meatballs in flour; then egg; then bread crumbs.

Fry for approximately 2 minutes in preheated oil until golden brown. Drain on paper towels. Serve with toothpicks. May be cooked in advance and reheated in the oven.

18 to 20 servings

ARTICHOKE PUFF PASTRY

2 to 4 tablespoons butter or
    margarine
32 or more medium firm
    mushroom caps
1 cup canned, drained chopped
    artichoke hearts
½ to 1 cup crumbled bleu cheese,
    or to taste
1 package frozen puff pastry, thawed
    according to package directions
Salt and freshly ground pepper

Preheat oven to 375°.

Wipe mushroom caps with damp paper towels and remove stems. In a large skillet, melt butter and sauté mushroom caps for 2 to 3 minutes. Drain on paper towels. Mix chopped artichoke hearts and bleu cheese and spoon into mushrooms.

On a lightly floured surface, roll 1 sheet of puff pastry to a 16-inch square. With a sharp knife, cut into 32 4-inch squares.

Working with one square at a time, place a filled mushroom cap in the center, filled side down. Brush edges with water and bring corners together to enclose mushroom completely and seal. Put seam side down on baking sheet.

Bake for 15 to 20 minutes, or until puffed and golden.

These puffs may be frozen. Thaw before cooking or cook a little longer.

32 appetizers

MUSTARD-HAM BITES

1¼ cups flour
1 tablespoon baking powder
8 tablespoons unsalted butter, cold,
    cut into 8 pieces
2 tablespoons shortening
1¼ cups finely chopped ham
¼ cup finely chopped green onions
½ cup grated Romano cheese
⅓ cup milk
3 tablespoons mayonnaise
3 tablespoons prepared mustard,
    of choice

Preheat oven to 375°. Grease 2 baking sheets.

In food processor work bowl, mix flour and baking powder. Add butter and shortening, mix until the size of coarse meal. Add ham, green onions and Romano cheese. Mix until blended. Add milk and mix until dough holds together.

Shape dough into 1-inch balls. Place on prepared baking sheets. With a wet finger, press an indentation into the center of each ball.

Bake for 10 minutes. Remove from oven and with handle of a wooden spoon, press indentations again.

Bake an additional 10 minutes or until golden.

In a small bowl, mix mayonnaise and mustard. Fill center of indentations with mixture.

Bake for 3 to 5 minutes.

Hint: Biscuits may be frozen prior to adding mayonnaise/mustard mixture. Defrost and reheat at 375° for 5 to 10 minutes or until heated through.

42 biscuits

SESAME CHICKEN WINGS

2½ pounds chicken wings, separated
    at joints (discard tips)

Marinade:
½ cup soy sauce
½ teaspoon rosemary
½ cup ketchup
1 clove garlic, minced
3 thin slices onion
2 tablespoons vegetable oil
¼ cup white wine
¼ cup red wine
¼ teaspoon dry mustard
½ teaspoon Worcestershire sauce
Sesame seeds

Place chicken wings in a large glass bowl.

Marinade: In blender, combine soy sauce, rosemary, ketchup, garlic, onion, vegetable oil, white wine, red wine, dry mustard, and Worcestershire sauce. Blend well. Cover with marinade and refrigerate 3 hours or overnight.

Preheat oven to 350°.

Remove chicken wings from marinade. Place on cookie sheet. Brush with marinade.

Bake for 45 minutes. Sprinkle with sesame seeds and continue baking another 45 minutes.

MUSHROOM PALMIERS

5 tablespoons butter
18 ounces mushrooms,
    finely chopped
1½ medium onion, finely chopped
¾ teaspoon fresh lemon juice
2 tablespoons flour
1 teaspoon dried thyme, crumbled
Salt and freshly ground pepper
3 frozen puff pastry sheets, thawed

Glaze:
1 egg beaten with 2 teaspoons water

Melt butter in heavy large skillet over medium-high heat. Add mushrooms and onions; cook about 8 minutes, or until juices evaporate, stirring occasionally. Mix in lemon juice, then flour and thyme. Cook and stir for 2 minutes. Season with salt and pepper. Cool.

Unfold one pastry sheet on a lightly floured surface and roll to a slightly larger rectangle. Spread ⅓ of mushroom mixture evenly over the pastry sheet. Starting from one long side, roll up jelly roll fashion to center. Roll second long side to center. Press the rolls together. Repeat with remaining pastry sheets and mushrooms. Cover and chill until firm, at least 2 hours or overnight. This recipe can be prepared one week ahead and frozen. Thaw slightly before continuing.

Preheat oven to 400°. Line baking sheets with parchment paper.

Using a very sharp knife, slice pastry into ½-inch thick slices. Arrange cut side down, 1-inch apart, on baking sheet. Brush with glaze.

Bake 25 minutes, or until golden brown. Serve warm.

5 dozen

SKILLET SOMBRERO PIE

1 pound ground lean beef
1 10-ounce package frozen corn,
    thawed
1 8-ounce can tomato sauce
1 16-ounce can tomatoes
1 tablespoon minced onion
1 1¾-ounce package chili or taco
    seasoning mix
Corn chips
1 cup grated Cheddar cheese

In a large skillet, stir ground beef over medium heat until brown. Stir in corn, tomato sauce, tomatoes, onions and seasoning mix.

Simmer for 20 minutes.

Arrange chips around edge of skillet. Sprinkle cheese in center and cook until cheese melts slightly.

6 servings

M O L L E T E S

½ cup bacon fat or lard
1 cup minced onion
3 cloves garlic, crushed
2 teaspoons salt
½ teaspoon freshly ground pepper
2 1-pound cans pinto beans, drained
1 long, thin loaf French bread cut
    into ½-inch thick slices, buttered
    and toasted
2½ cups shredded Monterey Jack or
    mozzarella cheese

Preheat oven to 400°.

Heat bacon fat in medium skillet until hot. Cook onion, garlic, salt and pepper over low heat until tender. Add pinto beans and mash with fork. Cook and stir until beans are thick enough to spread. Spread 1 tablespoon beans on toasted French bread slices. Top each with 1 tablespoon cheese. Arrange on cookie sheet.

Garnish with any combination of green olives, green onions, black olives or tomatoes before baking.

Bake for 5 to 7 minutes, or until cheese is melted.

40 appetizers

T I R O P I T A
(B A K E D   C H E E S E   P I E)

6 eggs
1¼ cup feta cheese, crumbled
1 cup cottage cheese
2 ounces cream cheese or bleu cheese
1 pound frozen phyllo dough, thawed
1 cup butter, melted

Preheat oven to 350°. Grease a 9x13-inch baking pan.

In a bowl, beat eggs until fluffy. Add cheeses and mix well with beater.

Place half of the pastry sheets, one by one, in prepared pan, brushing each with melted butter. Pour in filling and top with remaining pastry sheets, brushing each sheet with butter. Brush top sheet with extra melted butter.

Bake for 30 minutes until golden brown. Allow to cool. Cut in squares and serve warm.

Hint: Tiropita can also be served as a side dish for a main course.

10 to 12 servings

S E S A M E   A S P A R A G U S

Fresh asparagus
Mayonnaise
Toasted sesame seeds

Snap woody ends off fresh asparagus and blanch in boiling water until barely tender. Dip ends in mayonnaise and sprinkle with toasted sesame seeds.

PHYLLO SPINACH DIAMONDS

12 sheets phyllo dough (18x14-inch),
    thawed
½ cup butter, melted
2 12-ounce packages frozen spinach
    soufflé, thawed
1 8-ounce can water chestnuts,
    drained, finely chopped

Preheat oven to 400°.

Arrange 6 sheets of phyllo in the bottom of a
15x10x1-inch baking dish, brushing melted butter between
each sheet. Allow edges of dough to overlap pan. Spread
soufflé evenly over dough. Sprinkle with water chestnuts.
Top with remaining phyllo sheets, brushing butter between
sheets. Fold edges of phyllo dough toward center. Brush
with remaining butter. Score top layers of phyllo into 48
diamonds.

Bake for 30 minutes, or until golden. Cool slightly. Cut
and serve warm or cool.

48 diamonds

SIMPLY ELEGANT ARTICHOKES

1 10-ounce package frozen artichoke
    hearts
1 4-ounce package bleu cheese or
    Gorgonzola cheese
8 tablespoons butter

Cook frozen artichoke hearts according to package
directions. Melt butter in saucepan; add cheese and cook
to blend. Add artichoke hearts and toss into melted butter
and cheese.

Serve warm, in chafing dish, with buttered toast points,
wafers or party breads. This recipe may be doubled.

CHILES RELLENOS CASSEROLE

2 4-ounce cans chilies, whole or
    chopped, drained
1 cup shredded mozzarella
2 cups shredded Monterey Jack
    cheese
1 cup half and half
2 eggs
⅓ cup flour
1 8-ounce can tomato sauce
Salsa or taco sauce

Butter a 2-quart baking dish and spread chilies on the
bottom. Mix together mozzarella and Monterey Jack cheese
and spread 2½ cups over chilies.

Blend half and half, eggs and flour into blender and blend
until smooth. Pour over the cheese layer. Top with tomato
sauce mixed to taste with your favorite salsa or taco sauce.

Place in cool oven set at 350°.

Bake for 1 hour. Sprinkle with remaining ½ cup cheese
and return to oven just until melted.

SHRIMP IN BEER

4 cups beer
6 whole peppercorns
1 bay leaf
3 tablespoons mixed pickling spices
¼ cup minced parsley
½ teaspoon salt
2 pounds raw, unpeeled shrimp,
    rinsed well

Hot Sauce:
1 cup ketchup
1 teaspoon prepared mustard
1 teaspoon prepared horseradish
Generous squeeze of fresh
    lemon juice

Put beer, peppercorns, bay leaf, pickling spices, parsley and salt in a large saucepan and bring to a boil. Add shrimp and return to a boil. Reduce the heat and simmer gently for 1 to 2 minutes, or until the shrimp turn bright pink. Do not overcook! Drain and serve with hot sauce and a lot of napkins.

Hot Sauce: Combine ketchup, mustard, horseradish, and lemon juice.

6 servings

LAMB SHISH KEBAB

3 to 4 tablespoons extra virgin
    olive oil
2 tablespoons "less salt" soy sauce
¼ cup cognac
½ lemon, zest and juice
2 cloves garlic, crushed
¼ cup "herbs de Provence"
Freshly ground black pepper
Ground red pepper to taste
1 pound lamb, cubed for shish kebab

Mix olive oil, soy sauce, cognac, lemon zest, lemon juice, garlic, "herbes de Provence" and peppers to taste. Pour over lamb in shallow glass baking dish. Marinate overnight in refrigerator.
    Place on short skewers for appetizers.
    Grill or broil shish kebabs. Be careful not to overcook.

SHRIMP PASTE

2 pounds shrimp, peeled and cooked
¾ cup butter, softened
½ teaspoon fresh lemon juice
2 tablespoons mayonnaise
1 teaspoon Worcestershire sauce
⅛ teaspoon mace

In food processor work bowl, combine all ingredients. Process until smooth. Spoon into pretty crock and chill. Remove from refrigerator 20 minutes before serving.
    Serve with crackers or long, thin baguettes of French bread.

CHICKEN LIVER PATÉ

1 pound chicken livers
1 medium onion, chopped
¾ teaspoon chopped fresh thyme
1 bay leaf, crushed
½ cup water
Zest of one lemon, grated
2 teaspoons salt, divided
1 cup unsalted butter,
    room temperature
Ground white pepper, to taste
1 tablespoon cognac or brandy

Combine livers, onion, thyme, bay leaf, water, lemon zest and 1 teaspoon salt in a 10-inch skillet. Cover and cook for 8 minutes or until the livers are just cooked through. Do not overcook. Let mixture cool for 10 minutes.

Remove liver mixture to food processor work bowl, leaving liquid in the pan. Puree the livers. Add softened butter, 2 tablespoons at a time, blending in well. Scrape down sides of bowl and add 1 teaspoon of salt, white pepper to taste and cognac. Blend again for 10 seconds.

Pour paté into a 1½-quart mold and chill thoroughly.

Serve with French bread, cornichons and spicy Dijon mustard.

Hint: May be prepared a day ahead. Recipe is easily halved or doubled.

18 to 20 servings

SALMON PATÉ

4 ounces skinned fresh salmon fillets
½ cup dry white wine
1 tablespoon olive oil
2 tablespoons cognac
Freshly ground pepper
4 ounces best quality smoked salmon
6 tablespoons safflower or rice oil

Cut fresh salmon into small pieces. In a small pan combine salmon and wine, and bring to a gentle boil over medium-low heat. Remove from heat and drain salmon, discarding wine.

In a small pan heat olive oil and add salmon. Cook gently over medium heat for about 5 minutes. Do not brown. Add cognac and pepper. Remove from heat and set aside.

Cut smoked salmon into small pieces. In a small saucepan, over medium heat, cook smoked salmon in 3 tablespoons oil for 3 to 5 minutes. Cool, then blend fresh salmon and smoked salmon in a food processor with the remaining oil. Refrigerate overnight.

Serve with thin slices of warm toast or sliced French bread.

12 appetizers or 4 luncheon servings

MUSHROOM NUT PATÉ

3/4 cup blanched almonds
1 small onion, chopped
2 tablespoons butter
3/4 pound fresh mushrooms, chopped
2 cloves garlic, minced
2 teaspoons fresh lemon juice
1 teaspoon fresh tarragon
Salt and freshly ground pepper
1/3 cup sour cream

Garnish:
Fresh tarragon
Thin lemon slices

Preheat oven to 350°.

Toast almonds on baking sheet in oven until light brown, about 10 minutes.

In a large skillet, lightly sauté onion in butter; add mushrooms, garlic, lemon juice, tarragon, salt and pepper. Cook two minutes longer.

Finely chop almonds in food processor. Add mushroom mixture and process until smooth. Add sour cream and mix. Pour into a 6-cup decorative mold. Refrigerate for four hours. Turn out on a serving plate and garnish with lemon slices and fresh tarragon.

Serve with cocktail bread and crackers.

HERB CHEESE SPREAD

1 8-ounce package cream cheese
3/4 cup butter
1/2 clove garlic
1 tablespoon fresh tarragon
1/2 teaspoon onion salt
1 1/2 teaspoons fresh thyme
1 1/2 teaspoons fresh dill
1/2 teaspoons freshly ground pepper
Juice of 1 lemon

In food processor work bowl, combine cream cheese, butter, garlic, tarragon, onion salt, thyme, dill, pepper and lemon juice; process until smooth. Pack in a crock or jar. Chill. Serve at room temperature.

Serving suggestion: Blanch pea pods. Slit open on one side and stuff with cheese spread. Serve as hors d'oeuvres.

Variation: Substitute 1 teaspoon dried tarragon, 1/2 teaspoon dried thyme, and 1/2 teaspoon dried dill for fresh herbs

VEGETABLE BRIE

1 tablespoon butter, melted
1 cup sliced mushrooms
1 or 2 cloves garlic, minced
1 or 2 green onions, chopped
1 8-ounce wheel Brie
1 sheet frozen puff pastry dough,
    thawed
1 egg yolk mixed with 1 tablespoon
    water

In skillet, melt butter and sauté mushrooms with garlic and green onions. Slice Brie in half or thirds horizontally. Layer with mushroom filling. Put back together. Enclose in puff pastry. Brush with egg yolk mixed with a little water. Wrap in aluminum foil sprayed with non-stick spray. Freeze overnight.

Preheat oven to 300°.

Bake frozen on oven-proof serving dish approximately 25 minutes.

BAKED PECAN BRIE

1 8-ounce wheel Brie
½ cup chopped pecans
¼ cup brown sugar
2 tablespoons cognac

Preheat oven to 300°.

Remove only the top rind from the Brie. Place Brie on an oven-proof serving plate as it is difficult to move. Sprinkle brown sugar and nuts on top, drizzle with cognac.

Bake for 4 to 6 minutes or until Brie softens and sugar melts into the cognac.

Hint: Brie may be cooked in microwave oven by using 30 second increments to control melting.

6 servings

TACO TARTLETS

1 pound ground lean beef
2 tablespoons taco seasoning
2 tablespoons ice water
1 cup sour cream
2 tablespoons taco sauce
2 ounces black olives, chopped
1 cup cheddar cheese

Preheat oven to 400°.

In a large bowl, mix beef, taco seasoning mix and water. Press into mini-muffin cups forming shell.

Combine sour cream, taco sauce and olives. Place spoonful of filling into uncooked beef shell. Sprinkle with cheese.

Bake for 7 to 8 minutes.

2 dozen tartlets

SPICY SALSA

1 large tomato peeled, seeded
    and chopped
1 teaspoon dried chili flakes
½ teaspoon ground red pepper
1 teaspoon finely diced red onion
2 tablespoons chopped fresh cilantro
½ teaspoon minced garlic
Salt and freshly ground pepper
Juice of 1 lime

Combine all ingredients. Season with salt and pepper to taste. Chill or serve at room temperature.

1 cup

SALSA VERDE

10 tomatillos
5 jalapeño chili peppers or to taste
Pinch of salt
1 slice of onion

Place tomatillos, jalapeños, salt and onion in saucepan. Barely cover with water. Simmer for approximately 20 minutes or until tomatillos and peppers are soft. Place in blender or food processor and process until pureed. Serve warm. Can be made in advance and held several days.

WATER CHESTNUT DIP

1 cup mayonnaise
1 cup sour cream
3 green onions, chopped
1 8-ounce can water chestnuts, drained and chopped
1 small clove garlic, chopped
1 tablespoon soy sauce
1/4 cup fresh parsley, chopped
2-3 drops Tabasco, optional

Mix mayonnaise, sour cream, green onions, water chestnuts, garlic, soy sauce, parsley and Tabasco in blender or food processor. Process until fine but not pureed. Chill overnight. Serve with crackers, melba rounds and raw vegetables.

3 cups

TUNA TAPENADE

1 3½-ounce can tuna, drained
1/4 16-ounce jar kalamata olives, pitted
4 anchovy fillets, rinsed and patted dry, or to taste
3 tablespoons capers, rinsed and patted dry
1/2 cup extra virgin mild olive oil
2 teaspoons fresh lemon juice
1/2 teaspoon Dijon mustard

Garnish:
Chopped parsley

In food processor work bowl, mix tuna, olives, anchovies and capers. Process until smooth, approximately 3 seconds. Scrape sides of bowl with a rubber spatula. Add olive oil to processor bowl in a slow, steady stream with the motor running. Mixture should be a thick, spreadable paste. Mix in lemon juice and mustard. Do not add salt.

Transfer tapenade to a bowl, cover and chill for several hours or overnight.

Stir before serving if the oil has begun to separate. Serve in a bowl lined with large green bok choy leaves. Cut the white stems into sticks for dipping. Surround the bowl with additional crudités (seasonal fresh vegetables) for dipping such as blanched green beans, mini peeled carrots, yellow squash slices and broccoflower florets.

6 to 8 servings

VEGETABLE SPINACH DIP

2 10-ounce packages frozen chopped
   spinach, thawed and drained
1 cup tomatoes, peeled, seeded
   and chopped
1 cup Bermuda onion, chopped
1 teaspoon crushed garlic
2 tablespoons lemon juice
1 teaspoon seasoned salt
1 teaspoon freshly ground pepper
1 tablespoon chili powder
½ cup sour cream
½ cup mayonnaise

In food processor work bowl, mix spinach, tomatoes, onions and garlic. Add lemon juice, salt, pepper and chili powder. Process until smooth. Transfer to mixing bowl, add sour cream and mayonnaise. Mix well and adjust seasonings. Chill before serving.

20 to 30 servings

BREAD POT FONDUE

1 large round loaf rye bread,
   unsliced
2 cups shredded cheddar cheese
6 ounces cream cheese
1½ cups sour cream, softened
1 cup diced cooked ham, optional
½ cup chopped green onion
3 ounces chopped green chilies
1 teaspoon Worcestershire sauce

Preheat oven to 350°.

   Slice one inch off top of bread and reserve. Pull out soft bread inside, leaving a shell of bread crust about one inch thick. Save soft bread and cut into cubes for dipping.

   In a small bowl combine remaining ingredients and spoon into bread shell. Cover with top slice of bread. Wrap in double thickness of foil and bake for 1 hour, 15 minutes. Unwrap and stir fondue.

   Place on a large tray and serve warm surrounded by bread cubes, fresh broccoli, cauliflower and celery for dipping.

8 to 10 servings

Soups
& Salads

CHILLED CUCUMBER AVOCADO SOUP

1 large cucumber, peeled, seeded and
    cut into chunks
1 large avocado, peeled, seeded
    and cut into chunks
2 green onions and tops, chopped
1 cup chicken stock
1 cup sour cream
Dash Tabasco
2 tablespoons fresh lemon juice
Salt and freshly ground white pepper
    to taste

In a blender jar, place cucumber, avocado, green onions, stock, sour cream, Tabasco, lemon juice and pepper; blend for 10 to 15 seconds or until smooth. Chill.

Pour into balloon wine glasses, float a thin slice of lemon on top, and sprinkle with chopped parsley.

4 to 6 servings

CHUNKY GAZPACHO

2 28-ounce cans tomatoes, drained,
    reserving juices
1 cucumber, peeled and halved
2 green peppers, quartered
    and seeded
1 small onion, chopped
1 clove garlic, chopped
2 tablespoons fresh parsley, chopped
2 tablespoons red wine vinegar
1 tablespoon olive oil
½ teaspoon salt
Freshly ground pepper
½ teaspoon Worcestershire sauce
3 to 4 drops Tabasco
Fresh lime, optional

Blend in food processor work bowl: 1 can tomatoes, ½ cucumber, and ½ green pepper. Add mixture to reserved juices in large bowl.

Mix onion, garlic, parsley, vinegar, olive oil, Worcestershire sauce, Tabasco sauce, salt and pepper. Add to tomato juice mixture. Adjust seasonings.

Coarsely chop the remaining can of tomatoes, green pepper and cucumber. Add to juice mixture. Add parsley. Mix well. Cover and chill.

Serve chilled with fresh lime sprinkled on top.

Variation: Substitute canned tomatoes with 4 large tomatoes, peeled and 1 12-ounce can tomato juice or vegetable juice cocktail. Also add 1 zucchini, peeled and chopped.

4 to 6 servings

COLD RED PEPPER SOUP

1 tablespoon margarine
2 carrots, pared and chopped
3 shallots, chopped
1¼ cups chicken broth
1 large red pepper, chopped
1 3-ounce package Neufchâtel
   cream cheese
½ teaspoon salt
¼ teaspoon ground red pepper
¼ teaspoon nutmeg
½ cup half and half

Cook carrots and shallots in butter until tender. Add broth and red pepper, simmer 15 minutes. Stir in cream cheese, salt, pepper and nutmeg. Puree in blender or processor. Chill at least 4 hours.

Add half and half. Serve with fruit salad and French bread for a luncheon.

Variation: Substitute 1 pear, peeled for carrots and use yellow pepper for red.

4 to 6 servings

CHILLED ITALIAN EGG LEMON SOUP

2 cups chicken broth
2 tablespoons cornstarch
1 cup half and half
5 egg yolks
Juice of 3 fresh lemons
Salt and freshly ground white pepper

Garnish:
¼ cup chopped fresh parsley
3 tablespoons freshly grated
   Parmesan cheese
Lemon zest

In a large saucepan, heat chicken broth. Dissolve cornstarch in half and half and slowly add to broth, stirring constantly until smooth. In a bowl, beat egg yolks. Slowly add lemon juice to eggs, mix well. Add 1 tablespoon at a time of hot cream to egg mixture to warm. Pour broth into egg mixture and mix well. Season with salt and white pepper. Cool and chill at least 4 hours.

Garnish with parsley, cheese and lemon zest.

4 to 6 servings

SWEET POTATO VICHYSSOISE

1 medium onion, sliced
1 celery rib, sliced
2 tablespoons butter
2 tablespoons flour
8 cups beef stock
1½ pounds sweet potatoes, peeled
   and thinly sliced
Salt and freshly ground pepper
1 cup whipping cream

In a large saucepan, sauté celery and onion in butter until soft, but not brown. Stir in flour. Gradually add stock, mixing well. Add potatoes and cook 30 minutes, or until soft.

Whirl in blender. Season with salt and pepper to taste. Chill.

Add cream just before serving.

6 servings

CHESTNUT SOUP

6 tablespoons butter or margarine
1 cup chopped celery
1 cup chopped carrots
1 cup chopped onion
¾ pound potatoes, peeled and
    chopped (about 2 medium
    potatoes)
3 cups chicken broth
2½ cups beef broth
¼ cup chopped fresh parsley
1 teaspoon dried thyme
1 teaspoon dried basil
1 teaspoon dried sage
1 15½-ounce can chestnuts in water,
    drained or 1 pound fresh
    peeled chestnuts
½ cup dry Madeira
1 cup whipping cream
Salt and white pepper

In a large soup pot, melt butter or margarine. Add celery, carrots, onion, and potatoes; cook covered over moderately low heat, stirring occasionally, for 20 minutes or until vegetables are very soft, but not brown. Stir in chicken and beef broth, parsley, thyme, sage and basil. Reserve ½ cup chestnuts for garnish. Add remaining chestnuts to soup. Simmer covered for 20 minutes. Cool slightly; puree in blender for a smoother soup or in batches in a food processor with metal blade.

May be refrigerated for 2 days or frozen.

Before serving: Place in soup pot. Add Madeira and cream; simmer 5 minutes. Season to taste with salt and white pepper. Sprinkle reserved crumbled chestnuts over each serving.

Hint: Fresh herbs may be used for dried. Substitute 1 tablespoon fresh for 1 teaspoon dried.

10 to 12 servings

CREAMY POTATO BROCCOLI SOUP

2 tablespoons butter or margarine
1 medium onion, coarsely chopped
7 to 8 cups chicken broth, homemade
    or canned
1 pound broccoli, trimmed and cut
    into 1-inch pieces
3 medium russet potatoes, peeled
    and quartered
Salt and freshly ground pepper

Garnish:
Fresh chives, chopped
Croutons
Freshly grated Parmesan cheese

In stock pot, over medium heat, melt butter; add onion and sauté until translucent. Add chicken broth and bring to a boil. Add broccoli and potatoes, add more broth if vegetables are not covered, and reduce heat to low. Simmer, covered for 35 to 45 minutes or until vegetables are very soft. Remove from heat and cool to room temperature.

Puree vegetables in blender or food processor until smooth. Return to heat and check for seasoning. Add salt and pepper to taste. If too thick add chicken stock.

Serve with chopped chives, croutons and grated cheese.

Hint: This soup freezes well.

6 to 8 servings

POTAGE FRANÇAIS

2 leeks, white part only, washed well,
    chopped
2 tablespoons unsalted butter
5 cups chicken broth
2 10-ounce packages frozen peas
4 cups chopped lettuce
¼ cup mint
1 cup whipping cream
¼ cup whipping cream, whipped

In large saucepan, melt butter and sauté leeks until tender. Add chicken broth and bring to boil. Add peas and lettuce. Cook about 6 to 7 minutes, or until peas are tender. Puree all ingredients and add mint. Allow to cool and add cream. Stir and refrigerate until ready to serve.

Garnish each bowl with dollop of whipped cream and a mint leaf.

6 servings

CREAM OF CHEESE SOUP

2 tablespoons butter or margarine
3 green onions with tops, thinly sliced
½ cup thinly sliced celery
1¼ cups water
½ cup half and half
⅔ cup cheddar cheese
1 teaspoon instant chicken bouillon
⅛ teaspoon ground nutmeg
⅓ cup dry white wine

In a 3-quart saucepan, over medium heat, sauté onions and celery in butter for 8 minutes, or until onions are tender. Stir in water, half and half, cheese, instant bouillon and nutmeg. Heat to boiling over medium heat, stirring constantly. Stir in wine. Heat to boiling. Boil and stir 1 minute.

Sprinkle each serving with paprika and garnish with croutons.

3 servings

SHRIMP AND MUSHROOM SOUP

¾ pound jumbo shrimp
¼ pound mushrooms, sliced
1 shallot, chopped
4 tablespoons butter, divided

Garnish:
Chopped chives

Shell and devein shrimp; cut into bite-size pieces. Place shells in a large pot of water and boil for 10 minutes. In a skillet, melt 2 tablespoons butter; sauté mushrooms and shallots until tender. In a separate skillet sauté shrimp in 2 tablespoons butter until opaque.

Remove shrimp shells from fish stock. Discard all but 3 cups of fish stock. Add mushrooms, shallots and shrimp. Bring to a boil. Serve immediately. Sprinkle with chives for garnish.

2 servings

H E A R T Y   W I N T E R   S T E W

2 pounds lean beef short ribs, cut in
    3-inch lengths
4 to 5 pounds beef brisket
3 cloves garlic
2 to 3 bay leaves
10 sprigs parsley
1 teaspoon whole peppercorns
1 medium onion studded with
    6 whole cloves
1 small head cabbage, cored
2 to 3 teaspoons salt
4 medium carrots, pared and halved
8 small onions, peeled
3 pounds chicken, trussed
2 kielbasa (polish) sausage, sliced
10 2-inch new potatoes, scrubbed
6 medium leeks, split to green,
    washed and sliced

Place short ribs and brisket in large pot. Add water to cover 1 inch above meats. Simmer, covered, for 45 minutes. Skim surface. Place garlic, bay leaves, parsley and peppercorns in a cheesecloth bag, add to meat and water along with clove-studded onion, cabbage, salt, carrots and onions. Cover and simmer for another 30 minutes.

Add chicken, sausages and new potatoes. Be sure all ingredients are covered with stock. Add water if necessary and simmer for 45 minutes more.

Preheat oven to 200°.

Add leeks and simmer for another 15 minutes. Check seasonings and make sure meat is tender and vegetables are cooked.

Carefully lift vegetables from broth with a slotted spoon and arrange on large platter. Place meat on platter, cover with aluminum foil and place in oven to keep warm. Meanwhile strain broth and discard bouquet garnishes and onion. Check seasonings and serve broth with vegetables and meat.

6 to 8 servings

L E E K   A N D   S Q U A S H   S O U P

3 pounds butternut squash
3 leeks, white parts sliced
1 tablespoon saffron oil
3 to 4 sprigs fresh thyme or 1 scant
    tablespoon dried thyme
4 cups chicken stock
Salt and freshly ground pepper

Garnish:
Crème fraîche
Cooked bacon, crumbled
Fresh chives

Preheat oven to 375°.

Halve and bake squash on baking sheet for 35 to 40 minutes, or until tender. Scoop out flesh.

In a large saucepan, heat oil and sauté leeks until tender. Combine squash, leeks, thyme, chicken stock, salt and pepper to taste. Cook about 30 minutes. Puree in blender or food processor.

Serve with crème fraîche and sprinkle with crumbled bacon or chives.

4 to 6 servings

HERBED FRESH TOMATO SOUP

2 tablespoons butter or margarine
2 tablespoons olive oil
2 medium onions, thinly sliced
2 pounds fresh tomatoes, peeled
    and quartered
1 6-ounce can tomato paste
2 tablespoons chopped fresh basil
4 teaspoons snipped fresh thyme
3 cups chicken broth
1 teaspoon salt
¼ teaspoon freshly ground pepper

In large saucepan, combine butter and oil; heat until the butter melts. Add onion; cook until translucent. Stir in tomatoes, tomato paste, basil and thyme, crush tomatoes slightly. Add chicken broth and bring to boil. Reduce heat; cover and simmer for 40 minutes. Cool slightly.

Press through food mill or puree a small amount at a time, in blender container; strain. Return mixture to saucepan; season with salt and pepper to taste and heat through.

Serve with a dollop of whipped cream and fresh herbs.

Hint: Substitute 2 teaspoons dried basil and 1 teaspoon crushed dried thyme for fresh herbs.

8 servings

POTATO CORN CHOWDER

3 tablespoons butter or margarine
2 medium onions, finely chopped
1 clove garlic, minced
1 large celery rib, finely chopped
3 cups chicken stock or broth
2 cups whole milk
5½ to 6 cups peeled and diced
    potatoes, about 5 medium
    potatoes
5 cups fresh cut corn, about
    6 medium ears
1½ teaspoons fresh chopped basil
¾ teaspoon dry mustard
½ teaspoon fresh marjoram leaves
⅛ teaspoon celery seed
Freshly ground pepper
¾ teaspoon salt
1 cup whipping cream or
    half and half

In large heavy pot, over medium-high heat, melt butter; add onions, garlic and celery. Sauté for 5 minutes or until onions are soft. Add stock, milk, potatoes, corn, basil, mustard, marjoram, celery seed, pepper and salt. Bring to a boil. Lower heat, cover and simmer for about 15 to 17 minutes, or until potatoes are tender.

Transfer 2 cups of mixture with slotted spoon from pot to blender or food processor. Blend or process until the vegetables are pureed. Add cream to remaining mixture in pot. Return puree to pot and stir to blend.

Bring soup to boil over medium-high heat, stirring frequently. Lower heat and simmer for 5 to 8 minutes, stirring occasionally, or until flavors are well blended.

6 to 8 servings

W H I T E   B E A N   A N D   B A C O N   S O U P

8 slices bacon, chopped
1 medium onion, chopped
½ head cabbage, sliced crosswise
    and shredded
1 10¾-ounce can chicken broth
⅛ teaspoon dried red pepper flakes
2 16-ounce cans Cannellini
    beans (white kidney),
    rinsed and drained
½ teaspoon ground sage
Pinch ground red pepper
Fresh parsley, minced
Salt and freshly ground pepper

In large saucepan, cook bacon until crisp. Add onion and sauté until translucent. Add cabbage. Cook until tender. Add broth, red pepper flakes, beans, sage, and ground red pepper. Simmer about 20 minutes.

Serve sprinkled with fresh parsley.

4 servings

O R A N G E   C A R R O T   B I S Q U E

¼ cup unsalted butter
2 cups finely chopped onion
1½ pounds carrots, pared and
    chopped
4 cups chicken broth, divided
1 cup fresh orange juice
Freshly grated orange zest
¼ cup Grand Marnier
Salt and freshly ground pepper

Garnish:
Whipping cream, whipped or
    sour cream
Freshly ground nutmeg
Fresh parsley

Melt butter in a large, heavy saucepan; add onions and stir well. Cover and cook over low heat for 25 minutes, or until onions are golden. Stir occasionally. Add carrots and chicken broth, bring to a boil, reduce heat and simmer covered for 30 to 35 minutes, or until carrots are tender.

Drain mixture in sieve over large bowl, reserving the broth. Puree vegetables in a food processor or blender with 1 cup of reserved broth. Return the puree to cleaned pan. Stir in orange juice, and enough of the reserved broth to thin the soup to desired consistency. Add orange zest and Grand Marnier.

Add salt and pepper to taste. Heat soup over moderately low heat, stirring until it is just heated through. Ladle soup into bowls and garnish with a dollop of unsweetened, stiffly whipped cream or sour cream, topped with a grind of fresh nutmeg. Sprinkle with chopped fresh parsley.

6 servings

PARSLEY SOUP

1 cup sour cream
1 cup whipping cream
2 large bunches parsley, stems
    removed and minced
2 tablespoons minced onion
1 small clove garlic, minced
2 tablespoons butter
2 cups chicken broth
1/2 cup dry white wine
1 teaspoon salt

In a small bowl, mix sour cream and whipping cream. Cover and let set at room temperature.

Measure 1 1/2 cups loosely packed parsley and reserve 2 tablespoons more.

In saucepan, over medium heat, melt butter and sauté onion and garlic until onion is translucent, about 5 minutes. Add parsley and cook for 3 minutes, stirring constantly. Pour in chicken broth; cover, reduce heat and simmer 10 minutes. Stir in wine and salt.

Puree in blender or food processor, 2 cups at a time, or press through a sieve. Return puree to heat, bring to boil, remove from heat and stir in 3/4 of the cream mixture.

Serve with dollop of remaining sour cream and whipping cream mixture.

2 to 4 servings

RICH CREAM OF ASPARAGUS SOUP

2 pounds fresh asparagus,
    woody ends trimmed, cut into
    bite size pieces
1 large onion, chopped
2 13 3/4-ounce cans chicken broth
2 cups whipping cream, divided
1/8 teaspoon ground red pepper,
    or to taste
Freshly ground white pepper, to taste

Place in a 3-quart saucepan, the asparagus, onion and broth. Simmer covered for 20 minutes or until asparagus is tender. Strain and reserve broth. Put asparagus in a blender or food processor. Add 1 1/2 cups of whipping cream; blend until smooth. Return broth to saucepan and stir in asparagus-cream mixture. Heat gently until soup starts to boil slightly. Add pepper to taste.

In a small bowl, whip remaining 1/2 cup cream until soft peaks form. Serve soup with a dollop of whipped cream on each serving.

Variation: Stir 2 tablespoons sherry into soup after adding the asparagus/cream mixture to broth.

8 servings

POTATO CHEDDAR SOUP

6 slices bacon, slivered
2 large onions, chopped
4 large baking potatoes, chopped
2 cups chicken stock
2 cups milk or half and half
2 cups shredded sharp
    cheddar cheese
Salt and freshly ground pepper

In a large saucepan, render drippings from bacon. Remove bacon to paper towels and reserve. Add onions to drippings and cook until tender. (Vegetable oil, margarine or butter can be substituted for bacon drippings.)

Stir in potatoes and sauté for a few minutes. Pour in stock and cook over low heat for 30 to 45 minutes, or until potatoes are tender. Add more stock or water as needed. Add milk and cheese and stir until soup is hot and cheese is melted. Season with salt and pepper. Serve hot.

Garnish with cooked bacon.

4 to 6 servings

OLD FASHIONED OXTAIL SOUP

2 pounds or more oxtails
2 tablespoons vegetable oil
1 28-ounce can tomatoes,
    coarsely chopped
1 bunch fresh parsley,
    coarsely chopped
Cut in 1/4-inch pieces:
    2 medium onions
    4 celery ribs
    3 parsnips
    3 carrots
    2 small turnips
2 tablespoons beef bouillon,
    or to taste
Salt and freshly ground pepper

In a large soup pot, brown oxtails in oil. Cover with water. Cook covered for 2 hours. Add tomatoes and continue cooking for 2 more hours. Place meat, water and tomato mixture in refrigerator and chill overnight.

Next day: Skim off solidified grease. Add parsley, onions, celery, parsnips, carrots, turnips, bouillon, salt and pepper to soup. Return soup to stove and continue cooking for 45 minutes. Remove oxtails. Remove fat and bone from the oxtails and discard. Cut meat into cubes and return to the soup. The soup can be eaten immediately or refrigerated one more day.

This soup gets better with age!

8 servings

PUMPKIN SOUP JAMAICA

1 16-ounce can pumpkin puree
5 cups chicken broth
2 tablespoons butter
4 teaspoons minced onion
2 tablespoons flour
2 teaspoons salt
2 teaspoons ground ginger
2 eggs
2 cups half and half or whole milk

Garnish:
Chopped fresh chives

Combine pumpkin puree and chicken broth in a heavy saucepan. Heat, but do not allow to boil.

In a small pan, sauté onions in butter for about 3 minutes. Blend in flour, salt and ginger. Beat in pumpkin liquid and cook stirring constantly until slightly thickened. Do not allow to boil.

May be made ahead to this point.

Just before serving beat eggs with half and half and gradually add to soup. Reheat soup without boiling, stirring constantly until soup is hot.

Garnish with chopped chives.

12 servings

BROCCOLI CHEESE SOUP

1 pound fresh broccoli, chopped,
    reserve 6 to 8 florets for garnish
5 cups chicken broth, fresh or canned
1 small onion, diced
¼ cup butter or slightly more
⅔ cup flour
1 8-ounce package cheddar with
    garlic cheese spread
1 cup hot milk
5 strips bacon, diced, sautéed
    and drained

In a medium saucepan, cook chopped broccoli in chicken stock until tender. Steam floret garnish in 1 inch water in a separate small saucepan until crisp tender. Remove from heat, drain and cool. Reserve.

Melt butter in a large saucepan; add onion and cook until soft. Add flour and cook 5 minutes stirring frequently. Stir in broccoli and bring to boil, stirring constantly. Reduce heat and simmer 10 minutes. Add cheese spread and stir to melt. Stir in hot milk and bacon. Pour into soup tureen and garnish with reserved florets.

Variation: Substitute English cheshire cheese for the cheddar cheese spread.

4 to 6 servings

FABULOUS FRENCH ONION SOUP

3 pounds onions, peeled and sliced
    1/8-inch thick
1/2 cup butter, melted
1 1/2 teaspoons diced green pepper
2 tablespoons paprika
3/4 cup flour
8 cups beef broth
4 cups water
1 bay leaf
French bread, cut in 1/2-inch slices
    and toasted
Gruyère cheese, sliced

In a large soup pot, sauté onions in butter over low heat for 1 1/2 hours. *Do not brown.*

Add green pepper, paprika and flour. Mix well. Sauté for 10 minutes over low heat. Add beef broth, water and bay leaf. Simmer 2 hours. Refrigerate overnight.

Next day: Remove from refrigerator, ladle into soup tureen or individual bowls. Float several slices of bread in tureen or 2 slices in each bowl. Top each piece of bread with slice of Gruyère. Place under broiler until brown.

10 to 12 servings

ENGLISH CREAM OF CARROT SOUP

4 slices bacon, chopped
1/4 cup butter or margarine
2 pounds carrots, pared and chopped
1 medium onion, thinly sliced
1 cup chopped celery
1/2 cup chopped turnip
1/2 cup flour
8 cups chicken broth
Bouquet garni: tie in cheesecloth,
    2 parsley sprigs,
    1 bay leaf,
    1/4 teaspoon thyme
1 1/2 cups milk
Salt and freshly ground pepper

Garnish:
Whipping cream, whipped
Carrot strips

Sauté bacon in 4-quart soup pot until limp; add butter. Add chopped carrots, onion, celery and turnip; sauté until onion is transparent, about 5 minutes. Stir in flour; cook and stir 2 minutes. Stir in chicken broth; heat to boiling, stirring constantly to prevent lumps. Reduce heat to simmer; add bouquet garni. Simmer covered for 15 minutes. Remove bouquet garni.

Place carrot mixture, 3 cups at a time, in blender and puree. Pour into 4-quart saucepan; stir in milk, salt and pepper. Heat to boiling, stirring constantly; reduce heat to low and cook, uncovered, stirring constantly for 10 minutes. Place in serving bowls and garnish with a tablespoon of whipped cream and carrot strips.

8 servings

FRESH MUSHROOM SOUP

1 pound mushrooms, ⅓ sliced,
    ⅔ finely chopped
6 tablespoons butter
2 cups finely chopped onions
½ teaspoon sugar
¼ cup flour
1 cup water
1¾ cups chicken broth
1 cup dry vermouth
1 tablespoon salt, or to taste
¼ teaspoon freshly ground pepper,
    or to taste

In large saucepan, melt butter; add onions and sugar. Sauté over medium heat, stirring frequently, for about 15 minutes or until golden. Add sliced and chopped mushrooms and sauté for 4 minutes. Stir in flour until smooth; cook for 2 minutes, stirring constantly. Pour in water and stir until smooth. Add chicken broth, vermouth, salt and pepper; heat to boiling, stirring constantly. Reduce heat and simmer uncovered 10 minutes.

May be prepared in advance; refrigerated and reheated to boiling.

Variation: Wild mushrooms may be substituted for mushrooms. Blend wild and domestic. Try shiitake, porcini and/or button mushrooms for an aromatic and full bodied flavor.

6 servings

BOUILLABAISSE

¼ cup olive oil
4 cups chopped tomatoes
2 tablespoons tomato paste
1 cup chopped onion
3 cloves garlic, minced
1 teaspoon salt
1 bay leaf
¼ teaspoon freshly ground pepper
½ teaspoon dried basil
½ teaspoon dried thyme
¼ teaspoon fennel seed
Dash saffron
2 cups water
1½ dozen small clams
1 pound cod fillets
½ pound king crab pieces
¾ pound shrimp, shelled
¼ cup butter
½ cup dry white wine

Heat oil in large soup pot. Add tomatoes, tomato paste, onion, garlic, salt, pepper, bay leaf, basil, thyme, fennel seed and saffron. Simmer 10 minutes. Add water and clams. Simmer 15 minutes or until clams open. Add cod fillets, crab, shrimp, butter and wine. Simmer 20 minutes or until fish flakes.

4 to 6 servings

BRUNSWICK STEW

2 5-6 pound chickens
½ cup tomato puree
2 28-ounce cans whole tomatoes
2 large mild onions, diced
2 8-ounce packages frozen green
    lima beans or baby lima beans
6 small okra pods, cut in pieces or
    ½ 8-ounce package frozen okra
2 small, dried hot red pepper pods
1 8-ounce package frozen whole
    kernel corn
4 tablespoons butter or margarine,
    optional
1 to 1½ tablespoons Tabasco
Salt and freshly ground pepper

Stew chickens until the meat can be removed from the bones. Drain, reserving the broth, and cool. Remove meat from bones and dice. Put chicken, tomatoes, onions, lima beans, okra and red pepper pods into a large kettle. Skim the reserved broth (or use broth previously skimmed from another chicken and freeze this broth for later skimming). Add 2 cups or more of chicken broth. Simmer gently until beans are tender. Remove red pepper pods and add the corn. Add margarine, Tabasco, salt and pepper to taste. Continue cooking for 15 minutes. The stew should be thick in consistency and be very highly seasoned with pepper.

Ladle in soup bowls and serve with cornbread.

Hint: If red peppers are too hot for your taste, reduce quantity, or omit them, but Brunswick stew is a peppery dish.

Variation: The taste is enhanced by adding another cooked meat. In Mississippi, squirrels are cooked with the chicken. Previously cooked venison, rabbit, or beef may also be added.

12 to 14 servings

ITALIAN SAUSAGE SOUP

2 pounds Italian sausage
2 tablespoons olive oil
2 medium onions, chopped
2 cloves garlic, minced
1 28-ounce can whole tomatoes,
    crushed
2 14-ounce cans beef broth
1½ cups red wine
½ teaspoon dried basil
3 tablespoons chopped fresh parsley
1 green pepper, chopped
2 medium zucchini, sliced
3 cups bow-tie noodles

Slice sausage into 1-inch slices. Heat olive oil in a large soup pot and brown sausage. Drain fat; add onions and garlic. Cook until translucent. Crush tomatoes and add with beef broth, wine, basil, and parsley to soup pot.

Simmer uncovered for 30 minutes. Add green pepper, zucchini, and noodles. Simmer covered for 25 more minutes.

Serve with freshly grated Parmesan cheese.

CHILLED SPICED RICE SALAD

2 cups raw rice
1 to 1½ cups raisins
¾ cup sliced blanched, toasted
    almonds
⅔ cup chopped green pepper
1 pound fresh mushrooms, sliced
¼ teaspoon nutmeg
¼ teaspoon cinnamon
4 tablespoons extra virgin olive oil
Salt and freshly ground pepper

Cook rice according to package directions. Do not overcook. Rinse rice several times with cold water; drain well.

Mix raisins, almonds, green pepper, mushrooms, nutmeg, cinnamon, and olive oil and add to rice. Season with salt and freshly ground pepper to taste. Cover and chill until serving time.

8 servings

ITALIAN BREAD SALAD

2 cloves garlic, finely chopped
1 cup chopped fresh basil
3 tablespoons red wine vinegar
½ cup extra virgin olive oil
8 slices dry Italian bread,
    cut in cubes
1 small red onion, diced
⅓ cup pitted black olives, halved
    lengthwise
2 medium tomatoes, peeled
    and diced
Salt and freshly ground pepper

Whisk garlic, basil, vinegar and oil in a bowl. Stir in bread cubes, onion, olives, tomatoes and season to taste with salt and freshly ground pepper.

Serve in large salad bowl tossed with dandelion greens and arugula.

APPLE AVOCADO SALAD

2 red delicious apples, cored, seeded
    and diced
¼ cup dark or golden raisins
¼ cup chopped walnuts, toasted
⅓ cup chopped celery
½ cup mayonnaise
¼ teaspoon salt
3 avocados, halved, seeded
    and skinned
Red or green leaf lettuce

In a large bowl, combine apples, raisins, walnuts, celery, mayonnaise and salt. Fill each avocado half with the apple filling.

Serve on individual leaf lettuce lined plates.

6 servings

A.B.C. SALAD
AVOCADO, BACON AND CHICKEN SALAD

Dressing:
1 tablespoons peanut oil
1 tablespoon white wine
¼ teaspoon fresh lemon juice

Romaine lettuce
2 chicken breast halves, poached
*   and cubed*
1 avocado, seeded, peeled and sliced
2 bacon strips, crisp cooked
Crumbled Bleu cheese or cheese
*   of choice*
1 tomato, peeled and seeded

Dressing: In a small bowl, whisk peanut oil, white wine and lemon juice.

Arrange romaine lettuce on two plates. Divide remaining ingredients and compose salad on lettuce. Drizzle dressing over each salad.

2 servings

ORANGE ASPARAGUS SALAD

Orange Dressing:
¼ cup fresh orange juice
½ cup good quality olive oil
1 teaspoon Dijon mustard, unsalted
1 clove garlic, finely minced
3 strips orange peel, julienned

6 naval oranges, peeled and sliced
24 fresh asparagus spears
Freshly ground pepper
Romaine, spinach or any dark
*   leaf greens*

Garnish:
Chopped fresh chives

Orange Dressing: In jar, combine orange juice, olive oil, mustard, garlic and orange peel; shake until blended. Refrigerate overnight or several days.

Salad: Remove woody ends of asparagus, if necessary. Blanch asparagus in hot water until just tender; cool under cold water and drain.

Overlap lettuce on platter or individual salad plates. Arrange orange slices in a circle. Arrange asparagus spears in a circle with stems to center. Arrange orange slices in another circle over asparagus. Drizzle a little dressing on top of asparagus. Refrigerate.

When ready to serve, drizzle remaining dressing over salad and sprinkle with freshly ground pepper. Garnish with chives.

Variation: Substitute 2 avocados, peeled, seeded and sliced for the asparagus. On the lettuce lined plate arrange orange slices in a circle with the avocado slices in another circle on top of orange slices. The avocado increases the fat content in the recipe, but it's good! Garnish with chopped chives. If salt is not a problem, Dijon mustard with salt can be used.

4 servings

ORANGE WALNUT SALAD
WITH CELERY SEED VINAIGRETTE

Celery Seed Vinaigrette:
1/2 cup good quality olive oil
2/3 cup cider vinegar
1 tablespoon sugar
2 tablespoons water
1 clove garlic, minced
1 teaspoon celery seed
1 teaspoon salt
1/4 teaspoon freshly ground
   white pepper

3/4 cup chopped walnuts
2 tablespoons butter, melted
1/4 teaspoon salt
10 cups torn greens
4 oranges, peeled, sectioned with
   membrane removed
6 thin slices onion, separated
   into rings

Celery Seed Vinaigrette: In covered jar, combine oil, vinegar, sugar, water, garlic, celery seed, salt and pepper; shake well.

In a skillet, sauté walnuts in butter and salt. Remove and set aside.

Toss greens with dressing. Place on chilled plates. Divide orange sections and onion rings and place on greens. Sprinkle with walnuts.

Suggestion: Try any combination of bibb lettuce with romaine, watercress, Boston, spinach, radicchio, Belgian endive and sorrel. Canned mandarin oranges may be substituted for the oranges.

8 servings

JICAMA, MANGO AND PAPAYA
WITH CITRUS DRESSING

Citrus Dressing:
1/2 teaspoon salt
1 tablespoon fresh lemon juice
2 tablespoons fresh lime juice
1/4 cup fresh orange juice
1/3 cup extra virgin olive oil
1/2 teaspoon ground red pepper
1/2 teaspoon cumin
2 tablespoons honey

1/2 cup julienned peeled jicama
1/2 mango, peeled and thinly sliced
1/2 papaya, peeled and thinly sliced
3 heads Bibb lettuce, torn
1/2 cup shredded red cabbage or
   red chicory

Citrus Dressing: In a small bowl, whisk salt, lemon, lime and orange juices together until salt is dissolved. Whisk in oil and remaining ingredients. Whisk again just before serving.

Place jicama, mango, papaya, lettuce and cabbage in a large salad bowl. Just before serving toss with enough dressing to coat.

4 servings

CHICKEN SALAD WITH RICE AND GRAPES IN LEMON-MUSTARD VINAIGRETTE

Lemon-Mustard Vinaigrette:
1 tablespoon sherry vinegar
1 tablespoon fresh lemon juice
1 teaspoon Dijon mustard
⅓ cup good quality olive oil
Salt and freshly ground pepper

2 whole chicken breasts
Salt to taste
¼ cup wild rice
2¼ cups reserved chicken stock
½ cup long-grain brown rice,
    long cooking
1½ to 2 cups seedless green grapes,
    halved
½ cup coarsely chopped
    pecans, toasted lightly
Lettuce leaves, washed and dried

Garnish:
Fruit of your choice
Parmesan cheese sticks

Lemon-Mustard Vinaigrette: Whisk, in small bowl, vinegar, lemon juice, mustard, oil, salt and pepper to taste.

In a large pan, place chicken, salt and enough water to cover chicken about 1 inch. Remove chicken. Bring salted water to a boil, replace chicken and poach at a low simmer for 20 minutes. Remove pan from heat and let chicken cool in liquid for 30 minutes. Remove chicken and keep 2¼ cups of liquid. Discard skin and bones from chicken. Cut chicken into small pieces.

In a large pan, bring reserved 2¼ cups liquid to boil; add wild rice and simmer covered for 10 minutes. Add brown rice to wild rice, simmer covered for 40 minutes, or until liquid is absorbed and rice is tender. Cool.

In large bowl, mix rice with chicken, grapes and pecans. Toss well with vinaigrette.

Serve on lettuce with fruit and Parmesan cheese sticks.

SAIPAN CHICKEN SALAD

Vegetable oil
1 package rice sticks
3 to 6 chicken breasts,
    boned and skinned
1 or 2 heads iceberg lettuce,
    shredded
¼ cup toasted sesame seeds
1 cup slivered almonds

4 tablespoons sugar
4 tablespoons rice vinegar
2 teaspoons salt
¼ teaspoon freshly ground pepper
3 tablespoons vegetable oil
1 tablespoon light sesame oil

Heat 2 to 3 inches of vegetable oil in a deep skillet to about 375°. Break rice sticks in 2-inch pieces and drop a few at a time into hot oil. They will explode instantly expanding to about 10 times their size. Remove immediately with a slotted spoon and drain in a large bowl lined with paper towels.

Gently poach chicken breasts. Cut into bite-size pieces.

Dressing: Whisk sugar, vinegar, salt and pepper together. Slowly whisk in oils.

Place shredded lettuce, sesame seeds, almonds, rice sticks and diced chicken in a large salad bowl and toss with dressing. Serve immediately.

GRILLED BREAST OF CHICKEN SALAD

1 cup dry white wine
4 tablespoons Dijon mustard
3 to 4 whole chicken breasts,
    skinned and halved

Dressing:
1 cup mayonnaise
2 tablespoons A-1 sauce
1 tablespoon Dijon mustard
½ teaspoon dill weed
Half and half
Salt and freshly ground pepper

Chopped lettuce
Green bell pepper strips
Red bell pepper strips
Onions

Blend white wine and mustard. Marinate the boneless, skinless chicken breasts for at least an hour.

Dressing: Combine mayonnaise, A-1 sauce, Dijon mustard, and dill weed. Blend and thin with half and half as necessary.

Cook onions and peppers over medium heat in a small amount of oil until very tender, about 10 minutes. Keep warm.

Grill chicken breasts about 5 minutes on each side. Sprinkle with salt and pepper.

Place bed of lettuce on individual plates and top with a few tablespoons of dressing. Slice grilled chicken breasts horizontally and place on top of lettuce. Spoon more dressing on top of the chicken. Top this with sautéed onions and peppers that are still warm from the frying pan.

4 to 6 servings

CURRIED CHUTNEY CHICKEN SALAD

Dressing:
1 cup mayonnaise
½ cup chutney, or to taste
1 teaspoon curry, or to taste
1 teaspoon lemon zest

4 whole chicken breasts, boned,
    skinned, cooked, cooled, and
    cut into cubes
3 to 4 Granny Smith apples,
    cored and chopped
¾ cup diced celery
1 cup chopped toasted walnuts
¼ cup golden raisins, optional

Dressing: Mix dressing ingredients until well blended.

Combine chicken, apples, celery, pecans and raisins. Pour dressing over chicken mixture and toss to mix. Chill.

Spoon salad into a lettuce-lined salad bowl or on individual salad plates.

Variation: Substitute 1 cup halved red grapes and ½ cup halved green grapes for apples and eliminate the raisins. Substitute toasted almonds for walnuts and add 1 tablespoon chopped fresh cilantro.

Variation: Substitute one 20-ounce can drained pineapple chunks for the apples. Add 1 cup sliced green onions and substitute toasted almonds or one 8-ounce can drained and sliced water chestnuts for walnuts.

6 servings

CORN AND CRAB SALAD WITH CANTALOUPE

Dressing:
2 tablespoons fresh lime juice
1 tablespoon fresh lemon juice
1 tablespoon soy sauce
1 shallot, minced
⅓ cup vegetable oil

1 pound crabmeat or crab blend
2 ears fresh corn, cooked and
    removed from cob
1 cantaloupe, peeled and
    thinly sliced
⅓ cup chopped cilantro
¼ cup toasted sesame seeds
1 red pepper, thinly sliced
1 yellow pepper, thinly sliced
Salad greens, torn
Radicchio lettuce leaves

Dressing: Whisk lime and lemon juices, soy sauce and shallot together in a small glass bowl. Slowly whisk in oil.

In large salad bowl, combine crabmeat, corn, cantaloupe, cilantro, sesame seeds and peppers. Pour dressing over salad and mix well.

Arrange a bed of crisp lettuce on 6 chilled salad plates. Set a radicchio leaf on each plate and spoon salad into center. Serve at once.

Variation: One cup frozen corn, cooked as directed on the package may be substituted for fresh corn.

6 servings

MUSHROOM, CHEESE AND CRANBERRY SALAD WITH MAPLE DRESSING

Dressing:
1 tablespoon maple syrup
½ tablespoon cider vinegar
2 tablespoons cranberry juice
1 teaspoon good mustard
½ cup vegetable oil

1 cup Jarlsburg cheese, julienned
8 ounces fresh white mushrooms,
    sliced
½ cup finely chopped parsley
⅓ cup dried cranberries
1 head Boston lettuce, torn
½ bunch watercress without stems

Dressing: Whisk syrup, vinegar, cranberry juice and mustard. Slowly add oil, whisking constantly.

Place all salad ingredients in a large salad bowl. Add just enough dressing to coat and toss gently. Serve at once.

4 servings

CRABACADO SALAD

1/2 cup mayonnaise
1/2 cup sour cream
1 tablespoon Dijon mustard
1 teaspoon fresh lemon juice
1 teaspoon Worcestershire sauce
1/4 cup minced celery
1/4 cup minced capers
1 hard-cooked egg, minced
2 tablespoons drained pimiento,
    minced
1 tablespoon fresh parsley, minced
1 head leaf lettuce
2 chilled ripe avocados,
    pitted and halved
2 6-ounce packages crabmeat
Paprika

Garnish:
4 chilled tomatoes, seeded
    and quartered
4 hard-cooked eggs, wedged
4 chilled artichoke hearts
16 pitted black olives

In a mixing bowl, blend mayonnaise, sour cream, mustard, lemon juice and Worcestershire. Stir in celery, capers, minced egg, pimiento and parsley. Chill.

Arrange leaf lettuce on salad plates. Place 1/2 avocado on each plate. Reserving some crabmeat for garnish, divide remaining crabmeat between the 4 avocado halves. Spoon dressing over each avocado. Place reserved crab on top of each. Sprinkle each salad lightly with paprika. Arrange tomatoes, eggs, artichoke hearts and black olives around avocado.
    Serve chilled.

4 servings

SPINACH-STRAWBERRY SALAD

Strawberry Vinaigrette:
1/2 cup sugar
2 tablespoons poppyseeds
1 teaspoon minced onion
1/2 teaspoon Worcestershire sauce
1/4 teaspoon paprika
1/2 cup vegetable oil
1/4 cup dry red wine vinegar
3 or 4 strawberries, crushed

Amounts according to number
    being served:
Spinach, washed and crisped
Halved strawberries

Strawberry Vinaigrette: In a jar with lid, mix sugar, poppyseeds, minced onion, Worcestershire sauce, paprika, vegetable oil and vinegar; shake well. Add a few crushed strawberries and shake.

In a large bowl, toss spinach and halved strawberries. Drizzle with dressing, toss and serve.

DUCK SALAD

Marinade:
½ cup red wine vinegar
1 cup red wine
3 tablespoons soy sauce
1 ounce fresh ginger
¼ cup olive oil
¼ cup chopped shallot
Juice of 1 orange

4 skinned boned duck breasts

Dressing:
5 ounces olive oil
¾ cup red wine vinegar
2 tablespoons Dijon mustard
2 tablespoons soy sauce
1 tablespoon chopped shallots
2 teaspoons finely chopped ginger
1 tablespoon chopped parsley
2 tablespoons marinade

Salad:
12 endive leaves
4 heads Boston lettuce
16 arugala leaves
2 leaves romaine
2 tablespoons cooking oil
½ papaya, sliced thin
1 cup toasted walnuts

Marinade: Place vinegar, wine, soy sauce, ginger, olive oil, shallots and orange juice in a large stainless steel or glass bowl and mix well. Add duck breasts and marinate in refrigerator for 12 hours, turning occasionally.

Dressing: Whisk olive oil, vinegar, mustard, soy sauce, shallots, ginger, parsley and 2 tablespoons marinade together in small glass bowl. Whisk again just before serving.

Salad: Arrange greens on a large chilled plate. Heat large sauté pan until very hot. Add cooking oil. Sauté duck breasts until browned but rare, 2 minutes per side. Remove and cut in julienne strips. Return to pan and toss with dressing just until warm. Remove from heat and toss with papaya and walnuts. Spoon on top of greens and serve at once.

4 servings

WARM SCALLOP SALAD
WITH ANCHOVY VINAIGRETTE

Anchovy Vinaigrette:

¼ cup sherry wine vinegar, balsamic
    or a very good red wine vinegar

Salt and freshly ground pepper

2 teaspoon anchovy paste, or to taste

2 cloves garlic, crushed

¼ cup freshly grated Parmesan
    cheese (or a little less)

1 tablespoon Dijon mustard

¼ cup extra virgin olive oil

½ cup vegetable oil

1 head Belgium endive, julienne

1 head Belgium endive, separated
    into spears

½ pound spinach, rinsed, dried and
    cut into julienne strips

1 pound fresh sea scallops or
    bay scallops

Seed and cut into fine julienne:

    1 yellow sweet pepper

    ½ green sweet pepper

    1 red sweet pepper

    2 large tomatoes, peeled

1 carrot, cut into thin strips
    with zester

2 large tomatoes, peeled, seeded and
    coarsely chopped

2 tablespoons toasted pine nuts
    (or toasted walnut pieces)

Anchovy Vinaigrette: Pour vinegar into medium bowl, add salt and pepper to taste. Swirl to dissolve. Whisk in the anchovy paste, garlic, cheese and mustard. Add oils in a slow stream whisking constantly. Season with additional pepper. Flavor is best if made several hours ahead.

Julienne one head of endive and soak in cool water for 30 minutes. Separate the other head into separate leaves and soak in a separate pan of cool water for 30 minutes. Drain both and pat dry with paper towels. Add julienned endive and spinach to a bowl and mix with some of the dressing.

Heat a large skillet until hot, add oil and heat until smoking, then sauté scallops for a minute or two, or until just cooked. *Do not overcook.*

Arrange endive spears around the edges of large serving platter, in a wagon wheel spoke fashion. Add julienned endive and spinach to the center of the plate. Scatter the scallops over the spinach and endive on serving plate. Garnish with pepper strips, carrots, tomato and pine nuts. Drizzle scallops and vegetables with a little more dressing and serve immediately.

6 servings

CRANBERRY-CHICKEN MOLD

1 package (1 tablespoon) unflavored
    gelatin
1/4 cup cold water
1 16-ounce can whole cranberry
    sauce
1 12-ounce can crushed pineapple
    with juice
1/2 cup chopped nutmeats
1 tablespoon fresh lemon juice

1 package (1 tablespoon) unflavored
    gelatin
1/4 cup cold water
1 cup mayonnaise
1/2 cup chopped celery
1 tablespoons chopped fresh parsley
3/4 teaspoon salt
1/2 cup water
2 cups chopped cooked chicken
Green grapes, optional

First layer: In top of double boiler, soften gelatin in cold water. Place over boiling water, heat until gelatin is dissolved, about 5 minutes. Add cranberry sauce, pineapple, nutmeats and lemon juice; mix well. Pour into 8x10-inch or similar shallow dish. Refrigerate until firm.

Second layer: In top of double boiler, soften gelatin in cold water. Place over boiling water, heat until gelatin is dissolved, about 5 minutes. Add mayonnaise, celery, parsley, salt, water and chicken, mix well. Pour over firm first layer. Refrigerate.

8 servings

ASPARAGUS SALAD

2 envelopes unflavored gelatin
1 1/2 cups cold water, divided
3/4 cup sugar
1/2 cup cider vinegar
1 teaspoon salt
2 tablespoons fresh lemon juice
1 tablespoon minced onion
1 10-ounce can asparagus pieces,
    drained
1 cup pimiento, finely chopped
1 5-ounce can water chestnuts,
    chopped
1 cup finely chopped celery

Dissolve gelatin in 1/2 cup cold water; set aside.
    In small saucepan, combine sugar, vinegar, salt and 1 cup water. Bring to boil, stirring until sugar dissolves. Remove from heat and add gelatin, onion and lemon juice. Set aside until mixture cools to lukewarm.
    Add asparagus, pimiento, water chestnuts and celery. Divide mixture into 8 individual molds or fill one 2-quart ring mold. Refrigerate 2 to 3 hours, or until gelatin is firm.
    Serve with creamy dressing, if desired.

8 to 10 servings

BEET AND HORSERADISH MOLDED SALAD

1 3-ounce package lemon gelatin
1 cup boiling water
1 16-ounce can pickled diced beets
1 cup beet juice, reserved from beets
¾ cup chopped celery
2 tablespoons chopped green onion
1 tablespoon horseradish

Buttermilk Dressing:
¾ cup mayonnaise
½ cup buttermilk
1 tablespoon chopped fresh parsley
½ teaspoon minced onion
1 small clove garlic, crushed
½ teaspoon salt
Freshly ground pepper

Dissolve gelatin in 1 cup boiling water. Drain beets reserving liquid in measuring cup. Run boiling water through beets, if necessary, to equal 1 cup beet juice. Add juice, beets, celery, onion and drained horseradish to gelatin. Refrigerate until thickened but not set, about 1½ hours. Stir and pour into an oiled 3-cup or 6 individual ½-cup molds. Refrigerate until firm.

Buttermilk Dressing: Combine all ingredients and mix well. Chill at least 2 hours.

Unmold onto lettuce lined platter or individual salad plates. Spoon a dollop of the dressing on top or pass dressing separately.

6 servings

BLEU CHEESE SPINACH SALAD

Dressing:
2 tablespoons tarragon vinegar
¾ teaspoon salt
1 teaspoon fresh basil
Freshly ground pepper
3 tablespoons extra virgin olive oil

1 pound fresh spinach, torn in bite
    size pieces
1 14-ounce can hearts of palm,
    drained, sliced
½ pound bacon, diced and cooked
    until crispy
4 ounces bleu cheese, crumbled

Dressing: Whisk vinegar and salt in a small bowl until salt is dissolved. Add basil and pepper. Add oil in a thin stream and whisk until smooth.

Combine spinach, hearts of palm, bacon and bleu cheese in a large salad bowl. Pour dressing on salad and toss gently. Cover and chill. Can be prepared several hours before serving. Gently toss again before serving.

6 to 8 servings

SPINACH, CABBAGE SALAD WITH LEMON VINAIGRETTE

Dressing:
2½ tablespoons red wine vinegar
1 tablespoon fresh lemon juice
2 tablespoons sugar
½ teaspoon salt
½ cup olive oil
½ teaspoon minced onion
½ teaspoon dry mustard

½ head cabbage, torn into bite-size
    pieces
1 medium red onion, thinly sliced
1 pound spinach, torn into bite-size
    pieces
½ pound bacon, diced and cooked
    until crisp
3 hard cooked eggs, chopped
Freshly ground pepper

Dressing: Combine vinegar, lemon, sugar and salt. Whisk until salt and sugar are dissolved. Whisk in oil, onion and dry mustard. Can be made ahead and whisked again just before serving.

Layer cabbage, onion, spinach, bacon and eggs in large salad bowl. Cover and chill.

Pour dressing over salad and toss gently. Season with pepper and serve immediately.

4 to 6 servings

MARINATED BROCCOLI AND MUSHROOM SALAD

Marinade:
1 cup mayonnaise
1 tablespoon sugar
2 tablespoons wine vinegar

1 large bunch broccoli, cut into
    florets
1 cup fresh mushrooms
½ to ¾ cups raisins
½ cup chopped celery or
    water chestnuts
½ cup chopped red onion
½ pound bacon, diced and cooked
    until crispy
½ cup sunflower seeds or walnuts,
    toasted
Leafy green lettuce

Marinade: Whisk mayonnaise, sugar and vinegar in small bowl.

Combine the broccoli, mushrooms, raisins, celery, and onion in a large salad bowl. Pour marinade over vegetables. Toss. Cover and marinate in refrigerator for 4 hours, stirring occasionally.

Stir in bacon and sunflower seeds. Arrange salad on a bed of leafy green lettuce.

Variation: Substitute 1½ cups of red seedless grapes for the raisins.

4 to 6 servings

WALNUT AND HEARTS OF PALM SALAD

Dressing:
1 tablespoon red wine vinegar
2 teaspoons Dijon mustard
3 tablespoons corn or safflower oil
1 tablespoon walnut oil, optional
Salt and freshly ground pepper

1 7½-ounce can hearts of palm,
*   drained*
½ cup walnuts, broken into small
*   pieces*

Dressing: Whisk together vinegar and mustard. Slowly pour in oils, whisking continuously. Add salt and pepper to taste.

Slice hearts of palm into ½-inch rounds. Place in bowl with walnuts. Gently toss with the Walnut Vinaigrette. Serve.

2 servings

CAESAR SALAD WITH LIME

Dressing:
3 cloves garlic, crushed
1 to 2 teaspoons anchovy paste
2 egg yolks
1 tablespoon white wine vinegar
2 teaspoons balsamic vinegar
1½ teaspoon Dijon mustard
1 teaspoon Worcestershire sauce
¼ teaspoon salt
2 teaspoons fresh lime juice
¾ cup extra virgin olive oil

1 clove garlic
3 tablespoons butter
1 cup ½-inch French bread cubes
2 heads romaine lettuce, torn into
*   pieces, rinsed and spun dry*
¼ cup freshly grated Parmesan
*   cheese*

Dressing: In small bowl, mix garlic with anchovy paste. Whisk yolks, vinegar, mustard, Worcestershire sauce, salt and lime juice in same bowl. Add the oil in a stream, whisking constantly. Whisk the dressing well until it is emulsified.

Croutons: Rub a heavy skillet with cut side of garlic. In skillet, cook garlic with butter over moderately low heat for 5 minutes or until it is golden. Discard garlic, add 1 cup of ½-inch cubes of French bread. Cook croutons, tossing until they are toasted lightly. Sprinkle with salt to taste and transfer to a paper towel to drain. Makes about 1 cup.
In large bowl, toss romaine with Parmesan and croutons, add dressing and toss until it is well combined.

Variation: Use Mock Caesar Dressing (see page 72).

4 servings

NUTTY CHILLED PEAS

1 16-ounce bag frozen petit pois
    peas, thawed and drained
1 cup sour cream
2 green onions, chopped
6 slices bacon, cooked and crumbled
$\frac{1}{2}$ teaspoon salt
Freshly ground pepper
$\frac{1}{2}$ cup cashews or macadamia nuts,
    chopped
$\frac{1}{2}$ cup celery or water chestnuts,
    chopped

In large bowl, combine peas, sour cream, onions, bacon, salt, pepper, nuts and water chestnuts. Mix well and serve in lettuce cup.

8 servings

INSALATA PRIMAVERA

Dressing:
1 cup mayonnaise
$\frac{1}{2}$ cup sour cream
2 tablespoon Dijon mustard
$\frac{1}{2}$ teaspoon garlic powder
$\frac{1}{2}$ teaspoon basil, ground
1 teaspoon freshly ground pepper
$\frac{1}{4}$ cup crumbled Fontina cheese

1 16-ounce bag frozen petit peas,
    thawed
1 pound fresh green beans, blanched
    until tender
$\frac{1}{2}$ pound new red potatoes, cooked
    and sliced
1 cup sliced carrots, cooked until
    tender
1 cup chopped dill pickles
1 2-ounce jar pimentos, drained
1 6$\frac{1}{2}$-ounce jar marinated artichoke
    hearts, drained
$\frac{1}{2}$ cup sliced black olives
$\frac{1}{2}$ cup sliced scallions
Red cabbage leaves

Dressing: Whisk together, in small bowl, mayonnaise, sour cream, mustard, garlic powder, basil, pepper and cheese.

In a large bowl, combine peas, beans, potatoes, carrots, pickles, pimentos, artichoke hearts, olives, and scallions. Pour dressing over vegetables. Toss gently and chill 2 to 3 hours.

Line salad bowl with red cabbage leaves. Spoon salad into bowl and garnish with chopped parsley.

8 servings

MARINATED BRUSSELS SPROUTS, ZUCCHINI AND TOMATO SALAD

Vinaigrette Marinade:
1 cup salad or olive oil
¼ cup lemon juice
¼ cup white wine vinegar
2 cloves garlic, crushed
2 teaspoons seasoned salt
1 teaspoon sugar
½ teaspoon dry mustard
½ teaspoon salad
¼ teaspoon crushed dry red chilies
  or Tabasco sauce

1 pound fresh Brussels sprouts
1½ pounds zucchini, sliced
  (about 3 medium)
¼ cup sliced green onions

1 pound cherry tomatoes
1 head Boston or red leaf lettuce

Vinaigrette Marinade: Mix oil, lemon juice, vinegar, garlic, salt, sugar, mustard, salt and chilies together in glass jar or food processor with metal blade. Marinade may be refrigerated up to 2 days.

In a medium saucepan, bring small amount of salted water to a boil. Add Brussels sprouts, return to boiling, and simmer until crisp tender, about 5 minutes. Do not overcook, as they will continue to cook in marinade. Plunge immediately into a bowl of ice water to stop cooking. Drain well; slice into 4 to 5 slices each. Toss with zucchini and onions. Pour marinade over vegetables and refrigerate covered for at least 12 hours, stirring occasionally. May be refrigerated overnight.

One hour before serving, add tomatoes to marinade. Line a serving platter with lettuce leaves. Spoon vegetables onto lettuce.

8 servings

HERBED CREAMY CUCUMBERS

4 cucumbers, peeled, seeded,
  quartered, sliced in ¼ to ½-inch
  chunks

Dressing:
1 small yellow onion, thinly sliced
1½ cups sour cream
1 tablespoon fresh dill
2 to 3 tablespoons chopped
  fresh chives
¾ cup mayonnaise
Salt and freshly ground pepper

Salt cucumbers and allow to drain in a colander, pressing out excess liquid before adding dressing.

Dressing: In a bowl, add onion to sour cream, dill, chives, mayonnaise, salt and pepper. Mix well. Add cucumbers and chill. These cucumbers may be made a day ahead.

ORIENTAL SLAW

1 package chicken flavored Chinese
    ramen noodles
2 tablespoons sugar
Salt and freshly ground pepper
3 tablespoons red wine vinegar
1/3 cup vegetable oil

1 teaspoon butter
1 3-ounce package slivered almonds
2 tablespoons sesame seeds
1 medium head red cabbage,
    shredded
4 scallions, sliced

Add chicken flavoring packet from noodles, sugar, salt and pepper to vinegar and whisk until dissolved. Slowly add vegetable oil, whisking constantly.

Melt butter in a small skillet. Add almonds and toast until light, stirring constantly. Remove from skillet; add sesame seeds and toast until lightly colored. Remove and cool.

Mix cabbage and scallions together. Add crumbled uncooked noodles, almonds and sesame seeds. Toss to mix. Pour dressing over salad and toss well. Serve immediately.

Variation: Cooked chicken or shrimp can be added to make this a luncheon entree.

GREEK SALAD

Dressing:
4 tablespoons extra virgin olive oil
Juice of 1 fresh lemon
1 teaspoon fresh oregano, chopped
1 teaspoon fresh parsley, chopped
Salt and freshly ground pepper

Salad:
1 head Boston or bibb lettuce, torn
    in bite-size pieces
1 1/2 cups watercress, remove lower
    stem portion
1 cup escarole, torn in bite-size pieces
Greek olives, to taste
Feta cheese, to taste

Dressing: Whisk together in a small bowl the olive oil, lemon juice, oregano, parsley, salt and pepper to taste.

Salad: Toss salad greens with dressing. Top with Greek olives and crumbled feta cheese.

6 servings

NEST OF TOFU WITH GINGERY ORIENTAL DRESSING

Gingery Oriental Dressing:
3 tablespoons low-sodium soy sauce
2 tablespoons fresh lemon juice
2 tablespoons white wine vinegar
2 tablespoons brown sugar
1 tablespoon freshly grated peeled
*   ginger, or to taste*
2 tablespoons dark sesame oil
1 tablespoon chopped green onion

¾ pound bean sprouts
4 firm or tender tofu cakes, rinsed
*   and cubed*
3 to 4 carrots, shredded in food
*   processor*

Garnish:
Cabbage flowers
Chopped green onions
Fresh parsley

Gingery Oriental Dressing: In medium bowl, whisk soy sauce, lemon juice, vinegar, brown sugar, ginger, sesame oil and chopped green onion until well mixed.

Place bean sprouts in colander and pour boiling water over, rinse in cold running water. Dry sprouts and refrigerate.

In medium bowl, gently fold tofu cubes with ½ salad dressing, using a rubber spatula to prevent breaking. Chill overnight.

Using a round tray, center salad with cabbage flowers or parsley, next arrange bean sprouts, tofu cubes and shredded carrots. Sprinkle chopped onions over top. When ready to serve, drizzle with remaining dressing.

CRUNCHY SPICY COLE SLAW

Dressing:
2 cups mayonnaise
2 teaspoons mustard
3 tablespoons sugar
1 onion, finely chopped
¼ teaspoon freshly ground pepper
Dash of paprika
1 pound cabbage, shredded

Dressing: In a large bowl, whisk mayonnaise, mustard, sugar, onion, pepper and paprika. Add cabbage and toss. Serve garnished with sliced green pepper.

Hint: Choose your favorite mustard.

Variations: Combine 2 or 3 varieties of shredded cabbage to equal 3½ to 4½ cups. Try red, white and green cabbages. Vary the peppers using yellow and/or red pepper for additional color.

6 servings

FRESH TOMATO AND CHÈVRE WITH VINAIGRETTE

4 large tomatoes, cut in wedges
1 cup extra virgin olive oil
⅓ cup red wine vinegar
¼ cup fresh basil, snipped
2 cloves garlic, crushed
½ teaspoon salt
¼ teaspoon freshly ground pepper
½ teaspoon Parisian or
    Dijon mustard
8 ounces chèvre, crumbled
1 large red onion, minced
Italian parsley, minced

Place tomato wedges in a shallow dish. Combine oil, vinegar, basil, garlic, salt, pepper and mustard. Pour over tomatoes. Cover and marinate 2 to 3 hours in refrigerator.

Arrange tomatoes on a lettuce lined platter or on individual salad plates. Sprinkle with chèvre, onion and parsley.

Variation: Use fresh mozzarella for cheese.

Hint: A Bermuda or Spanish onion, when in season, may be substituted for the red onion. Italian parsley is a flat-leaf parsley.

8 servings

CUCUMBER, TOMATO AND ONION SALAD

Dressing:
⅓ cup vegetable oil
4 teaspoons red wine vinegar
1 teaspoon Dijon mustard
Several dashes of
    Worcestershire sauce
Dash of garlic powder
1 tablespoon sugar
3-4 drops of hot sauce
Salt and freshly ground pepper

3 fresh tomatoes, sliced
2 large cucumbers, sliced
½ cup chopped onions

Dressing: Whisk together in small bowl, vegetable oil, vinegar, mustard, Worcestershire sauce, garlic powder, sugar, hot sauce, salt and pepper to taste.

Combine tomatoes, cucumbers and onions. Toss with dressing. Chill.

8 to 10 servings

MOCK CAESAR DRESSING

8 cloves garlic, minced
1 teaspoon salt
1 teaspoon freshly ground pepper
1 tablespoon Dijon mustard
1 cup extra virgin olive oil
¼ cup fresh lemon juice
½ cup freshly grated Parmesan
    cheese
Croutons
4 anchovies, rinsed and patted dry,
    optional

Whisk together garlic, salt, pepper, Dijon, olive oil, and lemon juice. Let stand for at least 1 hour. Just before serving add cheese and mix.

Toss romaine with croutons and dressing, top with anchovies.

1 cup dressing

CRACKED PEPPER DRESSING

2 cups mayonnaise
¾ cup sour cream
½ cup freshly grated Romano cheese
1 tablespoon cracked pepper
1 tablespoon cider vinegar
1 teaspoon fresh lemon juice
¼ cup minced onion
1 small clove garlic, minced
1 dash red pepper sauce
2 dashes white wine
    Worcestershire sauce

In a large bowl, whisk mayonnaise, sour cream, cheese, pepper, vinegar, lemon juice, onion, garlic, red pepper sauce and Worcestershire sauce. Chill.
    Serve over mixed greens.
    Toss with bibb lettuce, romaine and radicchio.

3 cups

DIJON CHUTNEY DRESSING

½ cup wine vinegar
5 tablespoons chutney
1 to 2 cloves garlic
4 tablespoons Dijon mustard
3 to 4 teaspoons sugar
⅔ to 1 cup vegetable oil
Salt and freshly ground pepper

In food processor work bowl, combine vinegar, chutney, garlic, mustard and sugar. Process. Add oil slowing while processor is running. Make 1 day ahead to blend flavors. Season with salt and pepper to taste.

2 cups

WALNUT VINAIGRETTE

2 tablespoons Balsamic vinegar
1 teaspoon Dijon mustard
1/4 cup olive oil
1 tablespoon ground walnuts
Salt and freshly ground pepper

Combine vinegar and mustard in a small bowl and whisk well. Slowly drizzle in the oil, whisking constantly until smooth. Add ground walnuts and season with salt and pepper to taste. Blend well.

Drizzle over various greens: Boston, bibb, red leaf or arugula. Garnish with chopped, toasted walnuts and pimiento strips or tomatoes.

1/2 cup

BLEU CHEESE DRESSING

1 cup sour cream
1 teaspoon dry mustard
1/2 teaspoon freshly ground pepper
1/2 teaspoon salt
1/3 teaspoon garlic powder
1 teaspoon Worcestershire sauce
1 1/3 cups mayonnaise
4 ounces crumbled imported
    bleu cheese
1/4 cup chopped fresh parsley

In the large bowl of an electric mixer, combine sour cream, dry mustard, pepper, salt, garlic powder, and Worcestershire sauce and beat two minutes at low speed. Add mayonnaise and beat 1/2 minute at low speed, then increase speed to medium and beat an additional two minutes. Slowly add bleu cheese and parsley and beat at low speed for four minutes. Refrigerate overnight before serving.

3 cups

HAZELNUT VINAIGRETTE

2 teaspoons Dijon mustard
2 tablespoons chopped fresh tarragon
    or 2 teaspoons dried tarragon
2 tablespoons hazelnut liqueur
    or 2 tablespoons sugar
4 teaspoons tarragon vinegar
2 egg yolks
1/2 teaspoon salt
1 cup olive oil

In a small bowl, whisk mustard, tarragon, liqueur, vinegar, egg yolks and salt. Add oil, whisk until incorporated.

In a large bowl, toss spinach, hazelnuts and crumbled bacon. Drizzle dressing over and serve immediately.

RASPBERRY DRESSING

1 tablespoon Dijon mustard
½ cup to ¾ cup honey
1 cup olive oil, or ½ cup vegetable oil
    and ½ cup olive oil
2 tablespoons raspberry vinegar
Dash freshly ground white pepper
1 teaspoon Worcestershire sauce
1 tablespoon fresh lemon juice
3 to 4 tablespoons crushed
    raspberries, strained to
    remove seeds
4 tablespoons half and half

Combine all ingredients in a blender or food processor. Will be a beautiful pink color.

Drizzle on bibb lettuce, avocado and red onion slices.

2 cups

TERIYAKI DRESSING

1 clove garlic, minced
¼ cup red wine vinegar
½ cup olive oil
2 tablespoons Dijon mustard
1 teaspoon soy sauce
½ teaspoon ground ginger
Toasted sesame seeds, optional

In a jar combine garlic, vinegar, olive oil, mustard, soy sauce and ginger. Shake well.

1 cup

SUN-DRIED TOMATO BALSAMIC VINAIGRETTE

2 sun-dried tomatoes
1½ tablespoons balsamic vinegar
1½ tablespoons red wine vinegar
⅓ extra virgin olive oil
1 tablespoon chopped fresh basil

Cook sun-dried tomatoes in water to cover for 10 minutes. Cool and chop.

In a jar, combine sun-dried tomatoes, vinegars, olive oil and basil; shake well.

In large salad bowl, combine spinach, radicchio, watercress, chèvre and pine nuts; drizzle dressing on top, toss and serve immediately.

¾ cup dressing

EGGS & PASTA

Eggs

Asparagus Quiche 84
Basque Eggs 80
Cheese and Chilies Strata 82
Chicken Pecan Quiche 81
Deviled Eggs with Three Fillings 81
Egg White Omelette 86
Eggs Benedict Casserole 82
Hot Crab Soufflé 87
Huevos Rancheros 79
Marbleized Eggs 83
Mexican Ham and Scrambled Eggs 79
Mushroom Sausage Strata 77
Poached Eggs in Curry Cream 77
Potato and Leek Frittata 86
Puff Pastry Omelette with Spinach,
    Mozzarella and Sausage 85
Scrambled Eggs with Asparagus
    and Sweet Red Pepper 78
Scrambled Egg Tostados 80
Spinach Omelette 78
Spinach and Ricotta Tart 78
Vegetable Custard Pie 84
Wild Mushroom Crustless Quiche 83

Pasta

Angel Hair Pasta
    with Tomato Basil Shrimp 98
Antipasto Tortellini 88
Carbonara Sauce with Tortellini 89
Chicken Normandy Rigatoni 102
Chicken, Sausage and Red Pepper
    with Rotelle Pasta 90
Chicken Tortellini Salad
    with Pesto Sauce 89
Chicken with Pasta,
    Artichokes and Olives 102
Country Noodles 97

Crabmeat Fettucini 97
Eggplant Pasta 92
Hearty Stir Fry 94
Linguine with Grilled Chicken,
    Sun-dried Tomatoes and Pesto 96
Mushroom Italia Fettucini 95
Mustard Greens and Pasta
    with Anchovy-Garlic Sauce 94
Oriental Noodles with Hot and
    Spicy Peanut Sauce 93
Pasta Salad with
    Ham and Bleu Cheese 90
Pasta, Scallops and
    Leeks with Beurre Blanc 91
Pasta with Zucchini,
    Red Pepper and Onion 92
Pasta with Smoked Turkey
    and Sun-dried Tomatoes 95
Roselline (Pasta Roses) 100
Scallop and Spinach Penne Salad 88
Scallop and Vegetable Lasagna 99
Shrimp Scampi 99
Three Meat Ravioli 101
Three Cheese Pasta with Walnuts 98
Tomato and Sausage Pasta Salad 87
Tortellini Bruschetta 93
Vermicelli with Sun-dried Tomatoes
    and Spinach Sauce 91
Walnut Asparagus Linguine 96

Snips & Tips

Cheeses 243
Flavored Butters 246

P O A C H E D   E G G S   I N   C U R R Y   C R E A M

2 English muffin halves, toasted
*   and buttered*
2 thin slices cooked ham
½ cup half and half
½ teaspoon curry powder
¼ teaspoon salt
2 very fresh large eggs,
*   room temperature*

Garnish:
Paprika
Chopped fresh parsley

Place muffin halves in shallow serving dish (or individual serving dishes) and top each with one slice of ham. Keep warm.

In a small skillet combine half and half, curry powder and salt. Bring the mixture to a boil over moderately low heat; reduce heat and simmer for 30 seconds.

Break eggs into a small custard cup and slip them, one at a time, into the cream. Spoon cream over eggs for 3 to 4 minutes or until poached to desired doneness.

With a slotted spoon remove the eggs one at a time and place on top of the ham. Spoon sauce over each and sprinkle with paprika and chopped parsley.

Serve immediately.

2 servings

M U S H R O O M   S A U S A G E   S T R A T A

1 pound mushrooms, sliced
3 green onions, chopped
2 tablespoons butter
2 pounds mild bulk pork sausage
1 teaspoon dry mustard
18 slices white bread, crusts removed
6 eggs
3 cups milk
1 tablespoon Worcestershire sauce
Salt and freshly ground pepper
12 ounces grated cheddar cheese

Preheat oven to 350°. Butter a 9x13-inch baking dish.

In a large skillet, melt butter; sauté mushrooms and green onion. Remove from skillet and set aside.

In same skillet, cook sausage, breaking up with a fork. Drain. Stir in dry mustard and mix with mushrooms and green onion.

Place 9 slices of bread in baking dish. Spread sausage mixture over bread. Cube remaining 9 slices of bread and sprinkle on mixture.

In separate bowl, beat eggs; add milk, Worcestershire sauce, salt and pepper to taste. Pour over bread cubes.

Bake for 50 to 60 minutes or until top is light brown. Sprinkle cheese over top and bake for an additional 10 minutes or until cheese melts.

Hint: Casserole is great for brunch! It can be frozen before baking and defrosted the night before cooking.

12 servings

SCRAMBLED EGGS WITH ASPARAGUS AND SWEET RED PEPPER

1 pound fresh asparagus, cut into 1-inch pieces
½ large sweet red pepper, seeded and chopped
12 eggs
1 cup half and half
1 teaspoon marjoram
Salt and freshly ground pepper
4 tablespoons unsalted butter, melted

Steam asparagus and red pepper until tender crisp. Beat eggs with half and half, marjoram, salt and pepper to taste.

Melt butter in a large skillet; scramble egg mixture until set. Toss eggs with cooked asparagus and adjust seasonings to taste.

6 to 8 servings

SPINACH AND RICOTTA TART

2 10-ounce packages frozen chopped spinach, thawed, drained
1 small onion, minced
3 tablespoons butter
½ teaspoon salt
¼ teaspoon nutmeg
Dash freshly ground pepper
1 pound ricotta cheese
½ cup grated Romano cheese
1 cup half and half
3 eggs, slightly beaten

Preheat oven to 350°. Coat a 2-quart glass baking dish with non-stick spray.

In a large saucepan, sauté onion in butter. Stir in spinach. Add salt, nutmeg and pepper.

In a large bowl, combine cheeses, half and half and eggs. Beat lightly. Stir in spinach mixture. Pour in baking dish.

Bake for 50 minutes.

6 to 8 servings

SPINACH OMELETTE

3 eggs
¼ teaspoon salt
¼ teaspoon pepper
1 tablespoon butter
2 2-inch pieces cream cheese, room temperature
1 package frozen chopped spinach, cooked and drained

In a large bowl, beat eggs with salt and pepper. In omelette pan, melt butter over very high heat (do not burn). Pour in eggs and cook gently until they begin to set. Place pieces of cream cheese on omelette. Spoon on heaping tablespoon of spinach. Fold omelette over to enfold cheese and spinach.

1 serving

HUEVOS RANCHEROS

Oil
2 corn or flour tortillas
2 eggs

Salsa Verde (page 37)
Spicy Salsa (page 36)

Garnish:
Fresh tomato and avocado slices

In a large skillet, heat oil and lightly sauté tortillas. Set aside and keep warm. Add eggs to skillet and cook to taste (i.e. over-easy, over-medium). Place eggs on top of warm tortillas. Pour salsa verde over eggs and tortillas.

Serve hot with spicy salsa (page 36) and sour cream. Garnish plate with tomatoes and avocado slices.

1 serving

MEXICAN HAM AND SCRAMBLED EGGS

8 round onion, poppy seed or
    kaiser rolls
1/2 cup minced onion
4 tablespoons butter
2 3-ounce packages cream cheese
1/2 cup mayonnaise
1 4-ounce can green chilies, drained
1/4 cup chopped black olives
Freshly ground pepper
1 pound bulk chorizo or other spicy
    sausage, cooked and drained
8 large eggs, scrambled and cooked
2 cups shredded Monterey Jack
    cheese

Preheat oven to 350°.

Cut a 1/2-inch slice from tops of rolls and scoop out insides, leaving a 1/4-inch shell. Place rolls and tops on baking sheet and bake for 10 minutes or until lightly toasted.

In a small skillet, sauté onion in butter until tender. Stir in cream cheese; cook over very low heat, stirring constantly until cheese melts. Remove from heat and stir in mayonnaise, green chilies, black olives and pepper. Divide cream cheese mixture evenly among toasted rolls. Using back of spoon, spread mixture over bottom and up sides of each roll. Divide sausage and scrambled eggs evenly among the rolls. Sprinkle each with cheese and replace tops. Wrap individually in aluminum foil. Place on a baking sheet.

Bake for 30 minutes or until cheese is melted. Remove from oven and let stand 5 minutes before unwrapping. Serve at once.

These rolls can be partially prepared the night before. Wrap well and refrigerate overnight. Return to room temperature and fill with freshly cooked sausage and eggs just before baking.

8 servings

SCRAMBLED EGG TOSTADOS

Vegetable oil
6 small flour tortillas
8 eggs, slightly beaten
½ cup sour cream
½ cup shredded Monterey Jack
  cheese
1 4-ounce can chopped green chilies,
  drained
½ cup chopped onion
1 small clove garlic, minced
2 tablespoons butter, melted
¼ teaspoon ground cumin
2 cups shredded lettuce
1 large fresh ripe tomato, chopped
Sour cream
2 to 3 tablespoons chopped
  black olives
2 ripe avocados, chopped
Salsa

Preheat oven to 200°.

Pour 1-inch oil into a large skillet and heat until very hot. Fry tortillas, one at a time, for a minute or two, or until crisp and lightly browned. Remove and drain on paper towels. Place in oven to keep warm.

Combine eggs, ½ cup sour cream, cheese and green chilies; mix well. In a large skillet, sauté onion and garlic in butter until tender. Add ground cumin and stir for 1 minute. Pour egg mixture into skillet and cook over medium heat, stirring occasionally, until eggs are firm but still moist.

Place tortillas on serving plates and top each with equal portions of the following: lettuce, scrambled egg, chopped tomatoes, additional sour cream, chopped avocados and olives. Serve immediately with salsa.

6 servings

BASQUE EGGS

2½ tablespoons olive oil
4 shallots, finely chopped
2 cloves garlic, crushed
2 green peppers, julienned
3 average size tomatoes,
  skinned and seeded, cut into
  small pieces or cherry tomatoes
  cut in half
1 bay leaf
¼ teaspoon thyme
¼ teaspoon salt
Freshly ground pepper
8 eggs
4 tablespoons butter
4 slices bacon, gently fried

Heat olive oil in a saucepan; add shallots and garlic and sauté for two minutes. Add green peppers and sauté for 30 minutes. Add tomatoes, bay leaf, thyme, salt and pepper. Simmer for 15 minutes, uncovered, stirring occasionally.

In a large bowl, whisk eggs, salt and pepper lightly. In a large skillet, melt butter and pour in egg mixture. Cook over medium heat, stirring occasionally, until eggs are firm but still moist. Place eggs on a hot dish, make a well in the center and fill with vegetables. Arrange bacon around eggs.

4 to 6 servings

D E V I L E D   E G G S   W I T H   T H R E E   F I L L I N G S

12 eggs
¼ cup mayonnaise
¼ cup unsalted butter, softened

2 tablespoons minced prosciutto
1 tablespoon freshly grated
    Parmesan cheese

3 tablespoons sun-dried tomatoes,
    packed in oil

1 tablespoon unsalted butter
1 scallion, thinly sliced
1 large mushroom, minced

Garnish:
Sliced black olives
Sprigs of fresh parsley
Fresh basil leaves
Radish sprouts

Place eggs in a large pan in one layer. Add water to cover eggs by one inch. Bring to a full boil, cover and remove from heat. Let stand at least 20 minutes. Peel eggs and slice in half.

Put yolks in food processor work bowl with mayonnaise and butter. Process until very smooth. Add more mayonnaise or butter, if needed. Yolks should be soft, but should hold their shape. Divide into 3 small bowls.

First filling: Stir prosciutto and Parmesan into yolk mixture.

Second filling: Drain sun-dried tomatoes and pat dry with paper towels. Chop and add to yolk mixture.

Third filling: Melt butter in a small skillet, add scallion and mushroom; cook until tender. Mix in yolk mixture.

Using a pastry bag, fitted with a star tip, or a teaspoon; fill 8 egg halves with each filling. Garnish eggs with sliced black olives, sprigs of fresh parsley, a shred of fresh basil leaf or chives.

Cover lightly and chill.

To serve, line a basket with a brightly colored napkin. Fill halfway with fresh radish sprouts. Nest eggs in the sprouts.

24 halves

C H I C K E N   P E C A N   Q U I C H E

1 9-inch pie crust, baked and cooled
1 cup cooked chicken, finely chopped
1 cup grated Swiss cheese
¼ cup chopped onion
1 tablespoon flour
½ cup chopped toasted pecans,
    divided
2 eggs, beaten
1 cup milk
½ teaspoon Dijon mustard

Preheat oven to 325°.

Mix chicken, cheese, onion, flour and ¼ cup pecans. Spread into pie crust.

Mix eggs, milk and mustard; pour over chicken mixture. Top with remaining ¼ cup pecans.

Bake for 50 minutes or until knife inserted in center is withdrawn clean. Cool on wire rack. Serve warm.

Hint: This casserole may be frozen before baking and defrosted the night before baking.

6 servings

CHEESE AND CHILIES STRATA

12 slices bread, buttered and cut
    into cubes
¾ pound shredded cheddar cheese
1 pound bacon, cooked and crumbled
½ cup chopped fresh parsley
1 4-ounce can chopped green chilies
6 eggs, beaten
2 tablespoons minced onion
½ teaspoon dry mustard
½ teaspoon salt
Freshly ground pepper

Preheat oven to 350°. Butter 9x13-inch baking dish.

    Spread bread cubes over bottom of prepared baking dish. Sprinkle with shredded cheese, bacon, parsley and green chilies. In a large bowl, beat eggs with onion, dry mustard, salt and pepper. Pour over cheeses. Cover and refrigerate overnight.

    Bake uncovered for 45 minutes.

    Variation: Substitute 1 pound diced ham or 1 pound chopped cooked shrimp for bacon.

8 servings

EGGS BENEDICT CASSEROLE

Mornay Sauce:
¼ cup butter, melted
½ cup flour
½ teaspoon salt
⅛ teaspoon nutmeg
2½ cups milk
1½ cups Gruyère cheese, shredded
½ cup freshly grated Parmesan
    cheese

1 pound fresh asparagus, woody
    ends removed
5 whole English muffins
10 slices Canadian bacon
10 eggs
¼ teaspoon freshly ground pepper
1 cup corn flakes
1 tablespoon butter, melted

Preheat oven to 350°.

    Mornay Sauce: In a saucepan, heat butter over low heat until melted; stir in flour, salt and nutmeg. Cook over low heat, stirring constantly, until smooth and bubbly. Remove from heat. Stir in milk and heat to boiling, stirring constantly. Boil and stir 1 minute. Add cheeses. Cook and stir until cheese melts and mixture is smooth.

    Trim and blanch asparagus for 3 minutes in boiling water. Cool under cold water and drain well.

    Halve, toast and butter English muffins. Arrange halves in ungreased baking dish with bacon slice on top of each half. Place asparagus spears on top of each bacon slice. Prepare poached eggs in pan in oven for 3 minutes. Remove from water with slotted spoon and place on top of asparagus spears. Sprinkle with pepper. Spoon sauce over eggs. Mix cornflakes and butter; sprinkle over mornay sauce. Cover and refrigerate no longer than 24 hours.

    Preheat oven to 350°.

    Bake uncovered for 35 to 40 minutes until hot and bubbly. Serve with sliced tomatoes and fresh fruit.

10 servings

MARBLEIZED EGGS

12 eggs, hard boiled
2 cups beet juice

Gently roll eggs between hands until shells are evenly cracked. Put whole eggs in cracked shells in big bowl with beet juice to cover. Let stand in juice for 3 hours in refrigerator.

Remove from juice and peel shells. Cut top off marbleized egg and flatten bottom, so it will stand up.

Remove yolk to bowl. Fill whites with your favorite deviled egg mixture or use one of the recipes on page 81.

Serve on glass platter.

12 eggs

WILD MUSHROOM CRUSTLESS QUICHE

2 tablespoons butter
2 or 3 zucchini, sliced
1 large onion, thinly sliced
½ pound wild mushrooms, sliced
10 eggs
¼ pound butter, melted
½ cup all-purpose flour
1 teaspoon baking powder
¼ teaspoon salt
1 pound large curd cottage cheese
1 pound shredded Monterey Jack cheese

Preheat oven to 400°. Butter large quiche pan or shallow glass baking dish.

Sauté zucchini, onion and mushrooms in butter and set aside. Beat eggs until very fluffy. Add cooled butter, flour, baking powder, salt, cottage cheese and Monterey Jack cheese.

Place sautéed vegetables in bottom of pan. Pour egg mixture over vegetables.

Bake for 15 minutes; reduce heat to 350° and continue baking for 35 to 40 minutes or until top is golden brown. Cool and cut into squares.

Serve with a platter of seasonal fresh fruit and smoked ham or turkey, flavorful muffins and an assortment of mustards.

Variation: Substitute ½ pound Swiss or Muenster cheese for half of the Monterey Jack cheese. Blend well.

6 servings

VEGETABLE CUSTARD PIE

1 pound eggplant, cut in ½-inch cubes
¼ cup vegetable oil
1 medium onion, chopped
3 large mushrooms, sliced
1 small zucchini, sliced
2½ teaspoons chopped fresh basil
2½ teaspoons chopped fresh oregano
½ teaspoon salt
Freshly ground pepper
1 16-ounce can tomatoes, crushed

4 eggs
½ cup grated Parmesan cheese,
    divided
½ pound mozzarella, shredded
    and divided
Paprika

Preheat oven to 375°. Butter 8x8-inch glass baking dish.

In a large saucepan, sauté eggplant and onion in oil until soft. Add mushrooms, zucchini, herbs and seasonings. Cook until mushrooms are soft. Add undrained crushed tomatoes. Simmer for 15 minutes or until almost dry. Cool.

Beat eggs and add ¼ cup Parmesan. Stir into vegetables. Pour ½ mixture into prepared dish. Top with ½ mozzarella and remaining vegetable mixture. Sprinkle with the remaining cheese and paprika.

Bake for 25 minutes, or until puffed and brown. Cool 10 minutes and cut into squares.

Hint: Substitute ¾ teaspoon dried basil and ¾ teaspoon dried oregano for fresh herbs.

ASPARAGUS QUICHE

1 9-inch pastry shell, unbaked
1 10½-ounce can cut asparagus
    spears, drained
1 2½-ounce jar sliced mushrooms,
    and drained
4 ounces (1 cup) shredded
    Swiss cheese
2 tablespoons all-purpose flour
1½ cups half and half
3 eggs, slightly beaten
½ teaspoon salt
⅛ teaspoon freshly ground pepper
⅛ teaspoon nutmeg

Preheat oven to 350°.

Arrange asparagus and mushrooms in unbaked pastry shell.

In a large bowl, toss cheese with flour; add half and half, eggs, salt, pepper and nutmeg, mixing well. Pour over asparagus and mushrooms.

Bake for 55 to 60 minutes or until knife inserted in center is withdrawn clean. Let stand before cutting.

8 servings

PUFF PASTRY OMELETTE WITH SPINACH, MOZZARELLA AND SAUSAGE

1 package frozen puff pastry, thawed
2 tablespoons oil, divided
1 tablespoon butter
2 10-ounce packages frozen spinach,
  thawed, drained and pressed dry
1 clove garlic, minced
½ teaspoon nutmeg
Salt and freshly ground pepper
4 large red peppers
2 pounds Italian sausage,
  casings removed

Omelettes:
8 eggs
2 or 3 green onions, chopped
2 teaspoons chopped fresh parsley
1½ tablespoons chopped fresh
  tarragon
Salt
2 tablespoons butter, divided
1 to 2 cups shredded mozzarella
  cheese

1 egg beaten with 1 teaspoon water

Lightly grease 9 or 10-inch springform pan with non-stick spray. Roll out 1 piece of pastry and line bottom and sides of pan. Keep remaining pastry refrigerated.

In a skillet, heat 1 tablespoon oil and butter. Add spinach and garlic; sauté 2 to 3 minutes. Season with nutmeg, salt and pepper to taste; set aside.

In a skillet, heat 1 tablespoon oil. Sauté red peppers until almost cooked. Remove from pan; set aside. In same pan, cook sausage and break in pieces; remove from pan and drain.

Omelettes: Beat eggs with onions, parsley, tarragon, and salt. In omelette pan, melt 1 tablespoon butter and coat bottom evenly. Add ½ egg mixture. Lift edges so liquid can run under. When eggs are completely set and top is no longer moist, slide omelette onto plate. Repeat, making 2 separate omelettes.

Preheat oven to 350°. Position rack in lower third of oven.

To assemble: Layer ingredients in prepared springform pan in the following order: puff pastry, 1 omelette, ½ spinach, ½ cheese, ½ sausage and all red peppers. Repeat layering in reverse order.

To cover: Roll remaining pastry ¼-inch thick. Place over omelette and cut along edges. Pinch edges of crust. Decorate with pastry pieces.

Brush with beaten egg. Place pan on baking sheet and bake for 1 hour and 10 minutes, or until golden brown. Cool slightly before releasing from pan and cutting. Serve warm but not hot, slicing with a sharp thin knife.

6 to 8 servings

POTATO AND LEEK FRITTATA

1½ pounds boiling potatoes
3 cups thinly sliced leek (white and
    pale green part), washed well
    and drained
2 tablespoons unsalted butter
Salt and freshly ground pepper
12 large eggs
1 cup freshly grated Parmesan
    cheese, divided
1 cup coarsely grated Gruyère,
    divided
2 tablespoons fresh chives
2 tablespoons minced fresh parsley
2 tablespoons olive oil

In a steamer set over boiling water, steam the potatoes, covered, for 20 to 25 minutes, or until tender. Let cool. Peel potatoes and cut crosswise into thin slices.

In a 12-inch non-stick skillet, cook leeks in butter over moderately low heat, stirring for 12 to 15 minutes, or until very soft. Add salt and pepper to taste.

In a large bowl whisk the eggs. Add ½ cup Parmesan, ½ cup Gruyère, chives, parsley, salt and pepper to taste; mix well. Stir in leeks and potatoes.

In clean skillet, heat the oil over moderate heat until it is hot, but not smoking. Pour in egg mixture, distributing the potatoes evenly and cook frittata, without stirring, for 14 to 16 minutes, or until the edge is set but the center is still soft. Sprinkle remaining ½ cup Parmesan and ½ cup Gruyère over the top. If skillet handle is plastic, wrap it in a double thickness of foil. Broil frittata under a preheated broiler about 4 inches from heat for 4 to 5 minutes, or until cheese is bubbling and golden. Let frittata cool in the skillet for 5 minutes, run a thin knife around edge, and slide frittata onto a serving plate. Cut frittata into wedges and serve warm or at room temperature.

6 servings

EGG WHITE OMELETTE

½ cup diced green or red pepper
½ cup diced onion
½ cup diced tomatoes
2 tablespoons olive oil
6 egg whites
1½ teaspoon curry powder
¼ teaspoon salt-free seasoning
½ teaspoon basil or parsley

In omelette pan on medium heat, sauté pepper, onion and tomatoes in olive oil. Slightly beat egg whites and add curry, salt-free seasoning and parsley. Combine eggs with ingredients in pan and cook 5 minutes. Place on serving plates.

2 servings

H O T   C R A B   S O U F F L É

8-12 ounces imitation crab, flaked
1 tablespoon fresh lemon juice
1 or 1¼ cups finely chopped celery
2 tablespoons grated onion
2 tablespoons cream sherry
3 eggs, beaten
2 tablespoons chopped green pepper
1 cup mayonnaise
1 cup seasoned croutons, crushed
½ to 1 cup shredded cheddar cheese

Preheat oven to 350°. Grease quiche dish.

Mix crabmeat, lemon juice, celery, onion, sherry, eggs, green pepper and mayonnaise. Pour into prepared pan. Mix croutons and cheddar cheese; sprinkle on top.

Bake for 25 minutes or until knife inserted in center comes out clean. If using a pie crust, bake at 400°.

Variation: Use a pie crust and bake at 400°.

6 to 8 servings

T O M A T O   A N D   S A U S A G E   P A S T A   S A L A D

Dressing:
¼ teaspoon freshly ground pepper
1 tablespoon Dijon mustard
4½ tablespoons red wine vinegar
1¼ teaspoons sugar
½ teaspoon salt
2 tablespoons chopped fresh parsley
½ cup olive oil

1 8-ounce box macaroni twists or
    1 10-ounce package fresh
    macaroni
2 medium onions, sliced and halved
½ pound baby Swiss cheese, sliced
    or chunked
1 green pepper, sliced
20 cherry tomatoes, halved
2 pounds mild Italian sausage,
    cooked, drained and sliced at
    an angle in small pieces

Dressing: In a small bowl, whisk pepper, mustard, vinegar, sugar, salt and parsley. Slowly add olive oil and whisk well.

Cook macaroni according to package directions; drain.

In a large bowl, combine onion, Swiss cheese, green pepper, tomatoes, sausage and macaroni. Toss with dressing. Chill until cold and serve.

8 to 10 servings

SCALLOP AND SPINACH PENNE SALAD

½ pound bay scallops
⅓ cup olive oil
1 cup chopped fresh spinach
1 tomato, peeled, seeded and diced
½ zucchini, diced
4 ounces spinach penne, cooked
    al dente
1 fresh lemon
Salt and freshly ground pepper

Sauté scallops in oil until opaque, about 2 or 3 minutes. Do not over cook. Cool. Place in a large salad bowl with spinach, tomato, zucchini, and penne. Squeeze fresh lemon over salad. Season with salt and pepper to taste. Toss gently.

Garnish with fresh thyme. Delicious with warm French bread.

Hint: To peel tomato, immerse in boiling water for 1 minute. Remove and immerse in cold water, drain and slip off skin.

2 servings

ANTIPASTO TORTELLINI

Dressing:
¼ cup red wine vinegar
6 tablespoons olive oil
1 tablespoon finely chopped
    fresh basil
1 tablespoon finely chopped
    fresh parsley
1 tablespoon grated fresh Parmesan
    cheese
1 teaspoon minced garlic
½ teaspoon salt
Pinch ground red pepper

1 9-ounce package fresh cheese
    filled-tri-color tortellini
4 ounces Provolone cheese,
    not aged, cubed
4 ounces pepperoni, thinly sliced
1 14-ounce can artichoke hearts,
    drained and halved

Dressing: In a jar, combine vinegar, olive oil, basil, parsley, cheese, garlic, salt and pepper; mix well.

Cook tortellini according to package directions; drain.
In a large bowl, combine tortellini, cheese, pepperoni and artichoke hearts. Toss with dressing. Chill.

You may wish to double or triple this recipe.

4 servings

CHICKEN TORTELLINI SALAD WITH PESTO SAUCE

Pesto Sauce:

2 cloves garlic

½ cup loosely packed parsley leaves

¼ cup chicken broth

3 tablespoons freshly grated
    Parmesan cheese

2 tablespoons chopped walnuts

1 tablespoon fresh lemon juice

1 tablespoon olive oil

⅛ teaspoon white pepper

Chicken-Tortellini Salad:

9 ounces fresh cheese tortellini

2 whole chicken breasts, halved,
    boned and skinned

1 tablespoon butter

½ cup minced shallots

½ cup thinly sliced green onions

2 cloves garlic, minced

1 cup dry white wine

¼ cup fresh lemon juice

½ cup yellow bell peppers, cut
    into strips

½ cup red bell peppers, cut into strips

Pesto Sauce: In food processor work bowl with steel knife, drop garlic through food chute with blade running and process 10 seconds. Add parsley, chicken broth, Parmesan cheese, walnuts, lemon juice, olive oil and white pepper. Process until well combined.

¾ cup pesto sauce

Chicken-Tortellini Salad: Cook tortellini according to package directions; drain and cool.

Broil chicken and cut into ½-inch strips. In a large saucepan, melt butter and sauté green onions, shallots and garlic for 2 to 3 minutes or until tender. Add wine, lemon juice and chicken. Simmer for 10 minutes to reduce.

In a large bowl, combine cooked tortellini, chicken mixture and pepper strips, adding pesto sauce. Chill for 1 hour.

8 servings

CARBONARA SAUCE WITH TORTELLINI

1 pound fresh meat or cheese-filled
    tortellini

6 slices bacon, finely diced

2 tablespoons olive oil

⅓ cup dry white wine

3 eggs, room temperature

⅓ cup freshly grated Parmesan
    cheese

⅓ cup freshly grated Romano cheese

½ cup whipping cream

3 teaspoons chopped red pepper

In a large skillet, fry bacon in olive oil until crisp. Add wine and cook until wine evaporates. In bowl, beat eggs; add cheeses, cream and red pepper. Beat well. Cook tortellini according to package directions and drain. Slowly add bacon/wine mixture to egg mixture. Pour over tortellini. Serve on hot plates.

PASTA SALAD WITH HAM AND BLEU CHEESE

3 cups uncooked bow tie pasta
6 ounces cooked ham, cut into
    1-inch cubes
1 cup coarsely chopped pecans
2 ounces bleu cheese, crumbled
2 tablespoons fresh rosemary or
    2 teaspoons dried
1 clove garlic, minced
½ teaspoon coarsely ground pepper
¼ cup extra virgin olive oil
⅓ cup grated fresh Parmesan cheese

Cook pasta according to directions. Drain. Refresh with cold water, drain.

Combine pasta, ham, pecans, bleu cheese, rosemary, garlic, pepper, and olive oil. Toss well. Sprinkle Parmesan cheese over salad. Serve immediately or chill, if desired.

8 servings

CHICKEN, SAUSAGE AND RED PEPPER WITH ROTELLE PASTA

2 whole chicken breasts, boned,
    skinned, cooked and cut
    in chunks
4 tablespoons butter
2 mild Italian sausages,
    casing removed
2 fresh red bell peppers, cut in
    thin strips
½ teaspoon dried basil
¼ teaspoon dried oregano
½ teaspoon dried thyme
½ teaspoon dried marjoram
2 cups whipping cream
Salt and freshly ground pepper
1 pound fresh Rotelle or fusilli pasta,
    cooked and drained

Garnish:
Grated fresh Parmesan
Chopped fresh parsley

Chicken breasts can be poached, steamed or microwaved to cook.

In a large skillet, melt butter and sauté Italian sausage, peppers and herbs. Stir and cook about 7 minutes, or until sausage is browned. Add cream, chicken, salt and pepper to taste. Heat to a simmer over low heat. Simmer about 7 minutes, or until slightly thickened, stirring constantly.

Spoon over cooked pasta and sprinkle with cheese and parsley.

Hint: 1½ teaspoons of fresh basil, oregano, thyme and marjoram can be used to replace ½ teaspoon dried herbs.

PASTA,   SCALLOPS   AND   LEEKS
WITH   BEURRE   BLANC

1½ pounds leeks, whites and several
    inches of green, cut in
    julienne strips
6 tablespoons unsalted butter,
    divided
½ cup whipping cream
Salt and freshly ground pepper

Poaching liquid:
1 cup milk or ½ cup water and
    ½ cup white wine
¾ pound fresh sea scallops, cut in
    half horizontally

½ pound fresh mushrooms, cleaned
    and sliced
1 cup Beurre Blanc (page 230)
1 pound pasta, cooked al dente

Garnish:
Red peppers, julienned

In saucepan, melt 2 tablespoons butter and sauté leeks about
2 minutes. Add 2 tablespoons butter, cover and cook without
browning for 30 minutes, stirring occasionally. Add cream
and reduce to thicken. Season with salt and pepper to taste;
set aside.

   In a large saucepan, bring poaching liquid to a boil, add
scallops, cover immediately, remove from heat and let stand
5 minutes. Drain.
   While scallops poach, sauté mushrooms in skillet with 2
tablespoons butter until just losing color. Add poached
scallops and mushrooms to leeks. Adjust seasonings.
   Cook pasta, drain and portion onto hot serving plates.
Arrange scallop/leek mixture on top and spoon a thin veil of
Beurre Blanc (page 230) over all.
   Garnish with red pepper strips.

4 to 5 servings

VERMICELLI   WITH   SUN-DRIED   TOMATOES
AND   SPINACH   SAUCE

1 cup hot water
1 3-ounce package sun-dried
    tomatoes
3 or 4 cloves garlic, minced
Olive oil
1 10-ounce package fresh spinach,
    cleaned and dried
Vermicelli, cooked according to
    package directions

Garnish:
Freshly grated Parmesan cheese
Pine nuts or walnuts, toasted

Pour hot water over sun-dried tomatoes. Let stand 30
minutes to soften; drain.
   Sauté garlic in a generous amount of olive oil until light
brown; add softened drained tomatoes and sauté. Stir in
spinach; cover and cook until softened.
   Serve over cooked vermicelli. Sprinkle with Parmesan
cheese and pine nuts.

EGGPLANT PASTA

1 cup eggplant, sliced ¼-inch thick
    and chopped coarsely
2 tablespoons fresh parsley, minced
1 tablespoon butter, melted
1 cup fresh mushrooms, chopped
3 cloves garlic, minced
3 tablespoons extra virgin olive oil
1 chicken bouillon cube dissolved in
    1 tablespoon warm water
Freshly ground pepper
1 package fresh angel hair or
    fettucine pasta

In a skillet, sauté eggplant and parsley in butter. When soft, add mushrooms and continue cooking. Stir in garlic, olive oil and dissolved bouillon. Let sit for 10 minutes. Season with salt and pepper.

Cook pasta according to package directions until al dente. Drain.

Combine pasta with the eggplant mixture and a little extra olive oil. Toss and serve immediately.

Delicious with broiled meat or fish and a salad.

4 to 6 servings

PASTA WITH ZUCCHINI, RED PEPPER AND ONION

1 8-ounce package tubular pasta
    such as mostaccioli
4 tablespoons olive oil
4 cloves garlic, pressed
2 small zucchini
1 large red or green bell pepper,
    chopped
1 medium red onion, chopped
10 to 12 mushrooms, sliced
⅛ teaspoon crushed red pepper
    flakes
¼ cup chopped fresh basil
¼ cup chopped fresh oregano
1 large tomato, chopped
⅜ cup pine nuts, toasted
1¼ cup grated fresh Romano cheese

Cook pasta according to package directions and drain.

While pasta cooks, heat olive oil in large saucepan and sauté garlic, zucchini, bell pepper, onion, mushrooms and crushed pepper flakes, about 10 minutes.

When pasta is al dente, remove from heat. Drain, rinse and return to pan. Add cooked vegetables and basil, oregano, tomato, pine nuts and Romano cheese. Toss and serve immediately.

Hint: Can be served as a main dish, but is light enough to serve as a side dish.

Hint: This dish is best when using only fresh ingredients. Be sure to have all ingredients chopped, sliced or grated prior to cooking.

4 servings

O R I E N T A L   N O O D L E S
W I T H   H O T   A N D   S P I C Y   P E A N U T   S A U C E

*1 pound Chinese noodles, vermicelli
    or angel hair pasta, cooked
    according to package directions*
¼ cup smooth peanut butter
3 tablespoons sugar
¼ cup soy sauce
1 teaspoon red pepper flakes
Pinch of ground red pepper
3 tablespoons sesame oil
3 tablespoons corn oil

In a small bowl, whisk peanut butter, sugar, soy sauce, red pepper flakes, pinch of red pepper, and oils.

In a large salad bowl, place drained pasta and toss with peanut sauce. Top with assorted crunchy vegetables and toasted nuts.

Garnish with any combination of chopped or julienned vegetables such as carrots, cucumber, green onions, red and/or green bell peppers; and toasted sesame seeds or peanuts.

4 to 6 servings

T O R T E L L I N I   B R U S C H E T T A

Marinade:
2 tablespoons minced garlic
1 cup fresh basil leaves
2 tablespoons minced shallots
⅓ cup extra virgin olive oil
Salt and freshly ground pepper
10-12 fresh tomatoes, diced

Cream Sauce:
¾ cup whipping cream
½ cup grated fresh Parmesan cheese

*1 9-ounce package fresh cheese-filled
    tortellini*

Marinade: Mix garlic, basil, shallots, olive oil, salt and pepper together. Pour over tomatoes, Marinate for ½ hour.

Cream Sauce: Cook cream and parmesan cheese in double boiler until thickened.

Cook tortellini in large pan of boiling salted water according to package directions. Drain.

Arrange pasta on serving platter or individual plates. Top with tomato mixture and drizzle with cream sauce. Serve immediately.

8 servings

MUSTARD GREENS AND PASTA
WITH ANCHOVY-GARLIC SAUCE

3 pounds mustard greens, cleaned
    and rinsed
½ pound thin spaghetti,
    broken in half

Sauce:
1 large clove garlic, sliced
1 cup olive oil
3 small cans flat anchovies, in oil
    and drained

Remove tough ends and large leaves from mustard greens. Make a vertical cut 2 inches from base of stems to ease cooking. In a large saucepan, bring water to a boil, add spaghetti and cook 5 minutes. Add raw prepared mustard greens. Cook until pasta is al dente or to your taste. Drain and set aside. Pasta and greens may be cooked separately and then combined.

Sauce: Using a small saucepan, brown garlic in olive oil. Remove garlic. Carefully add 1 can drained anchovies (oil will be hot), cook and stir until anchovies are blended into the olive oil.

Put a small amount of anchovy sauce in bottom of serving bowl, add a layer of drained greens and spaghetti, place 5 or 6 anchovy fillets on top. Drizzle a small amount of anchovy and oil sauce over pasta. Layer as above until all ingredients are used. Pour remaining sauce over top. Serve hot.

4 to 6 servings

HEARTY STIR FRY

1 pound bulk pork sausage
4 cups thinly sliced cabbage
1 medium onion, cut into wedges
1 medium apple, cut into wedges
1 clove garlic, minced
1 teaspoon salt
1 2-ounce jar sliced pimiento
¼ teaspoon crushed red pepper
½ pound good quality spaghetti,
    cooked al dente
1½ cups (6 ounces) shredded
    Monterey Jack cheese
1½ cup (6 ounces) shredded
    cheddar cheese

In a large skillet, cook sausage until no longer pink. Drain, reserving 2 tablespoons of drippings. Add cabbage, onion, apple and garlic. Stir fry until tender. Stir in salt, pimiento and red pepper. Add spaghetti. Cook and stir until hot.

Remove from stove. Add cheeses. Toss and serve immediately.

4 to 6 servings

PASTA WITH SMOKED TURKEY AND SUN-DRIED TOMATOES

½ pound butter
1 pound Gorgonzola cheese, broken
  into pieces
1 cup whipping cream
1 pound smoked turkey, cut into
  irregular pieces
1 cup sun-dried tomatoes, julienned
¼ teaspoon freshly ground pepper
1½ pounds penne pasta

Garnish:
Freshly grated Parmesan cheese
Freshly ground pepper

In a deep saucepan, melt butter. Add Gorgonzola cheese and stir until melted. Be careful not to burn. Add cream. Blend well. Cook 3 minutes, stirring constantly. Add smoked turkey, sun-dried tomatoes and pepper. Cook another 3 minutes, stirring continuously.

Cook pasta according to package directions; drain and toss with the sauce. Serve with Parmesan cheese and freshly ground pepper.

Hint: Gorgonzola cheese can vary in taste. Taste before using and use amounts according to individual taste.

6 to 8 servings

MUSHROOM ITALIA FETTUCINI

2 pounds fresh white or wild
  mushrooms, wiped and sliced
3 tablespoons butter, divided
4 tablespoons chopped fresh parsley
2 tablespoons chopped fresh cilantro
Salt and freshly ground pepper
1 tablespoon flour
1 egg yolk
Juice of 1 lemon

Enough excellent fettucini for 6
  cooked al dente

In a large skillet, melt 2 tablespoons butter and sauté mushrooms lightly; add parsley, cilantro, salt and pepper.

In a small skillet, melt 1 tablespoon butter and stir in flour, egg yolk and lemon juice. Pour sauce over mushrooms and cook over low heat until sauce thickens.

Serve lemon mushrooms on top of fettucini.

Hint: Substitute 2 tablespoons dried parsley and 1 tablespoon dried cilantro for fresh herbs.

6 servings

LINGUINE WITH GRILLED CHICKEN, SUN-DRIED TOMATOES AND PESTO

Chicken:

2 whole chicken breasts, skinned
    and boned
1 clove garlic, crushed
2 tablespoons fresh lemon juice
Salt and freshly ground pepper
1 tablespoon extra virgin olive oil
2 tablespoons sesame seeds

1½ pounds linguine

Pasta Sauce:

3½ ounce jar high quality sun-dried
    tomatoes in olive oil
1 cup pesto sauce, homemade
    (page 89 or 233) or high quality
    prepared pesto
⅓ cup sliced black olives
½ cup pine nuts

Chicken: Rub chicken breast with garlic. Sprinkle with lemon, olive oil, salt and pepper. Sprinkle with sesame seeds and grill over coals or in the oven. Slice into thin strips, approximately ½-inch by 4-inches. Keep warm.

Prepare linguine according to package directions, drain.

Pasta Sauce: Drain sun-dried tomatoes, reserving 4 tablespoons of the oil, and thinly slice tomatoes. Toss pasta with 3 to 4 tablespoons olive oil from sun-dried tomatoes. Toss with pasta and pesto sauce (page 89 or 233) and place on warm platter. Arrange chicken fingers, tomato strips and black olives attractively on top of pasta. Sprinkle with pine nuts. Toss pasta just before serving.

Serve pasta with additional Parmesan or Romano cheese.

6 servings

WALNUT ASPARAGUS LINGUINE

2 dozen asparagus tips
1 cup butter
4 ounces walnuts, toasted
12 ounces fresh or 8 ounces
    dried linguine
Freshly grated Parmesan cheese

Cook asparagus tips, in boiling salted water, for 5 minutes. Drain.

In a saucepan, melt butter and cook until lightly brown. Stir in asparagus tips and toasted walnuts.

Cook pasta according to package directions, drain. Pour sauce over linguine and top with Parmesan cheese. Serve immediately.

Hint: Preheat oven to 250° and toast walnuts on baking sheet for 30 minutes.

4 servings

C R A B M E A T   F E T T U C I N I

1 12-ounce package fettucini
½ cup butter or margarine
1 clove garlic, minced
¾ cup half and half or
    whipping cream
½ cup grated fresh Parmesan cheese
½ teaspoon freshly ground pepper
1 7½ ounce crabmeat or imitation
    crabmeat
1 tablespoon finely chopped onion,
    optional
1 tablespoon finely chopped sweet
    red pepper, optional
1 tablespoon chopped fresh parsley

Cook pasta according to package directions; drain.

In a heavy skillet, heat butter and sauté garlic. Stir in half and half, Parmesan cheese and pepper. Stir until well blended. Add crabmeat. (If adding onion and pepper, do so now.) Pour sauce over hot cooked fettucini and toss well. Sprinkle with parsley and serve at once.

Great with tossed salad and crusty bread.

4 servings

C O U N T R Y   N O O D L E S

1 pound thin spinach noodles
½ pound bacon, cooked and crumbled
1 cup cottage cheese
3 cups sour half and half
3 cloves garlic, crushed
2 onions, minced
Dash of Tabasco or hot pepper sauce
1 teaspoon horseradish
1 tablespoon Worcestershire sauce
3 teaspoons salt
½ cup freshly grated Parmesan
    cheese

Preheat oven to 350°. Butter 2-quart baking dish.

Cook noodles according to package directions; drain. In a large bowl, mix bacon, cottage cheese, sour half and half, garlic, onions, hot pepper sauce (or Tabasco), horseradish, Worcestershire sauce, salt and Parmesan cheese. Add noodles and mix well. Place in prepared baking dish.

Bake for 30 to 40 minutes. May be prepared a day ahead of serving.

Variation: Substitute fusilli or penne pasta for noodles. Tri-colored, spinach or tomato flavored pasta would add color and flavor. Ricotta cheese can be a substitute for cottage cheese.

6 to 8 servings

PASTA CON TRE FORMAGGI E NOCE
(THREE CHEESE PASTA WITH WALNUTS)

6 ounces Gorgonzola cheese
    crumbled (see note)
4 ounces fontina cheese
    shredded (see note)
⅔ cup milk
6 tablespoons unsalted butter
1 teaspoon salt
1 pound angel hair pasta
1 cup half and half
⅔ cup freshly grated Parmesan
    cheese
¼ cup torn Italian parsley
½ cup coarsely chopped, toasted
    walnuts

Heat Gorgonzola, fontina, milk, butter and salt in large pan over medium-low heat. Cook, stirring until creamy and cheeses are melted. Remove from heat.

Bring large pot of water to a rolling boil. Add salt and pasta, return to a boil. Cook until al dente, about 1 minute. Drain.

Return sauce to low heat and stir in half and half. Add pasta and Parmesan cheese. Mix well. Toss with parsley.

Place in a large bowl and top with walnuts.
Serve at once.

Note: Domestic variety of Gorgonzola is milder than imported. Domestic and Danish fontina cheeses are milder than Italian.

6 servings

ANGEL HAIR PASTA
WITH TOMATO BASIL SHRIMP

½ cup loosely packed parsley leaves,
    divided
2 cloves garlic
1 35-ounce can Italian plum
    tomatoes, drained, or 3 pounds
    fresh plum tomatoes, peeled
½ cup plus 1 tablespoon extra virgin
    olive oil, divided
1 teaspoon dried oregano
Salt and freshly ground pepper
2 cups tightly packed fresh
    basil leaves
Coarse salt, to taste
1 pound medium shrimp, shelled,
    deveined, split lengthwise and
    dried on paper towels
1 pound angel hair pasta

Finely chop parsley in a food processor. Reserve.

Chop garlic in food processor. Add tomatoes and coarsely chop. Heat ¼ cup olive oil in a large saucepan. Add tomato-garlic mixture, 2 tablespoons parsley, oregano, salt and pepper. Cook stirring often until liquid has evaporated, about 20 minutes.

Finely chop basil with 2 tablespoons olive oil in food processor.

Sprinkle shrimp with coarse salt.

Heat remaining 3 tablespoons olive oil in large skillet. Cook the shrimp in oil, tossing, until they are pink and just cooked through, about 2 minutes. Reduce heat; stir in tomato mixture and basil oil paste. Keep warm.

Cook pasta according to package directions. Drain well. Add pasta to the shrimp mixture and heat through, tossing to coat with sauce.

Sprinkle with the remaining parsley and freshly ground pepper. Serve hot.

4 servings

SCALLOP AND VEGETABLE LASAGNA

⅓ cup butter or margarine, divided
1 cup chopped green onion
1 clove garlic, minced
1 zucchini, shredded
2 carrots, shredded
½ pound mushrooms, sliced
2 pounds scallops, rinsed well
    and drained
¼ teaspoon dried or ¾ teaspoon
    chopped fresh thyme
⅓ cup flour
1 cup chicken broth
1 cup whipping cream
½ cup dry white wine

1 12-ounce package lasagna noodles,
    cooked according to package
    directions, rinsed with cold
    water and drained
2 cups shredded Swiss cheese

Preheat oven to 350°. Butter a 9x13-inch baking dish or lasagna pan.

In a large sauté pan, melt 3 tablespoons butter. Add onion, garlic, zucchini, carrots and mushrooms; sauté over medium heat for 2 minutes. Add scallops and thyme; cook for approximately 3 minutes, or until scallops are opaque. Pour the scallop mixture into a strainer and drain for 15 minutes, reserving liquid.

Melt remaining butter and add flour, cooking over medium heat until it thickens. Remove from heat and mix in broth, whipping cream and white wine. Return to heat and cook, stirring constantly until mixture is thickened; set aside.

Pour reserved scallop juices into a saucepan and boil over high heat until reduced to approximately 2 tablespoons. Add reduced juices to cream sauce.

To assemble: Line bottom of prepared pan with ⅓ lasagna noodles; top with ⅓ thickened sauce, ⅓ scallops and ⅓ cheese. Repeat the layers twice more, ending with cheese on top. Cover pan with foil. May be assembled one day ahead to this point.

Bake for 20 minutes; remove foil and bake for approximately 20 additional minutes, or until cheese on top is browned and bubbly.

Let stand for 10 to 15 minutes before cutting.

6 to 8 servings

SHRIMP SCAMPI

¾ cup butter, room temperature
2 cloves garlic, crushed
3 tablespoons chopped fresh parsley
3 tablespoons Parmesan cheese
Salt and freshly ground pepper
¾ pound fresh shrimp, cleaned
    deveined and butterflied
Fettucini, cooked according to
    package directions

Preheat oven to broil.

Melt butter in shallow baking dish under broiler (watch to prevent burning). Remove from oven; stir in garlic, parsley, Parmesan, salt and pepper. Add shrimp and toss to cover. Place under broiler for 3 minutes; turn shrimp and broil another 3 to 4 minutes longer or until shrimp is just opaque. Do not overcook.

Place fettucini on a heated platter; spoon shrimp mixture over top. Garnish with chopped fresh parsley and serve immediately.

2 to 3 servings

ROSELLINE
(PASTA ROSES)

Pasta Dough:
3 eggs
2 tablespoons water
1 tablespoon olive oil
Pinch of salt
2 cups flour

Cream Sauce:
1 cup butter
4 cups whipping cream
4 tablespoons tomato paste
1 teaspoon grated nutmeg

Filling:
1 pound imported prosciutto or
*   smoked ham, very thinly sliced*
1 pound fontina cheese, shredded

Egg wash: 1 egg mixed with
*   1 tablespoon water*

6 tablespoons freshly grated
*   Parmesan cheese*

Pasta Dough: In a bowl, combine eggs, water, olive oil, salt and flour. Mix well. Knead pasta dough until it is elastic and pliable, about 5 minutes. Thin pasta in a pasta machine, stopping at next to last setting on machine. Do not make too thin. Trim pasta strips into straight-sided rectangles. Cut rectangles into about 6-inch lengths.

In a pot of boiling water, add salt and as water returns to a boil, drop in pasta strips 2 or 3 at a time. Cook for just seconds and remove pasta with a perforated scoop. Plunge into a bowl of cold water and then rinse each strip under cold running water. Gently squeeze as much moisture as possible from each strip with your hands, then spread flat to dry on clean cloth towels. Repeat until all pasta is cooked.

Cream Sauce: In a small sauté pan, over medium heat, combine butter and cream. Cook, stirring occasionally, until slightly reduced. Add tomato paste and nutmeg; cook stirring constantly until tomato paste has completely dissolved and the sauce is the consistency of buttermilk. Spread just enough cream sauce into baking dish to cover bottom with a thin film, reserving the rest.

Preheat oven to 450°.

On each strip of pasta, place a single layer of sliced ham without overlapping and trim the ham to size where necessary. Cover ham with a layer of shredded cheese. Roll up pasta, tightly, jelly-roll fashion. Seal with egg wash. With a sharp knife, slice the roll into rings, about ¾ to 1 inch wide. On one cut side of each ring, make 4 equidistant cuts (can use scissors), each about ½ inch deep, forming a cross pattern. Place the rings in the baking dish, sides with cross-cuts facing up. Do not crowd. Top with some of remaining sauce. Press down on the tops of the rings to spread them slightly more open. Sprinkle with grated Parmesan. Cover loosely with foil. Place the dish in the uppermost level of the oven.

Bake approximately 15 minutes watching closely. Allow to settle a few minutes before serving. Spoon some of the remaining warmed sauce on individual plates. Top with three or four pasta roses.

THREE MEAT RAVIOLI

Pasta Dough:
3 eggs
2¼ cups all-purpose flour
3 teaspoons milk

Sauce:
1 large pork neckbone
1 large beef neckbone
1 tablespoon vegetable oil
¼ cup red wine
1 cup chopped onion
2 cloves garlic, minced
½ cup finely chopped celery
½ cup finely chopped carrots
2 tablespoons fresh basil
Freshly ground pepper
1½ pounds ground beef
3 16-ounce crushed tomatoes
*   in puree*
1 5-ounce can tomato sauce

Filling:
3 chicken breasts, skinned and boned
2 slices veal cutlet
½ pound ground lean beef
2 cloves garlic, do not crush
2 tablespoons butter
3 eggs, slightly beaten
⅔ cup grated Parmesan cheese
⅛ teaspoon cinnamon
⅛ teaspoon nutmeg
Freshly ground pepper
Chopped parsley

Pasta Dough: In a large bowl, combine eggs, flour and milk. Mix well. Knead dough until elastic and pliable, about 5 minutes. Thin in pasta machine, stopping at the next to last setting on the machine. Cut dough in 4-inch rounds with a glass.

Sauce: Sauté bones in vegetable oil. Remove bones. Sauté ground beef; add onions, garlic, celery, carrots, basil and pepper to taste. Skim oil from liquid. Simmer until onions are translucent. Add wine and tomatoes and tomato sauce. Simmer very slowly for 30 minutes. Add neck bones and cook 1 hour.

Filling: Sauté meat in butter with garlic. Drain. Remove garlic. Grind all meat until very fine. Add 3 eggs, Parmesan cheese, cinnamon, nutmeg, pepper and parsley. Place teaspoon of filling on one-half of ravioli circle, fold over, and crimp edges.

Bring water to a boil in a large saucepan, with a dash of olive oil. Cook ravioli in small batches until they rise to top of pan. Ravioli should be al dente.

CHICKEN NORMANDY RIGATONI

4 to 5 chicken breasts, boned
    and skinned
¾ teaspoon salt
Margarine to brown chicken
1 onion, chopped
2 tablespoons celery, chopped
2 tablespoons chopped fresh parsley
2½ cups peeled tart apple slices,
    McIntosh or Granny Smith
¼ teaspoon dried thyme or
    1 teaspoon fresh
½ teaspoon salt
¼ teaspoon nutmeg
¼ cup whipping cream
1 12-ounce package rigatoni pasta

Sprinkle chicken with salt. In a large skillet, melt butter and brown chicken. Remove from pan. Add onion and celery. Cook about 5 minutes. Add parsley, apple, thyme, salt, nutmeg and chicken and cook over low heat for 40 to 45 minutes, or until chicken is tender, stirring occasionally.

Before serving, remove chicken from pan and stir cream into pan juices. Add more cream or milk, if more sauce is desired. Cook pasta according to package directions; drain.

Place pasta on serving dish. Top with cooked chicken and pour sauce over chicken.

4 servings

CHICKEN WITH PASTA, ARTICHOKES AND OLIVES

½ pound fresh small shell pasta or
    angel hair pasta
4 tablespoons extra virgin olive oil,
    divided
1 pound chicken breasts, skinned,
    boned and cut into strips
¼ cup flour
Salt and freshly ground pepper

2 tablespoons flour
1 tablespoon Dijon mustard
⅓ cup brandy
1 10-ounce can chicken broth
1 package frozen artichoke hearts,
    defrosted and drained
25 black olives, medium and pitted

Cook pasta according to package directions; drain well. Toss with 2 tablespoons olive oil.

In a large bowl, mix ¼ cup flour, salt and pepper and toss chicken to coat. In a large skillet, heat 2 tablespoons oil, sauté chicken until cooked. Remove from pan; set aside.

Add 2 tablespoons flour to drippings and stir until flour is cooked and incorporated. Add brandy and Dijon mustard; stir until smooth. Add broth and artichokes. Simmer about 5 minutes. Add chicken and olives. Simmer 2 additional minutes.

Pour over pasta in large bowl or deep platter. Toss and serve.

Hint: Easy to double or triple.

4 servings

Breakfast

Croissant French Toast 106
German Apple Pancakes 105
Golden Breakfast Puffs 106
Maple Banana French Toast 107
Meltaway Pancakes 106
Really French Toast 107
Swiss Muesli 105
Zucchini Sausage Biscuits 115

Coffee Cakes

Golden Coffee Cake (Hungarian Galuska) 110
Nut Streusel Coffee Cake 108
Pfirsich Kuchen (Peach Coffee Cake) 109
Swedish Coffee Braid 108

Muffins

Caraway Cheese Muffins 113
Double Berry Muffins 111
Lemon Streusel Muffins 111
Low-Fat Fruit Oat Bran Muffins 112
Medley Muffins 110

Yeast Breads

Basic Olive Oil Bread 117
Cinnamon Crisps 123
French Bread Baguettes 118
Honey Whole Wheat Bread 119
Italian Parmesan Bread 121
Old World Black Bread 122
Pizza di Verdura 120
Prairie State Corn Bread 119

Quick Breads

Beneficial Banana Bread 114
Brunch Banana Nut Bread 107
Buttermilk Scones 109

Caraway Rye Beer Bread 114
English Cherry Tea Loaf 117
Irish Soda Bread 115
Lettuce Bread 116
Mexican Spoon Bread 113
Plum Bread 116
Poppyseed Tea Bread 115
Rhubarb Bread 112
Strawberry Bread 113
Tea Room Carrot Bread 118

Savory Accompaniments

Bruschetta 125
Celery Loaf 122
Fines Herbes Toast 124
Orange Toasts 123
Pita Toasts 121
Roasted Garlic
    with Pumpernickel Bread 123

Sandwiches

Cool Dilled Chicken Sandwiches 124
Curried Chicken Almond
    Tea Sandwiches 126
Strawberry Cream Cheese
    Tea Sandwiches 126
Turkey Taco Sandwich 125
Watercress Lemon Pinwheels 126

Snips & Tips

Flavored Butters 246

GERMAN APPLE PANCAKES

4 eggs
½ cup all-purpose flour
½ teaspoon baking powder
1 tablespoon sugar
Salt to taste
1 cup milk
1 teaspoon vanilla
2 tablespoons melted butter
⅛ teaspoon nutmeg

½ cup sugar
½ teaspoon cinnamon
⅛ teaspoon nutmeg
4 tablespoons butter, melted
2 large tart green apples, sliced

Blend eggs, flour, baking powder, sugar and salt in a large bowl.

Add milk, vanilla, butter and nutmeg; mix well. Let stand 30 minutes at room temperature or refrigerate overnight.

Preheat oven to 425°.

Melt butter in a skillet and brush up sides of pan. Combine sugar, cinnamon and nutmeg in a small bowl. Sprinkle ¼ cup of mixture over butter. Spread apples in the skillet. Sprinkle remaining ¼ cup of sugar mixture over apples. Place pan over medium heat until mixture bubbles. Pour batter gently over apples.

Bake for 15 minutes. Reduce heat to 375° and cook for 10 more minutes. Invert on serving platter.

3 servings

SWISS MUESLI

1½ cups whole milk
2 cups uncooked rolled oats
¼ cup oat bran
¼ cup grated coconut
2 Granny Smith or firm apples,
   peeled, cored and chopped
Juice of 1 lemon
2 tablespoons sugar
½ cup diced dates
½ cup raisins
½ cup slivered or sliced almonds,
   toasted
1 banana, sliced
1 cup whipping cream, whipped

Garnish:
6 to 8 fresh strawberries, sliced

In a large mixing bowl, combine the milk oats, oat bran and coconut. Let stand for 10 minutes, stirring once or twice.

Sprinkle the chopped apples with lemon juice and toss with sugar. Add the dates, almonds, raisins and banana to the apples.

Stir the fruit and nut mixture into the oatmeal mixture. Fold the whipped cream into the fruit and oatmeal mixture.

Garnish with fresh strawberries.

Variation: Substitute yogurt and fresh grapes.

CROISSANT FRENCH TOAST

2 teaspoons sugar
1/8 teaspoon ground cinnamon
2 eggs
1/4 cup milk
1/2 teaspoon vanilla
2 fresh croissants
1 tablespoon butter or margarine
Powdered sugar
Apricot or peach jam

Mix sugar and cinnamon in a large wide bowl. Whisk in eggs, milk and vanilla. Slice croissants in half horizontally. Place in egg mixture, cut side down. Let soak a few minutes.

Melt butter on a griddle or large frying pan over medium high heat. Add croissants and brown on both sides.

Heat apricot or peach jam and spoon over croissant toast. Sprinkle with powdered sugar. Serve immediately.

2 servings

GOLDEN BREAKFAST PUFFS

1/2 cup sugar
1 teaspoon cinnamon

1 egg, beaten
1/4 cup oil
3/4 cup milk
2 cups all-purpose flour
1/4 cup sugar
3 teaspoons baking powder
1 teaspoon salt
1/2 teaspoon nutmeg
Oil for frying

Combine sugar and cinnamon in a small bowl; set aside.

Beat egg; add oil and milk in a large bowl.

Combine flour, sugar, baking powder, salt and nutmeg. Add to egg mixture. Beat just until smooth.

Heat oil in a heavy saucepan or a deep fryer to 375°. Drop batter by teaspoonfuls into hot oil and fry 4 or 5 at a time until golden brown, about 3 to 4 minutes, turning to brown on both sides. Drain on paper towels.

Roll warm puffs in sugar and cinnamon. Serve at once.

2 dozen puffs

MELTAWAY PANCAKES

3 egg yolks, well beaten
1/2 cup sour cream
1/4 cup sifted all-purpose flour
1 teaspoon sugar
1/4 teaspoon salt
3 egg whites, stiffly beaten

In a large bowl, mix egg yolks and sour cream. Stir in flour, sugar and salt. Fold in egg whites.

Drop from large spoon onto hot griddle. Cook until top is bubbly and bottom is brown. Turn and brown other side.

2 servings

MAPLE BANANA FRENCH TOAST

2 ripe bananas
1/4 cup milk
3 eggs
1 tablespoon sugar
2 teaspoons maple-flavored syrup
1/2 teaspoon vanilla
Salt to taste
10 bread slices
Melted butter

Peel and slice bananas into blender container. Add milk, eggs, sugar, syrup, vanilla and salt. Blend well. Turn into a shallow pan.

Dip bread into mixture and fry in melted butter until browned on one side, turn and brown other side.

5 servings

REALLY FRENCH TOAST

4 eggs
1 1/3 cup milk
1 1/4 tablespoons sugar
1 teaspoon cinnamon
French sourdough bread, sliced
    1-inch thick
4 tablespoons melted butter
1/2 cup powdered sugar
1 cup fresh sliced strawberries
    or blueberries

Beat eggs, milk, sugar and cinnamon in a large bowl.

Dip bread slices in batter and fry on a preheated griddle or non-stick skillet. Turn once and fry until golden brown on both sides.

Drizzle with melted butter and top with fresh fruit and a dusting of powdered sugar.

6 servings

BRUNCH BANANA NUT BREAD

8 tablespoons butter,
    room temperature
3/4 cup sugar
2 eggs
1 cup all-purpose flour
1/2 teaspoon salt
1 teaspoon baking soda
1/2 teaspoon cinnamon
1 cup whole wheat flour
3 ripe bananas, mashed
1 teaspoon spiced rum
1/2 cup chopped toasted pecans

Preheat oven to 350°. Grease a 9x5x3-inch loaf pan.

In a large bowl of electric mixer, cream butter and sugar until light and fluffy. Add eggs, one at a time, beating after each addition.

Sift flour, salt, baking soda and cinnamon. Stir in whole wheat flour and add to creamed mixture, mixing well. Fold in bananas, rum and pecans. Pour into prepared pan.

Bake for 50 to 60 minutes, or until tester inserted in center of bread comes out clean. Cool in pan for 10 minutes. Remove from pan. Cool on rack.

1 loaf

SWEDISH COFFEE BRAID

2 packages active dry or 2 cakes
    compressed fresh yeast
3 cups sifted regular all-purpose
    flour
$\frac{1}{2}$ teaspoon salt
1 cup sugar
$\frac{1}{2}$ to $\frac{3}{4}$ teaspoon ground cardamom
3 eggs, divided
$1\frac{1}{2}$ cups milk, scalded
1 cup butter, melted
$\frac{1}{2}$ cup slivered almonds

Sprinkle yeast into $\frac{1}{2}$ cup warm water; stir until dissolved. In a large bowl, combine flour with salt, sugar and cardamom; stir in 2 beaten eggs and yeast. Gradually add milk and melted butter. Beat until smooth. Cover, let rise in warm place until double in bulk. Turn onto lightly floured board and knead 10 minutes. Divide dough in half. Cut one half of dough into 3 pieces. Roll each piece into a rope about 12 inches long; then braid together. Place braid on a greased cookie sheet; cover and let rise until almost doubled.

Preheat oven to 350°.

Brush with 1 beaten egg, then sprinkle with half of almonds. Repeat the same with the other roll of dough.

Bake for 25 minutes or until golden. Cool on wire rack.

2 braids

NUT STREUSEL COFFEE CAKE

$\frac{1}{2}$ cup butter
1 cup sugar
1 cup sour milk or 1 cup milk with
    1 teaspoon vinegar
2 eggs
2 cups sifted all-purpose flour
1 teaspoon baking soda
1 teaspoon baking powder
$\frac{1}{2}$ teaspoon salt
1 teaspoon vanilla

Topping:
$\frac{1}{3}$ cup packed brown sugar
$\frac{1}{4}$ cup granulated sugar
1 teaspoon cinnamon
1 cup finely chopped toasted pecans

Preheat oven to 325°. Lightly grease 9x9-inch baking pan.

In a large bowl of electric mixer, cream butter until soft. Add sugar and sour milk, mixing until light and fluffy. Add eggs one at a time, beating well after each addition.

Sift flour, baking soda, baking powder and salt. Add to butter and cream mixture, mix well. Stir in vanilla.

Combine brown sugar, sugar, cinnamon and pecans; mix well.

Pour $\frac{1}{2}$ of batter into prepared baking pan. Sprinkle $\frac{1}{2}$ nut topping over mixture. Pour remaining batter on top and sprinkle with remaining nut mixture.

Bake for 40 minutes, or until tester comes out clean.

6 to 8 servings

PFIRSICH KUCHEN
(PEACH COFFEE CAKE)

1 package hot roll mix
½ cup butter, softened
¼ cup sugar

3½ pounds fresh peaches, peeled
    and sliced
1 to 1½ cups sugar (according to
    ripeness of peaches)
Cinnamon, to taste
1 cup sour cream
Cream or milk, to thin

Preheat oven to 400°.

Prepare roll mix according to package directions, adding butter and ¼ cup sugar. Allow to rise in a warm place in a covered bowl.

Combine sugar with cinnamon and toss with peaches, coating them thoroughly; set aside. Thin sour cream slightly with a little milk or cream.

After dough has risen, punch down and knead for a minute until smooth. Spread or stretch into a 9x13-inch pan and arrange peaches on top of the dough, in rows close together. Drizzle sour cream over all and dust with cinnamon. Allow to rise again.

Bake for 45 minutes, or until golden brown around the edges. Cool for juices to settle. Cut into squares to serve.

12 servings

BUTTERMILK SCONES

1¾ cups all-purpose flour
1 teaspoon sugar
1 teaspoon salt
2 teaspoons baking powder
½ teaspoon baking soda
5 tablespoons unsalted butter
½ to ¾ cup buttermilk

Whipping cream, whipped
Strawberry jam

Preheat oven to 450°.

Combine flour, sugar, salt, baking powder and baking soda in a large bowl and mix thoroughly. Cut in the butter until mixture resembles coarse crumbs. Add just enough buttermilk to form a soft dough. Knead very lightly on a floured board and roll out to 1/2 to ¾-inch thick. Cut the dough with a sharp knife or with a 2-inch round cutter and place on an ungreased baking sheet.

Bake for 10 to 12 minutes, or until golden brown. Serve with whipping cream and strawberry jam.

Variation: Fold 2 tablespoons golden raisins or currants into dough before rolling.

Variation: Add 1 tablespoon orange zest with flour.

12 scones

GOLDEN COFFEE CAKE
(HUNGARIAN GALUSKA)

2 packages active dry yeast or
   2 cakes of compressed yeast
1/2 cup shortening
1/2 cup sugar
1 1/2 teaspoons salt
1/2 cup scalded milk
4 3/4 to 5 cups all-purpose flour,
   sifted and divided
2 eggs, well beaten

1 cup sugar
3/4 to 2 cups finely chopped
   toasted walnuts
3/4 cup melted butter or margarine

Soften dry yeast in 1/2 cup warm water (110°-115°) or compressed yeast in 1/2 cup of luke warm water (80°-85°). Let yeast stand 5 to 10 minutes.

Stir shortening, sugar, and salt in a large bowl. Add scalded milk and mix well. Cool to luke warm and mix in 1/2 cup flour. Beat until smooth. Stir yeast and add to dough; mix well. Add 2 cups flour and beat until very smooth. Add eggs and beat in enough flour to make soft dough.

Turn dough out on a lightly floured surface and let rest for 5 to 10 minutes. Knead dough until smooth and elastic. Form dough in ball and put in well greased bowl. Turn dough over to bring greased surface to top. Cover bowl with wax paper and towel. Let stand in warm area until doubled in size. Punch down, pull edges to center. Cover bowl and let rise until double.

Preheat oven to 375°.

Mix sugar and walnuts in a small bowl. Pour melted butter in a separate bowl.

Form dough in balls about 1 1/2-inches in diameter. Roll in butter; then in sugar mixture and layer in a 10-inch tube pan. Sprinkle remaining butter and sugar on top. Cover pan with wax paper and towel; let rise for 30 to 40 minutes.

Bake for 35 to 40 minutes or golden brown. Invert on a large plate and serve warm.

10 servings

MEDLEY MUFFINS

2 cups self-rising flour
1/2 cup finely chopped zucchini
1/2 cup finely chopped tomatoes,
   peeled, seeded and drained
1 tablespoon dried onion
1/2 teaspoon celery salt
1 1/2 teaspoons dill weed
1 egg, beaten
3/4 cup water
3 tablespoons vegetable oil
1/4 teaspoon Tabasco

Preheat oven to 425°. Grease muffin cups.

In a large bowl, stir flour, zucchini, tomato, onion, salt and dill weed together. Blend egg, water, Tabasco and oil; add to flour mixture. Stir until blended.

Fill prepared muffin cups 2/3 full.

Bake for 15 to 20 minutes or until golden brown.

12 muffins

DOUBLE BERRY MUFFINS

1½ cups blueberries, fresh or frozen,
    thawed and divided
½ cup butter, at room temperature
1 cup sugar
2 large eggs
1 teaspoon vanilla
2 teaspoons baking powder
¼ teaspoon salt
1 cup raspberries, fresh or frozen,
    thawed and divided
2 cups all-purpose flour, divided
½ cup milk, divided
1 tablespoon sugar
¼ teaspoon cinnamon

Crush ½ cup of blueberries; set aside.

Preheat oven to 375°. Grease medium-size muffin cups or use foil baking cups. (Greasing the area between the cups will help in the removal of the muffins, if there is an overflow.)

In a medium bowl, beat butter until creamy. Add sugar and beat together until light in color and fluffy. Beat in eggs, one at a time; add vanilla, salt and baking powder. Stir in reserved ½ cup crushed berries. Fold in 1 cup flour, then ¼ cup milk. Repeat with remaining flour and milk. Fold in remaining berries. Spoon batter into muffin cups. Stir together sugar and cinnamon; sprinkle on muffins.

Bake for 25 to 30 minutes, or until golden brown. Allow to cool in the pan for 30 to 40 minutes before removing.

12 muffins

LEMON STREUSEL MUFFINS

Streusel Topping:
6 tablespoons sugar
5 tablespoons all-purpose flour
2 tablespoons butter or margarine

2 cups all-purpose flour
½ cup sugar
2 teaspoons baking powder
½ teaspoon baking soda
½ teaspoon salt
1 8-ounce container lemon yogurt
½ cup vegetable oil
1 tablespoon grated fresh lemon zest
2 eggs
1 cup blueberries or red raspberries,
    fresh or frozen and thawed

Preheat oven to 400°. Grease or paper line medium-size muffin cups or mini-muffin cups.

Topping: Combine sugar, flour and butter and mix until crumbly. Sprinkle over top of batter.

In a small bowl, combine flour, sugar, baking powder, baking soda and salt; mix well. In a large bowl, combine yogurt, oil, lemon zest and eggs; mix well. Add dry ingredients and stir until just moistened. Gently fold in fruit. Fill prepared muffin tin three-fourths full with batter.

Bake for 12 to 13 minutes for mini-muffins and 20 minutes for medium-size muffins. Cool 5 minutes and remove from pan.

Variation: Eliminate fruit and add ¼ cup poppy seeds or 1 cup finely chopped pecans.

Variation: For low cholesterol version, substitute equivalent egg substitute or egg whites for whole eggs.

12 medium muffins or 24 mini-muffins

LOW-FAT FRUIT OAT BRAN MUFFINS
(no cholesterol)

2¼ cups uncooked oat bran
1 teaspoon ground cinnamon
1 teaspoon baking powder
½ teaspoon baking soda
¼ teaspoon salt
1 8-ounce package dried fruit, diced
2 egg whites
1 cup unsweetened applesauce
½ cup brown sugar
½ cup plain or strawberry/ banana
    low-fat yogurt
2 tablespoons vegetable oil

Preheat oven to 350°. Spray medium-size or mini-muffin cups with a non-stick spray.

In a large bowl, combine oat bran, cinnamon, baking powder, baking soda, salt and dried fruits. In a small bowl, whisk egg whites, applesauce, brown sugar, yogurt and vegetable oil until smooth. Combine both mixtures in large bowl and mix well.

Fill medium-size muffin cups ⅓ full. Bake for 30 minutes.
Fill mini-muffin cups ½ full. Bake for 18 to 20 minutes.

Hint: Muffins will keep 5 to 7 days in refrigerator and can be frozen.

12 medium muffins or 24 mini-muffins

RHUBARB BREAD

1½ cups firmly packed brown sugar
⅔ cup vegetable oil
1 egg, beaten
1 cup buttermilk
1 teaspoon salt
1 teaspoon baking soda
1 teaspoon vanilla
2½ cups all-purpose flour
2 cups diced rhubarb
½ cup chopped walnuts

Topping:
¼ cup granulated sugar
1 tablespoon butter, softened

Preheat oven to 350°.

Combine brown sugar and oil; beat until smooth. Stir in egg, buttermilk, salt, baking soda, vanilla and flour. Blend just until moistened. Fold in rhubarb and nuts. Pour into two 8x4x2½-inch loaf pans.

Topping: Combine sugar and softened butter until crumbly. Sprinkle over batter.

Bake for 55 to 60 minutes, or until tester inserted in center of cake comes out clean. Let stand 10 minutes and remove from pan. Cool.

Hint: If top begins to burn while baking, cover with aluminum foil.

2 loaves

C A R A W A Y   C H E E S E   M U F F I N S

2 cups all-purpose flour
3 teaspoons baking powder
½ teaspoon salt
¾ teaspoon freshly ground pepper
2 tablespoons caraway seeds
1 cup milk
2 eggs
2 tablespoons oil
8 ounces sharp cheddar
    cheese, cubed

Preheat oven to 400°. Generously grease 12 muffin cups.
    Sift together flour, baking powder, salt and pepper. Stir in caraway seeds.
    Beat together the milk, eggs and oil. Stir into dry ingredients until just moistened. Do not over mix. Fold in cheese cubes.
    Spoon into prepared muffin cups.
    Bake for 15 minutes or until golden.

12 muffins

S T R A W B E R R Y   B R E A D

3 cups sugar
4 eggs, beaten
1¼ cups oil
2 10-ounce packages frozen
    strawberries, thawed
3 cups all-purpose flour
3 teaspoons cinnamon
1 teaspoon baking soda
1 teaspoon salt

Preheat oven to 350°.
    In a large bowl, mix sugar, eggs and oil; stir in strawberries. Add flour, cinnamon, baking soda and salt; mix well. Pour into 2 ungreased 9x5-inch loaf pans.
    Bake for 1 hour.

2 loaves

M E X I C A N   S P O O N   B R E A D

1 16-ounce can cream-style corn
¾ cup milk
⅓ cup melted shortening
1½ cups cornmeal
2 eggs, slightly beaten
½ teaspoon baking soda
1 teaspoon baking powder
1 teaspoon salt
1 teaspoon sugar (optional)
1 4-ounce can green chilies, chopped
1½ cups grated cheddar cheese

Preheat oven to 400°. Grease a 9x9-inch pan.
    In a large bowl, combine corn, milk, shortening, cornmeal, eggs, baking soda, baking powder, salt and sugar; mix well. Pour half the batter into prepared pan. Sprinkle on half of the cheese and chilies. Add remaining batter and top with remaining cheese and chilies.
    Bake for 45 minutes. Cool slightly and serve.

8 to 10 servings

CARAWAY RYE BEER BREAD

2 cups rye flour
1½ cups all-purpose flour
3½ teaspoons baking powder
1 teaspoon salt
2 tablespoons sugar
2 tablespoons caraway seeds,
    or dill seeds
1 tablespoon vegetable oil
1 12-ounce can beer

Preheat oven to 375°. Butter 8 or 9-inch round pan, or 1½-quart round baking dish.

In electric mixer, mix rye flour, all-purpose flour, baking powder, salt, sugar, caraway seeds, vegetable oil and beer. Mix until moist. Turn into pan or bowl.

Bake for 45 to 55 minutes or until bread sounds hollow when tapped. Remove from pan. Serve warm with winter soups, stews and sliced for sandwiches.

Variation: Substitute all-purpose flour with whole wheat flour.

1 loaf

BENEFICIAL BANANA BREAD

1¼ cups sugar
½ cup sunflower or safflower oil
¾ cup egg substitute or equal
    to 3 eggs
3 bananas (very ripe)
⅓ cup chopped walnuts
1½ cups all-purpose flour
1½ cups whole wheat flour
1½ teaspoons baking soda
1½ teaspoons salt

Preheat oven to 350°. Prepare two 4x8-inch loaf pans with cooking oil spray.

Cream sugar and oil together in food processor or mixer. Slowly add egg substitute and beat well. Crush bananas with pastry cutter or fork. Mix in nuts and combine with sugar mixture; set aside.

Sift together all-purpose flour, whole wheat flour, baking soda and salt. Add to batter, a little at a time, beating well after each addition. Pour into prepared pans.

Bake for 50 to 60 minutes, or until internal temperature registers 190° on an instant-read thermometer. Cool in pan for 5 minutes. Turn out on racks to cool completely.

2 loaves

I R I S H   S O D A   B R E A D

1¾ cup buttermilk
2 eggs
⅔ cup sugar
2 tablespoons butter, melted
3 cups all-purpose flour
1 tablespoon baking powder
1 teaspoon baking soda
1 teaspoon salt
1 cup seedless raisins
1 tablespoon caraway seed

Preheat oven to 350°. Butter and flour a 9x5-inch pan.

In a large bowl, beat eggs with buttermilk. Add sugar and melted butter. Sift flour into a small bowl, add baking powder, baking soda, and salt; mix well. Stir into egg mixture and blend until just incorporated. Add raisins and caraway seeds; stir to lightly mix. Overbeating will toughen batter. Pour batter into prepared pan.

Bake for 1 hour.

1 loaf

P O P P Y S E E D   T E A   B R E A D

3 large eggs
1¼ cup milk
¾ cup vegetable oil
1 teaspoon vanilla
2¼ cups all-purpose flour
1½ cups sugar
1 tablespoon baking powder
¾ cup poppy seeds

Preheat oven to 350°. Butter and flour two 6x3x3-inch loaf pans.

In a large bowl, beat eggs; add milk, oil and vanilla. In separate bowl mix flour, sugar, baking powder, and poppyseeds. Add dry ingredients to egg mixture and gently stir until smooth and well blended. Pour into prepared pans.

Bake for 50 to 60 minutes.

Hint: Substitute lightly toasted sesame seeds or 4 tablespoons of caraway seeds for the poppyseeds.

2 loaves

Z U C C H I N I   S A U S A G E   B I S C U I T S

⅓ cup packaged biscuit mix
¼ cup grated Parmesan cheese
⅛ teaspoon pepper
2 eggs, slightly beaten
¼ cup diced onion
2 cups shredded unpared zucchini
    (2 medium)
1 cup diced cooked Polish sausage
    or leftover meat
Olive oil

In a mixing bowl, stir together biscuit mix, cheese and pepper. Stir in beaten eggs, until mixture is just moistened. Fold in zucchini and onion. Add meat.

In a 10-inch skillet, heat olive oil over medium heat. Using 2 tablespoons mixture for each round, cook four rounds at a time about 2 to 3 minutes on each side or until brown. Keep warm while cooking remaining rounds.

Can be served at breakfast or dinner.

6 servings

PLUM BREAD

1 cup butter or margarine
1½ cups sugar
1 teaspoon vanilla
4 eggs (egg substitute may be used)
¾ cup lemon yogurt
1 teaspoon grated fresh lemon zest
3 cups all-purpose flour
1 teaspoon salt
1 teaspoon cream of tartar
½ teaspoon baking soda
2 cups diced plums (nectarines
     can be substituted)
1 cup chopped walnuts or
     pecans, toasted

Preheat oven to 350°. Grease two 5x9-inch loaf pans or four 4x8-inch loaf pans.

Cream butter or margarine with sugar and vanilla in a large bowl. Add eggs, one at a time, beating well after each addition; set aside. Blend yogurt with lemon zest. In a separate bowl, combine flour, salt, cream of tartar and baking soda. Add yogurt alternately with the dry ingredients to the butter mixture. Stir until blended. Fold in plums and nuts. Pour into prepared loaf pans.

Bake for 55 minutes or until internal temperature registers 190° on an instant-read thermometer.

Variation: Egg substitutes are an alternative to fresh eggs. Nectarines may be substituted for plums.

2 large loaves or 4 small loaves

LETTUCE BREAD

1 cup sugar
½ cup vegetable oil
1½ teaspoon grated fresh lemon zest
2 eggs
1½ cups sifted all-purpose flour
2 teaspoons baking powder
½ teaspoon baking soda
½ teaspoon salt
⅛ teaspoon mace
⅛ teaspoon ground ginger
1 cup finely shredded iceberg lettuce
½ cup chopped toasted pecans

Preheat oven to 350°. Line 8½x4½-inch loaf pan with aluminum foil.

Combine sugar, oil and lemon zest. Add eggs, beating well. Sift flour with baking powder, baking soda, salt, mace and ginger; add to creamed mixture. Fold lettuce and pecans into batter. Turn into pan.

Bake for 50 to 55 minutes, or until tester inserted in bread comes out clean. Cool in pan for 15 minutes. Invert and cool completely before serving.

1 loaf

BASIC OLIVE OIL BREAD

3 tablespoons active dry yeast
4 cups warm water (110° to 115°)
2 tablespoons salt
¾ cup olive oil
6 to 8 cups hi-gluten bread flour,
    divided

Onion Focaccia:
Thinly sliced onions
Coarse salt
Freshly ground pepper
Dried basil
Freshly grated Parmesan cheese

Rosemary Focaccia:
Olive oil
Dried rosemary
Coarse salt

Sprinkle yeast over warm water; let stand 5 to 10 minutes until foamy. Stir in salt and olive oil. Add 4 cups flour and mix well. Stir in remaining flour, ½ cup at a time until too stiff to stir. Turn out on lightly floured surface and knead, adding more flour as necessary, a small amount at a time, until dough is smooth and elastic, about 10 minutes. Put dough into a warm, oiled, ceramic bowl, turn over so top is oiled. Cover, set in a warm place, and let rise until doubled, or about 1 hour.

Punch down and turn out on oiled surface.

Onion Focaccia: Preheat oven to 375°. Line baking sheets with parchment paper sprinkled with corn meal.

Shape dough into balls the size of a large baseball. Roll out and place on lined baking sheets.

Brush surface with olive oil. Cover with thinly sliced onions, coarse salt, freshly ground pepper, dried basil and freshly grated Parmesan cheese.

Bake for 15 to 20 minutes, or until nicely browned.

Rosemary Focaccia: Preheat oven to 375°. Oil a 15x18-inch jelly roll pan.

Roll dough out to fit pan. Press with finger tips to leave indentations. Heat olive oil with dried rosemary and paint surface of dough. Sprinkle with coarse salt.

Bake for 15 to 20 minutes or until browned.

ENGLISH CHERRY TEA LOAF

⅔ cup butter
1 cup sugar
4 eggs
2 cups all-purpose flour
½ teaspoon baking powder
1½ to 2 cups halved candied cherries
Zest of 1 fresh lemon

Preheat oven to 300°. Butter and line a 9x5-inch loaf pan with waxed paper.

Cream butter with sugar in mixing bowl. Beat in eggs. Sift flour and baking powder together. Add to butter and egg mixture. To prevent cherries from sticking together, coat with flour. Stir cherries and lemon zest into batter. Pour into prepared loaf pan.

Bake for 1 to 1½ hours. The loaf is done when a crack forms on top and a tester inserted in center comes out clean.

1 loaf

FRENCH BREAD BAGUETTES

2½ tablespoons active dry yeast
5 cups warm water
6 to 8 cups high-gluten bread flour,
    divided
2 tablespoons salt
1 egg white
1 to 2 tablespoons cold water

Combine water and yeast in a warm mixing bowl and stir to dissolve. In the bowl of an electric mixer, outfitted with a dough hook, place 5 cups flour. Add water and yeast mixture to flour, stirring constantly with the dough hook or with a wooden spoon. Continue adding flour until the dough leaves the sides of the bowl almost clean. Remove from bowl and knead until elastic, about 10 minutes.

Place ball of dough in oiled warm bowl and turn in bowl to cover lightly with oil. Cover bowl with towel, let rise in warm place until double (about 1 or 1½ hours).

Punch down dough and divide into 2 or 3 rectangle long forms, pinching along seams. Spray baguette pans with non-stick cooking spray and place dough in pans. Place uncovered in warm place and let stand until double in bulk.

Preheat oven to 450°.

Using a razor blade or sharp knife, slash each loaf lengthwise. The cut should be about ⅛-inch deep.

Whisk together egg white and water for egg wash. Brush dough with egg wash.

Bake for 15 minutes, reduce heat to 350° and continue baking for 30 minutes or longer. Spray with water for "crusty" crust. Remove loaves from oven and cool on racks.

3 loaves

TEA ROOM CARROT BREAD

2 cups all-purpose flour
2 teaspoons baking soda
2 teaspoons cinnamon
½ teaspoon salt
1 cup vegetable oil
3 eggs, beaten
1½ cups sugar
1 teaspoon vanilla extract
¼ cup nuts, chopped
2 cups grated carrots
½ cup coconut
½ cup raisins
Cream cheese

Preheat oven to 350°. Grease and flour two 6x3x3-inch loaf pans (tube or any other pan is fine).

Sift flour, baking soda, cinnamon and salt into a large bowl. Make well in dry mixture. In separate bowl, mix oil, eggs, sugar and vanilla. Stir in nuts, carrots, coconut and raisins. Pour into well in dry ingredients. Mix lightly. Pour into prepared pans. Let stand 20 minutes before baking.

Bake for 1 hour, or until tester inserted in middle comes out clean. Remove from pan and cool on rack.

Slice and spread with cream cheese.

2 loaves

HONEY WHOLE WHEAT BREAD

3 tablespoons active dry yeast
4 cups warm water (110° to 115°)
½ cup honey
4 cups whole wheat flour, divided
8 cups hi-gluten white flour, divided
1 egg, beaten
1 tablespoon water

Sprinkle yeast over warm water and let stand 5 to 10 minutes or until bubbly. Add honey, 2 cups whole wheat flour and 2 cups white flour. Beat well. Gradually add additional flour until dough is stiff enough to knead. Turn out on floured surface and knead, adding small amounts of both flours as necessary, until dough is smooth and elastic, about 10 minutes. Place dough in an oiled, warm ceramic bowl; turn once to coat with oil. Cover and let rise, in a warm place, until doubled, about 1 hour.

Punch down and turn out onto work surface. Divide and shape into 4 loaves or 1 long baguette. Place in four 9x5-inch loaf pans or on a baking sheet. Cover and let rise until doubled, about 45 minutes.

Preheat oven to 325°. Beat egg and water together and brush on top of dough.

Bake for 25 minutes or until internal temperature registers 190° on an instant-read thermometer. Turn bread out on sides to cool on racks.

1 baguette loaf or 4 loaves

PRAIRIE STATE CORN BREAD
SOURDOUGH CORN BREAD

Sourdough Starter:
2 cups warm water
2½ cups unbleached flour
1 package active dry yeast

Bread:
1 cup sourdough starter
1½ cups yellow corn meal
1 cup sweetened condensed milk
2 eggs, beaten
¼ cup butter, melted
½ teaspoon salt
1 teaspoon baking soda
1 tablespoon water

Sourdough Starter: Combine water, flour, yeast and let stand 12 hours or more. Can be kept, covered, in the refrigerator for months. Just stir thoroughly before use.

Preheat oven to 425°. Grease a 10-inch pan or iron skillet.

In a large bowl, combine sourdough starter, corn meal, condensed milk, eggs and butter. Mix well. Dissolve baking soda in water and add salt. Fold into cornmeal mixture. Pour into prepared pan.

Bake for 25 minutes or until a tester is withdrawn clean from the center.

PIZZA DI VERDURA
(VEGETABLE PIZZA)

Sauce:
1 28-ounce can crushed tomatoes
    packed in puree
$1/2$ cup vegetable oil, plus
    1 tablespoon olive oil
4 drops Worcestershire sauce
1 dash ground red pepper
1 tablespoon dry red wine, optional
1 tablespoon dried oregano or
    3 tablespoons fresh
    chopped oregano
1 tablespoon dried basil or
    1 tablespoon fresh chopped basil
Freshly ground pepper

Crust:
2 packages active dry
    "quick rise" yeast
1 pinch sugar
$3^{1}/2$ cups all-purpose flour
$1/2$ teaspoon salt
$1^{1}/4$ cups lukewarm water
$1/4$ cup vegetable oil, plus
    1 tablespoon olive oil
Corn meal

Topping:
1 pound scamorza or mozzarella
    cheese, shredded
Freshly grated Parmesan cheese

Fresh vegetables:
    Spinach, sautéed, drained
    and finely chopped; Mushrooms,
    sliced, sautéed; Sliced onion;
    Cauliflower, chopped and
    blanched; Zucchini, sliced and
    sautéed

Sauce: In a large saucepan, combine and heat tomatoes, oil, Worcestershire sauce, red pepper, wine, oregano and basil. Season with pepper to taste. Simmer until ready to use.

Crust: In a small bowl, sprinkle yeast and sugar on $1/4$ cup water, swirl to mix. Cover with dish; let stand for 3 minutes to increase volume.

In a large mixing bowl, combine flour and salt; mix with whisk. Make a well in center of flour and pour in yeast mixture, 1 cup water and oil mixture. Mix until dough starts to stick together. Knead dough for 5 to 6 minutes, or until smooth and elastic. Smooth a drop of oil over the dough; place in a mixing bowl to rise. Place mixing bowl into warmed oven, not hot! Also place a cup of boiling water in the oven, next to bowl, to add humidity to the rising process. After 30 minutes remove mixing bowl and cup of water. Knead dough several times and let rest for one minute.

Preheat oven to 475°. Grease with oil or shortening a 16-inch pizza pan or 18 to 24 medium muffin tins and sprinkle with corn meal.

Grasp dough and hold it up to stretch it. Continue turning and stretching dough. Place stretched dough into prepared pizza pan. Press dough to meet the pan's edges. Patch any holes that may occur. If using muffin tins use ping-pong size balls of dough and stretch to make "cups of dough". Place crust in oven for 7 to 8 minutes (4 to 5 minutes for muffins) to pre-cook and seal crust. Dough can be frozen at this point.

Place $1/2$ cheese mixture on the hot pizza crust. Cover with sauce. Layer with vegetable combination of your choice. Cover vegetables with remaining cheese. Return to oven.

Bake for 8 to 10 minutes (5 to 7 minutes for muffins), or until crust is golden. Let sit for 4 minutes before cutting. Serve as a main course.

Variation: Substitute scamorza cheese with $3/4$ pound scamorza and $1/4$ pound brick cheese.

1 16-inch pizza or 18 to 24 individual pizzas

ITALIAN PARMESAN BREAD

1 package active dry yeast
¾ cup warm water
2 tablespoons sugar
1 teaspoon salt
3 cups all-purpose flour, divided
4 eggs, room temperature, divided
½ cup soft butter
1 cup freshly grated Parmesan
    cheese
1 cup shredded Monterey Jack cheese
1 teaspoon dried oregano or
    1 tablespoon chopped fresh
    oregano, optional

Sprinkle yeast into warm water (110°-115°) in large mixing bowl. Let stand until dissolved and foamy. Add sugar, salt and 1 cup flour. Beat well. Add 3 eggs, one at a time. Beat until smooth. Beat in butter. Gradually add enough remaining flour to make a soft dough. Turn out on a lightly floured board. Knead until smooth and satiny. Place in a greased bowl and butter top of dough lightly. Cover with a kitchen towel and let rise in a warm place until doubled in size. Turn out on a floured board. Knead lightly. Roll out into a rectangle about 10x16 inches.

In a large mixing bowl, beat remaining egg. Blend in cheeses and oregano. Spread cheese filling over dough. Roll up firmly from narrow end. Shape into a ball by folding ends underneath. Place in a greased 2-quart round baking dish (preferably one with straight sides about 3 inches high, such as a souffle dish). Cover. Let rise in warm place until doubled in size.

Preheat oven to 350°.

Bake for 40 minutes, or until golden brown and loaf sounds hollow when tapped. Cool 10 minutes. Remove from pan.

Variation: Substitute 2 cups freshly grated Romano cheese for the Parmesan and Monterey Jack cheeses.

This mushroom-shaped loaf, streaked with cheese, is a fine companion to an Italian dinner.

1 round loaf

PITA TOASTS

¾ cup unsalted margarine, softened
2 tablespoons minced fresh parsley
1 tablespoon chopped chives
2 large cloves garlic, minced
1 tablespoon fresh lemon juice
6 loaves pita bread, sesame preferred

Preheat oven to 450°.

In a small bowl, mix together margarine, parsley, chives, garlic and lemon juice; let mixture stand at room temperature at least two hours. Halve pita loaves horizontally. Cut each half into two pieces and spread with margarine mixture. Cut each half again. Arrange pita on two baking sheets.

Bake in top third of oven for 5 to 10 minutes or until golden brown and very crisp. Serve warm or at room temperature.

OLD WORLD BLACK BREAD

3¾ cups rye flour
3¾ cups all-purpose flour
2 packages active dry yeast
½ cup warm water
½ cup unsweetened cocoa
¼ cup sugar
2 tablespoons caraway seeds
2 teaspoons salt
2 teaspoons instant coffee
2 cups water
¼ cup vinegar
¼ cup dark corn syrup
¼ cup butter

Combine rye flour and all-purpose flour in a large bowl. Reserve 3 cups of the flour mixture. Sprinkle yeast over ½ cup warm water, stir until dissolved; set aside. In a large bowl, stir together reserved 3 cups flour mixture, cocoa, sugar, caraway seeds, salt and instant coffee.

Combine 2 cups water, vinegar, corn syrup and butter in a medium saucepan; heat over low heat just until warm. (Butter does not need to be completely melted.) Add to cocoa mixture and blend well. Add dissolved yeast and stir until thoroughly combined. Stir in additional flour mixture, 1 cup at a time, until dough no longer clings to side of bowl.

Turn dough onto a lightly floured board. Cover and let rest 10 minutes. Knead dough until smooth and elastic, about 15 minutes. Place in a greased bowl. Turn dough greased side up. Cover. Let rise in a warm place about 1 hour or until doubled. Punch down and turn onto lightly floured board. Divide dough in half. Shape each half into a smooth ball. Place each ball in center of a greased 8-inch round cake pan. Cover. Let rise in warm place about 1 hour or until doubled.

Preheat oven to 350°.

Bake for 45 to 50 minutes or until loaves sound hollow when tapped lightly. Remove from pans and place on wire racks. Brush with melted butter or milk for a soft crust.

2 loaves

CELERY LOAF

1 loaf unsliced white bread
½ cup butter or margarine, softened
1 teaspoon celery salt
½ teaspoon paprika

Garnish:
Fresh parsley, chopped

Trim crusts from top, sides and ends of loaf. Cut loaf at 1-inch intervals lengthwise and crosswise, almost to bottom of crust. Mix butter and seasonings. Spread over entire surface of cuts. Wrap in foil. (Can do ahead to this point and refrigerate).

Preheat oven to 400°.

When ready to bake, open foil slightly at top.

Bake for 15 to 18 minutes, until top is golden. Garnish with minced parsley just before serving.

1 loaf

C I N N A M O N   C R I S P S

1 package active dry yeast
²⁄₃ cup warm water
1 tablespoon sugar
¾ cup margarine
2 cups all-purpose flour
¼ teaspoon salt
1 egg yolk, beaten

Garnish:
Cinnamon
Sugar

Soften yeast in warm water; set aside. Using a pastry cutter or a fork, cut margarine into sugar, flour and salt until crumbly. Stir egg yolk into softened yeast and add to flour mixture. Roll out dough on waxed paper to a 9x13-inch rectangle. Sprinkle generously with cinnamon. Roll up jelly roll fashion, cover and chill overnight.

Preheat oven to 350°. Grease cookie sheets.

Slice dough into very thin slices. Sprinkle a piece of waxed paper generously with sugar. Place slices on sugar and roll with rolling pin until flat. Coat both sides with sugar. Place on prepared cookie sheet.

Bake for 10 minutes or until browned.

35 crisps

R O A S T E D   G A R L I C   W I T H   P U M P E R N I C K E L   B R E A D

1 cup olive oil, divided
8 whole garlic heads
1 teaspoon salt
¼ teaspoon freshly ground pepper
1 pound round loaf dark
    pumpernickel bread, torn
    in 8 pieces

Preheat oven to 200°. Use 1 tablespoon olive oil to grease bottom of 8-inch square baking pan.

Make shallow incision all around each garlic head, halfway between top and bottom, cutting through skin, but not into meat of garlic. Lift off pointed top of each head.

Arrange garlic in prepared pan. Pour remaining olive oil over garlic heads. Sprinkle with salt and pepper.

Bake, uncovered, for 15 minutes. Cover pan with foil and continue baking 1 hour or until garlic is tender. Serve warm with pumpernickel bread.

O R A N G E   T O A S T S

1 cup butter, melted
1 cup sugar
2 tablespoons grated orange zest
2 teaspoons cinnamon
1 loaf thin sliced white sandwich
    bread

Preheat oven to 250°.

Combine butter, sugar, orange zest and cinnamon and spread on bread (1 teaspoon to a slice). Cut into thirds. Place on ungreased cookie sheet.

Bake for 1 hour. Store in airtight container.

COOL DILLED CHICKEN SANDWICHES

4 chicken breasts, skinned and boned
1 carrot, sliced
1 celery rib, chopped
1 onion, chopped
½ teaspoon ground white pepper
4 ounces cream cheese
¼ cup mayonnaise
3 tablespoons chopped fresh dill
    (or 1 tablespoon dried dill)
2 tablespoons fresh lemon juice
1 teaspoon grated lemon zest
½ teaspoon Beau Monde seasoning
    or seasoned salt
Salt
Arugula
4 English muffins, toasted and
    buttered
2 tomatoes (8 slices)
1 20-ounce can pineapple slices
1 large green pepper (8 slices)
Chopped macadamia nuts

In a large saucepan, cook chicken, carrots, celery, onions and white pepper with water to cover for approximately 30 minutes, or just until chicken is opaque throughout. Do not overcook. Cool in stock and refrigerate until ready to use.

In a medium bowl, whip together cream cheese, mayonnaise and dill. Add lemon juice and lemon zest. Continue beating until smooth. Season with Beau Monde seasoning and salt.

Layer on plates as follows: arugula leaf, English muffin, tomato slice, pineapple slice, green pepper slice, chicken breast half, dressing, chopped macadamia nuts.

Variation: Substitute toasted almond slices, parsley, or cut pieces of green pepper and tomato for macadamia nuts.

8 servings

FINES HERBES TOAST

1 cup butter, melted
2 teaspoons "herbes de Provence"
1 teaspoon onion salt
1 loaf rye or whole wheat bread
Parmesan cheese

Preheat oven to 250°.

Mix butter with fines herbs and onion salt. Brush on bread slices and place on ungreased cookie sheets. Sprinkle with cheese.

Bake for 1 hour. Serve with salads and soups.

B R U S C H E T T A

1 1-pound French bread loaf,
    16-inches long
1 large clove garlic, halved
¼ cup extra virgin olive oil

Topping:
2½ pounds or 4 large ripe
    fresh tomatoes
14 kalamata olives, pitted
⅓ cup julienned fresh basil
¼ cup balsamic vinegar
¼ cup extra virgin olive oil
¼ cup minced onion
½ teaspoon salt
¼ teaspoon sugar
Freshly ground black pepper

Preheat grill or oven broiler.

Cut bread in half horizontally. Grill cut side down, over medium hot grill, until lightly toasted. (If using oven broiler, grill cut side up until toasted.) Rub toasted side with garlic and brush with olive oil. Cut each half into equal sections.

Topping: Peel tomato. Remove inside of tomato (use only outer shell) and cut into ½-inch dice. Mix tomatoes, olives, basil, vinegar, oil, onion, salt, sugar and pepper in a bowl. Tomato mixture may be made 2 hours before serving. Using a slotted spoon, divide mixture among slices of toasted bread.

Garnish with sun-dried tomatoes or mixture of sun-dried and fresh tomatoes and basil leaves.

T U R K E Y   T A C O   S A N D W I C H

½ cup coarsely chopped ripe olives
½ teaspoon chili powder
½ teaspoon ground cumin
¼ teaspoon salt
½ cup mayonnaise
½ cup sour cream
½ cup sliced green onions
1 large tomato, sliced
4 large oval slices French bread,
    about ½-inch thick
1 pound turkey breast, thinly sliced
1 ripe avocado, peeled, seeded
    and sliced
¾ cup cheddar cheese, shredded
¾ cup Monterey Jack cheese,
    shredded
Lettuce leaves
Salsa

Preheat oven to 350°.

Combine olives, chili powder, cumin and salt in medium bowl; mix well and reserve 2 tablespoons. Stir mayonnaise, sour cream and onion into remaining olive mixture. Use half the mayonnaise mixture and spread on each bread slice. Top with tomato and turkey. Spread remaining mayonnaise mixture on top of turkey. Top with avocado slices; sprinkle with cheeses. Place on baking sheet.

Bake for 15 minutes.

Serve on lettuce leaves. Top sandwiches with reserved olive mixture and several spoonfuls of salsa.

4 servings

CURRIED CHICKEN ALMOND TEA SANDWICHES

1 cup finely chopped or shredded
    cooked chicken breast meat
1 teaspoon curry powder or to taste
1/4 cup mayonnaise
Pinch salt
Freshly ground white pepper
Butter
1/4 cup toasted chopped almonds
Whole wheat bread, crust removed

In a small bowl, combine chicken, curry powder, mayonnaise, salt and white pepper; mix well. Butter each slice of bread. Spread each diamond with chicken mixture. Cut into diamond shapes. Top with chopped almonds.

STRAWBERRY CREAM CHEESE TEA SANDWICHES

4 ounces cream cheese, softened
1/8 teaspoon vanilla
1/4 teaspoon superfine sugar
Milk
Thin sliced white bread,
    crusts removed

Garnish:
Fresh strawberries
Mint leaves

In a small bowl, add vanilla and sugar to cream cheese; mix well. Add enough milk until consistency to spread. Spread cream cheese mixture on each slice of bread. Quarter bread slices. On top of each square, fan out 3 slices of strawberries with a piece of mint garnish used as stem.

WATERCRESS LEMON PINWHEELS

Fresh white bread, crusts removed
1/4 cup butter, softened
1 teaspoon finely minced onion
1/8 teaspoon fresh lemon zest
Pinch salt
2 bunches watercress, rinsed, dried
    and coarsely chopped

Place slices of bread between waxed paper and roll thinner with a rolling pin. Remove waxed paper.

In a small bowl, combine butter, onion, lemon zest and salt; mix well. Spread butter on bread slices. Place watercress on buttered slices; be generous and allow watercress to extend beyond edges of bread. Roll each slice jelly roll fashion. Wrap rolls in plastic wrap and chill.

To serve, cut across rolls into slices.

ENTREES

Beef

Arancini (Rice Balls) 129
Beef Filet with Peppercorns and Chutney 131
Beef Chili with Limes 133
Beef Fajitas 129
Crock Pot Barbecue Beef 133
Individual Beef Wellingtons 132
Italian Beef Roll-Up 137
Lobster-stuffed Tenderloin of Beef 131
Russian Stuffed Cabbage 134
Sauerbraten 136
Stuffed Flank Steak with Bleu Cheese 135
Tenderloin Chasseur 130

Pork

Potatoed Pork Loin 137
Pork Tenderloin in Dijon Sauce 138
Pork Tenderloin Medallions
    with Lemon Glaze 139

Chicken

Chicken, Mushroom
    and Spinach Strudel 150
Chicken Mole 146
Chicken Crab Supreme 153
Chicken à la Suisse 145
Chicken with Red Pepper Salsa 147
Fruit Glazed Chicken with
    Gazpacho and Tortilla Crisps 144
Fruit-Glazed Roast Chicken 147
Gingered Chicken Breasts 148
Lemon Chicken 146
Marghi with Indian Curry Sauce 149
Roast Chicken with Black Pepper Glaze 145
Rock Cornish Hens Bourguignon 148
Stuffed Chicken Breasts Saltimbocca 152
Vermouth Chicken Scallopine 151

Turkey

Grilled Ginger Turkey Breast 151
Turkey and Cheese Enchiladas 153
Turkey Vegetable Gratin 152
Viking Burgers 154

Lamb

Lamb and Bean Stew 136
Leg of Lamb with Artichoke Stuffing 138
Marinated Grilled Leg of Lamb 139
Mixed Marinated Grill 135

Veal

Stuffed Breast of Veal with Wild Rice 140
Veal Ragout 141
Veal Scallopine with Mushroom and
    Sun-dried Tomato Cream Sauce 140

Game

Divine Pheasant Breasts 142
Duck l'Orange 141
Midwestern Stuffed Duck 142
Venison Steaks 143

Fish

Baked Fish Parmesan
    with Tomato Sauce 156
Grilled Red Snapper 157
Grilled Salmon
    with Mustard Dill Sauce 155
Macadamia Salmon 157
Spicy Sweet and Sour
    Grilled Tuna 156
Stuffed Baked Trout
    in Horseradish Cream 154
Teriyaki Swordfish 157
Tuna Steaks in Marinade 155

Seafood

Baked Stuffed Shrimp 161
Le Crabe Excellent 160
Moules Marinière 158
Paella 162
Scallops and Mushrooms au Gratin 159
Seafood Risotto 161
Shrimp in Almond Sauce 159
Shrimp Creole 158
Spicy Crab Cakes with Corn 160

ARANCINI (RICE BALLS)

1 medium onion, chopped
3 pounds ground beef
1 6-ounce can tomato paste
2 6-ounce cans water
1/4 teaspoon pepper
1 teaspoon salt
3 tablespoons chopped fresh parsley,
    optional

2 pounds uncooked white rice
1 cup grated Romano or Parmesan
    cheese
1/2 cup butter or margarine, softened
4 eggs, beaten
Flour
6 eggs, well-beaten
Bread crumbs

2 15-ounce cans tomato sauce

Preheat oven to 350°. Line a jelly roll pan with aluminum foil.

In a large saucepan, brown onion and ground beef. Add tomato paste and cook for 5 more minutes. Add water, pepper, salt and parsley. Taste and adjust seasonings, if necessary. Mix well and let cool for 15 minutes.

Cook rice in salted boiling water until almost done. Drain well and mix in cheese, butter and eggs. Form rice into balls the size of an orange, putting a "light" tablespoon of meat mixture in the center of each ball. Roll ball first in flour, then in beaten eggs, and finally in bread crumbs. Place on cookie sheet.

Bake for 30 minutes (45 minutes if frozen).

In a large saucepan, mix tomato sauce with remaining meat mixture and heat. Serve sauce over arancini.

This is a delicious Italian dish. It is great for a buffet. The recipe is easily halved or doubled. If doubling, prepare only 2 pounds of rice at a time.

36 arancini or 18 servings

BEEF FAJITAS

1 pound round steak, cut in strips
3 cloves garlic, minced
4 tablespoons chili powder
2 teaspoons cumin
2 tablespoons olive oil
1 green pepper, cut in strips
1 large onion, sliced
3 fresh tomatoes, peeled and chopped
8 tortillas

In a large bowl, place steak strips and coat with garlic, chili powder and cumin. Let marinate 15 minutes.

In a large skillet, over medium heat, sauté green pepper and onion in olive oil until crisp-tender. Remove from pan. Sauté beef until cooked. Add tomatoes and cooked vegetables. Simmer for 5 minutes.

Heat tortillas. Fill tortillas with meat mixture. Serve with sour cream, guacamole and spicy salsa. Serve at once.

6 servings

16 filet mignons, 6 or 8-ounces each
3 cloves garlic, divided and crushed
1 tablespoon seasoned salt
1 teaspoon freshly ground pepper
9 tablespoons butter, divided
4 tablespoons brandy
6 tablespoons flour
4 teaspoons tomato paste
1½ cups dry red wine
2 cups chicken broth
1 cup beef broth
½ teaspoon Worcestershire sauce
4 tablespoons currant jelly
1 pound mushrooms, sliced

One day ahead: Mix 2 cloves garlic, seasoned salt and pepper and rub both sides of steaks. In a large heavy skillet melt 3 tablespoons butter and sauté steaks over high heat until brown on each side. Do not crowd in skillet; add more butter if needed. Put steaks in two 9x13-inch baking dishes leaving ½-inch between steaks.

Add brandy to frying pan and stir well to scrape browned bits left in pan. Add 6 tablespoons butter. When foamy stir in flour and reduce heat. Whisk constantly until golden brown. Add 1 crushed clove garlic and tomato paste; stir in wine, chicken and beef broth. Bring to a boil over moderate heat, stirring constantly for 10 minutes. Add Worcestershire sauce, jelly, and mushrooms stirring to coat with sauce. If sauce is too thick add more wine; if too thin, cook longer to thicken. Taste to adjust seasonings. Pour cooled sauce over steaks, until the sauce is half way to top of dishes. Cover dishes with plastic wrap and refrigerate overnight. Reserve remaining sauce.

Next day: Two hours before serving, remove from refrigerator so steaks will return to room temperature.

Preheat oven to 400°. Put uncovered baking dishes in oven and bake:

   16 to 20 minutes for medium rare;
   20 to 25 minutes for medium well.

Serve meat, spooning mushrooms and sauce over steak. Heat remaining sauce and pass.

Hint: Recipe may be cut in half to serve 8.

16 servings

BEEF FILET WITH PEPPERCORNS AND CHUTNEY

Cracked black peppercorns
 (amount as desired)
4 6-ounce beef filet mignon,
 room temperature
5 tablespoons butter, divided
8 ounces chutney
2 ounces cognac

Press cracked peppercorns into filets with the heel of your hand. Heat 3 tablespoons butter in heavy skillet over high heat. Add filets just before butter begins to brown. Brown over high heat, approximately 3 minutes per side for rare.

Remove filets from skillet, reduce heat to low. Add remaining 2 tablespoons butter and chutney. Put cognac in a small saucepan and warm over low heat. Light cognac and carefully pour into chutney. After flames burn out, return filets to skillet and spoon sauce over them. Keep warm until serving.

4 servings

LOBSTER-STUFFED TENDERLOIN OF BEEF

3 to 4 pounds whole beef tenderloin
2 4-ounce lobster tails
1 tablespoon butter or margarine,
 melted
1½ teaspoons lemon juice
6 slices bacon, partially cooked

Béarnaise Sauce:
1 cup melted butter
4 egg yolks, room temperature
Juice of 1 medium lemon
1½ teaspoons Worcestershire sauce
Ground red pepper to taste
3 tablespoons dry white wine,
 divided
1 tablespoon finely minced shallots
2 teaspoons finely crumbled dried
 tarragon or 2 tablespoons
 chopped fresh tarragon
Salt to taste

Garnish:
Fluted mushrooms
Watercress

Preheat oven to 425°.

Cut beef tenderloin lengthwise to within ½-inch of bottom to butterfly. Place frozen lobster tails in boiling salted water to cover. Return to boiling. Reduce heat and simmer for 5 to 6 minutes. Carefully remove lobster from shells. Cut in halves lengthwise. Place lobster, end to end, inside beef. Combine the butter and lemon juice. Drizzle on lobster. Close meat around lobster. Tie roast together securely with kitchen string at 1-inch intervals. Place on rack in shallow roasting pan.

Bake for 45 to 50 minutes for rare. Lay bacon slices on top. Roast 5 more minutes.

Béarnaise Sauce: Whisk egg yolks, lemon juice, Worcestershire sauce and red pepper in top of double boiler over simmering water until thick and a sheen forms, approximately 3 minutes, but not more than 5 minutes. Begin adding melted butter in a steady stream, whisking constantly until all has been added. Add 2 tablespoons of wine and whisk well. The sauce should be light and fluffy. In a small saucepan heat the remaining wine, shallots and tarragon until liquid evaporates. Remove from heat and add to sauce, mixing well. Add salt to taste. Hold at room temperature until serving time.

Slice roast and arrange on platter. Spoon on Béarnaise sauce and garnish with fluted whole mushrooms and watercress.

8 servings

Mushroom Filling:
½ pound mushrooms
2 teaspoons lemon juice
2 tablespoons butter or margarine
1 scallion, chopped
¼ cup dry sherry
2 tablespoons chopped parsley
Salt and freshly ground pepper

2 6-ounce beef tenderloins
¼ teaspoon dried thyme
Salt and freshly ground pepper
1 tablespoon butter or margarine
2 tablespoons brandy

2 sheets frozen puff pastry, thawed
⅛ pound paté, room temperature
    (country paté or forester paté)
1 egg
1 teaspoon water

Preheat oven to 425°.

Mushroom Filling: Finely chop mushrooms and sprinkle immediately with lemon juice to preserve color. In a large skillet, melt 2 tablespoons butter and add mushrooms, scallion, sherry and parsley. Cook, stirring with a wooden spoon, until the onion is tender and sherry is absorbed. Season with salt and pepper to taste. Set aside to cool.

Tenderloin: Rub tenderloins with thyme, pepper and salt. Melt butter in a small skillet. Sear tenderloins on all sides, about 5 minutes. Pour one tablespoon of brandy over each. Remove from heat and allow to cool to room temperature.

Assembly: Place one sheet of puff pastry on a flat surface. Cut in half and roll to ⅛-inch thickness. Spread ½ of paté in middle of each pastry sheet. Top with ½ of the mushroom mixture. Place a tenderloin on top of the mushroom mixture. Enclose each tenderloin in the pastry. Brush edges with a little water and press to seal. Trim off excess pastry. Turn each tenderloin over and place on a cookie sheet.

 Cut out decorative shapes (flowers, diamonds, etc.) from pastry trimmings. Brush with a little water and decorate tops of tenderloins. Beat egg with water and brush over pastry to ensure a high gloss.

Bake for 15 minutes for medium rare; 20 to 25 minutes for medium. Serve immediately.

2 servings

CROCK POT BARBECUE BEEF

4½ pounds chuck or round bone
    beef pot roast
2 tablespoons oil
1 small onion, finely chopped
1 clove garlic, minced
2 tablespoons sugar
1 teaspoon dry mustard
1 teaspoon celery seed
1 teaspoon chili powder
½ teaspoon salt (optional)
¼ teaspoon pepper
¼ teaspoon Tabasco sauce
1 tablespoon fresh lemon juice
1 tablespoon Worcestershire sauce
¾ cup ketchup
¼ cup vinegar
1 cup water

Cook pot roast in a crock pot for 6 hours on high. Remove and shred beef.

In a large saucepan, heat oil until hot and sauté onion and garlic until translucent, not brown. Add sugar, dry mustard, celery seed, chili powder, salt, pepper, Tabasco, lemon juice, Worcestershire sauce, ketchup, vinegar, and water and cook slowly for 15 minutes. Season with salt, if necessary.

Return shredded beef to crock pot and add cooked sauce. Keep warm until serving.

Spoon barbecue beef onto toasted Kaiser rolls or mini-Italian bread loaves.

8 to 10 servings

BEEF CHILI WITH LIMES

3 pounds boneless chuck, or top
    sirloin, cut into 1-inch cubes
2 tablespoons vegetable oil
2 to 3 cloves garlic, chopped
4 to 6 tablespoons chili powder
2 teaspoons ground cumin
3 tablespoons flour
1 tablespoon leaf oregano
2 13¼-ounce cans beef broth
1 teaspoon salt
Freshly ground pepper
1 15-ounce can pinto beans, optional

Garnish:
1 cup dairy sour cream
Limes, cut into wedges

Heat oil in 4-quart kettle or heavy-bottom pan over medium heat. Add beef, stirring frequently with a wooden spoon until meat changes color, but does not brown. Lower heat, stir in garlic. Combine chili powder, cumin seed and flour. Sprinkle meat with mixture, stirring until meat is evenly coated. Crumble oregano over meat. Add 1½ cans of broth and stir until liquid is well blended. Add salt and pepper. Bring to a boil, stirring occasionally. Add remaining broth; cook 30 minutes longer or until meat is almost falling apart.

Cool thoroughly. Cover. Refrigerate overnight to ripen flavor.

Reheat chili in top of double boiler, placed over boiling water. Optional: heat beans; drain; stir into chili.

Garnish chili with sour cream and wedges of lime to squeeze over portions.

8 servings

RUSSIAN STUFFED CABBAGE

Sauce:
1 medium onion, chopped fine
2 tablespoons olive oil
1 clove garlic, minced
6 cups tomato sauce
1 6-ounce can tomato paste
1 teaspoon Worcestershire sauce
½ teaspoon Tabasco, or to taste
2 tablespoons packed brown sugar
1 8-ounce can sauerkraut, drained,
    rinsed and chopped
½ cup grated fresh cabbage
Salt and freshly ground pepper

Filling:
1 medium onion, chopped fine
2 tablespoons olive oil
1 clove garlic, minced
1 pound ground lean beef
1 egg
Salt and freshly ground pepper
Fresh parsley, chopped

1 large head cabbage
¾ cup chicken stock
Sour cream
Chopped fresh parsley

Sauce: Cook onion in olive oil until soft. Add garlic and cook until tender. Add tomato sauce, tomato paste, Worcestershire, Tabasco, brown sugar, sauerkraut, cabbage, salt and pepper to taste. Bring just to a boil. Reduce heat and simmer, uncovered, for about 45 minutes.

Filling: Cook onion in olive oil until soft. Add garlic and cook until soft. Drain well. Place ground beef, egg, parsley, salt and pepper to taste in food processor and process until well mixed. Add onion and garlic and process until blended; set aside.

Cabbage: Set a large pan of water over high heat and bring to a boil. Meanwhile, remove core from cabbage. Gently remove whole leaves and drop several at a time into boiling water. Cook for 1 minute, remove and drain well. Pat dry.

Place about 1 heaping tablespoon of filling mixture at the base of each cabbage leaf and roll up envelope fashion. Put rolls in a single layer in a large skillet. Add chicken stock and spoon a little tomato sauce over each roll. Sauce does not have to be completely cooked at this time. Cover and simmer about 45 minutes. When cooked, add pan juices to tomato sauce and stir well.

Place rolls on plates, cover with sauce and top with a dollop of sour cream. Sprinkle with chopped parsley.

4 to 6 servings

STUFFED FLANK STEAK WITH BLEU CHEESE

Stuffing:
4 tablespoons butter or margarine
½ cup chopped onion
¾ cup chopped celery
½ cup chopped celery leaves
2 cups chopped mushrooms
Salt and freshly ground pepper
¼ teaspoon dried thyme
4 tablespoons chopped fresh parsley
2 cups fresh bread crumbs
4 ounces bleu cheese, crumbled
¼ cup milk

1½ pounds flank steak
2 tablespoons oil
2 tablespoons butter
1 cup beef stock or beef bouillon

Preheat oven to 350°. Butter a 9x13-inch baking dish.

Stuffing: Melt butter in a large skillet and cook onions and celery until tender. Add celery leaves, mushrooms, salt, pepper, thyme, parsley, bread crumbs, bleu cheese and milk. Toss well and remove from heat.

Carefully cut steak in half horizontally, so it will lay open like a book. Spread stuffing mixture over steak, to within 1 inch of edges. Starting with the short side, roll steak up jelly-roll fashion. Fasten with skewers or tie with kitchen string at 2-inch intervals.

Wipe skillet and heat remaining oil and butter. Place rolled steak in skillet and brown on all sides, over medium-high heat. Place in prepared baking dish and add stock. Cover loosely with a sheet of foil.

Bake for 1½ hours.

Slice in thin slices and, if desired, serve with gravy made from pan drippings.

4 to 6 servings

MIXED MARINATED GRILL

Marinade:
4 tablespoons wine vinegar
2 tablespoons lemon juice
4 teaspoons prepared mustard
6 tablespoons olive oil
2 cloves garlic, minced
½ teaspoon ground ginger
1½ teaspoons ground rosemary
½ teaspoon salt
1 small onion, sliced, optional

Allow 1 piece per person:
 Chicken and ribs, cut into pieces
 Lamb Chops, trimmed
 Sausage

Marinade: Whisk together vinegar, lemon juice, mustard, oil, garlic, ginger, rosemary, salt and onion.

Place meat and poultry pieces in glass dish, cover with marinade. Marinate in refrigerator, covered, for 4 to 5 hours.

Broil over coals or in oven/broiler for 15 to 20 minutes, basting with marinade during broiling. Broil sausage for 5 minutes just before other meats are done.

SAUERBRATEN

3 to 31/2 pounds round steak, cut
    2½-inches thick (or thicker)
Salt and freshly ground pepper
Garlic powder (rub into meat)

½ teaspoon peppercorns
4 bay leaves
8 whole cloves
2 medium onions, sliced
1 small carrot, minced
1 celery rib, chopped

Marinade:
1½ cups red wine vinegar
2½ cups water or 1¼ cups wine
    and 1¼ cups water

¼ cup butter or oil

Sauce:
4 tablespoons sugar
4 tablespoons flour
6 gingersnaps, crushed

Rub garlic powder into meat and season with salt and pepper.

Place meat in deep earthenware crock or glass bowl with peppercorns, bay leaves, cloves, onions, carrot, and celery. Heat vinegar and water to boiling point and pour immediately over meat. Cover tightly and refrigerate for 48 hours. Turn meat twice a day.

When ready to cook, remove meat from marinade and pat dry with paper towels. Heat butter or oil in large pan; add meat and brown well. Drain. Stir marinade and pour over meat. Bring to a boil, reduce heat, cover and simmer for 2½ to 3 hours or until tender.

Remove meat from pan and keep warm. Discard peppercorns, bay leaves and cloves. Strain marinade and puree vegetables in food processor or blender. Add marinade to puree to equal 6 cups of sauce.

In heavy pan, heat sugar until it caramelizes; carefully stir in ½ cup of sauce. Mix flour and 1 cup sauce until smooth; whisk into sugar mixture. Cook until smooth and bubbly. Mix gingersnaps with remaining sauce and add to pan. Mix well. Return meat to sauce and reheat over low heat.

Slice meat and serve with noodles or spaetzle. Pass sauce.

6 servings

LAMB AND BEAN STEW

1 cup dried kidney beans
3 cups water
3 pounds lamb shoulder on the bone
    or 6 lamb foreshanks
3 to 4 tablespoons oil
½ cup butter
1 large onion, finely chopped
1 teaspoon turmeric
½ cup tomato puree
1 tablespoon fresh lemon juice
Salt and freshly ground pepper

Soak kidney beans in water overnight.

Cut lamb into bite-size pieces. Heat oil in large pan and brown lamb, a few pieces at a time. Remove and keep warm. Heat butter in pan and cook onions until transparent. Add turmeric and cook 2 minutes. Stir in lamb, beans and water, tomato puree, lemon juice, salt and pepper. Cover pan and simmer for 1 hour, add more water, if needed. Check for doneness and adjust seasonings.

Serve with rice, pickles, and flat bread.

I T A L I A N   B E E F   R O L L - U P

2 pounds ground lean beef

2 eggs

1 cup soft, fresh bread crumbs

⅓ cup milk

½ cup chopped onions

¼ teaspoon oregano

1 clove garlic, minced

4 ounces thin-sliced Italian dry
    salami

1 cup shredded mozzarella cheese

Sauce:

1 16-ounce can chunky tomato sauce
    with tomato bits

½ cup sliced fresh mushrooms

1 clove garlic, minced

¼ cup chopped green pepper

¼ cup chopped red pepper

Tabasco, to taste

Fresh oregano, to taste

Freshly grated Parmesan cheese

Preheat oven to 350°.

Mix ground beef, eggs, bread crumbs, milk, onions, oregano and garlic in a large bowl.

Place meat mixture on wax paper and pat flat into a 9x12-inch rectangle. Spread salami slices and cheese on top. Roll up jelly roll fashion, using the wax paper to help form roll. Place 9x5-inch loaf pan on top of meat roll and turn over. Place grated cheese on top of meat loaf.

Bake for 55 to 60 minutes.

Sauce: Combine sauce ingredients in saucepan and simmer over low heat for 5 minutes.

Remove meat from oven and let set for 5 to 10 minutes. Slice with an electric knife for a clean cut and lift carefully from pan with a spatula and place on plate.

To serve: Top with tomato sauce and garnish with Parmesan cheese.

Tastes like pizza! Looks great!

6 servings

P O T A T O E D   P O R K   L O I N

2 tablespoons oil

1 medium Idaho potato, julienned

Salt and freshly ground pepper

2 tablespoons butter

5 2-ounce pork loin slices

2 tablespoons Marsala wine

Potatoes: Heat oil in sauté pan, over high heat. Let pan become very hot. Toss potato sticks into pan. Season with salt and pepper. Allow potatoes to cook until they form one large crust. Flip over to cook other side. They are finished on each side when they break free from the pan when shaken. Remove from pan and keep warm.

Melt butter in same pan. Season pork with salt and pepper; place in pan. Sauté until done, about 2 minutes. Remove pork from pan and place over potato crust. Deglaze pan with Marsala. Pour over pork to serve.

1 serving

LEG OF LAMB
WITH ARTICHOKE STUFFING

Stuffing:
½ cup chopped onion
1 or 2 cloves garlic, chopped
2 tablespoons butter or olive oil
1 15-ounce can artichoke hearts,
*   drained and chopped*
1 cup fresh bread crumbs
¼ cup chopped fresh parsley
2 or 3 sprigs dill, chopped
Salt and freshly ground pepper

3 to 3½ pound leg of lamb, boned
Dry white wine

Stuffing: Sauté onions and garlic in butter for 5 minutes. Add chopped artichoke hearts. Cook 2 to 3 minutes. Remove from heat. Stir in the bread crumbs, parsley, dill, salt and pepper to taste. Add a little melted butter if stuffing seems too dry. Chill.

Preheat oven to 325°.

Open leg of lamb and place stuffing in middle. Roll and tie lamb.

Bake for 30 minutes per pound. Baste with a little white wine during the last 30 minutes.

Hint: Take the cold stuffing to the butcher and have him stuff and tie the leg of lamb.

Hint: Leg of lamb can also be done easily on a covered grill. Use a meat thermometer to determine cooking time.

4 to 6 servings

PORK TENDERLOIN IN DIJON SAUCE

4 tablespoons butter, divided
1 tablespoon vegetable oil
1½ pounds pork tenderloin, cut in
*   1-inch slices*
1 onion, chopped
1 cup dry white wine
⅓ cup cider vinegar
10 peppercorns, crushed
Salt
1½ cups whipping cream
2 tablespoons Dijon mustard

Sauté tenderloin slices in 2 tablespoons butter and oil in large heavy skillet over medium heat. Brown pork for 1 minute on each side. Add onion and sauté until translucent. Add wine, bring to a boil, reduce heat to lowest setting, partially cover and let gently simmer for about 30 minutes or until meat is cooked through. Transfer meat to platter and keep warm.

Add vinegar to pan along with peppercorns. Let cook until sauce is reduced to no more than ⅔ cup. Add salt to taste and cream; simmer for about 5 minutes. Stir in Dijon mustard, simmer for several minutes longer and swirl in butter.

Spoon sauce over medallions and serve with rice.

MARINATED GRILLED LEG OF LAMB

Marinade:
½ cup vegetable oil
½ cup fresh lemon juice
1 clove garlic, crushed
1 teaspoon salt
1 teaspoon rosemary
¼ cup grated onion
1 tablespoon Worcestershire sauce
¼ cup sweet vermouth, to taste
½ teaspoon pepper

Leg of lamb, boned and butterflied

Marinade: Whisk together oil, lemon juice, garlic, salt, rosemary, onion, Worcestershire sauce, sweet vermouth and pepper.

Place lamb in a 16x12-inch roaster. Pierce with a large fork. Pour marinade over lamb and marinate in refrigerator for 6 hours. Turn, pierce and baste every hour. Marinate for an additional 2 hours at room temperature.

One hour before serving, prepare fire in grill.

Cook 40 minutes with cover on, turning every 10 minutes. Remove from grill. Let rest for 10 minutes.

Slice into ¾-inch pieces and arrange on a large serving platter. Pass juices separately. Rice is an excellent accompaniment.

8 servings

PORK TENDERLOIN MEDALLIONS WITH LEMON GLAZE

2 pounds whole pork tenderloins
Flour
2 large eggs
6 tablespoons flour
2 tablespoons freshly grated
*   Parmesan cheese*
½ cup milk or cream
Salt and freshly ground pepper
Freshly grated nutmeg to taste
1 cup butter, divided
6 tablespoons fresh lemon juice

Garnish:
6 tablespoons chopped fresh parsley

Slice tenderloin into ¼ to ½-inch slices. Pound slices between plastic wrap into thin medallions. Dredge in flour, shake off excess and set aside.

Place in blender eggs, flour, Parmesan cheese, milk, salt, pepper, nutmeg and blend until smooth.

Melt 4 tablespoons butter in a large heavy skillet. When butter is very hot, dip pork medallions in batter and sauté a few at a time until golden brown on both sides. Remove to a serving plate and keep warm. Continue until all medallions are cooked, adding more butter to skillet as needed. Deglaze pan with lemon juice and reduce to a thick glaze. Pour over pork and serve immediately.

Sprinkle with chopped parsley.

4 to 6 servings

VEAL SCALLOPINE WITH MUSHROOM AND SUN-DRIED TOMATO CREAM SAUCE

6 veal cutlets

Sauce:
6 to 8 sun-dried tomatoes
2½ tablespoons unsalted butter
¼ pound field or porcini mushrooms,
    sliced
¼ cup dry white wine
½ to 1 cup whipping cream
Salt and white pepper

5 tablespoons flour
1 tablespoon freshly ground pepper
2½ tablespoons unsalted butter

Pound veal until thickness is reduced by ½ and cut into 1x2-inch pieces.

Sauce: Place sun-dried tomatoes in a small saucepan and just cover with water. Bring to a boil and simmer for 18 minutes. Drain tomatoes, reserving liquid, and julienne.
   Add 2½ tablespoons butter and mushrooms to a large skillet and sauté until just beginning to brown. Add white wine to skillet and boil to reduce to a glaze. Add cream, sun-dried tomatoes and liquid; reduce by ⅓. Season to taste with salt and white pepper. Set aside and keep warm.

Combine flour and black pepper. Flour veal. Melt remaining butter in separate large skillet over medium high heat and sauté veal 30 seconds on each side.
   Arrange veal on platter and spoon sauce over top.

6 servings

STUFFED BREAST OF VEAL WITH WILD RICE

One whole veal breast, have butcher
    cut pocket in breast
¾ pound mushrooms, finely minced,
    extract moisture by squeezing
4 tablespoons butter, melted
4 ounces wild rice, cooked
6 ounces white rice, cooked
Shallots, minced
Salt and freshly ground pepper
Dry white wine
Cashew nuts, optional
Veal or chicken stock

Preheat oven to 350° to 375°.
   In a skillet, combine mushrooms with butter and cook until golden. Mix wild rice and white rice by hand, adding chopped shallots, salt and pepper to taste. Combine with mushroom mixture for dressing.
   Braise veal breast briefly in less than ⅛ inch of dry white wine in deep roasting pan. Just before stuffing, add optional cashew nuts to dressing. Stuff as much dressing as possible into pocket of veal breast. If there is additional dressing, bake in a separate casserole, keeping moist with stock.
   Roast loosely covered, adding stock as needed with small amounts of white wine. Roast for 25 to 30 minutes per pound, or until meat thermometer reaches 170°. Uncover and roast 10 to 15 minutes to brown.

4 to 6 servings

VEAL RAGOUT

4 tablespoons margarine
3 to 4 pounds veal steaks, cut in
    small pieces
1½ cups chopped onions
1 cup sliced mushrooms
3 teaspoons flour
2 cups water
1 6-ounce can tomato paste
⅛ teaspoon marjoram
⅛ teaspoon allspice
1½ teaspoons salt
2 tablespoons sugar
1½ cups green beans, cut or
    1 package frozen cut green
    beans, thawed

In a large saucepan, melt margarine. Add veal, onions and mushrooms and cook over low heat for 5 to 7 minutes until brown. Sprinkle with flour. Combine water and tomato paste; add to meat mixture. Stir in marjoram, allspice, salt and sugar. Cook over low heat about 1 hour until veal is tender. Add green beans and mix well. Cook until soft.

Serve over rice.

4 to 6 servings

DUCK L'ORANGE

2 cups vegetable oil
4 tablespoons butter, divided
2 4 to 5 pound ducks, trimmed
Onion and garlic salt to taste
Salt and freshly ground pepper
½ cup fresh orange juice

Sauce:
1 cup fresh orange juice
1 cup honey
1½ teaspoons soy sauce
½ teaspoon cinnamon
Pinch ground cloves

Garnish:
Orange slices
Chopped parsley

Preheat oven to 375°. Pour oil into large roasting pan to depth of ½ inch; set aside.

Rub 2 tablespoons butter into cavity of each duck. Season cavities with onion and garlic salt, salt and pepper. Add ½ cup orange juice to roasting pan. Set ducks in pan breast side up. Cover and roast 1 hour. Uncover, turn ducks over, roast 30 minutes. Turn breast side up and roast another 30 minutes. Transfer ducks to serving plate and let cool to room temperature. Can be prepared ahead to this point and refrigerated.

Preheat oven to 450°.

Slice through breastbone of each duck, peel meat back from rib cage and remove ribs, retaining leg and wing bones. Split ducks in half.

Sauce: Combine 1 cup orange juice, honey, soy sauce, cinnamon, and cloves in large saucepan over medium heat. Dip duck halves in sauce, turning to coat well. Remove ducks from sauce and arrange in 9x13-inch glass baking pan, skin side up.

Bake for 10 minutes to brown.

Arrange on platter with orange slices and parsley.

4 to 6 servings

DIVINE PHEASANT BREASTS

6 thin slices Canadian bacon
3 whole pheasant breasts, split,
    boned, and skinned

Sauce:
4 tablespoons butter
4 tablespoons flour
1/4 teaspoon freshly ground
    white pepper
1/2 teaspoon salt
1 cup milk
1 cup half and half cream
6 slices Swiss cheese
Oregano

Preheat oven to 350°.

Place Canadian bacon in single layer in 9x13-inch glass baking dish. Place pheasant breast on top of bacon, tucking under uneven edges.

Sauce: Melt butter in saucepan. Add flour, pepper and salt. Stir 1 to 2 minutes. Remove from heat. Gradually add milk and half and half. Return to heat and cook until thickened, stirring constantly. Pour over pheasant.

Place one slice Swiss cheese on each breast and sprinkle with oregano to taste (about 1/4 teaspoon per breast). Can prepare 1 day ahead.

Bake uncovered for 50 minutes.

Variation: Excellent with chicken breasts.

4 to 6 servings

MIDWESTERN STUFFED DUCK

Stuffing:
6 tablespoons tart applesauce
1 medium onion, chopped
2 strips bacon, cooked crisp
1 tablespoons grated orange zest
1 teaspoon salt
1 tablespoon celery salt
2 celery ribs, diced
2 tablespoons butter, melted
3 cups cubed day-old bread
6 tablespoons diced carrots,
    parboiled
4 tablespoons slivered almonds
1/4 cup melted butter

4 wild midwest ducks
4 strips bacon
1/2 cup dry sherry
1/2 cup chicken bouillon
1/2 cup orange juice
1/2 cup melted butter

Preheat oven to 250°.

In food processor work bowl, blend applesauce, onion, bacon, orange zest, salt and celery salt.

In a large saucepan, melt butter and sauté celery until soft, or about 10 minutes. Combine bread, carrots, almonds, 1/2 cup melted butter and applesauce mixture. Stuff birds.

Place stuffed ducks, breasts up in a roaster with a strip of bacon on each breast. In a small bowl, whisk sherry, bouillon, orange juice and 1/2 cup butter, pour over ducks. Cover.

Roast for 4 hours, or until meat is tender.

Serve with wild rice and fruit salad with white French dressing.

4 servings

VENISON STEAKS

Dijon-Honey Sauce:
1 tablespoon margarine or butter
2 tablespoons all-purpose flour
¾ cup canned unsalted chicken broth
¼ cup white wine
1 tablespoon Dijon mustard
1 tablespoon honey
¼ teaspoon fresh lemon juice
¼ teaspoon grated fresh lemon zest
1 tablespoon minced fresh parsley

Peppercorn-Shiitake Sauce:
¼ pound fresh shiitake mushrooms,
*   wiped*
1 tablespoon margarine or butter
4 cloves garlic, minced
1½ teaspoons whole green
*   peppercorns, crushed*
5 tablespoons dry white wine,
*   divided*
¼ teaspoon beef flavored bouillon
*   granules*

4 4-ounce lean, boneless venison
*   loin steaks*

Dijon-Honey Sauce: In a medium saucepan, melt margarine over medium heat; add flour. Cook 1 minute, stirring with a whisk. Gradually add broth and wine, stirring constantly. Add mustard, honey, lemon juice and lemon zest and cook 10 minutes or until thickened and bubbly, stirring constantly. Stir in parsley. Serve warm.

Peppercorn-Shiitake Sauce: Trim mushrooms and discard stems; set caps aside. In a small skillet, melt margarine, combine garlic and peppercorns; sauté 1 minute. Add mushroom caps; sauté 1 minute. Add 2 tablespoons wine; cook 1 minute, stirring constantly. Add remaining 3 tablespoons wine and bouillon granules; cook until thoroughly heated, stirring constantly. Serve sauce over steaks.

Venison: Trim fat from steaks. Place each steak between two sheets of heavy-duty plastic wrap; flatten to ⅛-inch thickness, using a meat mallet or rolling pin.
Coat skillet with non-stick cooking spray; place over medium-high heat until hot. Add steaks; cook 30 seconds on each side. Do not overcook! Serve with Dijon-Honey Sauce or Peppercorn-Shiitake Sauce.

4 servings

FRUIT GLAZED CHICKEN WITH GAZPACHO RELISH AND TORTILLA CRISPS

Gazpacho Relish:
1 avocado, peeled, seeded and cut
    into ½-inch pieces
1 tomato, cut in thin wedges
1 tomato, peeled, seeded and cut in
    thin wedges
1 cucumber, chopped
1 small onion, diced
1 clove garlic, crushed
1 tablespoon chopped fresh parsley
2 tablespoons fresh lime juice
½ teaspoon salt
Freshly ground pepper

Tortilla Crisps:
1 teaspoon salt
½ teaspoon chili powder
¼ teaspoon or less ground red
    pepper
4 large corn or flour tortillas, cut in
    ½-inch strips
2 tablespoons oil

Fruit Glazed Chicken:
4 boneless chicken breasts, skinned,
    boned and halved
1 tablespoon butter
1 tablespoon oil
2 tablespoons orange marmalade
1 tablespoon lime juice

Garnish:
Green leafy lettuce
Lime Wedges

Gazpacho Relish: Combine avocado, tomatoes, cucumber, onion, garlic, parsley, lime juice, salt and pepper. Chill until ready to serve.

Tortilla Crisps: Combine salt, chili powder and red pepper in small bowl. Place tortilla strips in separate bowl and toss with half of the chili seasoning mixture. Heat oil in 10-inch skillet over medium high heat and fry the tortilla strips until they are crisp and golden. Remove and drain on paper towels; set aside. Wipe skillet with a paper towel.

Fruit Glazed Chicken: Lightly score chicken breasts with sharp knife in a crosshatch pattern. Rub chicken on both sides with the remaining chili seasoning mixture. Melt butter and oil in 10-inch skillet over medium high heat and cook chicken about three minutes on each side until browned and cooked through.

Remove chicken to a serving plate. Add orange marmalade and lime juice to the drippings in the skillet. Heat and stir, loosening browned bits on bottom of pan. Return chicken to the pan and cook 2 to 3 minutes more until heated through and glazed on both sides.

Arrange chicken on lettuce-lined platter accompanied by the gazpacho relish and tortilla crisps. Garnish with lime wedges.

4 servings

CHICKEN À LA SUISSE

1½ tablespoons butter
1½ tablespoons flour
½ cup milk
½ cup half and half
¼ teaspoon nutmeg
Salt and freshly ground pepper
¾ cup shredded Swiss cheese,
    divided
1 cup freshly grated Parmesan
    cheese, divided

4 chicken breasts, boned and skinned
¼ cup freshly chopped parsley

Preheat oven to 350°. Lightly butter 9x13-inch glass baking dish.

Melt butter in saucepan. Whisk in flour until smooth, add milk and half and half. Whisk continually, until thickened. Add nutmeg, salt and pepper to taste and ½ cup Swiss cheese. Stir until cheese melts. Sprinkle baking dish with ½ cup Parmesan cheese. Place chicken on top of cheese. Pour sauce over chicken. Sprinkle with remaining Parmesan and Swiss cheese.

Bake for 30 to 35 minutes. Sprinkle with parsley to serve.

4 servings

ROAST CHICKEN WITH BLACK PEPPER GLAZE

2 3½-pound chickens
8 to 10 large cloves garlic
2 teaspoons extra virgin olive oil
2 teaspoons fresh lemon juice
Extra virgin olive oil
2 lemons, halved
Salt to taste
Freshly ground black pepper

Fit a meat rack in a large baking dish or jelly roll pan.

In a mini-food processor or blender, make a paste of garlic, olive oil and lemon juice. Gently loosen skin on chicken legs, thighs and breast. Slip garlic paste under skin and spread with fingers to cover flesh evenly. Using kitchen string, tie wings firmly against sides and legs together. Place chickens on rack and rub generously with additional olive oil. Squeeze lemon juice over chickens and put lemons in cavities. Sprinkle with salt. Grind enough black pepper over chickens to make skin black. Let chickens marinate at room temperature for 30 to 45 minutes. During this time pepper will lose most of its heat and the flavor will remain.

Preheat oven to 375°. Pour ½-inch water in bottom of baking dish to prevent drippings from smoking.

Place chickens on sides on rack and bake 30 minutes. Turn chickens to other side and bake 30 minutes. Place chickens on backs and bake 20 to 30 minutes longer or until nicely browned. Carve and serve hot or at room temperature on a bed of curly endive.

8 servings

CHICKEN MOLE

3 fryer chickens, cut up
Salt and freshly ground pepper
Flour
¾ cup butter, melted
¾ cup olive oil
3 cups chopped onions
6 cloves garlic, crushed
¾ cup tomato paste
⅓ cup chili powder
3 tablespoons fresh lemon juice
2 tablespoons chopped leaf oregano
1 tablespoon cinnamon
1 tablespoon salt
1½ teaspoons ground cloves
1½ teaspoons coriander
1½ teaspoons cumin
¼ teaspoon ground red pepper
3 cups chicken broth
2¼ cups dry white wine
9 tomatoes, peeled, seeded
    and chopped
3 1-ounce squares semi-sweet
    chocolate, grated
6 tablespoons chopped fresh parsley

Preheat oven to 400°.

Season chickens with salt and pepper. Dredge in flour; shake off excess. Brown chicken in 3 large skillets (or 1 large skillet in 3 batches) in combination of butter and olive oil. Remove chicken from skillet to large roasting pan. Add onions and garlic to drippings; cook until tender. Stir in tomato paste, chili powder, lemon juice, oregano, cinnamon, salt, cloves, coriander, cumin and red pepper. Blend in chicken broth, wine and tomatoes; heat to a boil. Pour over chicken in roasting pan and cover.

Bake for 30 minutes or until chicken is tender. Arrange chicken on serving platter. Stir chocolate into sauce until melted; pour sauce over chicken. Sprinkle with parsley.

12 servings

LEMON CHICKEN

3 whole chicken breasts, halved,
    boned and skinned
½ cup seasoned bread crumbs
½ teaspoon paprika
½ cup grated Parmesan cheese
Salt and freshly ground pepper
2 eggs, beaten with 2 tablespoons
    water
4 tablespoons butter
1 small clove garlic, crushed
½ cup fresh lemon juice

Preheat oven to 375°.

Mix crumbs, paprika, cheese, salt and pepper in a large bowl. Dip chicken breasts in egg wash, then in crumb mixture. Recipe can be made ahead to this point.

Melt butter in a large skillet and brown chicken breasts on both sides. Arrange in 9x13-inch baking dish. Add garlic and lemon juice to skillet and cook 2 minutes, scraping bottom of pan. Pour over chicken.

Bake for 25 to 30 minutes.

6 servings

146

C H I C K E N   W I T H   R E D   P E P P E R   S A L S A

3 to 4 tablespoons olive oil
1 teaspoon salt
2 cloves garlic, crushed
1 large ripe tomato, chopped
2 medium onions, chopped
1/2 teaspoon cumin
1/2 teaspoon crushed red pepper
2 bay leaves
3 tablespoons chopped fresh parsley
4 chicken breasts, skinned and boned
2 cups cooked white rice

In a 3-quart saucepan, sauté garlic in oil and salt. Add onions, tomato, cumin, crushed red pepper, bay leaves and parsley; stir to mix. This becomes a rich and thick sauce. Thin by adding a 1/2 cup of water if necessary.

Cut chicken open to less than 1/2-inch thick and divide each piece in two. Add chicken and mix well. Cover and cook at medium heat for 20 to 25 minutes. Remove bay leaves.

Serve over white rice.

2 to 3 servings

F R U I T - G L A Z E D   R O A S T   C H I C K E N

3 1/2 pound whole frying chicken
Salt and freshly ground pepper
1/4 cup water
1/4 cup dry white wine, divided

3/4 cup apricot, pineapple or peach
   preserves or jam

Preheat oven to 350°. Butter 9x9-inch glass baking dish and line the bottom with parchment paper. (Do not substitute foil or wax paper for parchment paper.)

Rinse and dry chicken. Season inside with salt and pepper. Fold wings under back and tie legs together. Place breast side down in prepared baking dish. Mix 1/4 cup wine and water together and pour over chicken.

Bake for 45 minutes, basting occasionally with juices. Turn chicken breast-side up and continue to bake and baste for another 45 minutes.

Mix the preserves and remaining 1/2 cup wine in a small saucepan and bring to simmering. Brush generously over the chicken every 5 minutes during the last 15 minutes of baking.

Carve and serve hot.

4 to 6 servings

GINGERED CHICKEN BREASTS

8 chicken breasts, boned with
    skin intact
Flour
Salt and freshly ground pepper
¼ cup butter
2 tablespoons oil
1 teaspoon ground ginger
1 teaspoon curry powder
¼ cup chopped crystallized ginger
½ cup chicken broth
¼ cup white wine
½ cup orange juice
2 tablespoons brown sugar

Preheat oven to 350°.

Dredge chicken breasts with flour, salt and pepper. Melt butter in large sauté pan; add oil, ground ginger and curry powder. Let mixture boil for 20 seconds, add chicken breasts and sauté for 5 minutes on each side. Place in baking dish. Sprinkle chicken with crystallized ginger. To the butter mixture left in the pan, add chicken broth, wine, orange juice and brown sugar. Simmer for 5 to 10 minutes. Pour over chicken and bake 8 minutes. Just before serving, put chicken under broiler for 2 minutes, or more if necessary, to crisp and glaze skin.

4 to 6 servings

ROCK CORNISH HENS BOURGUIGNON

1 teaspoon salt
¼ teaspoon ground cloves
¼ teaspoon ground nutmeg
¼ teaspoon freshly ground pepper
¼ teaspoon ground thyme
4 Rock Cornish hens
    (about 1 pound each)
4 slices bacon, halved
1¼ cups red Burgundy or other
    dry red wine
½ teaspoon instant chicken bouillon
½ cup boiling water
2 tablespoons finely chopped onion
2 tablespoons chopped fresh parsley
3 to 4 cups cooked brown or
    white rice
⅓ cup currant jelly

Preheat oven to 350°.

Mix salt, cloves, nutmeg, pepper and thyme; rub on skins and in cavities of hens. Place hens breast side up on rack in a shallow baking dish. Crisscross bacon slices over hens. Mix wine, bouillon, water, onion, and parsley; pour into baking dish.

Roast uncovered for 1 hour. Increase oven temperature to 400°. Roast until drumstick meat feels very soft when pressed, about 10 minutes.

Transfer hens to warm serving platter. Remove bacon, dice and stir into rice. Strain hot juices from baking dish into a saucepan and skim off fat. Stir in currant jelly and heat, stirring constantly, until jelly is melted.

Arrange rice around hens on platter; spoon some sauce over hens. Garnish with sprigs of watercress. Pass remaining sauce.

MARGHI WITH INDIAN CURRY SAUCE

Marinade:
2 cups buttermilk
1 tablespoon salt-free seasoning
1 clove garlic, minced
1 teaspoon fennel, ground
1 tablespoon lemon juice

8 chicken breasts, boned and skinned

Seasoning:
1 cup flour
1/2 cup sesame seeds
1 cup chopped walnuts
1 to 2 tablespoons paprika

Curry Powder:
2 tablespoons coriander powder
2 tablespoons cumin
1 teaspoon ginger
1 teaspoon turmeric
1/2 teaspoon cardamom
1 teaspoon fennel seeds, ground
1/2 teaspoon ground cloves
1/2 teaspoon ground red pepper
1 teaspoon fenugreek, optional

Indian Cider Curry Sauce:
4 tablespoons corn oil
2 small onions, sliced
2 to 3 tablespoons prepared
    curry powder
2 tablespoons cornstarch with
    2 tablespoons water
1 1/2 cups unsalted chicken broth
1 cup cider
1 cup dry white wine
2 to 3 cups dried mixed fruit, divided

Garnish:
Chopped green onions

Marinade: In a small bowl, whisk buttermilk, salt-free seasoning, garlic, fennel and lemon juice; mix well.

Marinate chicken in buttermilk marinade. Place in refrigerator overnight or at least five hours.

Preheat oven to 350°. Coat 9x13-inch baking dish with non-stick spray.

Seasoning: Place flour, sesame seeds and walnuts on flat plate and dredge chicken, coating especially with nuts. Dust with paprika and arrange in baking dish.

Bake for 45 minutes to 1 hour.

Curry Powder: In a small bowl, mix coriander, cumin, ginger, turmeric, cardamom, fennel, cloves, ground red pepper and fenugreek.

Indian Cider Curry Sauce: In a large skillet, heat oil and add onion rings. Cook until soft. Stir in curry powder and sauté for several minutes to bring out flavor. Add cornstarch mixture. Blend in broth, cider and wine. Bring to a boil, stirring constantly. Add some of the dried fruit and simmer, gently, for 20 to 30 minutes. Before serving, add the remaining dried fruit and warm through. Garnish with green onions.

Hint: Substitute 1 3 1/2-pound chicken, cut up, skinned for chicken breasts.

CHICKEN, MUSHROOM AND SPINACH STRUDEL

Dough:
2 cups all-purpose flour
½ package active dry yeast
Dash of salt
6 ounces butter, cut in pats
2 egg yolks
½ cup sour cream

Filling:
¾ cup butter, divided
4 tablespoons flour
1 cup chicken broth
1 cup half and half
¼ cup grated Parmesan cheese
¼ cup grated Swiss cheese
1 pound mushrooms, sliced
Salt and freshly ground pepper
3 onions, chopped
4 chicken breasts, skinned, boned,
    cooked and cubed
1 10-ounce package chopped
    spinach, thawed and drained

Place flour in food processor and sprinkle with yeast. Add salt and butter. Process until crumbly. Add egg yolks and sour cream. Process until large crumbs form. Remove and press into a ball. Cut into 4 equal parts and wrap each ball of dough securely in plastic wrap. Refrigerate for at least an hour.

Preheat oven to 350°.

Filling: Make roux with ¼ cup butter and flour. Whisk in chicken broth and half and half. Cook until thickened. Add cheeses, cook until melted and blended into sauce. Set aside.

In a large skillet, sauté mushrooms in ¼ cup butter. Add mushrooms and juices to sauce. Season with salt and pepper.

Brown onions in ¼ cup butter; stir in cubed chicken and spinach. Add half of sauce to the chicken mixture. Chicken mixture will fill at least 2 strudels.

Roll one ball of dough out into a rectangle about ⅛-inch thick. Fill with ½ chicken filling. Place half of filling along the long edge of the dough, leaving ½-inch border at side and end. Turn edge of dough over the filling and roll up. Tuck ends under the strudel. Repeat, using one additional ball of dough and remaining filling. Use remaining dough for Apricot, Raisin and Walnut Strudel (see page 212).

Bake on ungreased cookie sheet for 30 minutes.

Thin remaining sauce with milk or chicken broth and serve warmed over strudel.

V E R M O U T H   C H I C K E N   S C A L L O P I N E

*2 pounds chicken breasts, skinned
    and boned*
Salt and freshly ground pepper
Flour
¼ cup olive oil, divided
2 cloves garlic, crushed
6 green onions, minced
½ cup vermouth
2 tablespoons fresh lemon juice

Garnish:
Parsley sprigs

Place chicken between two sheets of wax paper and flatten to ⅛-inch with a steak mallet. Season with salt and pepper. Dredge in flour. Heat skillet and add 2 tablespoons oil. When hot, sauté garlic and onion 1 minute. Remove and reserve. Heat another 2 or more tablespoons oil.

When hot, sauté chicken on both sides until browned, adding more oil if necessary. Remove chicken from skillet and keep warm. Return onion and garlic to skillet and add vermouth and lemon juice; bring to boil and reduce slightly. Season with salt and pepper.

Arrange chicken on platter and spoon sauce on top. Garnish with sprigs of fresh parsley and serve immediately.

4 to 6 servings

G R I L L E D   G I N G E R   T U R K E Y   B R E A S T

1 3-pound turkey breast
*1 piece peeled fresh ginger, about
    1x1x½-inch*
1 clove garlic
¼ cup fresh lemon juice
2 tablespoons oil
*½ to ¾ teaspoon freshly ground
    pepper*
½ teaspoon dried thyme
¼ teaspoon salt
1 bay leaf, broken into small pieces

Place turkey breast, skin side up, in a low, flat baking dish.

Use the metal blade of a food processor and, with the machine running, drop ginger and garlic through the food tube and process until finely chopped. Scrape down the bowl. Add remaining ingredients and process until mixed, about 5 seconds.

Pour over turkey, spreading to coat well. Let stand 2 hours at room temperature, turning occasionally.

One hour before cooking, preheat grill.

Place turkey breast, skin side down on grill.

Cook for 1½ hours, turning occasionally and basting with marinade, until the turkey is done or the internal temperature registers 170°. Let stand 10 minutes before slicing. The turkey may be placed on rack in roasting pan in preheated 325° oven for 1½ to 2 hours.

Rice and sautéed bananas make appropriate side dishes.

6 to 8 servings

STUFFED CHICKEN BREASTS SALTIMBOCCA

4 chicken breasts, split, boned
    and pounded thin
8 slices prosciutto
4 slices mozzarella cheese, halved
1 tomato, chopped and drained
1 teaspoon sage
½ cup bread crumbs
3 tablespoons grated Parmesan
    cheese
3 tablespoons chopped fresh parsley
4 tablespoons butter, melted

Preheat oven to 350°. Grease a 9x13-inch baking dish.

Place chicken breasts, skin side down. Top each breast with slice of prosciutto and ½ slice mozzarella cheese. Sprinkle each breast with equal amounts of chopped tomato and sage. Roll up each breast to enclose filling. Secure with wooden picks or tie with kitchen string. Combine bread crumbs, Parmesan cheese and parsley. Coat chicken in crumbs. Arrange seam side down in single layer in prepared baking dish. Drizzle with butter.

Bake for 40 to 45 minutes.

Garnish with parsley sprigs. Serve immediately.

6 servings

TURKEY VEGETABLE GRATIN

1 9-ounce package frozen artichoke
    hearts, cooked and drained
1 6-ounce jar marinated artichoke
    hearts, drained
2 cups chopped, cooked turkey breast
2 10-ounce packages frozen chopped
    spinach, thawed
1 10-ounce package frozen broccoli
    florets, thawed

Sauce:
2 8-ounce packages cream cheese
4 tablespoons mayonnaise
½ cup butter
¾ cup milk
Freshly ground pepper
⅓ cup freshly grated Romano cheese

Preheat oven to 375°.

Place artichoke hearts on bottom of a 3-quart baking dish or 9x13-inch glass baking dish. Squeeze moisture from spinach and drain broccoli; place on top of artichoke hearts. Arrange turkey over vegetables.

With electric mixer, blend cream cheese, mayonnaise and butter until fluffy. Gradually beat in milk and spread over vegetables. Sprinkle with pepper and cheese.

Bake uncovered for 40 minutes or until lightly browned.

Hint: This casserole can be made ahead and refrigerated. If chilled, slightly increase baking time.

Variation: Substitute 1 14-ounce can artichoke hearts for frozen artichoke hearts.

10 to 12 servings

CHICKEN CRAB SUPREME

4 chicken breasts, boned and skinned
2 tablespoons fresh lemon juice
1 teaspoon salt
¼ teaspoon freshly ground pepper
6 tablespoons butter, divided
7 ounces flaked crabmeat
1 tablespoon flour
¼ teaspoon dried tarragon
¼ teaspoon salt
1 cup whipping cream
1 egg yolk, slightly beaten

Preheat oven to 400°

Place chicken between two sheets of wax paper. Flatten slightly with a steak mallet. Sprinkle with lemon juice, salt and pepper. Melt 4 tablespoons melted butter in shallow baking dish. Place chicken in dish, turning once to coat with butter. Cover.

Bake for 20 minutes or until tender.

Put remaining butter in medium size pan. Add crabmeat and heat for 5 minutes. Blend in flour, tarragon and salt. Add cream, cook slowly, stirring constantly until slightly thickened. Blend in egg yolk. Pour over chicken.

Broil until slightly browned.

4 servings

TURKEY AND CHEESE ENCHILADAS

Filling:
2 cups chopped cooked turkey
2 cups shredded Monterey Jack
   cheese
6 green onions, chopped with part
   of the green tops

Sauce:
1 large onion, chopped
1 large clove garlic, minced
2 tablespoons olive oil
2 cups tomato sauce
1 cup beef broth
1 to 2 tablespoons chili powder
2 teaspoons cumin
Salt and freshly ground pepper
12 tortillas

Topping:
1½ cups grated cheddar cheese

Filling: Combine turkey, cheese and onions in a large bowl.

Sauce: In medium saucepan, sauté onion and garlic in olive oil until onion becomes transparent. Add tomato sauce, beef broth, chili powder, cumin, salt and pepper to taste. Simmer for 15 minutes over low heat.

Preheat oven to 350°.

Assembly: Warm tortillas in microwave for 1 minute. Place a thin layer of sauce in the bottom of 9x13-inch baking dish. Spread 1 tablespoon sauce, then 3 tablespoons filling on each tortilla. Roll each tortilla and place in baking dish with seam side down. Pour remaining sauce over tortillas and sprinkle with cheddar cheese.

Bake for 30 minutes or until cheese is melted and sauce is bubbly.

Hint: Look in Snips & Tips for Mexican menu additions, page 239.

4 servings

VIKING BURGERS

1 pound ground turkey
1½ tablespoons horseradish
1½ teaspoons Dijon mustard
1½ teaspoons paprika
⅛ teaspoon salt
¼ teaspoon freshly ground pepper
4 whole wheat hamburger buns

Combine turkey, drained horseradish, mustard, paprika, salt and pepper; shape into 4 patties, about ½-inch thick. Place on grill over hot coals, about 6 inches from heat, and cook 3 to 4 minutes per side or until no longer pink in center.

Serve on buns.

4 servings

STUFFED BAKED TROUT IN HORSERADISH CREAM

Horseradish Sauce:
2 tablespoons minced shallots
⅔ cup dry white wine
2½ tablespoons drained horseradish
1 cup whipping cream
Salt and freshly ground pepper
3 tablespoons butter, softened

Stuffing:
⅓ pound bacon
1 tablespoon butter
1 cup chopped onions
½ pound fresh mushrooms, chopped
Salt and freshly ground pepper

Fish:
4 small trout, about 6 to 8 ounces
*   each, or other small whole fish,*
*   or 4 large thin fish fillets*
Salt and freshly ground pepper
1 tablespoon butter

Garnish:
Minced fresh parsley

Horseradish Sauce: In a small saucepan, combine shallots and wine; reduce to 2 to 3 tablespoons. Add horseradish, cream, salt and pepper; simmer until thickened; set aside.

While fish is baking, bring sauce to simmer. Remove from heat and cool slightly. Stir in softened butter.

Stuffing: In a large skillet, fry bacon until crisp, drain on paper towels; crumble and set aside. Drain all but 1 tablespoon bacon drippings and add 1 tablespoon butter. Stir in onions and sauté until soft. Add mushrooms and cook until they just lose their color. Season with salt and pepper. Transfer to a bowl and stir in reserved bacon.

Preheat oven to 400°. Butter a baking dish large enough to hold fish in one layer.

Fish: Rinse fish and pat dry. Sprinkle each cavity with a little salt and pepper. Place equal amounts of stuffing into cavity of each fish. Press closed as tightly as possible. (If using fish fillets, spread stuffing down center of each fillet and roll up starting with wide end of fillet. Secure with wooden picks.) Arrange fish in prepared baking dish, in one layer, and dot with butter.

Bake for 12 to 15 minutes.

Transfer fish to serving plate. Spoon some sauce over top and sprinkle with chopped parsley. Pass remaining sauce in separate bowl.

4 servings

GRILLED SALMON WITH MUSTARD DILL SAUCE

Mustard Dill Sauce:

4 tablespoons dark, spicy prepared mustard

1 teaspoon dry mustard

3 tablespoons sugar or honey

2 tablespoons white wine vinegar

⅓ cup vegetable oil

3 tablespoons fresh chopped dill, or 1½ teaspoons dried dill

4 salmon, swordfish or haddock steaks

Extra virgin olive oil

Mustard Dill Sauce: In a small bowl, mix mustards, sugar and vinegar to a paste. Slowly whisk in oil until sauce is consistency of mayonnaise. Stir in dill. Store in refrigerator and serve with fish or grilled chicken.

¾ cup sauce

Fish: Rinse salmon under cool water; drain and pat dry with paper towels. Sprinkle steaks with olive oil.

Heat barbecue grill, grill pan, cast iron skillet or a non-stick skillet until very hot. Place steaks in pan and grill for about 4 to 5 minutes per side. They should be browned and just done. Transfer to serving platter and serve immediately with mustard dill sauce.

4 servings

TUNA STEAKS IN MARINADE

4 1-inch thick fresh red tuna steaks

Marinade:

¼ cup vegetable oil

1 teaspoon hot chili sesame oil

¼ cup rice wine vinegar

1 tablespoon packed brown sugar

2 tablespoons Madeira wine or sweet Vermouth

¼ cup soy sauce

¼ teaspoon ground ginger

¼ teaspoon minced garlic

Place tuna steaks in shallow glass dish, large enough to hold steaks in one layer.

Marinade: Whisk oil, sesame oil, rice wine vinegar, brown sugar, Madeira wine, soy sauce, ginger and garlic in a small bowl. Pour over tuna steaks. Cover and let marinate in refrigerator at least 3 hours, turning occasionally.

Grill over charcoal or gas grill until just cooked through, 5 to 6 minutes per side. Do not overcook. Baste with marinade while cooking to keep moist.

4 to 6 servings

SPICY SWEET AND SOUR GRILLED TUNA

Sauce:
2 tablespoons oil
¾ cup ketchup
1 cup freshly squeezed orange juice
¼ cup fresh lemon juice
¼ cup white wine vinegar
2 cups sugar
2 tablespoons honey
2 tablespoons cornstarch mixed with
    2 tablespoons water
2 teaspoons ground red pepper
4 8-ounce tuna steaks
Salt and freshly ground pepper

Heat grill.

Sauce: In large saucepan, heat the oil and add ketchup, cooking until hot. Add orange juice, lemon juice, vinegar, sugar and honey. Bring to boil and thicken with cornstarch mixture, stirring until thick. Season with red pepper.

Steaks: Season tuna with salt and pepper. Rub entirely with oil to coat. Place on hot grill for about 3 minutes on each side or until there is no more pink color in center.
Serve immediately, spooning sauce over steaks.

Excellent served with saffron rice and snow peas with shiitake mushroom caps.

4 servings

BAKED FISH PARMESAN WITH TOMATO SAUCE

Tomato Sauce:
⅓ cup minced prosciutto fat
2 tablespoons olive oil
1 tablespoon butter
3 large onions, chopped
4 tablespoons dried basil
3 28-ounce cans Italian
    plum tomatoes
Salt and freshly ground pepper

2 pounds flounder, sole, orange
    roughy or other mild,
    fresh white fish
⅓ cup unsalted butter, softened
¼ cup freshly grated Parmesan
    cheese
½ cup fresh bread crumbs
½ cup sour cream
½ teaspoon salt
Freshly ground pepper

Tomato Sauce: Sauté prosciutto fat in oil and butter until drippings are rendered. Add onions and dried basil. Cook until onions are tender. Stir in tomatoes; simmer uncovered for 30 minutes, stirring frequently. Season with salt and pepper. This sauce is wonderful for pasta and freezes well.

Preheat oven to 350°. Butter a 9x13-inch baking dish.
Arrange fish in one layer in baking dish. Mix butter, Parmesan, bread crumbs, sour cream, salt and pepper and spread gently over each fish fillet.
Bake for 20 minutes, or until fish is cooked through. Do not overcook.
Remove fish to serving platter. Surround with tomato sauce and sprinkle with chopped parsley.

4 to 5 servings

MACADAMIA SALMON

2 salmon fillets, 1-inch thick, tail
    section preferred
Juice of 1 fresh lemon
2 small sprigs fresh dill,
    finely chopped
2 shallots, finely chopped
2 tablespoons olive oil
6 sun-dried tomatoes, preserved in
    oil, drained and chopped
8 macadamia nuts, coarsely chopped

In a small bowl, whisk lemon juice, dill, shallots and olive oil. Place salmon in shallow bowl, pour marinade over top, cover and refrigerate for 2 hours.

Preheat barbecue grill or broiler.

Remove salmon from marinade, reserving marinade. Grill salmon for 5 minutes on each side. Warm marinade, adding tomatoes. When hot, pour over salmon. Sprinkle with macadamia nuts.

2 servings

GRILLED RED SNAPPER

Juice of 4 lemons
1/2 cup olive oil
1/4 cup soy sauce
4 red snapper fillets

Whisk together the lemon juice, olive oil and soy sauce. Place fillets in a glass baking dish that will just hold them in one layer. Pour marinade over fillets and turn over. Marinate for 1 hour in refrigerator.

Preheat grill. Place in a fish griller and cook over hot coals 5 to 7 minutes per side, brushing with marinade every 2 to 3 minutes.

4 servings

TERIYAKI SWORDFISH

4 swordfish steaks, 1 1/4 to
    1 1/2-inches thick

Marinade:
1 1/3 cups light soy sauce
2/3 cup sherry
2 teaspoons sugar
4 teaspoons freshly grated
    ginger root
2 cloves garlic, crushed

Place swordfish in one or two low flat dishes that will hold them in one layer. In a small saucepan, bring soy sauce, sherry, sugar, ginger root and garlic to a boil over medium heat. Strain marinade over steaks. Cover lightly and refrigerate for at least 2 hours.

Heat gas or charcoal grill. Grill steaks 5 to 6 minutes per side. Baste with marinade several times while grilling. Serve immediately.

Variation: Try salmon steaks.

6 to 8 servings

MOULES MARINIÈRE

4 dozen mussels, well scrubbed
    and debearded
4 cups white wine
1 medium onion, finely chopped
1 tablespoon fresh lemon juice
1 teaspoon salt
1 teaspoon freshly ground pepper
4 cloves garlic, finely chopped
4 fresh basil leaves
3 parsley sprigs
4 tablespoons butter
1 16-ounce can pureed tomatoes

Place mussels in large kettle with all ingredients except butter and tomatoes. Bring to boil and cook until mussels open. Discard any that do not open. Remove mussels. Add butter to liquid and reduce. Pass liquid through sieve lined with cheesecloth. Warm liquid with tomatoes. Pour over mussels, arranged in individual bowls.

Serve with crusty Italian or French bread.

3 servings

SHRIMP CREOLE

1 tablespoon mild olive oil
2 tablespoons flour
2 onions, chopped
2 cloves garlic, chopped
1 large green bell pepper, chopped
1 28-ounce can tomatoes; drain
    and reserve juice
½ teaspoon ground red pepper
2 bay leaves
⅓ teaspoon celery seeds
¼ teaspoon dried powdered thyme
2 pounds fresh shrimp, shelled
    and deveined
2 teaspoons Worcestershire sauce

In a large heavy heated saucepan, make a roux by mixing olive oil and flour to paste consistency. Add onions, garlic and green pepper. Stir until onion browns slightly. If mixture is too thick, add more oil. Coarsely chop the canned tomatoes. Add tomatoes with half of the can's reserved juice; retain the remaining liquid. Season mixture with red pepper, bay leaves, celery seeds and thyme. Add shrimp and cover tightly.

Cook slowly for an hour. After 30 minutes of cooking add Worcestershire sauce. Add remaining tomato liquid as needed during cooking.

Serve with Indian, Basmati or plain fluffy rice in a separate dish and crusty French bread.

6 servings

SHRIMP IN ALMOND SAUCE

2½ cups fresh bread crumbs
1½ cups milk
1 small onion, minced
½ cup butter
1 teaspoon garlic salt
½ teaspoon white pepper
1 teaspoon paprika
¼ teaspoon ground red pepper
1 cup chicken broth
1 cup slivered almonds
1 pound medium shrimp, cooked,
    shelled and split lengthwise

In a small bowl, soak crumbs in milk for 5 minutes. Beat until smooth.

In a large skillet, sauté onion in butter until soft; add garlic salt, white pepper, paprika, red pepper, chicken broth, almonds and shrimp. Add bread crumb-milk mixture and heat.

Serve over parsley rice.

Hint: Substitute 2 cloves garlic, crushed and salt to taste for garlic salt. Saute garlic with onion.

4 servings

SCALLOPS AND MUSHROOMS AU GRATIN

2 pounds bay scallops or sea scallops,
    halved
1 cup chicken broth
4 tablespoons butter, divided
¾ pound mushrooms, sliced
1 tablespoon fresh lemon juice
1 onion, sliced
6 tablespoons flour
½ cup whipping cream
⅛ teaspoon nutmeg
1½ cups grated Swiss cheese, divided
¼ cup fresh parsley, chopped
Salt to taste

Place scallops and broth in a large saucepan. Quickly bring to boil, reduce heat, cover and simmer until scallops are opaque about 1 or 2 minutes. Cool in broth. Drain and reserve liquid (should be 2 cups, if not, add more chicken broth). Cover and chill scallops.

Heat 2 tablespoons butter in a large skillet. Add mushrooms and lemon juice and sauté over high heat until lightly browned. Remove from skillet. Heat remaining butter and onion; cook until transparent. Stir in flour. Remove from heat and gradually whisk in cooking liquid. Return to heat and bring to boil, stirring until thickened. Add mushrooms, cream, nutmeg, ¾ cup of cheese. Cool sauce slightly and chill.

Stir scallops into cooled sauce along with parsley and salt. Divide among 6 individual baking dishes; top with remaining cheese. Cover and chill until ready to serve.

Preheat oven to 400°.

Bake, uncovered, for 12 to 15 minutes, or until browned and bubbling.

6 servings

SPICY CRAB CAKES WITH CORN

1 pound lump crabmeat (fresh or
    frozen, thawed and drained)
1 cup cooked corn
½ cup finely diced onion
½ cup finely diced green pepper
½ cup finely diced celery
1 teaspoon finely diced jalapeño
    chili pepper
1 cup mayonnaise
½ teaspoon dry mustard
Pinch of ground red pepper
½ teaspoon seafood seasoning
Salt and freshly ground pepper
1 egg, lightly beaten
1 cup crushed saltine cracker,
    divided
2 tablespoons butter or margarine,
    divided
2 tablespoons vegetable oil, divided

Combine the crab, corn, onion, green pepper, celery and jalapeño. Toss well.

In a separate bowl, combine the mayonnaise, dry mustard, red pepper and seafood seasoning. Add to the crab mixture and blend, adding salt and pepper to taste. Gently fold in the beaten egg and ¼ cup cracker crumbs. Form the crab into eight patties. Carefully coat with the remaining cracker crumbs. Sprinkle both sides of crab cakes with seafood seasoning. Cover and chill for approximately 30 minutes.

In large skillet, heat 1 tablespoon butter and 1 tablespoon oil. Cook the crab cakes over medium heat for approximately 3 minutes per side, or until golden. Sprinkle with additional seafood seasoning while frying. It is best to cook only 3 to 4 at a time. Add more oil and butter as needed.

Serve immediately with lemon or tartar sauce.

4 servings

LE CRABE EXCELLENT

1 cup butter, melted
8 tablespoons flour
2 pounds fresh crabmeat
1 teaspoon paprika
1 teaspoon nutmeg
2 teaspoons salt
½ teaspoon white pepper
3 cups milk
3 tablespoons fresh lemon juice
2 tablespoons chopped fresh parsley
½ cup coarsely chopped pecans
Long-grained white rice, cooked

Preheat oven to 350°.

In a large saucepan, melt butter, add flour to make a roux. Stir in crabmeat and simmer briefly. Add paprika, nutmeg, salt, pepper and milk. Remove from heat and add lemon juice and parsley. Spoon into shallow, 8x12-inch baking dish.

Bake for 30 minutes.

Serve over rice and sprinkle with chopped pecans.

6 servings

S E A F O O D   R I S O T T O

Risotto:
¼ cup butter or margarine
½ cup olive oil
2 small onions, chopped
1 pound Italian risotto
½ cup dry white wine
8 cups chicken broth

Seafood Sauce:
¼ cup butter or margarine
¼ cup extra virgin olive oil
1 onion, chopped
3 cloves garlic, chopped
3 6½-ounce cans minced or
    chopped clams
½ cup chopped fresh parsley
¼ teaspoon oregano
½ cup dry white wine
1 cup sliced mushrooms
Salt and freshly ground pepper
1 pound fresh shrimp, shelled and
    deveined or frozen shrimp,
    thawed and drained

Grated fresh Parmesan cheese

Risotto: In separate large skillet, heat butter and olive oil. Sauté onion until golden. Stir in rice and cook for about 2 minutes. Add wine and cook for another 2 minutes. Heat chicken broth in saucepan. Begin adding broth to rice, ½ cup at a time. Continue adding broth until rice is soft in texture, approximately 15 minutes.

Seafood Sauce: In a large skillet, heat butter and olive oil. Sauté onion and garlic until golden. Stir in clams with juice, parsley, oregano, wine and mushrooms. Simmer mixture 5 minutes. Season to taste with salt and pepper. Set aside.
Bring seafood sauce to a boil, add shrimp and simmer for 4 minutes. Add seafood sauce mixture to risotto and continue heating for 1 to 2 minutes. Sprinkle cheese on top.

4 to 6 servings

B A K E D   S T U F F E D   S H R I M P

16 large shrimp, raw, cleaned,
    deveined and butterflied
20 butter-flavored crackers, crushed
1 6-ounce can crabmeat, drained
½ cup butter, melted
¼ cup chopped fresh parsley
2 cloves garlic, crushed
¼ cup finely chopped onion
¼ cup finely chopped green pepper

Preheat oven to 350°.
Mix together cracker crumbs, crabmeat, butter, parsley, garlic, onion and green pepper to make stuffing.
Arrange shrimp on ungreased baking pan. Spoon stuffing equally onto each shrimp.
Bake for 20 to 25 minutes or until shrimp is pink.

4 servings

PAELLA

Chicken and Pork Marinade:
1 cup dry white wine
1 teaspoon salt-free seasoning
2 tablespoons fresh lemon juice
2 tablespoons chopped green onions
8 to 10 chicken breasts, skinless
 and boneless
1 pound pork tenderloin, sliced
 in strips

Broth:
6 cups homemade chicken broth
 (see hint)
1 teaspoon unsalted bouillon
½ cup brandy
½ teaspoon saffron
1 tablespoon fresh coriander or
 1 teaspoon dried
1 teaspoon ground cumin
1 tablespoon minced onion
1 teaspoon salt-free seasoning
½ cup chopped fresh parsley
Juice of ½ fresh lemon
2 strips of lemon zest

Special Oil:
1 cup safflower or corn oil
1 teaspoon fennel seeds
¼ teaspoon hot red pepper flakes
1 clove garlic, crushed

Flour
½ cup chopped onion
2 red bell peppers, chopped
2 green bell peppers, chopped
1 large fresh tomato, peeled, seeded
 and cubed
3 cups uncooked white rice
1 pound shrimp
1 pound scallops
2 clams per person
1 10-ounce package frozen Italian
 green beans, thawed
1 10-ounce frozen peas, thawed

Marinade: In a bowl, whisk together wine, salt-free seasoning, lemon juice and green onion. Add chicken and pork to marinade. Marinate for the day in the refrigerator.

Broth: In a large kettle, combine chicken broth, bouillon, brandy, saffron, coriander, cumin, onion, salt-free seasoning, parsley, lemon and lemon zest. Heat to boiling. Remove lemon peel.

Special Oil: In a paella pan or deep sided skillet, stir together oil, fennel, hot red pepper and garlic.

Remove chicken from marinade; pat dry. Dredge in flour. Heat special oil in paella pan; sauté chicken until brown; set aside. Remove pork from marinade and sauté pork in same oil; set aside. Sauté onion and peppers in same oil until almost tender; set aside. Lightly sauté fresh tomato. Add rice to residue in pan; add additional oil, if needed, to coat grains. May be prepared ahead to this point.

Preheat oven to 350°.

Arrange chicken, pork, onion, peppers and tomatoes over rice in paella pan. Bury shrimp and scallops in mixture. Place clams with hinged side down, allowing clams to open as they cook. Add boiling broth to paella mixture and cook on top of stove for a few minutes.

Cover with aluminum foil and bake for 45 minutes to 1 hour, or until rice is cooked. Check every 15 to 30 minutes. The last 15 minutes, add Italian green beans and sprinkle peas over all. Bake until done. Do not overcook rice. It should be firm.

Hint: Substitute 3 13-ounce cans unsalted chicken broth for homemade chicken broth.

VEGETABLES, POTATOES & RICE

Vegetables

Potatoes

Rice

ARTICHAUTS À LA BARIJOULE

Mushroom Duxelle:
1 pound white mushrooms
Lemon juice
3 shallots, chopped
2 tablespoons butter

4 artichokes
1 tablespoon diced carrot
1 tablespoon diced leek
1 tablespoon diced celery root
⅛ cup olive oil
2 ounces brandy
2 cups chicken stock
¾ cup butter

Mushroom Duxelle: Wipe mushrooms and coat with lemon juice to keep white. Finely chop mushrooms. In a skillet, melt 2 tablespoons butter and lightly sauté shallots, add mushrooms and cook until water evaporates.

Remove leaves of artichokes starting from bottom. Holding the artichoke by the stem, carve and remove the choke. In a large skillet, lightly sauté vegetables in olive oil; add artichokes and sauté over low heat for 2 or 3 minutes. Deglaze skillet with brandy and reduce slightly. Add chicken stock and cook until tender. Reduce cooking juices to syrupy consistency and whisk in butter. Fill artichokes with some duxelle and pour sauce around.

4 servings

LEMON ARTICHOKES

2 packages frozen artichokes, thawed
½ cup finely chopped green onion
    or chives
½ cup extra virgin olive oil
2 tablespoons butter, melted
¼ cup fresh lemon juice
Salt and freshly ground pepper

Layer artichokes in bottom of skillet, cover with green onions, olive oil, melted butter and lemon juice. Simmer about 2 minutes, or until artichokes are tender. Adjust the seasonings with salt and pepper.

AUBERGINE À LA PROVENCALE

1 eggplant, peeled and cubed
Flour
Salt and freshly ground pepper
5 tablespoons olive oil, divided
4 large (or 6 small) tomatoes, peeled,
    seeded and coarsely chopped
2 small cloves garlic, minced
Chopped fresh parsley

Shake eggplant cubes in flour, salt and pepper. In a small skillet, heat 2 tablespoons olive oil and sauté tomatoes with garlic for 4 minutes. Season with salt and pepper to taste. Remove from heat.

In a large skillet, heat remaining 3 tablespoons oil, sauté eggplant until golden and add tomatoes. Mix well. Cook about 3 minutes. Sprinkle with parsley and serve. Can be frozen.

6 servings

BEANS À LA POITOU

2 pounds dried white beans,
    (Great Northern), washed
½ cup butter
2 onions, finely chopped
3 cloves garlic, peeled,
    coarsely chopped
Salt and freshly ground pepper
1 bouquet garni
3 firm ripe tomatoes
2 pounds ham, cubed
2 tablespoons butter, cubed
2 to 4 tablespoons wine vinegar

Place beans in a large pot with 5 quarts of hot water; cover and bring to a boil. Cook for 3 minutes and soak overnight. Drain and reserve beans.

Heat butter in a large pot; add onion and garlic and sauté until golden. Add beans, salt, pepper, bouquet garni and whole tomatoes; pour in enough cold water to cover. Bring to a boil.

Simmer covered for 2 hours or until beans are tender. Add ham for last 15 minutes of cooking. Just before serving, remove bouquet garni, dot with remaining butter and drizzle with vinegar to taste.

Hint: To make bouquet garni, tie 3 sprigs parsley, 1 sprig thyme, 1 bay leaf, 2 celery ribs together in cheesecloth.

6 to 8 servings

FRIJOLES DE OLLA
(RANCH BEANS)

1 cup pinto beans
2 jalapeño chili peppers
Salt and freshly ground pepper

Place beans in large pot; cover with water to 5 inches above level of beans. Add peppers. Bring to boil and simmer for 2 to 2½ hours. Add water as necessary to keep beans covered. Do not add additional water during the last 45 minutes of cooking. This allows the juices to thicken. Season with salt and pepper.

FRESH GREEN BEANS WITH
BUTTERY BROWNED MACADAMIA NUTS

1½ pounds fresh green beans
4 tablespoons butter
1 3½-ounce jar macadamia nuts

Cook green beans until crisp tender. While green beans are cooking, melt butter in a small saucepan until butter begins to brown. Quickly add macadamia nuts. Swirl until the nuts become brown. Toss butter-nut mixture with hot drained green beans. Serve immediately.

LUBIA POLO (GREEN BEAN RICE)

2 cups uncooked long-grain rice
4 cups water
1 teaspoon saffron
½ cup boiling water, divided
1 clove garlic, minced
2 small onions, sliced
3 tablespoons corn oil, divided
Sprinkle of turmeric
1 teaspoon cumin
1 teaspoon coriander
1 large package frozen green beans
2 tablespoons unsalted tomato paste
2 16-ounce cans unsalted tomatoes,
    drained (reserving juices)
    and chopped
½ tablespoon salt-free seasoning
Juice of ½ fresh lemon
Sprinkle of cinnamon
Freshly ground pepper
2 baking potatoes, sliced
    (called the "Tah-Deeg")

In a large saucepan, bring 4 cups water to boil, add rice and partially cook. Test rice; should be firm. Drain and rinse with cold water; set aside.

Grind saffron with mortar and pestle and mix with ¼ cup boiling water; set aside.

Spray skillet bottom with non-stick cooking spray. Sauté onions and garlic in 1 tablespoon oil until golden. Sprinkle with turmeric, cumin and coriander. Add green beans and stir-fry for 2 to 3 minutes. Add tomato paste and tomato juices. Reduce slightly. Add tomatoes and season with salt-free seasoning, lemon juice, cinnamon, pepper and 2 or more tablespoons saffron mixture. Taste for correct seasonings. Cook until juice has almost evaporated. May be prepared in advance to this point.

Spray bottom of 5-quart non-stick pot with non-stick cooking spray. Heat 1 tablespoon oil, 2 tablespoons boiling water and 2 tablespoons of saffron mixture. Arrange sliced potatoes on bottom of pot. This is called the "Tah-Deeg". Over the potatoes, layer rice and vegetables several times ending with rice. Poke air holes in rice. Keep heat on high until steam forms. Test pot with wet finger. If it sizzles, the steam is right. Be careful not to burn bottom of pot. Combine 1 tablespoon oil, 1 tablespoon boiling water and remaining saffron-water and drizzle over rice. Cover with pan lid lined with folds of paper toweling to absorb water.

Steam for approximately ½ hour over very low heat. Do not be tempted to lift lid. After cooking let stand 15 minutes before unmolding.

Turn onto round platter, making sure that the "Tah-Deeg" is on top of rice. Shape, if rice does not unmold properly.

CARROTS WITH WHITE GRAPES

1 13½-ounce jar small whole
    Belgium carrots
20 seedless white grapes
4 tablespoons butter
4 tablespoons Cointreau

Drain carrots. In a skillet, melt butter; add Cointreau, stir. Add grapes and carrots and heat through.

2 servings

CARROT SOUFFLÉ

2 cups pared and sliced carrots
½ cup chicken broth
1 tablespoon fresh orange juice
1 tablespoon orange zest
½ cup butter, softened
¼ cup brown sugar
1 tablespoon flour
½ teaspoon salt
1 cup milk
1 teaspoon grated fresh ginger
3 eggs

Preheat oven to 350°. Lightly butter a 2-quart baking dish.

In a large saucepan, cover and simmer carrots in chicken broth until soft. Drain well and puree in blender or food processor. Stir in orange juice and zest. Add butter, sugar, flour, salt, milk, ginger, and eggs. Process until smooth. Pour into prepared baking dish.

Bake for 45 minutes to 1 hour, or until the center of soufflé is firm to the touch.

8 servings

ASPARAGUS FOR SPRINGTIME

1 pound fresh asparagus
¼ pound unsalted butter
½ cup chopped walnuts
½ teaspoon marjoram
Salt and freshly ground pepper

Wash and cut asparagus in bite-size pieces. Steam until crisp-tender.

Melt butter in medium-size skillet. Sauté walnuts and marjoram together until walnuts are coated. Stir fry asparagus with butter and walnut mixture for 2 minutes. Season with salt and pepper to taste.

4 servings

GERMAN RED CABBAGE

½ pound bacon, diced
1 head red cabbage, cored
    and thinly sliced
2 teaspoons salt
2 cups dry red wine
1 cup water
½ cup sugar
6 tablespoons white vinegar
3 tart apples, peeled, cored, sliced

Brown bacon in a large Dutch oven. Add cabbage and stir over medium heat until cabbage starts to glisten and wilt. Add salt, wine and water. Bring to boil. Cover, reduce heat and simmer for 1 hour.

Add sugar, vinegar and apples. Cover and simmer for another hour. If mixture becomes too dry, mix 2 parts red wine to 1 part water and add as needed.

8 to 10 servings

LIMAS AND CHEDDAR IN TOMATO CUPS

4 or 5 medium tomatoes
2 tablespoons butter
1/4 cup chopped onion
2 tablespoons chopped fresh parsley
1/2 cup grated cheddar cheese
1 10-ounce package frozen baby
    lima beans, cooked and drained

Preheat oven to 350°.

    Slice top from tomatoes, remove seeds and membranes and drain.

    Melt butter in a small skillet. Add onion and parsley; cook until soft. Combine with cheese and limas. Spoon into lightly salted tomato shells.

    Bake for 15 to 20 minutes.

4 to 5 servings

CAULIFLOWER EXCELLENT

1 whole head cauliflower, cored
1/2 cup mayonnaise
1/4 cup grated Parmesan cheese
2 tablespoons chopped fresh parsley
1 tablespoon fresh lemon juice
1/4 teaspoon salt
2 egg whites, beaten stiff

Preheat oven to 350°.

    Cook cauliflower in salted boiling water about 20 minutes or until just tender. Place cauliflower head in baking dish.

    In a large bowl, mix together mayonnaise, cheese, parsley, lemon juice and salt. Fold in beaten egg whites. Frost cauliflower with mixture.

    Bake for 20 minutes or until golden brown. Serve immediately.

6 to 8 servings

SASSY BRUSSELS SPROUTS

2 10-ounce packages frozen Brussels
    sprouts, or 1 1/4 pound fresh,
    cooked and halved
1/2 cup butter or margarine
2/3 cup coarsely chopped
    salted peanuts
1 teaspoon salt
Freshly ground pepper
2 teaspoons lemon juice

Garnish:
Grated lemon zest

Sauté cooked Brussels sprouts in butter for 1 minute. Stir in peanuts, salt and pepper to taste. Cook 1 or 2 minutes longer or until sprouts are slightly brown. Remove from heat and stir in lemon juice. Serve immediately, garnished with lemon zest.

6 to 8 servings

SIMPLY SCRUMPTIOUS MUSHROOM STUFFING

½ cup butter
1 pound mushrooms, halved or
    quartered
1 large green pepper, seeded and
    coarsely chopped
1 large onion, coarsely chopped
10 slices of mixed bread varieties,
    torn in pieces

Preheat oven to 350°. Spray a 2½-quart baking dish with a non-stick cooking spray.

In a large skillet, melt butter and sauté mushrooms, green pepper and onion over medium heat until tender. Lower heat and cover mixture. Continue cooking for 20 minutes, stirring occasionally. Arrange torn broken pieces of bread in the baking dish. Pour hot mixture over bread and mix together.

Bake uncovered for 30 minutes.

Hint: Use a combination of French bread, dark rye and whole wheat breads for great flavor. Do not remove the crusts. Use the ends of the bread for great texture!

Variation: Wrap the mixture in well-sealed heavy duty aluminum foil and place on barbecue grill. Turn often. Cook about 30 minutes. Delicious!

12 servings

MUSHROOMS IN COGNAC HERB SAUCE

½ cup butter
2 pounds small mushroom caps
4 shallots, minced
Salt and freshly ground pepper
½ cup cognac, heated
3 cloves garlic
1 tablespoon chopped fresh parsley
1 teaspoon dried rosemary
1 teaspoon dried thyme
1 teaspoon dried basil
½ teaspoon turmeric
½ teaspoon cumin
½ teaspoon coriander
½ teaspoon ginger
½ teaspoon freshly ground pepper
3 cups whipping cream

In a large skillet, sauté shallots and mushroom caps in butter for 2 minutes. Season with salt and pepper. Stir in heated cognac, ignite and stir until flame dies; set aside.

In blender or food processor, process garlic, parsley, rosemary, thyme, basil, turmeric, cumin, coriander, ginger, pepper and cream. Add mixture to mushrooms. Put in heavy saucepan and cook over low heat until thick, approximately 3 hours, stirring occasionally.

Serve as a condiment with turkey or beef. It is also wonderful with wild rice.

Hint: Fresh herbs may be substituted for dried. Triple the amount.

8 to 10 servings

CORN CHEESE CHILE PIE

3 eggs, beaten
1 16-ounce can creamed corn
1 16-ounce can corn kernels, drained
1 4-ounce can chopped green chilies,
    drained
½ cup melted butter
½ cup yellow cornmeal
1 cup sour cream
4 ounces cheddar cheese, shredded
4 ounces Monterey Jack cheese,
    shredded
½ teaspoon salt
¼ teaspoon Worcestershire sauce

Preheat oven to 350°. Butter a 2-quart baking dish.

Combine eggs, creamed corn, corn kernels, green chilies, butter, yellow cornmeal, sour cream, cheddar cheese, Monterey Jack cheese, salt and Worcestershire sauce. Place in prepared baking dish.

Bake for 1 hour or until set.

GRILLED MEXICAN CORN CAKES

1 cup yellow cornmeal
4 tablespoons all-purpose flour
1 teaspoon baking powder
¾ teaspoon salt
1¼ cups milk
1 4-ounce can green chilies, drained
6 to 8 tablespoons vegetable oil
4 ounces Monterey Jack cheese,
    shredded
⅓ cup sour cream,
    room temperature
⅓ cup guacamole, room temperature
⅓ cup salsa
¼ cup chopped black olives
4 tablespoons minced fresh parsley
2 tablespoons chopped fresh cilantro

Combine cornmeal, flour, baking powder and salt. Add milk and chilies; stir to blend. Heat 1½ tablespoons of oil in a large heavy skillet over moderately high heat. Spoon batter by tablespoons into skillet to make 4 or 5 small pancakes. Fry until brown around the edges, about 4 to 5 minutes. Turn and fry until brown and crisp on second side, about 4 minutes. Turn only once. Drain on paper towels. Repeat, using remaining batter, adding oil as needed.

Place corn cakes on a broiler pan and top with cheese. Broil 6 inches from heat until cheese melts, about 2 minutes. Top with small dabs of sour cream, guacamole and salsa. Sprinkle with olives. Mix parsley and cilantro together and sprinkle over pancakes. Serve warm.

4 servings

CREAMED SQUASH AU GRATIN

2 pounds yellow squash, sliced
½ cup water
½ teaspoon salt
½ teaspoon sugar
¼ cup butter or margarine, softened
1¼ cups cubed sharp cheddar cheese
¼ cup grated Gruyère cheese
1 cup sour cream
½ cup chopped onion
¼ cup dry white wine, to taste
Salt and freshly ground pepper
1 cup fresh bread crumbs
4 tablespoons melted butter
Grated fresh imported Parmesan
    cheese

Preheat oven to 350°. Butter a 7½x11-inch baking dish.

Place squash in a large saucepan. Add water, salt and sugar. Cover and cook for 10 to 12 minutes, or until squash is just tender. Drain very well and return to pan. Add butter and cut into squash with a pastry blender until mixture is chunky. Add cheddar and Gruyère cheese, sour cream, onion and wine. Season with salt and pepper to taste. Mix well. Pour into prepared baking dish.

Stir crumbs and melted butter together and sprinkle over squash. Top generously with Parmesan cheese.

Variation: Add ½ cup chopped sweet red pepper.

Variation: Substitute 2 pounds zucchini, sliced for yellow squash. Parboil the zucchini for 7 minutes. Substitute ¼ cup chopped chives for the onion and add ⅛ teaspoon of paprika to the cheese mixture.

8 to 10 servings

SQUASH AND ZUCCHINI CASSEROLE

1 tablespoon butter or 1 tablespoon
    olive oil
2 large onions, chopped
1 green pepper, seeded and chopped
3 to 4 yellow squash, sliced
3 to 4 zucchini, sliced
2 teaspoons sugar
1 tablespoon oregano
1 teaspoon basil
½ cup chopped fresh parsley
½ pound grated cheese, any kind
    except American

Preheat oven to 350°. Butter a 2 to 3-quart baking dish.

In a large skillet, sauté onion and green pepper in butter or olive oil until golden, about 15 minutes. Mix in a large mixing bowl the yellow squash, zucchini, sugar, oregano, basil and parsley; add onions and green peppers. Spread in prepared baking dish. Sprinkle top with cheese, cover.

Bake for 30 to 35 minutes. Remove cover and cook an additional 10 minutes, or until liquid is absorbed.

Serve garnished with toasted sesame seeds.

Hint: See Snips & Tips - Cheese, page 243.

4 to 6 servings

SPINACH WITH TOMATOES, PROSCIUTTO AND BEANS

¼ cup olive oil
3 cloves garlic, minced
1 medium onion, chopped
½ to ¾ teaspoon dried red
    pepper flakes
1 pound fresh spinach leaves,
    coarsely chopped
¼ pound prosciutto, cut into
    ¼-inch dice
2 cups canned cannellini beans,
    rinsed and drained
12 cherry tomatoes, halved
¼ cup minced fresh parsley
Salt and freshly ground pepper

In a large skillet, heat olive oil. Sauté garlic and onion until onion is translucent; add red pepper flakes. Add spinach and prosciutto; cook a few minutes until spinach is wilted. Add cannellini beans, tomatoes, parsley, salt and pepper to taste.

Variation: Substitute smoked ham for prosciutto.

TOMATOES D'MEDICI

6 medium, ripe, firm tomatoes
2 10-ounce packages frozen
    chopped spinach
3 eggs, beaten
½ cup fresh bread crumbs
⅓ cup freshly grated Romano cheese
4 tablespoons butter, melted
½ teaspoon salt
1 teaspoon minced onion
¼ teaspoon garlic powder

Preheat oven to 350°.

Core and halve tomatoes. Drain with cut side down on paper towels. Cook spinach according to package directions and drain thoroughly in a strainer. Combine spinach with eggs, bread crumbs, cheese, butter, salt, onion and garlic powder and mix well. Arrange tomatoes on a baking sheet, cut side up. Generously spoon spinach mixture into tomato halves.

Bake for 20 minutes.

Hint: Can be prepared early in the day and baked just before serving.

12 servings

VEGETABLE CHIPS

4 beets, peeled
4 parsnips, peeled
3 sweet potatoes, peeled
2 cups vegetable oil
Salt and freshly ground pepper

Slice very thin with 1 millimeter blade on food processor or a very sharp knife.

Heat oil in a deep fryer or heavy saucepan to 375° and cook 4 to 5 vegetable slices at a time until crisp. Season with salt and pepper.

Serve warm as an accompaniment to meat dishes.

SPINACH MUSHROOM MEDLEY

1 pound fresh spinach, washed and
    coarse stems removed
2 tablespoons butter
1 cup sliced fresh mushrooms
¼ cup white Worcestershire sauce
2 cloves garlic, minced

In a large saucepan bring 2 cups of water to a boil and add spinach. Reduce heat and simmer covered for 20 minutes. Drain well.

    In another saucepan, melt butter and add mushrooms, Worcestershire sauce, and garlic. Cook on low heat until mushrooms are tender. Combine mixture with spinach and serve.

4 to 6 servings

FRESH TOMATO BASIL TART

1 pre-baked 9-inch pastry shell

Filling:
6 medium tomatoes seeded, drained
    and diced
3 to 4 tablespoons pesto (see index)
½ teaspoon salt
2 cups shredded cheddar cheese
2 cups shredded Swiss or
    mozzarella cheese
¾ cup good quality mayonnaise

Preheat oven to 375°.

    In a large bowl, mix tomatoes, pesto and salt. Spoon into pastry crust. In bowl, blend cheeses and mayonnaise. Pat evenly over tomato mixture.

    Bake for 20 to 25 minutes, or until filling is heated and cheese is melted and light brown.

10 servings

SCALLOPED TOMATO DELIGHT

4 medium tomatoes
4 tablespoons butter or margarine
1 cup diced celery
½ cup chopped onion
1 teaspoon salt
1 teaspoon sugar
⅛ teaspoon freshly ground pepper
1 cup plain croutons

Preheat oven to 350°.

    Core tomatoes and cut into ¼-inch slices. Overlap slices in 2 rows in buttered 8x12x2-inch baking dish; set aside.

    In a skillet, melt butter, add celery and onions, sauté 2 minutes. Stir in salt, sugar and pepper. Spoon all but ¼ cup of mixture over tomatoes. Toss croutons with remaining ¼ cup celery mixture and spoon down center between tomatoes.

    Bake covered for 30 minutes.

4 to 6 servings

SWEET POTATO SOUFFLÉ

3 pounds sweet potatoes
1/3 cup butter, melted
1 cup sugar, divided
6 eggs, separated
1 tablespoon grated lemon zest
1 cup fresh orange juice
1/4 teaspoon cinnamon

Preheat oven to 350°. Grease a 2-quart baking dish.

Boil the potatoes, peel and mash. Place in large mixing bowl. Add butter and 3/4 cup sugar. In separate bowl, beat egg yolks. Add yolks, lemon zest, orange juice and cinnamon to the potatoes. Mix well. Beat egg whites until stiff and fold into the potato mixture. Pour into prepared baking dish. Sprinkle the top with remaining sugar.

Bake for 1 hour.

Variation: Spoon potato mixture in hollowed out orange halves and bake.

6 servings

YAM AND APPLE CASSEROLE

1/4 cup sugar
1/2 teaspoon salt
1/4 teaspoon nutmeg
4 tablespoons butter or margarine, softened
4 medium yams, cooked, skinned and sliced
3 tart green apples, peeled, cored and sliced
1/4 cup hot water
1/2 cup brown sugar

Preheat oven to 350°. Butter a 2-quart baking dish.

Combine sugar, salt and nutmeg in a large bowl. Blend in butter with a fork. Add sliced yams and apples and toss gently. Spoon into prepared baking dish. Pour hot water over top and cover.

Bake for 1 hour or until apples are tender. Remove from oven and heat broiler. Uncover baking dish and sprinkle with brown sugar.

Broil for 2 to 3 minutes or until sugar melts and bubbles.

4 to 6 servings

SWEET POTATO PIE

1 sweet potato per pie
2 eggs
2 ounces half and half
1/2 teaspoon nutmeg
1 teaspoon baking powder
1 cup sugar
1 teaspoon lemon extract
1 tablespoon flour
1 9-inch uncooked pie pastry shell

Preheat oven to 300°.

In a large saucepan, boil sweet potato until tender. Drain and peel.

In food processor work bowl, process sweet potato, eggs, half and half, nutmeg, baking powder, sugar and lemon extract. Add flour. Mix well. Pour into crust.

Bake for 50 minutes, or until crust is light brown. Do not turn oven higher than 300°.

6 servings

HÄSSELBACK POTATOES

6 baking potatoes, peeled
1½ tablespoons butter, melted
Salt
¾ cup fresh bread crumbs
2 tablespoons butter, melted
Grated Parmesan cheese, optional

Preheat oven to 425°. Butter a 9x13-inch baking dish. To prevent discoloration, place potatoes in a large pan and cover with cold water until ready to roast.

Place 1 potato at a time on a wooden spoon, large enough to cradle it comfortably. Begin one inch from end of potato and slice down at ⅛-inch intervals. (The bowl of the spoon will prevent the knife from slicing completely through the potato.) Return to cold water. When ready to roast, drain potatoes and pat dry. Arrange in baking dish cut side up. Brush with 1½ tablespoons melted butter and sprinkle with salt. Place in prepared pan in oven and roast 30 minutes. Sprinkle with bread crumbs and baste with 2 tablespoons melted butter and butter in the pan.

Roast for 15 minutes or until tender and golden brown. Parmesan cheese can be sprinkled on potatoes during last 5 minutes of roasting.

VIDALIA ONION PIE

Pie Crust:
1½ cups all-purpose flour
½ teaspoon salt
½ cup chilled vegetable shortening
3 to 4 tablespoons ice water

Filling:
2 pounds Vidalia onions, thinly sliced
½ cup butter or margarine, melted
3 eggs, beaten
1 cup sour cream
¼ teaspoon salt
¼ teaspoon pepper
¼ cup freshly grated Parmesan
    cheese

Pie Crust: Mix flour and salt in a large bowl. Cut in shortening until mixture resembles coarse crumbs. Stir in water, 1 tablespoon at a time, until mixture forms a ball. Wrap in plastic and refrigerate for 30 minutes. Roll out the dough between 2 sheets of floured wax paper into a circle to fit a 9-inch pie pan. Fit the dough into the pan and flute the edges.

Preheat oven to 450°.

In medium saucepan, sauté onions in butter until tender; remove from heat. Whisk in eggs, sour cream, salt and pepper. Pour this mixture into the prepared pan. Sprinkle with Parmesan cheese.

Bake for 20 minutes; reduce heat to 325° and bake for 20 minutes until the top and crust are golden. Cool slightly before cutting.

8 servings

POTATO KUGELE
(LITHUANIAN POTATO CUSTARD)

12 large white potatoes, peeled
2 small onions
5 eggs
½ cup sour cream
2 tablespoons flour
⅔ cup margarine, melted
½ pound bacon, cooked and
    crumbled
½ cup cracker or bread crumbs
1 teaspoon baking powder
1 teaspoon salt
½ teaspoon freshly ground pepper

Preheat oven to 450°. Grease two 5x9-inch or three 4x8-inch loaf pans.

Grate potatoes and onions together in food processor work bowl using finest grating blade.

Mix together eggs, sour cream, flour, margarine, bacon, cracker crumbs, baking powder, salt and pepper in food processor with steel blade.

Combine two mixtures with steel blade, hand mixer or hands. Pour into prepared pans. Fill to 2½-inches deep.

Bake for 15 minutes. Reduce heat to 375° and bake 1 hour or until brown and firm. Serve with sour cream and/or butter.

12 servings

GNOCCHI VIAREGGIO
(ITALIAN POTATO DUMPLINGS)

2½ pounds or 4 large potatoes,
    peeled and quartered
1¾ cups all-purpose flour, if needed
    use an additional 1¼ cups
    all-purpose flour
2 eggs
1½ tablespoons butter, softened
¼ teaspoon salt
Freshly ground black pepper
Dash of ground red pepper

In a large pan of salted boiling water, cook potatoes until tender. Drain. Mash and return potatoes to pan over a low heat. Stir to dry out mixture.

Place dry mashed potatoes in a mixing bowl. Add 1¾ cups flour, eggs, butter, salt, black and red pepper. Beat into a soft dough, add additional flour if needed. Gently knead, with floured hands. Roll a portion of dough the size of a plum into a long sausage shape the width of a finger. Cut roll into ¾-inch slices. Pinch the edges together with thumb and finger to make a little pillow. Press side of pillow with the prongs of a fork. Place on a floured board.

In boiling salted water, drop 10 gnocchi at a time. As they rise to the surface, remove from pan with slotted spoon and drain.

Serve with favorite red sauce and top with favorite Italian grated cheeses.

6 to 8 servings

POTATO AU GRATIN

3 pounds medium potatoes,
    thinly sliced
2 cups milk
2 cups water
2 cloves garlic, minced
1 teaspoon salt, or to taste
1 cup whipping cream, divided
½ pound grated Gruyère or Swiss
    cheese, divided
Freshly ground nutmeg to taste
Freshly ground pepper to taste

Preheat oven to 375°.

Place the sliced potatoes in a large saucepan; cover with milk and water. Add the garlic and salt. Bring the potatoes to a boil; reduce heat and simmer until tender.

Drain the potatoes and place half in a large baking dish. Cover with half the cream and half the cheese. Sprinkle with nutmeg and pepper to taste. Cover with remaining potatoes, cream and cheese; sprinkle top with nutmeg and pepper.

Bake for 1 hour, or until top is crispy and bubbly.

6 to 8 servings

CATALAN VEGETABLE PAELLA

4 tablespoons olive oil
1 large Bermuda onion, peeled,
    quartered and sliced
1 large red bell pepper, seeded
    and thinly sliced
1 large green bell pepper, seeded
    and thinly sliced
2 large cloves garlic, minced
1½ teaspoons paprika
1 tablespoon thyme leaves
1 medium zucchini, trimmed
    and cubed
4 large ripe tomatoes, seeded
    and chopped
Salt and freshly ground pepper
1¼ cups arborio rice
2 cups chicken stock

In a large, deep, 12-inch skillet, heat olive oil over medium heat; add onion and peppers. Reduce heat to medium-low and cook 20 minutes or until vegetables are crisp-tender. Add garlic, paprika, thyme, zucchini and tomatoes. Season with salt and pepper to taste.

Cover skillet and simmer 15 minutes. Stir in rice and chicken stock. Bring to boil, reduce heat to medium-low; cover and simmer 20 to 25 minutes, or until rice is tender. Taste and correct seasoning.

Garnish with finely minced fresh parsley.

4 to 6 servings

R I S O T T O   A L L A   M I L A N E S E

1 cup dried Italian porcini mushrooms
2 cups hot chicken broth
1 tablespoon saffron threads
6 tablespoons butter
2 tablespoons olive oil
2 large onions, chopped
Salt and freshly ground pepper
1 cup long grain converted rice
½ cup freshly grated Parmesan cheese

Presoak mushrooms in hot water to cover for several minutes. Drain and slice mushrooms.

Dissolve saffron in hot chicken broth.

In a large saucepan, melt butter, add olive oil and sauté onions until golden brown. Add mushrooms to onions and season with salt and pepper to taste. Cook 10 minutes. Add rice. When rice is coated with butter mixture, slowly add hot saffron chicken broth to cover. Stir until broth is absorbed. Cover rice with remaining broth. When rice is very moist, not dry, and tender to taste, add grated Parmesan cheese. Serve immediately with extra cheese.

Hint: Do not cover pan while cooking. Mixture should be "soupy not dry".

Variation: Add diced prosciutto, vegetables of choice. Be creative! Will serve four people as entree.

6 servings

H O P P I N '   J O H N

1 cup rice
2 cups chicken broth
5 slices bacon, diced
1 medium onion, diced
½ cup diced celery
1 16-ounce can black-eyed peas, drained
¼ cup barbecue sauce
¼ teaspoon Tabasco
2 cups cubed ham, cooked shrimp, crab, cooked chicken or smoked sausage, or a combination of any of the above
Salt and freshly ground pepper

Cook rice according to package directions, substituting chicken broth for water.

In a large saucepan, fry bacon; add onions and celery, cook until soft. Stir in rice, black-eyed peas, barbecue sauce, Tabasco, meat or seafood, salt to taste and a liberal amount of pepper.

Serve immediately, or if made ahead, bake in a covered baking dish at 325° for 45 minutes if ingredients are at room temperature; 55 to 60 minutes if refrigerated.

6 servings

TOASTED MEXICAN RICE

1/3 cup oil
2 1/4 cups raw long grain rice
2 slices onion
2 cloves garlic, halved
6 cups chicken broth
3/4 teaspoon salt
1 1/2 cups almonds, toasted
3/4 cup seedless raisins

Heat oil in a large saucepan; add rice, onion and garlic. Cook on medium low heat, stirring continuously until rice is golden. Add chicken broth and salt. Heat to boil and reduce heat.

Cover and simmer 40 minutes, or until liquid is absorbed. Stir in almonds and raisins.

12 servings

WILD RICE FORESTIERE

1 cup raw wild rice*
1 cup mild white cheddar cheese,
    shredded, divided
3/4 cup sliced mushrooms, sautéed
1/2 cup chopped onion
1/2 cup hot water
1/2 cup vegetable oil
2 16-ounce cans tomatoes, drained,
    reserving juices and chopped
1 teaspoon salt
1/4 teaspoon freshly ground pepper
1/2 teaspoon basil
1/4 cup sherry

Rinse rice and soak in water for at least 24 hours, preferably 48 hours.* Drain rice.

Preheat oven to 350°.

In a large bowl, combine 1/2 cup cheese, mushrooms, onion, hot water, oil, chopped tomatoes, 1 cup reserved juice, salt, pepper, basil and sherry. Pour into 2-quart baking dish.

Cover and bake for 1 hour, 45 minutes.

During last 5 minutes, sprinkle remaining cheese on top of casserole to melt.

* Raw unprocessed rice requires long soaking. Not all wild rices require prolonged soaking.

8 to 10 servings

RED PILAF

1 tablespoon butter, melted
1 medium onion, chopped
1 cup rice
2 cups water or chicken broth
1 tablespoon tomato paste
Salt and freshly ground pepper

In a heavy saucepan, sauté onion in melted butter until soft. Add rice and sauté for several minutes. Add chicken broth or water, tomato paste, salt and pepper to taste.

Cook covered over low heat for 20 minutes. Toss rice with fork and serve.

4 to 6 servings

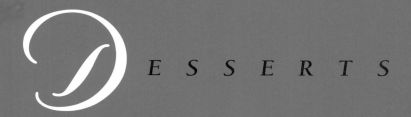

DESSERTS

Brownies and Dessert Bars

Chocolate Truffle Squares 188
Chocolate Date Bars 189
Coffee Liqueur Brownies 184
Fantasy Fudge Brownie Bars 186
Frost on the Pumpkin Bars 185
Frosterrific Brownies 183
Raspberry Almond Meringue Bars 185
Rhubarb Walnut Dessert 187
White Chocolate Brownies
    with Bittersweet Chocolate Chunks 183

Fruits

Flaming Bananas 209
Glazed Oranges in Cointreau 209
Strawberries Amaretto 208

Cakes

Black Forest Cherry Roll 189
Chocolate Zucchini Cake
    with Cinnamon Cream 195
Cinnamon Peach Cake 190
Coconut Sponge Cake 192
Flourless Chocolate Cake 197
Fresh Apple Cake with Brown Sugar Glaze 198
Frosted English Toffee Cake 193
German Apple Cake 190
Glazed Lemon Pound Cake 191
Ladyfingers 204
Layered Mocha Buttercream Cake 194
Nut Cream Cake 199
Simply Strawberry Shortcake 191
Superb Carrot Cake 192

Cookies

Honeyed Gingersnaps 195
Italian Anise Biscotti 197
Jan Hagel Dutch Cookies 193
Oatmeal Nut Cookies 198
Sour Cream Sugar Cookies 194
Swedish Spice Cookies 196

Pies

Blueberry Yogurt Pie 196
Chocolate Angel Pie 201
Frozen Lemon Cream Meringue Pie
    with Raspberry Coulis 200
Mystery Pecan Pie 201
Peach Cream Pie 202
Sour Cream Apple Pie Deluxe 199
Topsy-Turvy Apple Pie 200

Refrigerated Desserts

Apricot Bavarian
    with Raspberry-Apricot Sauce 205
Chilled Lemon Soufflé 203
Chocolate Zabaglione 204
Chocolate Charlotte 203
Flan de Queso 209
Mocha Mousse 202
White Chocolate Mousse 204

Cheesecakes

Almond Cheesecake with Fresh Nectarine 208
Country Inn Cheesecake 205
Delicioso Chocolate Grand Marnier Cheesecake
    with Raspberry Sauce 207

Tarts

Almond Toffee Tart 202
Edinburgh Currant Tarts 188
Fruit Tart Parisienne 187
Glistening Strawberry Tart
    with Whipped Cream 206
Pecan Lassies 206

Delicious Temptations

Apple Pecan Crisp 212
Apricot Rum Puffs 210
Apricot, Raisin and Walnut Strudel 212
Bread Pudding with Whiskey Cream
    or Vanilla Sauce 215
Chocolate Glazed Eclairs 216
Chocolate Sauce 215
Crème Anglaise 196
Galatobouriko (Custard Pastry) 213
Johnny Appleseed Soufflé 210
Lollipops & Roses Supreme 214
Megthalopita (Almond Pie) 213
Meringues with Lemon Curd 217
Pain Perdu 211
Paris Delight 211
Phyllo Baskets with Lemon Curd and Fruit 217

Frozen Desserts

Buster Bar Torte 219
Chocolate Truffle
    and Praline Ice Cream Bombe 218
Cinnamon Ice Cream 220
Coconut Sorbet 219
Intensely Raspberry Sorbet 219
Orange Chocolate Flower Pots 220
Pistachio Ice Cream 220
Sour Cherry Sorbet 220

FROSTERRIFIC BROWNIES

2 cups sugar
1 cup butter or margarine, softened
4 eggs, beaten slightly
½ cup half and half
1½ cups sifted all-purpose flour
½ teaspoon salt
3 1-ounce squares unsweetened
    chocolate, melted
1 cup chopped pecans or walnuts,
    optional

Frosting:
6 tablespoons butter or margarine,
    softened
1 teaspoon vanilla extract
2 cups powdered sugar
3 to 4 tablespoons half and half
1 1-ounce square semi-sweet
    chocolate, melted

Preheat oven to 325°. Grease and flour 9x13-inch baking pan.

Cream sugar and butter, add eggs and mix well. Add half and half. Mix flour and salt; add to sugar mixture. Blend in chocolate and nuts. Mix well. Pour into prepared pan.

Bake for 25 to 30 minutes. Cool.

Frosting: Cream butter and vanilla. Gradually add powdered sugar, beating thoroughly after each addition. Stir in half and half and beat until the frosting is of spreading consistency.

Frost the cooled brownies in pan and drizzle melted chocolate over frosting. Cut into bars.

These are sinfully rich and yummy!

2 dozen bars

WHITE CHOCOLATE BROWNIES WITH BITTERSWEET CHOCOLATE CHUNKS

8 tablespoons unsalted butter
10 ounces white chocolate, very
    finely chopped, divided
3 eggs, room temperature
Pinch of salt
½ cup sugar
1½ teaspoons vanilla extract
1 cup all-purpose flour
4 ounces (1 cup) bittersweet
    chocolate chunks
¾ cup chopped toasted pecans

Preheat oven to 350°. Lightly grease an 8-inch square pan.

Melt butter in a small heavy saucepan over low heat. Remove from heat, add half of the white chocolate and melt in the butter; set aside.

In a large mixing bowl, combine eggs and salt. Beat at high speed until foamy. Gradually add sugar and continue to beat for 2 to 3 minutes, or until light in color. Add white chocolate mixture, vanilla and flour. Beat until smooth. Stir in remaining white chocolate, bittersweet chocolate chunks and pecans. Pour batter into prepared pan.

Bake for exactly 35 minutes. Cool in pan. Cut into squares.

16 brownies

1 cup all-purpose flour
½ teaspoon baking powder
⅓ teaspoon salt
4 ounces semi-sweet chocolate
⅓ cup unsalted butter
¼ cup granulated sugar
½ cup light brown sugar
1 tablespoon instant coffee
1½ teaspoon vanilla
2 tablespoon coffee liqueur
1 egg
½ cup semi-sweet chocolate chips
    or toasted walnuts
2 tablespoons coffee liqueur

Glaze:
2 ounces semi-sweet chocolate
1 tablespoon unsalted butter
1 tablespoon whipping cream

Preheat oven to 350°. Line an 8x8-inch pan with foil and spray the foil with a non-stick spray.

In a small bowl sift the flour, baking powder and salt, set aside. Melt 4 ounces of chocolate in the microwave at 50% power, set aside to cool slightly.

In electric mixer bowl, beat butter and sugars until fluffy. Blend in instant coffee, vanilla and coffee liqueur. Blend in egg (mixture may look curdled). Stir in the melted chocolate and quickly fold in the flour mixture by hand, being careful not to over mix it. Fold in chocolate chips and spread batter evenly into prepared pan.

Bake for 25-28 minutes or until tester inserted one inch from the center comes out barely clean. The center will not look done; do not over bake. Cool brownies in pan.

When cooled, lift brownies out of pan and invert onto a flat surface. Carefully peel off foil. With a fork, prick entire surface of the brownies and sprinkle with remaining liqueur. Let stand for 30 minutes, invert and return to pan.

Glaze: Prepare glaze by combining all ingredients in a microwave safe bowl. Microwave at 50% power, stirring every 30 seconds until chocolate is melted and the glaze is smooth. Spread glaze evenly over the top and refrigerate for about an hour to let glaze harden and make cutting easier. Cut into 16 pieces, wipe knife after each cut.

16 brownies

R A S P B E R R Y   A L M O N D   M E R I N G U E   B A R S

¾ *cup butter or margarine, softened*
¾ *cup powdered sugar*
1½ *cups all-purpose flour*
¾ *cup seedless raspberry jam*
3 *egg whites*
¾ *cup sugar*
½ *cup shredded coconut*
1 *cup slivered blanched almonds*

Preheat oven to 350°. Grease 9x13-inch baking pan.

In a large bowl of electric mixer, cream butter and sugar, add flour; mix well. Press mixture into prepared pan.

Bake for 12 to 15 minutes or until lightly browned.

Spread jam over hot layer. Beat egg whites until foamy. Gradually add sugar, beating until stiff. Fold in coconut. Spread egg white mixture over jam. Sprinkle with almonds. Bake for 20 minutes. Cool and cut into squares. Store in metal tin with waxed paper between layers of bars.

48 bars

F R O S T   O N   T H E   P U M P K I N   B A R S

4 *eggs*
1⅔ *cups sugar*
1 *16-ounce can pumpkin*
1 *cup vegetable oil*
2 *cups sifted all-purpose flour*
2 *teaspoons baking powder*
2 *teaspoons cinnamon*
½ *teaspoon nutmeg*
¼ *teaspoon ground cloves*
¼ *teaspoon ginger*
1 *teaspoon salt*
1 *teaspoon baking soda*

Frosting:
1 *3-ounce package cream cheese,*
    softened
½ *cup butter, softened*
1 *teaspoon vanilla extract*
2 *cups powdered sugar*

Preheat oven to 350°.

Beat together in a large bowl the eggs, sugar, oil and pumpkin until light and fluffy. Sift flour, baking powder, cinnamon, nutmeg, ground cloves, ginger, salt and baking soda together; add to pumpkin and mix thoroughly. Spread batter evenly in a 15x10x1-inch baking pan.

Bake for 25 to 30 minutes, or until center springs back when lightly touched. Cool.

Frosting: In a small bowl, beat cream cheese and add butter. Mix until blended. Stir in vanilla. Add powdered sugar gradually, beating well after each addition.

Frost and cut into bars.

24 bars

FANTASY FUDGE BROWNIE BARS
(A.K.A. KILLER BROWNIES)

Brownie:

4 ounces unsweetened chocolate,
   broken into pieces

1¼ cups sugar

3 eggs

6 tablespoons unsalted butter,
   softened

2 teaspoons vanilla extract

½ cup all-purpose flour

Walnut Layer:

4 tablespoons unsalted butter

½ cup firmly packed light
   brown sugar

¼ cup sugar

2½ cups walnut halves

2 eggs

3 tablespoons all-purpose flour

1 tablespoon vanilla extract

Glaze:

½ cup unsalted butter

4 ounces semi-sweet chocolate

Butter a 9-inch square baking pan.

Brownies: Put chocolate in food processor work bowl with metal blade; add sugar and pulse to chop. Let machine run continuously until chocolate is as fine as the sugar. Add eggs, butter and vanilla and process 1 minute. Scrape sides of bowl. Add flour, pulse machine on and off 2 or 3 times until flour is mixed in.

To make brownies in electric mixer, melt chocolate in the top of double boiler over simmering water; cool. In a separate bowl, mix sugar, eggs and butter until light and fluffy. Stir in cooled chocolate, vanilla and flour.

Transfer the batter to prepared pan and spread evenly. Place in freezer at least one hour. This will keep the brownie and walnut layers separate.

Preheat oven to 325°.

Walnut Layer: Melt the butter in a small pan. Add both sugars and cook over high heat, stirring often until sugar is completely dissolved, about 2 minutes. Transfer to food processor work bowl and add walnuts, eggs, flour and vanilla (chop walnuts if using electric mixer). Mix just until blended.

Remove brownie layer from freezer and spread walnut mixture evenly on top.

Bake for 45 minutes, or until a tester, inserted in the center, comes out with moist but not wet crumbs. Transfer to wire rack and cool completely.

Glaze: Melt butter and chocolate in top of double boiler. Let cool until thickened slightly, then pour over cooled brownies. Refrigerate at least 4 hours or up to 4 days before serving. Cut into squares and serve chilled. May be frozen, if wrapped well, for several months.

3 dozen

RHUBARB WALNUT DESSERT

1 cup all-purpose flour
2 tablespoons sugar
½ cup butter or margarine
¼ cup finely chopped walnuts
    or cashews

¾ cup sugar
3 tablespoons flour
3 cups fresh rhubarb, finely chopped

3 egg yolks, slightly beaten
⅓ cup milk or half and half
½ teaspoon vanilla extract

3 egg whites
⅓ cup sugar

Preheat oven to 350°.

Crust: Combine flour and sugar, cut in butter with pastry cutter until crumbly. Stir in chopped nuts. Press into 9x9x2-inch baking pan.
Bake for 20 minutes.

Filling: Combine sugar and flour; stir in the rhubarb. In another bowl, combine egg yolks, milk and vanilla. Add to rhubarb mixture. Spoon over hot crust. Return to oven and continue baking for 35 to 40 minutes.
In a small bowl, beat egg whites until soft peaks form. Gradually add sugar, beating until stiff peaks form. Spread over hot rhubarb. Return to oven.
Bake for an additional 12 to 15 minutes, or until meringue is golden. Let cool and cut into 9 squares.

9 servings

FRUIT TART PARISIENNE

French Pastry Dough:
1¼ cups all-purpose flour
12 tablespoons cold unsalted
    margarine
1 tablespoon sugar
2 to 3 tablespoons ice water

Fruit Filling:
1 10-ounce package frozen
    raspberries, thawed
1 tablespoon rum
1 tablespoon unflavored gelatin
    softened in 1 tablespoon water
3 to 5 fresh peaches (or any other
    fresh fruit in season), peeled
    and sliced

Preheat oven to 350°.

French Pastry Dough: Put flour into work bowl of food processor with metal blade. Cut the margarine into small pieces and add with sugar to flour. Start processing while adding just enough water that pastry holds together. *Be sure not to over-process.* Form dough into a ball and place into a plastic bag. Flatten and roll dough in plastic bag. Remove from bag and carefully place in tart pan. Fold edges into pan. Prick edges and bottom of tart. Cover with piece of wax paper and pastry weights. Dried beans may be used for weights.
Bake for 15 minutes. Remove weights. Increase oven temperature to 400° and bake an additional 5 minutes.

Fruit Filling: Puree raspberries and rum in food processor. Strain to remove seeds. Heat raspberries, gelatin and water until thick. Set aside until cool. Paint raspberry mixture on bottom of cooled crust. Layer sliced fruit, overlapping slices. Brush remaining puree mixture over fruit, filling in between the fruit slices.

6 servings

CHOCOLATE TRUFFLE SQUARES

1 pound semi-sweet chocolate bits
   or squares
¾ cup butter
1 cup sifted powdered sugar
1 tablespoon all-purpose flour
4 eggs, separated, room temperature
1 teaspoon vanilla extract
1 cup sour cream

Preheat oven to 375°. Butter an 8-inch square baking dish.

    In a saucepan, over low heat, melt chocolate and butter. Remove from heat. Blend in sugar and flour, stirring constantly. Stir in egg yolks, one at a time, thoroughly incorporating. Add vanilla.

    Beat egg whites until stiff and gently fold into chocolate mixture. Remove one cup of chocolate mixture and mix with sour cream. Pour remaining mixture into prepared baking dish. Top with sour cream mixture.

    Bake for 25 minutes. Do not over bake; center will not be set. Chill at least 4 hours. Cut in 2-inch squares.

16 bars

EDINBURGH CURRANT TARTS

Pastry:
3 cups sifted all-purpose flour
1 cup butter or margarine
1 teaspoon salt
Ice water to moisten

Filling:
½ cup butter or margarine
1½ cups packed dark brown sugar
3 eggs, well beaten
1 teaspoon vanilla extract
1 cup currants

Preheat oven to 450°.

    Pastry: In work bowl of food processor, combine flour, butter and salt. While processing, add water as necessary to moisten dough and form a ball. Roll pastry on a floured surface, and cut with a 2 or 3-inch round cookie cutter. Place pastry rounds in muffin pans to form tart shells.

    Filling: In a mixing bowl, cream butter and sugar. Add eggs, vanilla and currants to butter mixture. Spoon 1 teaspoon mixture in each large tart shell or ½ teaspoon in each mini-tart shell. Do not use more.

    Bake for 10 minutes for large and 6 to 7 minutes for mini-tarts. Reduce heat to 350° and bake until done, about 10 minutes (6 to 7 minutes for mini-tarts). Store in covered container.

    Reheat to freshen.

100 year old recipe from Scotland.

32 tarts

BLACK FOREST CHERRY ROLL

2 16-ounce cans red pitted cherries,
    drained and marinated in
    ¼ cup kirsch

Cake:
Powdered sugar
3 eggs
1 cup sugar
¼ cup plus 2 tablespoons milk
1 teaspoon vanilla extract
1¾ cups biscuit or baking mix

Filling/Frosting:
2 cups whipping cream, whipped
3 tablespoons powdered sugar

Preheat oven to 375°. Butter a 10x15-inch jelly roll pan; line with aluminum foil. Butter foil.

Spread clean dish towel on counter and sprinkle entire surface with powdered sugar.

Cake: In a large bowl of electric mixer, beat eggs until thick, fluffy and pale. Add sugar and mix well. Add milk and vanilla and mix well. Add baking mix and mix until just blended; do not over beat! Pour batter into prepared pan and spread evenly.

Bake for 15 minutes, or until cake springs back when gently touched in center with finger. Remove from oven and immediately turn out of pan onto sugared dishtowel. Peel off foil, being careful not to burn fingers. Cool for 5 minutes. Then roll up with towel and cool completely.

Filling/Frosting: In mixing bowl, combine whipped cream and powdered sugar.

To assemble: Drain marinated cherries. Unroll cake. Spread half filling mixture on cake then half the cherries. Carefully roll cake without the towel, jelly roll fashion. Place on a serving dish and frost the roll with the remaining frosting. Place the remaining cherries in a row down center of frosted roll. Keep chilled until ready to serve.

8 to 10 servings

CHOCOLATE DATE BARS

1 8-ounce package dates
1 cup hot water
1 teaspoon baking soda
1 cup shortening
1 cup sugar
1 teaspoon vanilla extract
2 eggs
2 tablespoons cocoa
2 cups sifted all-purpose flour
1 12-ounce package chocolate chips
½ cup chopped walnuts or pecans

Preheat oven to 350°.

Chop dates and combine with water and soda; let mixture cool.

Cream sugar, shortening and vanilla until light and fluffy. Add eggs and beat well. Add sifted flour and cocoa; mix thoroughly. Stir in date mixture, chocolate chips and nuts. Spread in ungreased 15½x10x1-inch jelly roll pan.

Bake for 20 minutes.

36 bars

GERMAN APPLE CAKE

2 eggs
1 cup vegetable oil
1 teaspoon vanilla extract
2 cups sugar
2 cups all-purpose flour
2 teaspoons cinnamon
1 teaspoon baking soda
½ teaspoon salt
4 cups thinly sliced apples
½ to 1 cup chopped walnuts

Frosting:
2 tablespoons butter, softened
1 8-ounce package cream cheese,
   softened
1 teaspoon vanilla extract
1½ cups powdered sugar

Preheat oven to 350°.

In a large bowl, beat eggs by hand; add oil and vanilla. Blend in sugar. Sift sugar, flour, cinnamon, baking soda and salt together and add to mixture. Add apples and walnuts. Spoon into 9x13-inch baking pan.

Bake for 45 to 60 minutes, or until cake tester comes out clean. Remove from oven and frost while hot.

Frosting: In a small bowl, cream butter, cream cheese and vanilla. Mix in powdered sugar and blend until smooth. Frost cake.

24 squares

CINNAMON PEACH CAKE

3 cups fresh peaches, peeled
   and sliced
5 tablespoons brown sugar
5 teaspoons cinnamon
2 cups sugar
3 cups all-purpose flour
1 tablespoon baking powder
1 teaspoon salt
1 cup vegetable oil
4 eggs
¼ cup orange juice
1 tablespoon vanilla extract

Preheat oven to 375°. Grease a 10-inch bundt pan.

Toss peaches with brown sugar and cinnamon; set aside.

Sift sugar, flour, baking powder and salt together into a large bowl. Add the oil, eggs, orange juice and vanilla. Mix with a wooden spoon until well blended. Batter will be very thick.

Layer ⅓ of the batter into pan, ½ of the fruit, ⅓ of the batter, remaining fruit, and remaining batter on top. Do not let fruit touch sides of pan.

Bake for 50 minutes. Cool in pan before removing. Sprinkle with powdered sugar just before serving.

Variation: Substitute 3 cups peeled and coarsely chopped apples for fresh peaches.

12 to 14 servings

GLAZED LEMON POUND CAKE

1 cup vegetable shortening
½ cup butter or margarine
3 cups sugar
6 eggs
3 cups all-purpose flour
¼ teaspoon baking soda
1 cup buttermilk
1½ teaspoons lemon extract

Lemon Glaze:
½ cup sugar
2 tablespoons fresh lemon juice

Preheat oven to 350°. Butter a 10-inch bundt or tube pan.

Cream shortening and butter with electric mixer. Add sugar gradually, beating well. Add the eggs, one at a time, beating well after each addition. Combine flour and baking soda in a separate bowl and add to creamed mixture alternately with buttermilk, mixing well. Add lemon extract. Pour into prepared pan.

Bake for 1 hour, 10 minutes. Do not open oven while cake is baking. Remove cake from oven. Cool 10 minutes. Remove from pan and place on serving platter.

Lemon Glaze: Mix sugar and lemon juice. Microwave for 30 seconds. When sugar is dissolved, drizzle over the "warm" cake. Cool.

Slice and serve plain or with fresh strawberries or blueberries.

Variation: Add ¼ cup of poppyseeds to batter before baking.

10 to 12 servings

SIMPLY STRAWBERRY SHORTCAKE

4 cups all-purpose flour
½ cup sugar
2 tablespoons plus 2 teaspoons
    baking powder
½ teaspoon salt
⅛ teaspoon nutmeg
1 cup butter
4 egg yolks
1 cup milk
3 egg whites, beaten
6 to 8 tablespoons sugar
2 quarts strawberries, sliced
    and sweetened
2 cups whipping cream, whipped and
    sweetened with 3 tablespoons
    powdered sugar

Preheat oven to 450°. Butter a 12x15-inch jelly roll pan.

In food processor work bowl, process flour, sugar, baking powder, salt and nutmeg with butter. Process until crumbly. Blend yolks and milk in a small bowl and add to processor. Pulse until just blended. Pat dough into pan. Brush generously with egg whites and sprinkle with sugar.

Bake for 12 minutes or until golden. Cool in pan. Cut into squares. Top with strawberries and a dollop of whipped cream. Recipe can be cut in half.

Variation: Substitute other fresh fruits for the strawberries.

24 shortcakes

COCONUT SPONGE CAKE

10 egg whites
1½ teaspoons cream of tartar
½ teaspoon salt
1¼ cups sugar, divided
1 cup sifted cake flour
10 egg yolks, divided
1 teaspoon vanilla extract

Frosting:
½ cup milk, scalded
½ cup powdered sugar
¼ cup butter
Toasted coconut

Preheat oven to 350°.

Beat egg whites until foamy, then add cream of tartar and salt; beat until stiff. Fold in ¾ cup sugar and cake flour. Beat 7 egg yolks (reserve 3 egg yolks for frosting) with vanilla and ½ cup sugar. Fold into egg white mixture. Pour mixture into angel food cake pan.

Bake for 35 to 40 minutes.

Frosting: Mix milk, powdered sugar and egg yolks in saucepan. Cook over medium heat until thickened. Cool and add butter.

Frost cooled cake, then cover with toasted coconut.

SUPERB CARROT CAKE

1½ cups all-purpose flour
1½ teaspoons baking soda
½ teaspoon salt
2 eggs
1½ cups sugar
¾ cup corn oil
1½ teaspoons vanilla extract
1½ teaspoons cinnamon
½ cup crushed pineapple, drained
¾ cup chopped toasted walnuts
¾ cup shredded coconut
4 to 6 carrots, peeled, cooked, and
    roughly pureed to make ¾ cup

Frosting:
4 ounces cream cheese,
    room temperature
4 tablespoons unsalted butter,
    softened
½ teaspoon vanilla extract
1 or 2 tablespoons fresh lemon juice
1½ cups sifted powdered sugar

Preheat oven to 350°. Butter and flour a 9-inch square cake pan with 2-inch sides.

Cake: Stir flour, baking soda and salt together in a small bowl; set aside. Beat eggs until pale yellow, add sugar and beat well. Add corn oil, vanilla and cinnamon. Stir in pineapple, walnuts, coconut, carrots and dry ingredients. Stir to blend well without overbeating. Pour into prepared pan.

Bake for 50 minutes, or until cake has pulled away from sides of the pan. Cool and cut in half to make two rectangular layers.

Frosting: Beat cream cheese with butter. Add vanilla, lemon juice and powdered sugar. Beat until fluffy and spreadable. Spread frosting on middle and sides and set top layer on cake. Sprinkle top with additional powdered sugar.

FROSTED ENGLISH TOFFEE CAKE

5¾-ounce chocolate covered
    toffee bars
2½ cups sifted all-purpose flour
1 teaspoon double-acting baking
    powder
1 teaspoon baking soda
1 teaspoon instant coffee
½ teaspoon salt
1½ cups brown sugar, firmly packed
1 cup dairy sour cream
½ cup butter or margarine
1 unbeaten egg
2 unbeaten egg yolks
1 teaspoon vanilla extract
½ cup water

Frosting:
¾ cup sugar
¼ cup light corn syrup
2 tablespoons water
2 unbeaten egg whites
¼ teaspoon cream of tartar
¼ teaspoon salt
1 teaspoon vanilla extract

Preheat oven to 375°.

Crush toffee bars between sheets of waxed paper and reserve ¼ cup for a garnish for the frosting. Mix flour, baking powder, baking soda, instant coffee and salt; set aside.

In a large bowl, combine brown sugar, sour cream, butter, egg, egg yolks and vanilla. Beat for 1½ minutes at lowest speed of electric mixer, then beat at low speed. Add dry ingredients and water and beat 1½ minutes. Turn into two 8-inch square pans. Sprinkle candy mixture on top.

Bake for 25 to 30 minutes. Cool, frost and cut into bars.

Frosting: Heat, in top of double boiler over simmering water, sugar, corn syrup, water, egg whites, cream of tartar and salt. Beat with rotary beater until mixture holds in peaks. Remove from the heat, add vanilla and beat until mixture is of spreading consistency.

18 to 24 servings

JAN HAGEL DUTCH COOKIES

1 cup sugar
1 cup butter, softened
1 egg, separated
2 cups all-purpose flour
½ teaspoon cinnamon
½ cup sliced almonds

Preheat oven to 350°. Butter a cookie sheet.

Cream sugar, butter and egg yolk. Add flour and cinnamon. Roll out onto cookie sheet. Brush with a beaten egg white and sprinkle with sliced almonds.

Bake for 30 minutes. Cut into any size rectangular cookies you desire when slightly cooled.

So simple and so good!

3 to 4 dozen cookies

LAYERED MOCHA BUTTERCREAM CAKE

Cake:
2 cups sugar
2 eggs
1 cup sour milk
1 cup cocoa powder
1 cup margarine
2 teaspoons baking soda
1 teaspoon salt
2 teaspoons vanilla extract
3 cups all-purpose flour
1 cup hot coffee

Buttercream Frosting:
2 tablespoons instant espresso
 or coffee
1 teaspoon boiling water
6 egg yolks
¾ cup sugar
½ cup corn syrup
1 cup butter, softened
3 tablespoons coffee-flavored liqueur
5 ounces semi-sweet chocolate,
 melted

Preheat oven to 350°. Grease and flour 3 9-inch round cake pans.

Cake: In a large bowl of electric mixer, combine sugar, eggs, milk, cocoa, margarine, baking soda, salt, vanilla, flour and hot coffee and beat until smooth. Divide batter equally between 3 prepared pans.

Bake for 28 minutes. Cake is done when tester inserted in center of cake is dry when removed. Remove from oven and cool on rack.

Buttercream Frosting: Combine coffee and water; set aside. In a large mixing bowl, beat egg yolks until light in color.

In a small saucepan, combine sugar and corn syrup. Stir constantly until sugar mixture boils. Immediately remove from heat and pour in glass container to stop cooking.

Add syrup to egg yolks in a steady stream while mixing with electric mixer. Continue beating until completely cool. Gradually beat in butter. Stir liqueur and coffee mixture into melted chocolate. Slowly add to frosting. Frost cooled cake.

12 servings

SOUR CREAM SUGAR COOKIES

½ cup butter
1 cup sugar, softened
1 egg
1 teaspoon vanilla extract
3¼ cups sifted all-purpose flour
½ teaspoon baking soda
1 teaspoon baking powder
¾ teaspoon salt
¼ teaspoon nutmeg
½ cup sour cream

Granulated sugar

Preheat oven to 425°.

Cream butter and sugar until light and fluffy. Add egg and vanilla; beat well. Sift flour, baking soda, baking powder, salt and nutmeg together. Add to creamed mixture, alternately with sour cream, mixing until smooth after each addition. Roll out dough and cut with cookie cutters. Sprinkle with sugar. Place on cookie sheets.

Bake for 10 minutes.

Old fashioned and good!

4 dozen cookies

CHOCOLATE ZUCCHINI CAKE
WITH CINNAMON CREAM

3/4 cup all-purpose flour
1/4 teaspoon baking powder
1/4 teaspoon baking soda
1 teaspoon salt
1/4 teaspoon cinnamon
4 eggs, room temperature
3 cups sugar
1 1/2 cups vegetable oil
3 1-ounce squares unsweetened
    chocolate, melted and cooled
1 1/2 teaspoons vanilla extract
1/2 teaspoon almond extract
3 cups coarsely grated zucchini,
    drained and squeezed dry
1 cup chopped toasted walnuts
1/2 cup chopped dates

Cinnamon Cream:
1 cup whipping cream
1/4 cup powdered sugar
1/4 teaspoon vanilla extract
1/2 teaspoon cinnamon

Preheat oven to 350°. Grease and flour a 10-inch bundt or tube pan.

Sift together flour, baking powder, baking soda, salt and cinnamon. Set aside.

Beat eggs in a large bowl until frothy. Gradually beat in sugar and oil. Add chocolate, vanilla and almond extract. Fold in dry ingredients, then zucchini, nuts and dates. Pour into pan and bake 1 hour, 15 minutes or until tester comes out clean.

Let stand inverted on wire rack 20 minutes. Remove from pan and cool completely. Serve with Cinnamon Cream.

Cinnamon Cream: Beat whipping cream, powdered sugar, vanilla and cinnamon until stiff peaks form.

10 to 12 servings

HONEYED GINGERSNAPS

1/2 cup plus 2 tablespoons sugar,
    divided
2 1/4 cups all-purpose flour
3/4 cup butter or margarine, melted
1/4 cup unsulphured molasses
1/4 cup honey
2 teaspoons baking soda
2 teaspoons ground ginger
1/2 teaspoon ground cinnamon
1/4 teaspoon salt
1 egg

Preheat oven to 350°.

In a large bowl, combine 1/2 cup sugar with flour, butter, molasses, honey, baking soda, ginger, cinnamon, salt and egg. Mix until well blended.

Place 2 tablespoons sugar in a small bowl. Shape dough into balls the size of walnuts and roll in sugar. Place on ungreased cookie sheets.

Bake for 8 to 10 minutes. Cool on racks.

CRÈME ANGLAISE

2 cups milk
⅓ vanilla bean
7 egg yolks
¾ cup sugar

In a saucepan, boil milk and vanilla bean. In a bowl, whisk yolks and sugar until well blended. Pour hot milk over yolks, stirring constantly. Put back on heat, stirring constantly, until slightly thickened. Cool immediately.

BLUEBERRY YOGURT PIE

24 ounces nonfat vanilla yogurt
3 tablespoons all-purpose flour
3 tablespoons light brown sugar
1 8-ounce carton egg substitute
1 9-inch graham cracker pie crust,
    unbaked
2½ cups blueberries
½ cup light brown sugar

At least 12 hours before baking, strain the whey from the yogurt by placing yogurt in cheesecloth over strainer in bowl.
    Preheat oven to 400°.
    Combine strained yogurt with flour and sugar in a mixing bowl; add egg substitute and beat well. Spoon half mixture into graham cracker crust.
    Combine blueberries with ½ cup brown sugar in separate bowl and mix until coated. Spread over yogurt mixture. Top with remaining yogurt mixture.
    Bake for 25 minutes. Chill several hours before serving. Can be prepared a day before serving.

A low cholesterol dessert

One 9-inch pie

SWEDISH SPICE COOKIES
(PEPPAR-KAKOR)

¾ cup butter or margarine, softened
1 cup brown sugar
1 egg
¼ cup dark molasses
2¼ cups all-purpose flour
2 teaspoons baking soda
1 teaspoon ginger
½ teaspoon cloves
1 teaspoon cinnamon
Butter
Granulated sugar

Preheat oven to 375°. Grease a cookie sheet.
    In a large bowl of electric mixer, cream butter and sugar. Add egg and molasses.
    Sift flour, baking soda, ginger, cloves and cinnamon together. Stir into butter mixture batter. Chill for 1 hour.
    Make small balls, the size of walnuts. Flatten with bottom of flat glass which has been greased with butter and dipped in granulated sugar.
    Bake for 9 minutes.

50 cookies

FLOURLESS CHOCOLATE CAKE

9 ounces semi-sweet chocolate
1 ounce unsweetened
    chocolate
½ cup powdered sugar
1½ teaspoons cornstarch
4 eggs
½ tablespoon vanilla extract
2 tablespoons coffee liqueur
1½ cups whipping cream

Preheat oven to 350°. Butter and flour 10-inch springform pan and line with waxed paper.

Melt chocolates, in top of double boiler over simmering water. When melted remove from heat and let cool.

In a medium bowl, sift sugar and cornstarch.

In another bowl, beat eggs, vanilla and coffee liqueur. Add sugar mixture and beat until thick, foamy and tripled in volume. Blend a little egg mixture into cooled chocolate. Mix well, then fold in remaining egg mixture. Whip cream and lightly fold into chocolate. Pour into prepared pan.

Bake for 1 hour or until tester comes out clean. Turn off oven, leaving door partially open and let cake cool in oven.

Sprinkle with powdered sugar when ready to serve. Can also serve with Crème Anglaise (page 196).

12 to 16 servings

ITALIAN ANISE BISCOTTI

6 eggs
1 cup sugar
1 cup vegetable oil
5 cups all-purpose flour
    (more if necessary)
6 teaspoons baking powder
2 to 2½ teaspoons anise seed
1 small bottle anise extract

Preheat oven to 350°.

Beat eggs well in a large mixing bowl with an electric mixer. Add sugar slowly to eggs, beating well. Add oil a little at a time. Beat well after each addition.

Sift flour with baking powder. Add anise seeds to flour mixture. Add anise extract to egg mixture. Add flour a little at a time to the eggs; mixing well after each addition for a medium dough.

Divide dough into 6 portions, rolling each portion into a long narrow loaf. Place on cookie sheet.

Bake for 8 to 10 minutes, or until the bottom is brown. Increase oven temperature to 400°. Cook 5 minutes.

Slice each loaf on a diagonal in ½-inch slices. Place each slice on cookie sheet. Toast one side for about 6 minutes in the oven, watch carefully and toast to a golden brown. Remove from the oven and turn over and toast other side. Remove from oven and cool. Pack in containers.

FRESH APPLE CAKE
WITH BROWN SUGAR GLAZE

Cake:
1½ cups vegetable oil
2 cups sugar
3 eggs
3 cups all-purpose flour
1 teaspoon baking soda
2 teaspoons cinnamon
½ teaspoon nutmeg
½ teaspoon salt
3 cups diced tart apples
1 cup black walnuts (regular walnuts
    may be substituted)
2 teaspoons vanilla extract

Glaze:
2 tablespoons butter, softened
¼ cup packed brown sugar
2 tablespoons granulated sugar
2 tablespoons whipping cream
¼ teaspoon vanilla extract

Preheat oven to 325°. Butter and flour a 9-inch or 10-inch tube pan.

Combine oil and sugar in a large bowl. Add eggs, one at a time, beating well after each addition. Sift flour, baking soda, cinnamon, nutmeg and salt into the oil-egg mixture and combine thoroughly. Add apples and walnuts. Mix well by hand, then stir in vanilla. Pour batter in prepared pan.

Bake for 1 hour, 15 minutes, or until tester comes out clean.

Glaze: In a heavy pan, combine butter, brown sugar, granulated sugar and whipping cream. Boil for 1 minute. Remove from heat, add vanilla and spoon over the warm cake.

Let cake cool in pan before serving.

10 to 12 servings

OATMEAL NUT COOKIES

½ cup margarine, at room
    temperature
½ cup unsalted butter,
    room temperature
1 cup dark brown sugar,
    firmly packed
1 cup granulated sugar
2 eggs, lightly beaten
2 tablespoons milk
2 teaspoons vanilla
2 cups sifted unbleached flour
1 teaspoon baking powder
1 teaspoon baking soda
1 teaspoon salt
2 cups quick cooking oats
1 cup raisins
1 cup chopped pecans

Cream the margarine, butter, both sugars in a large mixer bowl until light and fluffy. Add eggs, milk and vanilla; beat until blended.

Sift the flour, baking powder, baking soda, and salt together. Add to butter mixture. Stir just until blended. Stir in the oats. Fold in raisins and pecans.

Refrigerate at least 1 hour.

Preheat oven to 350°. Grease cookie sheets.

Shape dough into balls using rounded teaspoon. Place on cookie sheets. Flatten slightly.

Bake for 8 to 10 minutes or until edges are lightly brown. Cool at least 10 minutes on cookie sheet. Remove and let cool. Cookies can be frozen.

Variation: Chocolate chips may be substituted for the raisins.

50 cookies

NUT CREAM CAKE

7 eggs, room temperature, divided
¾ cup sugar, divided
1 cup finely ground almonds
½ cup dry bread crumbs
1 teaspoon all-purpose flour

Frosting:
1½ cups whipping cream
1 tablespoon powdered sugar
1 teaspoon vanilla extract

1½ cups toasted sliced almonds

Preheat oven to 300°. Butter and flour two 8-inch cake pans.

Separate 6 eggs. Beat egg yolks plus one whole egg until pale. Add ½ cup sugar and beat until creamy and fluffy. Blend in ground almonds and bread crumbs. Beat 6 egg whites in a separate bowl until frothy. Continue beating and slowly add ¼ cup sugar. Beat until stiff but not dry. Sprinkle flour over egg/nut mixture. Add egg whites and fold until whites are well incorporated. Pour into pans.

Bake for 45 minutes or until cake shrinks away from the sides of pan. Cool and remove from pans.

Frosting: Whip whipping cream until fluffy. Add powdered sugar and vanilla. Put a thick layer of cream in between layers of cake and then frost all over. Sprinkle with toasted almonds and gently press onto sides of cake. Refrigerate until ready to serve.

8 to 10 servings

SOUR CREAM APPLE PIE DELUXE

1 9-inch unbaked pie crust
¾ cup sugar
2 tablespoons all-purpose flour
⅛ teaspoon salt
1 cup sour cream
½ teaspoon vanilla extract
1 egg, well beaten
2 cups apples, peeled and chopped

Topping:
⅓ cup sugar
⅓ cup all-purpose flour
1 teaspoon cinnamon
¼ cup butter

Preheat oven to 425°.

In a bowl, combine sugar, flour and salt; add sour cream, vanilla and egg; fold in apples and spoon into pie crust.

Bake for 15 minutes; reduce heat to 350° and bake an additional 30 minutes.

Topping: Blend sugar, flour, cinnamon and butter until crumbly and sprinkle over top of apples. Return pie to oven and bake 15 minutes more.

Refrigerate at once.

8 servings

FROZEN LEMON CREAM MERINGUE PIE
WITH RASPBERRY COULIS

Crust:
4 tablespoons butter, melted
1⅓ cups crushed vanilla wafer
*   crumbs*
½ cup finely chopped toasted pecans

Filling:
1 14-ounce can sweetened
*   condensed milk*
3 eggs yolks, beaten
Juice and zest of 1 lemon
1 cup whipping cream, whipped

Meringue:
3 egg whites, room temperature
4 tablespoons sugar

Raspberry Coulis:
1 10-ounce package frozen
*   raspberries thawed, or 1 cup*
*   fresh raspberries*
2 tablespoons superfine sugar
2 tablespoons raspberry liqueur,
*   optional*

Crust: Mix melted butter, crumbs and pecans. Press firmly on bottom and sides of a buttered 8-inch pie or cake pan.

Filling: Whisk milk, eggs, lemon juice and zest in a large bowl. Fold in whipped cream. Spoon into crust.

Meringue: Beat egg whites until foamy. Gradually add sugar and beat until stiff but not dry. Spread over lemon filling. Freeze. As soon as pie is solid, wrap in foil or plastic wrap and return to freezer until serving time.

Raspberry Coulis: Puree raspberries, sugar and liqueur. Strain. Refrigerate.

Preheat oven to 450°.
Remove pie from freezer and place in oven for 4 minutes to brown meringue. Watch closely.
Puddle raspberry coulis on dessert plate. Place a serving of pie on sauce and garnish with a lemon twist.

TOPSY-TURVY APPLE PIE

2 9-inch unbaked pie crusts
¼ cup butter, softened
½ cup pecans halves
½ cup brown sugar
5 large tart apples (6 cups) peeled,
*   cored, sliced*
1 tablespoon fresh lemon juice
1 tablespoon flour
½ cup sugar
½ teaspoon cinnamon
½ teaspoon nutmeg
Salt

Preheat oven to 400°. Spread butter evenly on bottom and side of a 9-inch pie plate.
Press nuts, rounded side down into butter on bottom. Pat brown sugar evenly over nuts. Place pie crust over sugar. Sprinkle apples with lemon juice. Combine flour, sugar, cinnamon, nutmeg and dash of salt. Toss with apples. Turn into pie plate and spread evenly. Place remaining crust on top and prick top.
Bake for 50 minutes. Cool for 5 minutes.
Place serving plate on top of pie and invert. Carefully remove pie plate. Serve warm or cool.

6 servings

M Y S T E R Y   P E C A N   P I E

1 8-ounce package cream cheese,
    softened
⅓ cup sugar
¼ teaspoon salt
1 teaspoon vanilla extract
1 egg
1 9-inch unbaked pie crust
1¼ cups chopped pecans

Topping:
3 eggs
¼ cup sugar
1 cup light or dark corn syrup
1 teaspoon vanilla extract

Preheat oven to 375°.

In a small bowl of electric mixer, combine cream cheese, sugar, salt, vanilla and 1 egg. Beat at medium speed until well blended. Spread in bottom of pie crust pan. Sprinkle with pecans.

Topping: In a small bowl, combine 3 eggs, sugar, corn syrup and vanilla. Beat at medium speed just until blended. Gently pour topping over pecan mixture.

Bake for 35 to 40 minutes, or until center is firm to touch. Refrigerate leftovers.

8 servings

C H O C O L A T E   A N G E L   P I E

Shell:
2 egg whites
¼ teaspoon cream of tartar
½ cup sugar
3 tablespoons chopped walnuts
    or pecans

Filling:
½ cup butter, softened
¾ cup sugar
1½ ounces unsweetened chocolate,
    melted and cooled
1 teaspoon vanilla extract
2 eggs
1 cup whipping cream
1 tablespoon Amaretto or
    Crème de Cacao

Garnish:
½ ounce shaved semi-sweet
    chocolate

Preheat oven to 275°. Grease 9-inch glass pie plate.

Shell: Beat egg whites with cream of tartar until soft peaks form. Beat in sugar gradually until very stiff. Spread in prepared pie plate. Sprinkle with nuts.
Bake for 1 hour. Cool.

Filling: Cream butter. Beat in sugar gradually. Add chocolate, vanilla and eggs, one at a time. Beat well. Pour into cooled shell. Whip cream and add liqueur. Spread cream over chocolate mixture; sprinkle with shaved chocolate. Chill at least 4 hours.

8 servings

PEACH CREAM PIE

1 9-inch unbaked pie crust
3 cups peeled and sliced
    fresh peaches
2 eggs
1 cup sugar
¼ cup sifted all-purpose flour
⅛ teaspoon salt
½ teaspoon cinnamon
1 teaspoon vanilla extract
1 cup whipping cream

Preheat oven to 375°.

Layer sliced peaches in crust. Beat eggs slightly. Blend in sugar, flour, salt and cinnamon. Stir in vanilla and cream. Pour over peaches.

Bake for 1 hour, or until tester inserted in middle comes out clean.

Serve warm.

8 servings

ALMOND TOFFEE TART

Crust:
2 cups all-purpose flour
3 tablespoons sugar
¾ cup butter
2 egg yolks

Glazed Filling:
1½ cups whipping cream
1½ cups sugar
½ teaspoon grated orange zest
Pinch of salt
2 cups sliced almonds
¼ teaspoon almond extract

Preheat oven to 325°.

Crust: Mix flour, sugar, butter and yolks in food processor until crumbly. Press onto bottom of an ungreased 12-inch tart pan with removable bottom.

Bake for 12 minutes or until golden brown.

Glazed Filling: Mix cream, sugar, zest, salt, almonds and almond extract in a large bowl. Pour into crust and spread to cover.

Bake for 35 minutes. Serve in wedges.

Variation: Drizzle tart with ½ cup melted semi-sweet chocolate.

MOCHA MOUSSE

4 1-ounce squares semi-sweet
    chocolate
4 tablespoons coffee or amaretto
4 jumbo eggs, separated

Garnish:
Whipped cream
Chocolate curls

Melt chocolate with coffee in double boiler over simmering water. Remove from heat.

Beat yolks into chocolate one by one.

In a large bowl, beat egg whites until stiff. Fold into yolk mixture. Spoon into stemmed glasses and refrigerate.

Garnish with whipped cream and chocolate curls.

4 servings

C H I L L E D   L E M O N   S O U F F L É

1 envelope unflavored gelatin
½ cup cold water
4 eggs, separated
Juice of 2 fresh lemons
1 cup sugar, divided
½ teaspoon salt
Grated zest of 1 lemon
1 cup whipping cream, whipped

Garnish:
Whipped cream
Lime slices

Sprinkle gelatin over cold water to soften. Combine egg yolks, lemon juice, ½ cup sugar and salt in the top of a double boiler over simmering water, stirring constantly until mixture has thickened and resembles custard. Remove from heat; stir in gelatin until dissolved. Add lemon zest. Cool.

Beat egg whites until soft peaks are formed. Gradually beat in the remaining ½ cup sugar and continue beating until shiny stiff peaks are formed.

Vigorously whisk about a third of the egg whites into the yolk custard. Fold in remainder of whites with a rubber spatula. Fold in the whipped cream.

Spoon into 1-quart soufflé dish, seal with saran wrap, and refrigerate for 2 to 3 hours or until firm. Decorate with whipped cream and curled slices of lime.

4 to 6 servings

C H O C O L A T E   C H A R L O T T E

2 3-ounce packages lady fingers
¾ cup butter
1¾ cup powdered sugar
6 egg yolks
¼ cup milk
1½ teaspoon vanilla
1 teaspoon rum extract
4 1-ounce squares unsweetened
  chocolate, melted
6 egg whites
1½ cups chopped nuts

1 cup whipping cream, whipped
1 to 3 tablespoons powdered sugar
1 teaspoon vanilla extract

Garnish:
1 1-ounce square sweet chocolate,
  shaved in curls

Butter a 9x5-inch loaf pan and line with wax paper. Butter paper and line bottom and sides of pan with lady fingers, cut side in.

Cream butter; add sugar and beat until fluffy. Add egg yolks, one at a time, beating until fluffy. Add milk, vanilla, rum extract and chocolate.

In a separate bowl, beat egg whites until stiff, but not dry. Fold into chocolate mixture. Add nuts. Pour into prepared pan. Refrigerate overnight.

At serving time, invert onto serving plate. In a small bowl, combine whipped cream, powdered sugar and vanilla. Frost cake. Decorate with shaved chocolate.

Variation: Substitute fresh lady fingers (page 204) for packaged.

10 to 12 servings

WHITE CHOCOLATE MOUSSE

18 ounces white chocolate, grated
1 cup plus 2 tablespoons
    melted butter
8 eggs, separated
1/2 cup plus 3 tablespoons sugar

Garnish:
Chocolate curls
Chocolate dipped strawberries

Melt chocolate in top of double boiler over simmering water. Mix chocolate and melted butter with mixer until blended. Add egg yolks one at a time. Mixture will separate, but keep beating. After about 5 minutes it will be creamy and thick.

Beat egg whites in separate bowl until soft, shiny peaks form, add sugar gradually throughout the process. On low speed, add half the egg whites to the chocolate. Stir until just blended. Fold in remaining whites by hand. Spoon into wine glasses or sherbet dishes.

Garnish with chocolate curls or chocolate dipped strawberries.

12 servings

CHOCOLATE ZABAGLIONE

3 1-ounce squares semi-sweet
    chocolate
2 tablespoons half and half
1/4 cup sugar
4 egg yolks
1/2 cup Marsala

1 cup whipping cream, whipped with
    2 tablespoons powdered sugar
    and 1 teaspoon vanilla extract

Melt chocolate in top of double boiler over simmering water. Combine with half and half; set aside.

Put sugar and egg yolks in top of double boiler, over simmering water; beat with wire whisk until pale yellow. Add Marsala and beat rapidly until mixture becomes foamy and thickened. Remove from heat and continue to beat until cooled slightly. With a spatula, fold in the chocolate mixture.

Spoon chocolate mixture into stemmed glasses layered or topped with sweetened whipped cream.

6 servings

LADYFINGERS

1/2 teaspoon vanilla extract
1/3 cup sugar
3 egg yolks
3 egg whites, room temperature
2/3 cup flour

Preheat oven to 400°. Line baking sheets with parchment paper.

Beat vanilla, sugar and egg yolks until pale yellow. In separate bowl, beat egg whites until stiff, but not dry. Very gently fold in yolks, along with flour. Spoon into a pastry bag, fitted with a 1/2-inch plain tip, and pipe out 4-inch strips on baking sheets. Sprinkle lightly with powdered sugar.

Bake for 15 to 20 minutes, or until just firm and lightly colored. Cool on racks.

48 ladyfingers

COUNTRY INN CHEESECAKE

Crust:
½ cup butter, melted
½ cup sugar
⅛ teaspoon cinnamon
16 pieces zwieback, crushed

Filling:
6 8-ounce packages cream cheese,
    softened
2½ cups sugar
¼ cup plus 2 tablespoons
    all-purpose flour
6 eggs
3 tablespoons fresh lemon juice
1 teaspoon vanilla extract
1½ cups half and half

Preheat oven to 350°. Butter a 10-inch springform pan.

Crust: In a large bowl, combine butter, sugar, cinnamon and zwieback; mix well. Press crust mixture into prepared pan, reserving 2 tablespoons for topping.

Filling: In a large bowl, blend cream cheese, sugar, flour, eggs, lemon, vanilla and half and half. Pour into pan. Sprinkle with reserved crumbs.

Bake for 1 hour. Leave cheesecake in oven for 1 hour with the door open and oven off. Refrigerate at least 3 hours.

12 servings

APRICOT BAVARIAN
WITH RASPBERRY-APRICOT SAUCE

2 envelopes unflavored gelatin
1 12-ounce can apricot nectar,
    drained, juice reserved
¼ to ½ cup apricot brandy
1 cup whipping cream, whipped

Raspberry Sauce:
2 cups fresh raspberries, divided or
    1 10-ounce package frozen
    raspberries, thawed
2 tablespoons superfine sugar
2 cups peeled, seeded, halved ripe
    fresh apricots or 1 16-ounce can
    apricot halves, drained
¼ cup toasted pecan halves

In a small bowl soften gelatin in ½ cup apricot nectar for 5 minutes. Bring remaining 1 cup of nectar just to a boil and add to gelatin. Stir to dissolve. Cool. Add apricot brandy and chill until consistency of unbeaten egg whites. Beat until light and fluffy. Fold in whipped cream. Pour into a lightly oiled 1-quart mold, cover with plastic wrap and chill at least 4 hours.

Raspberry Sauce: Puree 1½ cups fresh raspberries and sugar in a blender or food processor. Strain to remove seeds. Gently mix the puree with the apricots and pecans. (To peel fresh apricots, immerse in boiling water for 20 to 30 seconds and slip skins off.)

Unmold on lettuce, lined serving dish. Arrange apricot halves around mold. Spoon sauce and nuts over mold and apricot halves. Scatter remaining raspberries over all. Garnish with mint leaves.

GLISTENING STRAWBERRY TART WITH WHIPPED CREAM

Pastry Crust:
1 egg yolk
4 tablespoons water
1 tablespoon oil
1⅔ cups all-purpose flour
8 tablespoons butter
Pinch of salt
Apricot preserves

Pastry Cream:
2 tablespoons all-purpose flour
1 cup half and half, divided
6 tablespoons sugar
4 egg yolks
1 teaspoon vanilla extract

Strawberries, halved
Red currant jelly, melted
½ cup whipped cream, whipped

Preheat oven to 375°.

Pastry Crust: Whisk egg yolk with water and oil. In work bowl of food processor, combine egg mixture with flour, butter and salt. Process until a ball forms. Roll out, place on the bottom and sides of a 10 to 12-inch quiche pan. Brush the interior of the crust with apricot preserves before baking to waterproof the crust.

Bake for 15 minutes until done. Cool.

Pastry Cream: In a saucepan, combine flour and ¼ cup half and half; stir until smooth. Add another ¾ cup of half and half, plus the sugar to the mixture. Cook over medium heat, stirring until mixture becomes as thick as a medium white sauce. Add a few teaspoons of hot mixture to the egg yolks in a separate bowl. Stir quickly, add to mixture in saucepan. This ensures a smooth custard. Stir over heat for a few more minutes to cook the egg yolks. Remove from heat and stir in vanilla. Cool quickly. Pour into cooled crust.

Layer strawberries in concentric circles on top of the pastry cream and glaze with melted red currant jelly. Serve with a dollop of whipped cream.

Hint: For pastry cream glaze, a red transparent glaze mix can be substituted for red currant jelly.

10 servings

PECAN LASSIES

½ cup butter
1 cup sifted all-purpose flour
1 3-ounce package cream cheese
¾ cup firmly packed brown sugar
1 egg, slightly beaten
1 tablespoon melted butter
½ teaspoon vanilla extract
½ cup ground pecans, divided

Preheat oven to 350°.

In food processor work bowl, process flour, butter and cheese until dough forms a ball. Chill for 1 hour. Divide into 24 balls. Press each ball into 1¾-inch muffin tins.

In a small bowl, combine brown sugar, egg, butter, and vanilla. Divide half of pecans among pastry cups, spoon egg mixture on top. Sprinkle with remaining nuts.

Bake for 18 to 20 minutes. When cool, sprinkle with powdered sugar.

24 mini-tarts

FLAMING BANANAS

4 tablespoons butter
1/2 cup brown sugar
2 large bananas, sliced
1/4 cup rum
1/8 cup banana liqueur
Vanilla ice cream

In a large skillet, melt butter. Stir in brown sugar and bananas. Pour rum and liqueur into long-handled container and warm slightly. Ignite rum and liqueur mixture and pour gently over banana mixture. Stir gently and spoon over vanilla ice cream served in sherbet glasses.

4 servings

FLAN DE QUESO

1/2 cup granulated sugar
1 large can sweetened condensed
    milk
4 eggs
1 cup milk
1 8-ounce package cream cheese,
    softened

Preheat oven to 350°.

Spread sugar evenly in 8-inch pie pan or flan pan. Heat in oven until sugar is melted and is golden brown. Remove from oven and cool.

Place remaining ingredients in blender and mix until smooth. Pour over caramel syrup and set flan pan in pan of hot water.

Bake for 1 hour or until tester inserted in custard comes out clean. Chill overnight.

Run spatula around edge of pan and invert onto serving plate.

8 servings

GLAZED ORANGES IN COINTREAU

Syrup:
2 cups water
2 cups sugar
1/4 teaspoon cream of tartar
1/2 cup Cointreau, Grand Marnier
    or rum
1 tablespoon grenadine

8 large navel oranges

Syrup: Remove orange zest without white from oranges. Cut into fine slivers. Put slivers in saucepan with water, sugar and cream of tartar. Bring to a boil, then reduce heat to simmer and cook until thick and syrupy, about 25 to 30 minutes. Remove from heat, stir in liqueur, then add grenadine. Chill.

Oranges: Finish peeling oranges. Either leave whole, slice or section for easier eating. Place in glass bowl, add syrup, distributing peel evenly. Refrigerate, covered for at least 2 hours.

Serve with Florentines or Brandy snaps filled with vanilla-flavored whipped cream.

8 to 10 servings

JOHNNY APPLESEED SOUFFLÉ

2 pounds tart green apples, cored
    and peeled
1/2 cup Riesling, Gewurtraminer, or
    slightly sweet wine
1/2 cup water
1/2 cup plus 4 tablespoons sugar,
    divided
Grated zest of 1 lemon
4 tablespoons unsalted butter
4 ounces sliced leftover bread,
    no crust
1 egg
3/4 cup milk
1/2 teaspoon vanilla extract
3/4 teaspoon ground cinnamon,
    divided
2/3 cup raisins
2 tablespoons apricot jam

Place apples, wine, water, 1/2 cup plus 2 tablespoons sugar and lemon zest in a medium size heavy saucepan. Cook, covered, over medium heat, stirring occasionally until texture of applesauce, about 25 to 30 minutes.

Preheat oven to 350°. Butter a 2-quart soufflé dish.

Butter bread on both sides and toast on a baking sheet until lightly toasted. Transfer to a large flat dish. Mix the egg, milk, vanilla, 2 tablespoons sugar and 1/4 teaspoon of cinnamon and pour over the bread. Let stand about 30 minutes.

Place raisins in a small bowl and add boiling water to cover. Let stand 15 minutes. Drain and pat dry. Add raisins, apricot jam and remaining 1/2 teaspoon cinnamon to the applesauce and stir thoroughly.

Line bottom and sides of prepared soufflé dish with bread. Pour apple mixture into dish and smooth top. Trim bread so it is even with the apple mixture.

Bake about 45 minutes, or until set and light golden on top. Unmold and serve hot or warm.

8 servings

APRICOT RUM PUFFS

2 cups chopped dried apricots
2 cups dark seedless raisins
3/4 cup water
1/2 cup rum
2 tablespoons butter
2 3/4 teaspoons cornstarch with
    1 tablespoon water
1 cup chopped walnuts or pecans
1 teaspoon grated fresh lemon zest
1 tablespoon fresh lemon juice
1 teaspoon vanilla extract
1 package frozen puff pastry, thawed
1 egg beaten with 1 teaspoon water

In a large saucepan, bring apricots, raisins, water, rum and butter to boil. Stir in cornstarch mixture and cook until thick. Remove from heat and stir in walnuts, lemon zest, juice and vanilla. Cool completely.

Preheat oven to 375°.

Roll puff pastry and cut into 3-inch squares. Put 1 teaspoon filling in each center. Moisten corners and gather corners into a four-corner puff. Press firmly to seal. Brush top with egg wash before baking.

Bake for 25 to 30 minutes, or until golden and puffed.

Hint: These puffs may be frozen. This recipe will also make 24 puffs and one coffee cake.

48 puffs

PAIN PERDU

French or sourdough bread, sliced
    ½-inch thick
½ cup dried cherries or cranberries
Zest of 1 lemon
Zest of 1 orange
1 papaya, peeled and sliced
2 tart green apples, peeled, cored
    and sliced
2 ripe Bosc pears, peeled, cored
    and sliced
2 tablespoons corn oil
4 tablespoons applejack brandy,
    or to taste
6 eggs
6 cups half and half
3 teaspoons vanilla extract
¼ teaspoon freshly grated nutmeg
½ cup brown sugar, firmly packed

Preheat oven to 350°.

Cover bottom of a 9x13-inch baking dish with bread slices. Scatter cherries, lemon and orange zest; arrange papaya slices on top.

Cook apple and pear slices in corn oil in a large skillet until tender. Add applejack and cook 1 minute longer. Pour over bread slices. Gently press fruit into bread.

In a large bowl, whisk eggs, half and half, vanilla, nutmeg and brown sugar in a large bowl. Pour over bread and fruit.

Bake for 30 minutes. Serve with Crème Anglaise (page 196).

PARIS DELIGHT

1 12-ounce package chocolate chips
16 paper cupcake cups

1 cup whipping cream
2 tablespoons powdered sugar
1 teaspoon vanilla extract

12 champagne biscuits or
    macaroons, crumbled
3 tablespoons kirsch, divided
1 cup fresh strawberries, sugared
    and chopped
1 cup fresh raspberries, sugared

Garnish:
Strawberry slices
Shaved chocolate

Chocolate Cups: Melt chocolate in double boiler over simmering water. When melted, cool slightly and spoon 2 tablespoons into double thickness of a cupcake cup. Set in a muffin cup. With spoon spread evenly around bottom and up sides of cups. Chill until firm. Quickly remove paper and chill again.

When ready to serve, whip cream with sugar and vanilla until stiff. Set chocolate cup on dessert plate and crumble one cookie in bottom of each cup. Sprinkle with kirsch. Top with layer of strawberries and another of raspberries. Spoon whipped cream over filling. Garnish with slice of strawberry and shaved chocolate.

Variation: Fold 2 cups fresh raspberries into the sweetened vanilla flavored whipped cream and add 1½ tablespoons kirsch. Spoon into chocolate cups and garnish with mint leaves.

8 servings

A P R I C O T ,   R A I S I N   A N D   W A L N U T   S T R U D E L

Strudel:
2 cups all-purpose flour
1/2 package active dry yeast
Dash of salt
12 tablespoons butter, cut into pats
2 egg yolks
1/2 cup sour cream

Filling:
2 tablespoons apricot puree
    (or preserves)
1 tablespoon pineapple preserves
1/4 cup sugar
1/4 teaspoon cinnamon
1/2 cup raisins
1/2 cup chopped walnuts

Strudel: Place flour in food processor work bowl and sprinkle with yeast. Add salt and butter. Process until crumbly. Add egg yolks and sour cream. Process until crumbs form. Remove and press into a ball. Cut into 4 equal parts and wrap each ball of dough securely in plastic wrap. Refrigerate for at least one hour.

Preheat oven to 350°.

Roll out one portion of dough into a rectangle about 1/8-inch thick.

Filling: In a small bowl, combine apricot puree and pineapple preserves. Spread filling along the longer side of the rectangle in a strip. Sprinkle evenly with sugar, cinnamon, raisins and walnuts. Turn edge of dough over the filling and roll up. Tuck the ends under the strudel. Repeat using remaining filling.

Bake on an ungreased cookie sheet for 30 minutes. Sprinkle with powdered sugar just before serving.

A P P L E   P E C A N   C R I S P

1/4 cup butter or margarine, softened
1 cup sugar
1 egg, beaten
1 cup all-purpose flour
1 teaspoon baking soda
1/4 teaspoon salt
1 teaspoon vanilla extract
1/2 teaspoon nutmeg
1 teaspoon cinnamon
2 1/2 cups peeled and diced tart
    cooking apples
1/2 cup toasted pecan halves

Preheat oven to 350°. Grease a 9x9-inch baking pan or 10-inch pie pan.

In a large bowl, cream butter and sugar; add egg and beat well. Gradually mix in flour, baking soda, salt, vanilla, nutmeg and cinnamon. Mix. Fold in apples and pecans. Pour into prepared pan.

Bake for 30 to 40 minutes. Remove from oven and serve immediately with ice cream, hot caramel sauce and whipped cream.

8 servings

GALATOBOURIKO (CUSTARD PASTRY) MEGTHALOPITA (ALMOND PIE)

Syrup:
1½ cups water
3 cups sugar
6 cloves
1 cinnamon stick
2 pieces of fresh lemon zest

Custard Pastry:
1 cup sugar
1 quart milk
1¼ pounds butter, divided
¾ cup cream of wheat
1 teaspoon vanilla extract
9 eggs
1½ pounds phyllo dough
    (pastry sheets)

Almond Pie:
8 eggs, separated
1 cup sugar
1 pound almond paste
1½ teaspoons all-purpose flour
1¼ teaspoons baking powder
1 teaspoon almond extract
1¼ pounds unsalted butter
1 pound phyllo dough (pastry sheets)

Syrup: Boil water, sugar, cloves, cinnamon stick and lemon zest for 5 minutes to a medium consistency. Let cool.

Preheat oven to 350°.

Custard Pastry: Heat sugar, milk and 1½ cups butter in large saucepan, stirring constantly. When mixture comes to a boil, add cream of wheat slowly, stirring constantly. Boil until thick, remove from heat and add vanilla; set aside. In a large bowl, beat eggs until fluffy and light. Slowly add the hot milk mixture to the beaten eggs, stirring rapidly; set aside, stirring from time to time.

Almond Pie: Beat egg yolks with sugar. Break almond paste in pieces and add to egg yolks. Add flour, baking powder and almond extract. Beat well. In a separate bowl, beat egg whites until soft peaks form. Fold egg whites into egg yolk mixture.

Melt remaining butter from appropriate pastry/pie recipe. Brush either a 9x13-inch pan or a 15-inch round pan with 2-inch sides with a small amount of melted butter. Place one layer of pastry sheets in pan, covering the sides and brush with butter. Continue placing pastry sheets, brushed with butter, in pan until half the sheets are used. Spread one of the fillings on the dough and turn in the outer layers of the sheets.

Cover with remaining pastry sheets, each one brushed with melted butter. Fold in pastry edges to retain mixture. On top layer, place extra melted butter. Cut through top with 2-inch diagonal lines.

Bake for 50 minutes for the Custard Pastry or 1 hour for the Almond Pie, or until evenly browned. Remove from oven and drizzle with cool syrup. Let cool before slicing into squares.

28 servings

LOLLIPOPS & ROSES SUPREME
(LUSCIOUS FRUIT CUPS)

8 commercially prepared crêpes or
    4 homemade crêpes

6 ounces best quality white chocolate,
    chopped
1½ cups whipping cream, whipped

1 10-ounce package frozen
    raspberries, thawed
½ pint strawberries, hulled
½ pint raspberries
½ pint blueberries
1 teaspoon sugar, optional

Chocolate Sauce (page 215) or
1½ cups best quality chocolate
    sauce, warmed slightly to a thin
    consistency

Preheat oven to 350°. Spray bottom and outside of heat-proof glass 1 or 2 cup measuring cup with cooking spray. Invert and set on a cookie sheet.

Remove crêpes from package, 2 at a time, so they adhere to one another. Drape crêpes or 1 homemade crêpe over bottom of inverted measuring cup, pressing gently to follow the shape of the cup. The crêpe will flare out in at least 4 places. Arrange so the measuring cup handle fits in one of the flares. Toast in oven for 5 minutes; crêpe cup should be very crisp. Immediately remove, gently, from measuring cup and cool on rack. Repeat until 4 crêpe cups are formed.

Place chopped white chocolate in bowl over hot water. Stir until melted. Remove and allow to cool. Fold into whipped cream and chill.

Place thawed raspberries in a fine mesh strainer over a bowl. Press out all juices with the back of a spoon and strain the seeds from the juice. Add a little sugar to the raspberry juice, if you wish.

To assemble: Spoon whipped cream mixture into a pastry bag fitted with a star tip, pipe or spoon about 2 tablespoons of whipped cream mixture just off-center on each serving plate. Set bottom edge of a crêpe cup on the whipped cream so the cup is sitting at an angle. Spoon about 2 tablespoons of chocolate sauce in the bottom of each cup. Cool to room temperature.

Pipe, or spoon, equal amounts of the whipped cream mixture on top of the chocolate. Puddle the raspberry sauce on one side of the plate and the chocolate sauce on the other side. Scatter fresh fruit over the whipped cream and the sauces. Serve at once.

4 servings

CHOCOLATE SAUCE

1 cup butter
2 cups sifted cocoa
2 cups sugar
5 cups whipping cream

Melt butter in a large saucepan. Add cocoa and sugar slowly. When mixture is too thick to stir add a little cream. After all sugar and cocoa are added, slowly whisk in remaining cream. Bring to a simmer, turn heat to low and cook 10 minutes, stirring constantly. Strain before serving.

BREAD PUDDING WITH WHISKEY CREAM OR VANILLA SAUCE

1 16-ounce loaf stale French bread
    with crust, sliced 1-inch thick
1 cup butter
2 cups sugar
8 eggs
4 cups milk
2 teaspoons cinnamon
2 tablespoons vanilla extract
½ cup raisins
1 cup pecans, toasted

Butter a 9x13-inch baking pan and place half of bread slices on bottom of dish. Cream butter and sugar, add eggs and milk, then remaining ingredients and mix well. Pour ½ of sauce over bread slices. Place the remaining slices in baking dish. Pour remaining sauce slowly on top. Let stand one-half hour.
    Preheat oven to 375°.
    Bake, covered, for 30 minutes. Uncover and bake 15 minutes longer or until golden.
    Slice pudding while still warm and serve with Whiskey Cream or Vanilla Sauce.

Whiskey Cream Sauce:
7 egg yolks
2 cups sugar
1½ cups half and half
4 tablespoons whiskey, or to taste

Whiskey Cream Sauce: Beat sugar into egg yolks until pale in color. Heat half and half until scalding. Remove from heat and very slowly whisk in egg/sugar mixture. Return to low heat and cook until thickened, stirring constantly. Cool over ice and slowly add whiskey.

Vanilla Sauce:
2 cups whipping cream
½ cup sugar
4 egg yolks
1 tablespoon all-purpose flour
1 tablespoon vanilla extract
¼ teaspoon salt
2 scoops French vanilla ice cream

Vanilla Sauce: In a 2-quart saucepan combine cream and sugar. Bring to a boil. Remove from heat. In a bowl, whisk together egg yolks, flour, vanilla and salt. Stir in a little hot cream mixture. Add this mixture to the remaining hot cream. Return to heat and stir constantly until thickened. Do not overcook. Remove from heat. Add ice cream, stirring until melted. Strain. Sauce may be served hot or cold.

10 to 12 servings

CHOCOLATE GLAZED ECLAIRS

Choux Paste:
1 cup water
1 cup unsalted butter
½ teaspoon salt
1½ cups all-purpose flour
6 to 8 eggs

Pastry Cream:
1 teaspoon unflavored gelatin
1 teaspoon cold water
1⅓ cups milk
4 egg yolks
⅓ cup sugar
3 tablespoons all-purpose flour
2 teaspoons vanilla extract

Chocolate Glaze:
6 tablespoons water
3 ounces unsweetened chocolate
2 tablespoons butter
2 cups powdered sugar

Preheat oven to 400°. Cover cookie sheet with parchment paper.

Choux Paste: In a heavy saucepan, combine water, butter and salt. Heat until butter is melted. Bring to a rapid boil. Add all flour at once. Stir until a large ball of dough forms. While still on the heat, flatten dough on bottom of pan. Remove from heat and cool for 5 minutes. Place in a mixing bowl. Add one egg at a time until a smooth creamy, shiny paste appears. Spoon into pastry bag with a medium tip and pipe 1½-inch strips onto cookie sheet.

Bake for 10 minutes; reduce heat to 350° and bake for about 25 minutes longer, or until golden brown and sound hollow. Cool before filling.

Pastry Cream: Soften gelatin in water; set aside. In a small saucepan, heat milk. Combine yolks and sugar in a small mixing bowl. Beat until light color. Add flour and beat well. Add hot milk to flour mixture, pouring very slowly. Beat until all ingredients are incorporated. Place over medium heat. Whisk constantly until mixture boils. Boil for 1 minute. Remove from heat. Add vanilla. Stir in gelatin. Let cool completely, at least 6 hours. Before using, beat to remove any lumps. Fill choux with cream by poking a hole at one end and filling with a piping bag with a small round tip.

Chocolate Glaze: Combine water, chocolate and butter in saucepan. Heat, stirring constantly, until chocolate is melted. Whisk in sugar until glaze is smooth. Spoon over eclairs.

LEMON CURD

1 cup sugar
3 eggs
1 egg yolk
½ cup unsalted butter
6 tablespoons fresh lemon juice
1 tablespoon grated lemon zest

In heavy medium saucepan, whisk sugar, eggs, egg yolk, butter, lemon juice and lemon zest over low heat until butter melts. Cook 5 minutes, or until mixture thickens to consistency of lightly whipped cream, whisking constantly. Pour into bowl. Cover and refrigerate until cold, about 4 hours. Can be prepared 2 days ahead.

PHYLLO BASKETS WITH LEMON CURD AND FRUIT

Baskets:
4 frozen phyllo dough sheets, thawed
¼ cup unsalted butter, melted
2 tablespoons dry white
*   bread crumbs*

1 pint strawberries, sliced

Lemon Curd (page 216)

Preheat oven to 350°.

Place 1 phyllo sheet on work surface. Brush with butter. Sprinkle bread crumbs over the sheet. Continue with second phyllo sheet, repeating the steps for each sheet. Cut out twelve 4-inch squares from phyllo.

Brush every other cup of 2 twelve-cup ½-inch muffin tins with melted butter. Place 1 phyllo square in each buttered cup, pressing pastry down in center and around edges to mold to cup. Pastry corners should stick up.

Bake for 10 minutes, or until crisp and soft golden in color. Remove pastry from tins and cool completely.

Spoon berries into bottom of each phyllo basket; top each with 2½ tablespoons of lemon curd. Arrange remaining berries in petal fashion on top of the curd. Garnish with mint sprigs.

12 servings

MERINGUES WITH LEMON CURD

3 egg whites, room temperature
¼ teaspoon salt
½ teaspoon cream of tartar
1 cup sugar
1 teaspoon vanilla extract or
*   ¼ teaspoon almond extract*

Lemon Curd (page 216)

Garnish:
Fresh raspberries
Candied violets

Preheat oven to 225°. Line baking sheets with parchment paper or foil.

In a large bowl of electric mixer, beat egg whites until foamy. Add salt and cream of tartar and beat until whites hold a soft peak. Continue beating and add sugar, 1 tablespoon at a time, beating well after each addition. Add vanilla. Continue to beat at high speed for 5 minutes.

Using a pastry bag fitted with a ½-inch star tip, form a small concentric circle, about 2 to 3 inches in diameter, with raised edges and a depression in the center. Place meringues about 1 inch apart.

Bake for 1 hour. Turn off heat, prop oven door open slightly, and let cool in oven. Meringues should not color.

When cooled and just before serving, spoon a small amount of Lemon Curd into center of each meringue and garnish with fresh raspberries and candied violets.

To store unfilled meringues, place in an air-tight container and keep at room temperature. Do not try to make meringues on a rainy or humid day.

CHOCOLATE TRUFFLE AND
PRALINE ICE CREAM BOMBE

½ gallon praline ice cream
1 quart butter pecan ice cream

Chocolate Truffle Filling:
1¼ cups plus 1 tablespoon
    whipping cream
3 tablespoons unsalted butter, cut
    into pieces
10 ounces semi-sweet chocolate,
    finely chopped
5 tablespoons Frangelico, hazelnut
    liqueur

Cookie Crust:
1½ 6-ounce packages cappuccino
    cookies, broken
1 tablespoon unsalted butter,
    softened, cut into pieces
1 egg yolk

Topping:
1 pint whipping cream
2 tablespoons powdered sugar
1 teaspoon vanilla extract

Garnish:
5 strawberries, halved

Caramel Sauce:
¾ cup sugar
¼ cup water
1¼ cups whipping cream
¼ cup butter
2 tablespoons sour cream
4 teaspoons Frangelico liqueur

Line a 10-cup (9¾-inch diameter) bowl with two sheets of foil, overlapping sides slightly. Spread praline ice cream evenly up sides of bowl with back of dampened spoon. Freeze first layer.

Repeat with butter pecan ice cream forming 4-inch wide, 2½-inch deep hollow center. Freeze both layers.

Chocolate Truffle Filling: Bring cream and butter to simmer in saucepan. Remove from heat. Add chocolate and whisk until smooth. Mix in Frangelico. Cool to room temperature. Refrigerate, if necessary — must hold shape of spoon. Then spoon filling into hollow of bombe. Freeze.

Cookie Crust: In food processor work bowl, finely grind cookies; add butter and egg yolk; blend well. Press crumbs evenly and firmly over ice cream and truffle filling. Cover and freeze (can be prepared 4 days ahead or done in steps each day).

The day before serving, invert bombe onto 10-inch diameter cake plate.

Topping: Whip cream with sugar and vanilla until stiff. Spread over bombe.

Garnish: Make lengthwise cuts in strawberry halves, starting ¼-inch from stem and cutting through tips. Fan berries, placing on top and along sides. Freeze until ready to serve.

Caramel Sauce: Cook sugar and water in small saucepan over low heat, stirring until sugar dissolves. Increase heat and boil until sugar caramelizes. Remove from heat. Stir in cream (mixture will bubble). Return to heat and boil until smooth and slightly thickened, stirring frequently about 2 minutes. Whisk in butter and boil 2 minutes. Remove from heat. Whisk in sour cream and Frangelico. Can be prepared one day ahead. Cover and refrigerate. Rewarm slowly.

Serve bombe with warm sauce.

WARNING: Bombe weighs six pounds!

10 to 16 servings

BUSTER BAR TORTE

24 vanilla-filled chocolate sandwich
    cookies, crushed
⅓ cup butter, melted
½ gallon vanilla ice cream, softened
1 cup peanuts, chopped
2 1-ounce squares unsweetened
    chocolate
½ cup sugar
1 5⅓-ounce can evaporated milk
1 tablespoon butter

Grease 9x13-inch pan.

Mix cookies and melted butter. Press into prepared pan. Freeze. Pat softened ice cream on crust. Sprinkle peanuts on top. Freeze.

Combine chocolate, sugar, milk and butter in top of double boiler over simmering water. Cook until chocolate melts and mixture thickens. Cool.

Pour on torte. Freeze. Keep covered.

16 to 20 servings

INTENSELY RASPBERRY SORBET

⅓ cup sugar
⅓ cup water
3 10-ounce packages frozen
    raspberries, heavy syrup,
    thawed
1 cup club soda
3 tablespoons fresh lemon juice

In a small saucepan, combine sugar and water; bring to a boil without stirring until sugar is completely dissolved.

Process raspberries in a food processor and force through a fine meshed sieve to remove seeds or process berries through a vegetable juicer. Mix raspberries with sugar mixture, club soda and lemon juice. Chill in ice cream maker according to directions.

Serve in stemmed glasses.

8 servings

COCONUT SORBET

1 cup canned coconut milk
½ cup club soda
2 tablespoons dark rum
2 egg whites
½ cup sugar
Sliced bananas
Chocolate sauce (page 215)

Mix coconut milk, club soda and rum in a large bowl. In a separate bowl, beat egg whites until soft peaks form. Fold egg whites into the coconut mixture. Freeze in an ice cream maker following manufacturer's directions. (Or place in freezer until creamy.) Serve with bananas and chocolate sauce.

CINNAMON OR PISTACHIO ICE CREAM

Cinnamon Ice Cream:
12 egg yolks
1 cup sugar
4 cups half and half
2 cinnamon sticks
1 cup chopped walnuts, toasted

Pistachio Ice Cream:
12 egg yolks
1 cup sugar
4 cups half and half
2 cups pistachios
1 tablespoon almond liqueur

Cinnamon Ice Cream: In electric mixer small bowl, beat egg yolks and sugar at medium speed until pale. Bring half and half to a boil with cinnamon sticks. Pour slowly over egg mixture, stirring constantly. Pour back into pan and cook over low heat, stirring constantly until mixture starts to thicken. Do not allow to simmer or boil. Remove from heat. Strain through a sieve. Remove cinnamon sticks.

Freeze in an ice cream maker according to manufacturer's directions.

Fold in walnuts after ice cream is soft-frozen.

Pistachio Ice Cream: Follow same directions above; omitting cinnamon sticks while heating half and half. Fold in pistachios and almond liqueur after ice cream is soft-frozen.

SOUR CHERRY SORBET

¾ cup sugar
1 cup water
½ teaspoon ground cinnamon
4 cups pitted fresh sour cherries or
    2 16-ounce packages frozen
    sour cherries, thawed
Juice of ½ lemon
1 cup whipping cream, whipped
1 tablespoon sugar
1 teaspoon vanilla extract

Bring sugar, water and cinnamon to a boil in large sauce pan; set aside and cool. Puree cherries in blender or food processor. Stir in lemon juice and sugar syrup. Freeze in an ice cream maker, following manufacturer's directions. Or place in freezer until creamy consistency.

In a small bowl, combine whipped cream with sugar and vanilla. Serve with sorbet.

ORANGE CHOCOLATE FLOWER POTS

Terra cotta flower pots, ½ cup size
2 pints orange sherbet, softened
¼ cup Grand Marnier
½ cup whipping cream
Chocolate sprinkles
Fresh daisies or other flowers
Straws

Line flower pots with foil. Trim so foil is even with top of pot.

Stir softened sherbet, liqueur and cream together. Pack into flower pots. Insert a small straw in center to extend about two inches above top of pot. Freeze.

To serve: Place each flower pot on dessert plate. Scatter chocolate sprinkles on top of sherbet. Insert a daisy in the straw and serve at once.

6 servings

S NIPS & TIPS

Why name our cookbook "Sugar Snips & Asparagus Tips"? Many interpretations have been heard, but none speak as well as the age old children's nursery rhyme,

What are little girls made of?
Sugar and spice and everything nice.

What are little boys made of?
Snips and snails and puppy dogs tails.

What is Infant Welfare made of?
Beautiful little girls and boys,
   full of life that's short on joys.

So we made a cookbook for those little Sugar Snips, and filled it with recipes that are as fresh and healthy as Asparagus Tips. And we hope that all enjoy the natural, back to basics, easy to prepare meals from these pages that will please family and friends alike for a long time to come.

Bon Appétit

Nancy Petkunas
Infant Welfare Member

CHAMPAGNE FRUIT PUNCH

Juice of 12 fresh lemons
1 pound superfine sugar
4 cups seltzer water
1 pint cognac
½ pint curaçao
½ pint maraschino cherry juice
2 quarts champagne
Combination of fresh seasonal fruits

Combine lemon juice and sugar. Stir until dissolved. Add seltzer, cognac, curaçao, cherry juice and champagne.

Add cut up fruit, equal to: 1 quart strawberries (halved), 6 to 8 peaches peeled and sliced, ½ fresh pineapple, diced, or any combination desired.

16 servings

LEMON ZINGER
(A.K.A. SOUTH SIDER)

1 12-ounce can frozen lemonade
Vodka
10 mint leaves, or to taste
Ice
Club soda

Spoon frozen lemonade into blender. Use the lemonade can and pour an equal amount of vodka into the blender with the mint leaves. Blend well.

Fill individual glasses with ice cubes. Pour equal amounts of lemonade mixture with club soda to fill glass.

8 servings

MOCHA TODDIES

Mocha Base:
1 2-ounce jar or ¾ cup instant coffee
    crystals
¼ cup hot water
1 16-ounce can or 1½ cups
    chocolate syrup
1 cup rum
1 tablespoon vanilla extract

Toddies:
¾ hot milk per serving
Vanilla ice cream

In mixing bowl, combine coffee crystals and water. Stir to dissolve coffee crystals. Add chocolate syrup, rum and vanilla. Store covered in refrigerator.

To serve: Stir 2 tablespoons of mocha base into each hot milk serving. Top with ice cream.

Base for 22 servings

PLUM BRANDY "NECTAR OF THE GODS"

1 pound ripe red or purple plums
1 pound sugar
4 cups vodka

Prick plums all over with fork. Place plums in large glass container with screw top. Mix sugar and vodka, pour over plums and close top.

Turn container over every other day for six weeks. Ready to enjoy after six weeks.

Remove plums and strain.

CAFÉ CON LECHE

¼ cup firmly packed brown sugar
1 tablespoon water
2 whole cloves
1 stick cinnamon
3 cups strong hot coffee
1 cup half and half, warmed

In a small saucepan, combine sugar, water, cloves and cinnamon; stir over low heat until mixture comes to a boil and sugar dissolves. Add to coffee. Cover; steep for 15 minutes. Strain coffee.

Stir half and half into coffee.

4 servings

PERCOLATED PUNCH

2 32-ounce jars cranberry juice
1 46-ounce can pineapple juice
1 orange, sliced
5 to 6 sticks cinnamon
Handful of cloves

Pour fruit juices into large coffee pot. Place orange, cinnamon sticks and cloves in the "grounds holder" of pot. Turn on coffee maker and brew.

Serve hot.

32 servings

MEXICAN HOT CHOCOLATE

2 cups milk
Chocolate syrup to taste
⅛ teaspoon cinnamon
2 teaspoons sugar

Place milk, chocolate syrup, cinnamon and sugar in saucepan. Bring to a boil.

Serve very hot.

2 servings

FRESH FRUIT TEA

1½ cups sugar
25 whole cloves
Water
6 tea bags
16 cups water, divided
3 cups orange juice
6 to 8 tablespoons fresh lemon juice
2 cups pineapple juice

In a saucepan, combine sugar and cloves. Add enough water to cover and heat until sugar melts.

In separate large saucepan, place tea bags in 6 cups water and steep for 3 hours. Then add 6 additional cups of water to tea. Remove tea bags. Add sugar/clove mixture to tea and bring to a boil. Add orange, lemon and pineapple juices. Heat but DO NOT boil after adding juices. Serve hot.

1 gallon

GLAZED SPICED NUTS

8 ounces almonds
8 ounces cashews
8 ounces pecans
2 egg whites
1 teaspoon salt
1 cup sugar
1 teaspoon cinnamon
¼ teaspoon ground red pepper
¼ teaspoon allspice
½ cup butter

Preheat oven to 325°.

On a shallow baking sheet, roast nuts until lightly browned. Remove from oven. Reduce oven temperature to 275°.

In a large bowl, beat egg whites with salt until stiff peaks form. In a small, bowl mix sugar, cinnamon, red pepper and allspice. Gradually add sugar mixture to the egg whites and continue beating until very stiff. Fold in nuts.

Melt butter on a large baking pan in the oven. Be careful not to burn butter. Add nut mixture and bake for 45 minutes, stirring every 15 minutes while baking. The butter will be absorbed while baking. Be careful to avoid burning.

Cool and store in airtight container.

DEVILED WALNUTS

1 pound shelled walnuts
3 tablespoons unsalted margarine
⅛ teaspoon Worcestershire sauce
⅛ teaspoon sweet paprika
¼ teaspoon ground red pepper
⅛ teaspoon chili powder
⅛ teaspoon ground cumin
½ teaspoon Oriental five-spice
    seasoning

In large skillet, melt margarine, add Worcestershire sauce and sauté walnuts until brown. Cool on paper towel. Place paprika, red pepper, chili powder, cumin and five-spice seasoning in paper bag; add walnuts and shake.

Keep fresh in covered tin.

HOT SUGARED ALMONDS
(GEBRANNTE MANDELN)

2 tablespoons safflower oil
2 cups sugar
2/3 cup water
2 1/2 cups whole unblanched almonds
1 teaspoon cinnamon

Brush 2 baking sheets with safflower oil; set aside.

Combine sugar and water in a heavy 3-quart saucepan; heat over medium heat, stirring constantly with wooden spoon until sugar has melted and syrup begins to boil. Stop stirring and attach candy thermometer to saucepan. Boil syrup until thermometer registers 220°. Add almonds and cinnamon and begin stirring again. At 240° syrup will change consistency, becoming bubbly and granular in appearance. Watch carefully so syrup does not burn. When sugar begins to coat nuts, pour mixture onto prepared baking sheets. Immediately separate nuts with 2 forks. Let cool.

Store in airtight containers at room temperature.

FLORENTINE TOFFEE

1 cup unsalted butter, softened
1 cup sugar
1/3 cup honey
1/3 cup whipping cream
1 16-ounce package sliced almonds
   or chopped pecans or
   combination of both
2 1-ounce squares semi-sweet
   chocolate, melted, optional

Preheat oven to 375°. Butter four 9-inch metal pie pans.

In a large saucepan, combine butter, sugar, honey and cream. Bring to a boil over medium heat, stirring often. Boil 1 1/2 minutes, stirring constantly. Remove from heat and add nuts. Stir to keep mixture from separating while pouring into prepared pans.

Using back of spoon, spread mixture evenly over bottom of pan. Toffee should be 1/4-inch thick.

Bake 8 to 12 minutes, until golden brown. Cool slightly and refrigerate 5 to 10 minutes, until toffee is firm enough to separate from pie pans with tip of rounded knife. Hardened but chewy toffee should pop out of pan. Cut each round into 16 wedges or break into irregular pieces. If desired, spread melted chocolate over tops. Refrigerate in single layer in refrigerator until hardened before wrapping individually in wax paper. Store up to a month in airtight container at room temperature (except in summer) or indefinitely in refrigerator. May be frozen.

64 wedges

N I C A R A G U A N   B A N A N A S

8 bananas, slightly underripe
3 cups sugar
1½ cups wine vinegar
½ cup Burgundy or dry red wine
1 tablespoon whole cloves
2 teaspoons cinnamon

In a large skillet, combine sugar, vinegar, wine, cloves and cinnamon. Bring mixture to a boil. Drop bananas in mixture; turning once. Cook approximately 2 to 3 minutes until bananas are well-glazed, tender on the outside but firm inside.

Serve as a side dish with steaks, roasts or fowl. Excellent for brunch.

6 to 8 servings

I T A L I A   D I   F R U T T A
F R U I T   W I T H   C I T R U S   S A U C E

1 pound assorted seasonal fruits:
    apples, pears, plums, peaches,
    grapes, apricots, cherries,
    bananas, sliced
½ cup fresh orange juice
1½ tablespoons fresh lemon juice
1½ tablespoons superfine sugar

Combine assorted sliced fruit in large bowl. In a small bowl mix orange and lemon juice with sugar until sugar dissolves. Pour juice mixture over the fruit; cover with plastic wrap and refrigerate for at least 4 hours.

Before serving, toss fruits. Taste and add additional sugar if necessary. Serve with assorted Italian cheeses such as mascarpone, fontina and Gorgonzola.

F R U I T   M E D L E Y   W I T H   P O R T

½ cup sugar
¼ teaspoon whole cloves
½ cup water
½ cup port wine
1 cup melon balls
1 cup red seedless grapes, halved
1 large banana, peeled and sliced

Garnish:
Mint leaves

In a small saucepan, combine sugar, cloves and water. Bring to a boil and continue boiling for 5 minutes. Cool.

Stir port into cooled mixture. Combine melon balls and grapes. Pour port sauce over the fruit. Refrigerate for several hours. Before serving, add bananas. Serve in bowl or individual stemmed glasses. Garnish with mint leaves.

4 servings

CRANBERRY CONSERVE

1 12-ounce package fresh
    cranberries
½ cup golden raisins
½ cup sugar
¼ cup water
⅓ cup pear schnapps

Preheat oven to 300° to 325°.

In a 9x13-inch baking dish, combine all ingredients except schnapps. Cover with foil.

Bake 45 minutes. Remove foil and sprinkle schnapps on top. Cool. Can be made ahead.

2½ cups

SUGAR PLUMS

1 egg white
¼ cup cold water
1 teaspoon cream of tartar
1 teaspoon vanilla extract
6 cups sifted powdered sugar, divided
4 tablespoons butter, softened
½ cup unsweetened grated coconut
¼ cup chopped glacéed pineapple
¼ cup chopped glacéed cherries
1½ pounds prunes, pitted and
    halved lengthwise
Granulated sugar

Garnish:
Slivered glacéed cherries

In a bowl beat egg white, water, cream of tartar and vanilla until the mixture is frothy. Beat in powdered sugar, ¼ cup at time, and continue to beat the mixture until it is thick and smooth. Add butter and combine well. Stir in coconut, pineapple and cherries. Chill, covered, for at least 48 hours.

Stuff each prune with 1½ teaspoons of filling and roll the prunes in granulated sugar.

Garnish each sugarplum with a sliver of glacéed cherry and store confections in an airtight container.

7 dozen

SHERRIED BAKED CRANBERRY SAUCE

1 cup sherry
1 cup sugar
1 tablespoon grated orange zest,
    optional
¼ teaspoon salt
1 16-ounce package cranberries

Preheat oven to 350°.

In a large saucepan, bring sherry, sugar, orange zest and salt to a boil. Add cranberries. Pour into a 1-quart baking dish.

Bake 30 minutes. Cool and refrigerate.

6 to 8 servings

MARVELOUS MELON

1 cup blueberries
1 cup raspberries
2 cups small cantaloupe balls
⅓ cup shredded coconut
3 tablespoons coconut liqueur

Combine blueberries, raspberries, melon, coconut and coconut liqueur. Mix well. Refrigerate for several hours before serving.

Variation: Substitute for 1 cup cantaloupe, 1 cup of another in-season melon.

5 to 6 servings

APPLE PEACH GRATIN

4 large tart apples, peeled and sliced
½ cup sugar
2 peaches, peeled and sliced or
  1 16-ounce can peaches, drained
8 pecan cookies, crushed

Preheat oven to 350°. Butter an 8-inch square baking dish.
In a small saucepan, simmer apples, sugar and a little water until apples are browned and candied, stirring constantly. Spoon into baking dish, add peaches and sprinkle with cookie crumbs.
Bake, uncovered, 1 hour. Very good with pork, as a brunch side dish or with ice cream.

8 servings

FRUIT SALSA

Peel, core and chop:
  2 pineapples
  2 pears
Peel, seed and chop:
  1 papaya
  2 serrano chilies
  2 jalapeño chili peppers
2 tablespoons olive oil
6 to 7 green onions, chopped
¼ cup fresh lime juice
1 tablespoon chopped fresh cilantro
1 teaspoon cumin
1 teaspoon sugar
¼ teaspoon salt
½ teaspoon freshly ground pepper

Combine pineapple, pears, papaya, chilies, jalapeño peppers, olive oil, green onions, lime juice, cilantro, cumin, sugar, salt and pepper in a large bowl. Chill 1 hour.
Serve with grilled foods, such as red snapper, swordfish steaks, tuna, shrimp or chicken breasts.

WHIPPED HORSERADISH CREAM

2 tablespoons horseradish, or to taste
2 tablespoons sour cream
1 cup whipping cream, whipped

Fold horseradish and sour cream into whipped cream. Serve.

BEURRE BLANC

¼ cup white wine
¼ cup cider vinegar
1 tablespoon minced shallot
¾-1 pound cold unsalted butter
Salt and freshly ground pepper

Variation:
¼ cup orange juice
Zest of 1 orange

Variation:
½ cup pineapple juice
¼ cup white wine vinegar
¼ cup minced green onion
½ teaspoon salt
¼ teaspoon freshly ground
    white pepper

Combine wine, vinegar and shallot in saucepan. Reduce over high heat to 2 tablespoons. Cut butter into 1-inch cubes. Over very low heat, whisk into reduction. When smooth emulsion forms, remove from heat. Add salt and pepper to taste.

Serve over green vegetables, shellfish or fish.

Variation:
Add orange juice and orange zest to reduction. Then add butter. Serve sauce over fish, veal or chicken.

Variation:
Reduce pineapple juice, vinegar, onion, salt and pepper. Add butter. Serve over asparagus, broccoli, beans, scallops or chicken.

1 cup

CREAMY LEMON PARSLEY SAUCE

2 teaspoons freshly grated lemon zest
4 tablespoons fresh lemon juice
2 cups whipping cream
2 tablespoons butter
Salt and freshly ground pepper

Freshly chopped parsley

In a small bowl, combine lemon zest, lemon juice and cream.

Serving suggestion: Toss hot pasta and 2 tablespoons butter; add sauce, toss, and sprinkle with freshly chopped parsley. Season with salt and pepper to taste.

Serving suggestion: Use as a sauce over vegetables.

4 servings

BEST TOMATO SAUCE

2 pounds fresh tomatoes, peeled
    and crushed
2 pounds tomato sauce
¹/₄ cup tomato paste
2 tablespoons sugar
2 cloves garlic, crushed
1 tablespoon finely chopped:
    fresh basil
    fresh thyme
    fresh marjoram
    fresh oregano
Salt and freshly ground pepper
1 tablespoon butter
¹/₂ pound mushrooms, sliced

In large pan, combine tomatoes, tomato sauce, tomato paste, sugar and garlic. Crush basil, thyme, marjoram and oregano; add to tomatoes stirring well. Season with salt and pepper to taste. Simmer for 1¹/₂ hours.

In small skillet, sauté mushrooms in butter; add to sauce. Serve over pasta or chicken.

This sauce may be frozen.

Variation: Substitute 1 teaspoon dried basil, thyme, marjoram and oregano for fresh herbs.

4 servings

MAYONNAISE DE PROVENCE

1 cup mayonnaise
3 tablespoons chopped:
    fresh parsley
    fresh chives
    fresh tarragon
1 heaping tablespoon capers,
    finely chopped
1 small sour pickle, chopped
1 clove garlic, finely chopped

Whisk, in a large bowl, mayonnaise, parsley, chives, tarragon, capers, pickle and garlic until well blended. Chill.

Variation: Substitute 1 tablespoon dried parsley, dried chives, and dried tarragon for fresh herbs.

HOT MUSTARD SAUCE

¹/₂ cup sugar
2 tablespoons spicy mustard
1 tablespoon cider vinegar
2 egg yolks, beaten
1 cup half and half

In top of a double boiler, mix sugar and mustard. Add vinegar, egg yolks and half and half. Cook one hour over simmering water, stirring frequently.

Serve hot or cold. Excellent with ham, pork and as a sandwich spread. Can freeze or reheat.

RAISIN-NUT SAUCE

1½ tablespoons cornstarch
1½ cups fresh orange juice
⅓ cup firmly packed brown sugar
2 tablespoons butter
¼ cup raisins
¼ cup slivered almonds

In a saucepan, blend cornstarch with orange juice. Add sugar, butter, raisins and almonds and mix well. Cook and stir over medium heat until sauce thickens.

Pour sauce over cooked fowl.

CUMBERLAND SAUCE

1 jar raspberry jam
½ cup Dijon mustard
Fresh lemon juice to taste

Mix jam, mustard and lemon juice. Serve in gravy boat at room temperature with meat roasts. Best with cold beef, such as beef tenderloin.

CUCUMBER SAUCE

⅓ cucumber, seeded, grated and drained
2 teaspoons minced onions
¼ cup mayonnaise
1 cup sour cream
2 tablespoons white wine vinegar
2 tablespoons minced fresh parsley

In a bowl, mix all ingredients and chill. Serve cold.

Variation: For a spicy flavor, add ½ teaspoon red pepper and 1 tablespoon fresh lemon juice.

6 servings

DILL AND MUSTARD SAUCE

1 dry mustard
4 tablespoons dark, seasoned mustard
3 tablespoons sugar
2 tablespoons balsamic vinegar
3½ cups safflower oil
2 tablespoons chopped dill

In large bowl, mix two mustards, sugar and vinegar to a paste. Beat in oil with a whisk until sauce thickens. Stir in dill. Keeps well in refrigerator. Whisk well again before serving.

Hint: Try sauce with smoked turkey, ham or salmon.

MARINARA SAUCE

4 tablespoons good quality olive oil
3 large cloves garlic, minced
1 large onion, cut in half
   and sliced thin
2 28-ounce cans peeled plum
   tomatoes, Italian style,
   hand crushed
1 tablespoon fresh parsley
1 tablespoon fresh basil, divided
Salt and freshly ground pepper
2 tablespoons freshly grated
   Romano cheese

In a skillet, sauté garlic and onion in oil until soft and a little brown. Add crushed tomatoes, parsley, ½ tablespoon basil, salt and pepper. Heat to boiling. Lower heat and simmer uncovered for 20 to 30 minutes. Stir occasionally. Taste for flavor; add more salt and pepper. Add remaining fresh basil and grated cheese. Let stand covered about 10 minutes. Serve hot.

Serve over chicken, meat, pasta or cooked vegetables.

Variation: Substitute 1 teaspoon dried parsley and 1 teaspoon dried basil for fresh herbs.

4 to 6 servings

HEALTHY PESTO

2 cloves garlic
1 16-ounce carton soft tofu
2 cups fresh basil leaves
½ cup freshly grated Parmesan
   cheese
Salt and freshly ground pepper

Peel garlic. Place in food processor work bowl and process in bursts until chopped. Drain tofu. Add to processor and process until smooth. Add basil and Parmesan. Process until smooth. Sauce should be a light green. Add salt and pepper to taste.

Heat sauce in microwave, uncovered, until hot, stirring occasionally.

Do not use dried basil. Sauce may be heated on stove top at medium heat. Do not freeze. This sauce is especially good with shrimp or scallops added. Will keep in refrigerator about 4 days.

4 to 6 servings

MINT PESTO

1 cup parsley, chopped
1 cup mint leaves, chopped
1 clove garlic, crushed
¼ cup extra virgin olive oil
¼ cup vegetable oil

In food processor work bowl, process parsley and mint. Add finely crushed garlic and slowly add oils.

Serve with grilled meats, especially good with lamb.

BARBECUE SAUCE

1 cup fresh lemon juice
1 cup fresh orange juice
3 tablespoons Worcestershire sauce
3 teaspoons dry mustard
4 cloves garlic, chopped
1 cup chili sauce
¾ cup honey
¾ cup vegetable oil
1 teaspoon paprika
¼ teaspoon ground red pepper
Salt and freshly ground pepper

In large saucepan, combine lemon and orange juice, Worcestershire sauce, dry mustard, garlic, chili sauce, honey, vegetable oil, paprika and red pepper. Simmer uncovered for 45 minutes, stirring occasionally. Season to taste with salt and pepper. Cool and refrigerate.

MUSTARD RING

¾ cup vinegar
¼ cup water
¾ cup sugar
Salt and white pepper, to taste
½ teaspoon tumeric
2 tablespoons dry mustard
4 eggs, well beaten
1 tablespoon gelatin, dissolved
    in ½ cup water
1 cup whipping cream

In top of double boiler, mix vinegar, water, sugar, salt, pepper, turmeric and mustard. Add beaten eggs and cook over simmering water, stirring constantly until thickened. Add gelatin and stir to dissolve. Cool. Add cream, mixing well. Pour into a 4-cup mold and chill several hours or overnight.

Unmold on a lettuce-lined plate. Serve small portions with ham, smoked fish or turkey.

Variation: Whip cream and fold into cooled mustard mixture before pouring into mold. Chill. Serve on lettuce-lined plate garnished with drained pickled shoestring beets.

W I L D   M U S H R O O M S

Wild mushrooms can be substituted in any recipe calling for
mushrooms. A blend of wild and the cultivated mushroom with its mild
earthy flavor can provide a balance in flavor and texture.
Wild mushrooms are not necessarily strong in flavor, but are rather
aromatic and full bodied, so do not shy away from them.
They are excellent in soups, sauces, fruit and bread dressings, and
sautéed with vegetables or combined with pasta.

To clean fresh mushrooms, always brush or wipe with a cloth.
If they must be washed, dry completely.

Crimini

Earthy relative of the white mushroom. Has brown streaks
and darkens with age while also intensifying in flavor.
Excellent enhancement for cooked dishes. Trim stems and
slice for recipes. A half-pound slices into 2½ cups.

Dried Wood Ear

An Oriental dried mushroom. A crunchy texture with a
delicate, bland flavor. It is best used with strong-flavored
ingredients. Usually purchased dried, but sometimes it is
available fresh. If dried, rehydrate in liquid until soft.

Enoki

Clumps of long orangy-brown stems, which are topped with
tiny, shiny caps. The cultivated mushrooms have white stems
and caps. The crunchy texture and mild flavor is a perfect
garnish for soups. Cut off bottom stem where bunch is
attached; brush off dirt.

Oyster

Fan-shaped with convex caps from white to gray in color.
A fairly robust and peppery taste which becomes mild and
flavorful when cooked. Best purchased with 1½-inch or
smaller diameter caps and should be odorless. Completely
edible; trim stem.

Porcini (Cepe)

Pale brown ranging from 1 to 10-inch diameter cap with pale
undersides and a stout stalk. Superior taste. Trim stem, slice
for recipe.

Shiitake

Dark brown cap which average 3 to 6 inches in diameter.
Meaty, earthy flavor with a garlic pine aroma, that indicates it
is fresh! Remove woody stem, slice for recipe.

SALAD GREENS

Always wash all greens in cold water to remove sand and grit.
Pat dry completely.

Arugula

Bright green leaf with aromatic pepper-mustard flavor. Remove stems and add to salad. Combine with Bibb or Boston, endive, radicchio or romaine.

Bibb or Boston

Pale green, buttery textured, loose-leaf, small, round head lettuce of the butterhead family. Sweet and succulent flavor. Bibb is smaller than Boston. Gently wash, remove stem and tear into bite-size pieces. Combines well with any green.

Bok Choy (Chinese Mild flavored White Cabbage)

Crunch-white stalks with dark green leaves. member of the beet family. Leaves may be used for salads, while the stem may be used the same as celery.

Chinese Cabbage (Nappa Cabbage)

Crisp, crinkly green-tipped leaves with a mild, subtle flavor.

Cress

Mild to hot-flavor with varieties available during the year. Add to salads for texture.

Endives:
  Belgian

Firm, compact, 6-inch long head of cream-colored leaves with yellow tips. If tips are green, it is not fresh. Slightly bitter flavor. Remove stem end, separate leaves and rinse under cold water. May be combined with radicchio, arugula, watercress, Bibb or Boston.

  Curly

Lacy, green leaves with a slightly bitter flavor. Excellent with fruit and berries and a sweet-sour dressing.

  Escarole

A milder endive flavor with crisp, broad, pale green curly leaf. Use a small amount with a variety of greens.

Dandelion

Leaves are best eaten young, before the plant flowers and develops a pungent flavor. May be served with mild-flavored greens.

Kale

Mild relative of the cabbage family with many varieties and colors. Slightly bitter flavor but excellent for blending with other greens for taste and color. Remove leaves from stem and discard stem. Best eaten the same day purchased.

Iceberg	Bland flavor with crisp, wilt-resistant leaves. Use with other greens to add texture.
Leaf Lettuce	A loose leaf with red leaf and green leaf varieties. Delicate flavor with soft, tender leaves ranging from bright chartreuse green to deep bronze red with green. May be combined with many greens including watercress, sorrel or arugula.
Radicchio	Italian chicory with tender but firm pinkish leaves and a peppery flavor. Remove the core, tear or dice for salad. Excellent for color.
Romaine	Elongated, coarse, dark green outer leaves to pale green in the center with a slightly bitter flavor. Adds crunch and flavor to mixed greens and is the choice for Caesar salads.
Savoy Cabbage	Wrinkled dark to pale green leaves on a loose, full head with a mellow flavor. Slice to serve in salad.
Spinach	Crisp, tender dark green leaves with a slightly bitter taste. Remove large stems and add to greens.
Swiss Chard	See Oriental variety, Bok Choy. Slight difference in appearance, but they have the same flavor and texture.
Watercress	Member of the mustard family with small crisp, dark green leaves and a spicy flavor. Excellent addition to salads. Remove lower stem portion.

CRUDITÉS FOR DIPPING

Asparagus	Green variety and French white variety. Purchase stalks with tight, firm, pointed tips. If stem is thick, peel, blanch in hot water until barely tender, cool under cold water and drain.
Beets	Deep red color with crisp bright green leaves. Purchase firm and smooth-skinned small or medium size beets. Remove greens as soon as purchased. Wash, cook in boiling water until just tender; peel and slice.
Belgian Endive	Slightly bitter flavor with cream colored, yellow-tipped leaves. Rinse under cold water, cut bottom off and separate leaves.

Bok Choy	Mild flavored member of beet family. Use large green leaves to line bowl or platter. Cut white stems into sticks or slices for dipping.
Broccoflower	Hybrid of broccoli and cauliflower. Wash, remove core to separate florets and cut into bite size portions.
Brussels Sprouts	Tightly closed and compact heads resemble green cabbage in appearance and flavor. Purchase smaller size for tender vegetable. Wash, remove bottom stem, cut in half.
Cauliflower	"Cabbage flower". Most delicate flavor of the cabbage family. Choose firm compact florets with crisp, green leaves. Remove core to separate florets and cut into bite size portions.
Cherry Tomatoes	Red or yellow-gold color, 1-inch in diameter tomatoes. Yellow has a milder flavor. Wash, remove stems.
Daikon Radish	Crisp, juicy, white, very large member of the mustard family. Radish has sweet, fresh flavor with slightly spongy texture. Peel, cut into slices.
English Cucumber	Appealing green color, uniformly shaped with practically no seeds. Purchase dark green firm cucumbers. Soft cucumbers are bitter. Cut into slices or sticks.
Enoki Mushrooms	Delicate size and unusual flavor. Cut off bottom stem where bunch is attached, brush off dirt.
Fennel	Pale green stalks with feathery green foliage and a delicate licorice smell and flavor. Wash bulb, remove top stems, cut bulb in half and cut into slices.
Green Beans	Long, slender green pod with small edible seeds. Purchase crisp and brightly colored beans which are free of blemishes. Wash, remove top stem, serve raw or blanch in hot water briefly.
Jicama	Crunchy, juicy, sweet nutty-flavored root vegetable with light colored meat. Purchase smooth and unmarred roots. Peel outer skin completely. Cut into sticks, cubes or triangles.

Mini-Carrots

Very tender. Wash, peel, remove bottom root, leave top stem attached, if attractive.

Pattypan Squash

Round, flat, scalloped edge. Smaller squash are more tender with fewer seeds. Purchase firm and waxy skins. Wash and cut in half, if large.

Snow Pea Pods

Soft, flexible yet crisp green pods with small edible seeds. Wash, remove stem and string.

Sweet Potatoes

Pale yellow with dry flesh or dark orange with moist flesh. Peel, cut into cubes or sticks.

Yellow Squash

Very mild flavor. Best when purchased young. Wash, cut into slices.

Zucchini

Light tasting, firm flesh, crisp with glossy tender skin and faint stripes. Smaller size, 7 inches, tastes best. Wash, cut into slices.

M E X I C A N   M E N U
F R U I T S   A N D   V E G E T A B L E S

Avocado

Dark green smooth skin with a buttery, mild nut-like flavored pulp. Many sizes and varieties are available. Use in dressings, dips and spreads for variety.

Chayote

Member of gourd family. Pale green and pear-shaped with large edible seeds and white, bland, tasting flesh. Cut in half, remove seeds, parboil until almost tender. Stuff with vegetables and cheese and finish baking.

Cilantro

Related to the parsley family. The most popular herb used in Mexican cooking. Slice it fine and add it to guacamole, marinades and dressings.

Coconut

Edible meat and milk. Purchase one that is heavy and filled with liquid. After removing the meat from the shell, the milk and coconut meat can be used for making desserts.

Fresh Sugar Cane	Available peeled in sticks or whole cane segments. The sweet juice can be sucked from the cane or added to milk and simmered to extract juices.
Guava	Fragrant, sharply sweet, meaty white to yellow to pink flesh with light yellow skin and a gritty texture. Cut in half, remove seeds and scoop out flesh.
Jicama, orange, and lime	An interesting salad combination. Garnish salad with fresh and lime and cilantro.
Malanga	Root vegetable with nutty flavor when cooked. Choose firm, juicy, crisp vegetable without soft spots. After peeling, use in recipes calling for potato. Can be fried, mashed or baked.
Nopales (Cactus Leaves)	Pale to dark green, soft but crunchy, tangy, silky-textured pads. Delicate but slightly tart green bean-like flavor. Purchase small to medium-sized firm pads. Prepare by peeling stickers and eyes off the leaves. Wash well, and grill over hot coals. Slice and then marinate in vinegar and oil with cilantro leaves chopped fine. Serve as a condiment with meat and fish.
Plantains	Vegetable and fruit. When green prepare as appetizers and potatoes. When ripe prepare as bananas. Rinse, trim edges, cut, peel and remove woody fibers before cooking.
Poblano Chili	Dark almost black with rich flavor. The darkest have the richest flavor. These peppers are primarily used for preparing chiles relleno, a cheese stuffed pepper. They range from mild to very hot in flavor.
Red Banana	Short, soft with a hint of strawberry in banana flavor. Can be eaten cooked or raw. Can be blended with ice and fruit juice or ice cream for a refreshing drink.
Variety Chili	There is a range of peppers from the mildest to the world's hottest in this category. Look for labeled peppers explaining their use and heat level.

FRUIT

Fruits to serve with cheese as appetizers or desserts

Apples

Many varieties. From yellow to yellow-green to bright red smooth skins, they can be tender to crisp, and sweet to tart. Purchase firm, good color fruit with a fresh fragrance and no bruises. Wash, cut in half, remove seeds and slice.

Asian Pear

Firm lemon-green to brown in color in a wide range of sizes. Lightly sweet and fragrant with a hint of pineapple and a crisp, juicy flesh. Cut into thin wedges or rounds.

Berries

Many varieties. Purchase with good color, no mold or injured berries, or leaking. Use within a day or two of purchase.

Blood Orange

Small, sweet-tart citrus with brilliant red flesh. Extremely juicy, it has a rich flavor with a hint of raspberry. Peel, cut into slices.

Carambola (Star Fruit)

Thin skinned, glossy yellow with 5 ribs forming a star shape when sliced. Larger ribs indicate sweet and smaller ribs indicate tart fruit. Juicy, refreshing flavor and flowery scent when it is ripe. Does not require peeling. Cut into slices. The interesting star shape makes it an excellent garnish.

Fresh Figs

Soft flesh with tiny edible seeds. Best used soon after purchased. Wash and cut in half.

Grapes

Edible berries with a smooth skin and juicy flesh. Purchase only plump grapes, firmly attached to stem. Wash.

Kiwi

Fuzzy brown-skinned fruit with a bright lime-green flesh with spattered edible tiny black seeds. Fruit has smooth texture with an indescribably sweet-tart flavor. Delicious. Peel, cut into wedges or rounds.

Mango

Thin skinned green or yellow-red with exceedingly juicy inside. Flavor is sweet and fragrant. Purchase larger mango for better ratio of fruit to oversized seed. Peel, cut fruit from seed and cut into slices.

Melons	Many varieties. Sweet and fragrant member of the gourd family. Serve at any time. Peel, remove seeds, cut into slices or cubes.
Oranges	Juicy sweet to tart citrus fruit. Purchase firm oranges, heavy for size with no spongy spots. Peel, cut into slices and remove seeds.
Papaya	Large, pear-shaped, yellow skinned with yellow to red-orange juicy pulp. Sweet-tart flavor with a creamy firm texture. Purchase fruit that gives when slightly touched. Peel, remove seeds, and cut into slices or cubes.
Pears	Many varieties. Bell shaped, from green to yellow to red. Juicy with spicy to sweet to tart-sweet flavor. Purchase fragrant, free from blemishes and soft spots. Wash and cut in half, remove seeds and slice.
Pineapple	From yellow, to red-brown to green with deep green leaves. Exceedingly juicy, tangy, sweet-tart flavor with a bumpy patterned skin. Purchase plump and fresh fruit. Cut thick slice from top and bottom, pare skin from top to bottom. Cut in half, cube or slice.
Ugli Fruit	Tangerine-grapefruit hybrid with yellow-orange pulp and a puffy, thick, loose-fitting skin. Acid-sweet flavor, it is juicy and heavy for its size. Gives to pressure when ripe. Peel and cut into wedges.

CHEESE

Cheese is the perfect addition or accompaniment to foods
from appetizers to dessert. Use your creativity and interchange or add a cheese
to a recipe. Remember cheese is also delicious served with fruit.

(Fresh, Soft and Semi-Ripe)

Bel Paese

Italian. Cow's milk. Slightly sweet and buttery flavor. Melts well. Good with fruity wines for appetizer or dessert.

Boursin

French. Cow's milk. Triple-creme. Soft, spreadable; purchase plain, with herbs, peppercorns or mushrooms added. Top grilled meats at end of cooking time. Great with wine.

Brie

French. Cow's milk. Edible white rind with creamy-runny milk mild to tangy interior. Pungent when overripe. Excellent with fruit.

Camembert

French. Cow's milk. Edible white rind with smooth, spreadable, mild to tangy interior with a fruity fragrance. Excellent with fruit, melts well on chicken and meat, and in eggs and quiche.

Chèvre

French. Goat's milk. Pure white from moist and creamy to dry and semi-firm with mild to pungent flavor. Delicious served fresh and melts well. Domestics as Capriole from Greenville, Indiana and Californian Taupiniere.

Cream Cheese

American. Cow's milk. Smooth, creamy, spreadable with slightly tangy flavor. Use for cheesecakes, bagels and baking.

Feta

Greek. Sheep or goat's milk. White, crumbly, salty with slightly sour yet rich tangy flavor.

Fontina

Italian. Cow's milk. Rind with buttery, delicately sweet-nutty interior. Semi-firm but creamy. Melts well. Excellent on pasta.

Fontinella
Kasseri

Italian. Sheep's milk. Mild and slightly salty flavor.
Greek. Same as Fontinella.

Fresh Mozzarella

Italian. Cow or water buffalo's milk. Packed in water. Mild, delicate flavor. Spreadable. Melts well. Excellent for pizza or pasta.

Mascarpone	Italian. Cow's milk. Delicately sweet with a heavy whipped cream texture. Great with fruit.
Muenster	French. Cow's milk. Red-orange rinds with smooth, buttery, sharp flavor. Melts well.
Neufchâtel	French. Cow's milk. Interchangeable with cream cheese. Lower fat content.
Petit Suisse	French. Cow's milk. Interchangeable with cream cheese, but a bit sweeter and very soft.
Port-Salut	French. Cow's milk. Orange rind with creamy, full-flavored tang. Perfect with fruit or as an hor d'oeuvre with crackers.
Havarti	Danish. Cow's milk. Creamy with irregular holes and a mild tangy flavor.
Scamorza	Italian. Cow's milk. Firm texture but supple with mild nutty flavor, similar to mozzarella but saltier. Delicious as table cheese or use in cooking on pizza, pasta or antipasto.

(Firm Cheeses)

Brick	Wisconsin. Cow's milk. Reddish-brown rind with yellow-white mild, earthy-flavored interior. Drier than Muenster. Melts well. Also good grated.
Cheddar	American. Cow or sheep's milk. Many varieties. Mild to very sharp. Naturally cream colored. Popular. Melts well.
Cheshire	English. Cow's milk. Crumbly, mild, tangy. Similar to cheddar and interchangeable. Great in soups. Melts well.
Colby	Wisconsin. Cow's milk. Cheddar-like but moister and softer. Melts well and excellent sliced.
Derby or Derbyshire	English. Cow's milk. Natural or waxed rind with mild firm paste interior. Similar to cheddar. Melts well and great snack.
Edam	Dutch. Cow's milk. Natural rind with mild, buttery interior. Slightly harder but similar to Gouda. Low fat content.

Emmentaler or Emmenthal

Swiss. Cow's milk. Nutty or fruity with sweet mellow flavor. Real Swiss! Any use from appetizers to dessert.

Gloucester or Double Gouster

English. Cow's milk. Natural rind with mellow golden-yellow interior. Excellent with or after a meal.

Gouda

Dutch. Cow's milk. Natural rind with mild, buttery interior. Becomes tangy and full flavored with age. Excellent flavor. Great with fruit. Aged is great with beer, red wine and whole-grained breads.

Gruyère

Swiss. Cow's milk. Rind with medium hole interior of creamy but firm, mild-to-sharp flavor with nutty aroma. Melts well. Excellent for fondue, dinner cheese with wine, melted sandwiches or in eggs.

Jarlsberg

Norwegian. Cow's milk. Wax rind with large irregular hole interior with buttery, rich mild-to-nutty Swiss-style flavor. Excellent for cooking and eating.

Monterey Jack

American. Cow's milk. Mild and sweet. Softer than cheddar. Stronger flavor with age. Excellent melting cheese.

Provolone

Italian. Cow or water buffalo's milk. Rind with creamy, buttery to piquant flavor. Excellent for cooking. Aged cheese excellent for grating and on pizza.

Swiss

American. Cow's milk. Generic term. Very bland to very good with nutty flavor and large holes. Imitating Emmentaler and Gruyère.

Tilsit

German. Cow's milk. Dark yellow rind with mild to tangy flavored pale yellow, irregularly cracked, interior. Aged is more pungent. Excellent in sauces and vegetable dishes, for sandwiches and dessert.

(Premier Bleus)
Strong flavor and aroma that intensifies with age.

Gorgonzola

Italian. Cow's milk. Soft, creamy and crumbly. Fatter and moister than most but also considered by many as the best bleu cheese.

Maytag Blue	American, Iowa. Cow's milk. Very creamy, crumbly.
Roquefort	French. Sheep's milk. Strong flavor and crumbly.
Stilton	English. Cow's milk. Intensely flavored. Moist, creamy and crumbly.

(Grating Cheeses)
Aged and hard

Asiago	Italian. Cow's milk. Salty, nutty and sharp flavor. Grasso di Monte milder than d'Allevio.
Parmesan	Italian. Cow's milk. Sweet to sharp flavor.
Percorino Romano	Italian. Sheep, goat or cow's milk. Tangy and pungent flavor.
Sapsago	Swiss. Cow's milk. Pale green due to the addition of sweet clover. Mild, tangy, spicy flavor.

FLAVORED BUTTERS

Flavored butters make the ordinary meal a little more special
and add that extra touch to a gourmet meal. Experiment with proportions and
use your imagination. Several suggestions:

Mix butter with:	*Serve on:*
Chopped strawberries	Popovers
Apricots	French toast
Currants	Pancakes
Maple syrup	Pancakes
Honey	Biscuits or toast
Dijon mustard	Vegetables or pasta
Dill	Tomato soup
Champagne and ginger	Shrimp
Lemon and dill	Fish
Salmon	Cocktail rye and crackers
Herbs	Chicken and vegetables
Curry and garlic	Grilled beef
Herbs and cheese	French or sourdough bread

CELEBRITY CHEFS

GOVERNOR EDGAR'S FAVORITE BROWNIES

Governor James Edgar
Governor, State of Illinois

1½ squares bitter chocolate
½ cup butter
2 eggs
1 cup sugar
½ teaspoon baking powder
1 cup flour
1 cup chopped nuts
1 tablespoon vanilla

Frosting:
2 tablespoons butter
1 square bitter chocolate
1 cup powdered sugar

Preheat oven to 350°. Grease a 9-inch square pan.

Melt chocolate with butter and set aside. Beat eggs with sugar until fluffy. Sift baking powder with flour. Stir into egg and sugar mixture alternately with chocolate. Mix in nuts and vanilla. Pour into prepared pan.

Bake for 30 minutes.

Ten minutes before brownies are out of oven, melt butter and chocolate. Blend in powdered sugar. Thin with milk if too thick. Spread on brownies while still hot.

8 to 10 servings

CURRIED ZUCCHINI AND POTATO SOUP

Mayor Richard M. Daley
City of Chicago

4 large zucchini (about 2 pounds)
2 onions, chopped
½ teaspoon curry powder
½ cup chopped fresh parsley
4 cups chicken broth
1 cup cooked potatoes
½ cup light cream
Salt to taste
½ cup sour cream
    (plain yogurt can be substituted)

Garnish:
Chopped watercress or fresh parsley

Cook zucchini, onions, curry and parsley in chicken broth until vegetables are tender. Puree with potatoes in blender, 1 cup at a time. Stir in cream and salt to taste.

Serve hot or cold. Top with dollop of sour cream or plain yogurt and sprinkle with parsley or watercress.

May be frozen before cream is added. Defrost and serve cold with cream added, or heat, then add cream.

8 servings

ZUCCHINI SOUP

The White House
Luncheon with Barbara Bush

1 pound cleaned, unpeeled zucchini
2 tablespoons shallots (I use onion or leeks often)
1 clove garlic, minced
1¾ cups chicken broth
2 tablespoons butter or margarine
1 teaspoon curry powder
½ teaspoon salt
½ cup table cream

Chop unpeeled zucchini, shallots, and garlic. Put all three into a heavy frying pan. Cook for 10 to 20 minutes (stir to keep from burning—you don't want it to brown). Put all ingredients into blender and blend. Add table cream.

Heat and serve hot with croutons or chill and serve cold with chives.

6 to 8 servings

CAESAR SALAD

2 to 3 cloves garlic
½ cup olive oil
4 cups bread cubes (¼-inch)
4 quarts assorted lettuce greens
1 cup grated Parmesan cheese
½ cup crumbled bleu cheese
1 teaspoon salt
½ teaspoon freshly ground pepper
12 teaspoons olive oil
1 egg
7 tablespoons lemon juice
2 tablespoons Worcestershire sauce

Cut garlic into quarters and let sit in ½ cup olive oil overnight (out of refrigerator). Put bread cubes into shallow pan. Toast them in a slow oven (300°) for 30 minutes until golden brown, turning with a fork. After cooling, wrap cubes in wax paper until needed.

Sprinkle lettuce greens with Parmesan cheese, bleu cheese, salt and pepper. Add olive oil (not the oil treated with garlic). Mix together one egg, lemon juice, and Worcestershire sauce. Pour over salad and toss. Add croutons (flavored with garlic and oil mixed beforehand) to salad and toss. Do this at the last moment as the croutons get soggy.

8 servings

BLACKENED REDFISH
The White House
Luncheon with Barbara Bush

3 pounds redfish, filleted
Melted butter or margarine
1 tablespoon paprika
2½ teaspoons salt
1 teaspoon onion powder
1 teaspoon ground red pepper
1 teaspoon garlic powder
¾ teaspoon ground white pepper
¾ teaspoon freshly ground
   black pepper
½ teaspoon dry thyme
½ teaspoon oregano

Dip fish in melted butter or margarine and then in mixture of seasonings. Cook in cast iron skillet, preheated until pan is very hot. Cook 2 minutes on one side, turn, and cook for another minute.

This dish is very smoky to prepare; it cooks well outside on a grill or campstove.

LEMON BARS
For Lemon Lovers of America!

1 cup margarine, softened
2 cups powdered sugar
2 cups flour

4 teaspoons fresh lemon juice
Rind of 2 lemons, grated
4 eggs, well beaten
2 cups sugar
1 teaspoon baking powder
4 tablespoons flour
1 cup shredded coconut, optional

Preheat oven to 350°.

Mix margarine, powdered sugar and flour in a small bowl. Spread out (batter is stiff) in a jelly roll pan.

Bake 15 minutes or until pale tan or paler. Cool.

Mix together lemon juice, rind, eggs, sugar, baking powder, flour and coconut and pour over crust.

Bake for 25 minutes.

This is a favorite of ours . . . borrowed from a dear friend.

12 servings

PAVÉ OF SALMON, MUSHROOMS AND NAPA CABBAGE WITH BROWN BUTTER VINAIGRETTE

Charlie Trotter's – Chicago, Illinois
Chef Charlie Trotter

This dish has appeared in several forms on our menu, but I believe, that this is the best version which we have come up with yet. The mushrooms here are so concentrated and earthy in flavor that they make a powerful back-drop to the succulent salmon and clean refreshing cabbage. The brown butter vinaigrette is delicate and satiny and adds just the perfect acidity and unctuous touch to the other ingredients on the plate.

Mise-en-place:
5 pounds black trumpet mushrooms,
*   cleaned*
5 pounds Portabella mushrooms,
*   cleaned*
6 ounces foie gras butter

Vinaigrette:
1¼ cups butter
1 cup aged balsamic vinegar
¾ cup unsalted butter, cooled
*   and sliced*
Salt and freshly ground pepper

6 to 8 pounds Norwegian salmon,
*   skinned, boned,*
30 to 35 napa cabbage leaves,
*   blanched, center vein removed*
*   and thoroughly blotted dry*

Blanch, peel, seed and chop:
*   1 tomato*
*   1 yellow tomato*
2 tablespoons chopped fresh chives
2 tablespoons chopped fresh parsley

Foie Gras butter:
1 pound fresh foie gras, cleaned,
*   mashed, deveined*
Pinch of salt and sugar
Freshly cracked black pepper
Generous splash of best quality
*   port or sautérne*
3 cups sugar
3 cups salt
Freshly cracked black pepper
2 pounds unsalted butter

Mise-en-place: Puree black trumpet mushrooms and cook in 2 tablespoons bacon fat until all liquid is rendered. Puree Portabella mushrooms and cook with 2 tablespoons of bacon fat until all liquid is rendered. Divide foie gras butter and cook with mushrooms.

Vinaigrette: Cook butter over a medium high heat until thoroughly golden brown. While still hot, blend with the vinegar in blender. Gradually add sliced butter into running blender. Season to taste

Preheat oven to 350°.

Assembly: Slice salmon lengthwise into thin long pieces. In a 10x14-inch roasting pan, layer the salmon, cabbage, and mushrooms, creating many layers of each, or at least 2½ inches thick. Place weight on top over night and then the next day turn out and cut diamonds, or pavé pieces.
Roast for 10 minutes.
Place a pavé on a plate and strew the plate with concassé (chopped yellow and red tomatoes), chives and parsley. Drizzle with the warm vinaigrette.

Foie Gras Butter: Mix together the foie gras, pinch of salt and sugar, pepper and port. Roll into a log. Rinse a large piece of cheesecloth and squeeze dry. Wrap around the foie gras. Stir sugar, salt and pepper together; pour over foie gras. Let stand in refrigerator for 36 to 48 hours. Remove from sugar-salt mixture and unwrap. Place half of foie gras and half of butter in food processor and process 2 to 3 minutes. Repeat with remaining foie gras and butter. Store covered tightly in refrigerator until ready to use.

12 to 14 servings

FIG AND MASCARPONE TORTE

Calihan Gotoff Catering, Inc.
Chicago, Illinois
John Calihan

1 pound fresh mascarpone
1 pound cream cheese
¾ cup light brown sugar
1 tablespoon pure vanilla extract
½ pound dried figs
Marsala
¼ cup sugar

Gently blend mascarpone, cream cheese, brown sugar and vanilla in a large bowl taking care not to over mix. (The mascarpone can break if over mixed.) Poach dried figs in a small amount of marsala or maderia wine. Cool figs and split lengthwise.

Preheat oven to 300°. Butter a 2-quart baking dish and sprinkle with ¼ cup sugar.

Line bottom of baking dish with the halved figs. Pour in half of cheese mixture and smooth out evenly. Make another layer of halved figs and pour in the remaining cheese mixture.

Bake in a water bath for 35 to 40 minutes until the center is hot but still quite soft. Cool overnight.

Before serving, run a knife around the inner rim of baking dish and flip torte out onto a serving dish.

Serving suggestions:
*Set on a platter and surround with fresh cut figs, figs wrapped with prosciutto and sliced french bread.
*Surround with fresh whole strawberries and imported crackers.
*Serve a small dollop of fig/mascarpone mixture on individual endive leaves (no baking necessary for this).

8 servings

EGGPLANT DUXELLE
WITH ROQUEFORT GLAZE

Gordon Restaurant
Chicago, Illinois
Gordon Sinclair

1 pound mushrooms, sliced
3 tablespoons clarified butter,
    divided
2 large Bermuda onions, diced
3 tablespoons tomato paste
Salt and freshly ground pepper

2 medium eggplants
Salt and freshly ground pepper

2 cups olive oil
2 cups hollandaise sauce
1 cup bechamel sauce
3 to 4 ounces Roquefort cheese,
    crumbled

Hollandaise Sauce:
1/2 cup butter, creamed,
    room temperature
4 egg yolks
1 tablespoon fresh lemon juice
Salt
2 tablespoons boiling water

Béchamel Sauce:
1 quart whipping cream
1 tablespoon butter
2 tablespoons flour
5 egg yolks
1/2 teaspoon dried tarragon
1 teaspoon white wine
Salt and freshly ground pepper

Preheat oven to 350°.

Sauté mushrooms in 1½ tablespoons butter until soft in a heavy skillet; drain; dry. Finely chop mushrooms and wring them out in a towel.

Sauté onions in remaining butter until soft in a heavy skillet. Combine mushrooms, onions and tomato paste. Season with salt and pepper.

Cut eggplants across in ¾-inch pieces. Season with salt and pepper. Sauté eggplant in hot olive oil until eggplant is cooked half way. Remove eggplant and pat dry. Distribute mushroom/onion duxelle evenly over the six slices of eggplant. Place eggplant slices on a cookie sheet and bake for about 5 to 8 minutes. Remove from the oven and transfer to a gratin serving dish.

Hollandaise Sauce: Place creamed butter in top of double boiler, over warm water. Beat in egg yolks. Mix in lemon juice and salt. Whisk in the boiling water. Stir constantly until the sauce thickens.

Béchamel Sauce: In a heavy saucepan reduce cream for 15 minutes over low heat. Meanwhile, melt butter in a large pan; add flour and cook 2 to 3 minutes. Whisk in the cream and cook until thickened. Beat egg yolks in a cold bowl. Add tarragon, wine and salt and pepper to taste. Slowly whisk in the cream mixture. Remove from heat.

Combine the two sauces and pour over eggplant slices. Sprinkle with Roquefort. Place serving dish under the broiler and broil until they are brown and bubbly. Remove, sprinkle with chopped parsley and serve.

Eggplant has been cultivated in France since the beginning of the 17th century. It originated in India.

6 servings

CRAB CAKE WITH MUSTARD SAUCE

Le Francais
Wheeling, Illinois
Chef Patrick Chabart

3 green onions, sliced
Olive oil
6 medium shrimp
1 egg
1 cup whipping cream
Salt and freshly ground pepper
1 teaspoon Dijon mustard
1 dash Tabasco
3 dashes Worcestershire sauce
1 cup crabmeat (jumbo lump)

Sauce:
2 shallots, chopped
¼ cup white wine
2 tablespoons whipping cream
½ cup butter
Salt and freshly ground pepper
1 teaspoon Dijon mustard
1 teaspoon chopped herbs
    (tarragon, chives, parsley)

Preheat oven to 350°.

Cook, on low heat, the sliced green onions in olive oil until soft. Process the shrimp in food processor for 30 seconds. Add egg and process again. Place bowl in freezer for 5 minutes. Add green onions, process; add whipping cream and season lightly. Add mustard, tabasco, and Worcestershire sauce. Fold in crabmeat.

In a non-stick saucepan cook the crab cake in a ring (or shaped with a spoon) for 2 minutes on each side in oven.

Sauce: Reduce shallots and white wine to 1 tablespoon and add whipping cream. Reduce again to 1 tablespoon. Turn heat to very low. Whisk in butter, one tablespoon at a time. Season with salt, pepper and mustard. Add the chopped herbs.

Place crab cake in middle of plate and pour sauce around.

4 servings

GUACAMOLE DAVIES

Janet Davies
Chicago Television Personality

1 medium avocado, peeled
1 medium tomato, quartered
2 tablespoons mayonnaise
2 tablespoons fresh lime juice
2 tablespoons sour cream
¼ teaspoon salt
½ teaspoon ground red pepper
½ teaspoon garlic powder
⅓ cup chopped onion

Place avocado, tomato, mayonnaise, lime juice, sour cream, salt, red pepper, and garlic powder in food processor. Process one minute or until lumpy. Stir in onion.

Serve with tortilla chips. I prefer black bean tortilla chips.

2 cups

SMOKED SALMON WITH SMOKED SALMON MOUSSE AND LIME

Carlos
Highland Park, Illinois
Chef Don Yamauchi

1 fillet smoked salmon, front fillet
    (6-inch x 6-inch square)
½ cup shrimp stock
4 sheets gelatine*
Salt and freshly ground pepper
Tabasco, to taste
Dash Worcestershire sauce, to taste
Horseradish, to taste
1½ cups whipping cream
1 tomato, peeled and small diced
1 bunch chives
1 lime, juice and zest
4 ounces Osetra caviar
48 mache leaves
12 lime crowns

Cut smoked salmon fillet into 2-inch wide rectangles. Slice ⅛-inch from the top of each rectangle and put aside 7 ounces for the mousse mixture. You should have 6 rectangular pieces.

Heat shrimp stock and remove from heat, add gelatine* to the hot shrimp stock and cool mixture completely. After cool, process shrimp stock and 7 ounces of salmon trimmings in food processor until smooth. Pass mixture through a fine strainer. Season with salt, pepper, Tabasco, Worcestershire sauce, and horseradish to taste.

Whip 1 cup of cream until stiff. Fold the salmon mixture and whipped cream together with a spatula.

Cut the smoked salmon rectangles in thin slices, slicing horizontally on the filet, with an electric knife. Place salmon rectangles onto a sheet of plastic wrap. With a pastry bag, pipe one strip of the mousse mixture lengthwise onto each piece of smoked salmon. Cross the smoked salmon widthwise over the mousse using the plastic wrap to keep it as round as possible.

Whip the remaining cream to soft peaks, then fold in the tomato, chives, lime zest and juice.

Remove salmon rolls from plastic and place two rolls on each plate forming a v-shape. Between the rolls, place 4 leaves of mache beneath a lime crown. Using a pastry bag, border each plate with dots of flavored whipped cream mixture. Spoon a small amount of the caviar on each tip of the salmon rolls.

*One envelope unflavored gelatin can be substituted for gelatin sheets. Soften gelatin in cold shrimp stock for 5 minutes. Heat to dissolve. Cool. Process with salmon trimmings as directed.

12 servings

WARM CELERY ROOT PANCAKE WITH SMOKED SALMON AND FAVA BEAN SALAD

Fairmont Hotel
Chicago, Illinois
Chef John Coletta

Marinated Olive Oil:
4 cloves garlic, peeled
1/4 teaspoon hot red pepper flakes
3/4 cup olive oil, divided

Fava Bean Salad:
10 ounces fava bean pods
2 teaspoons julienned fresh basil
Marinated olive oil
Salt and freshly ground pepper

Celery Root Pancake:
2 medium celery roots, peeled
    and julienned
Salt and freshly ground pepper
2 tablespoons chopped fresh herbs
    (basil, oregano, parsley)
2 whole eggs
1/2 cup marinated olive oil
12 slices smoked salmon
1/2 cup olive oil
1/2 cup fava bean salad

Marinated Olive Oil: Over medium heat, pre-heat saucepan with 2 tablespoons olive oil. Add garlic cloves, fry until golden brown on all sides. Place in jar, add hot red pepper flakes and remaining olive oil. Cover. Let marinate at room temperature.

Fava Bean Salad: Carefully open pods, removing beans. Discard pods. In boiling salted water, cook beans until tender. Stop cooking process by immersing in ice water. Peel beans carefully, not damaging beans. Place beans and basil in mixing bowl, coat liberally with marinated olive oil. Mix well. Season with salt and pepper. Mix well and chill.

Celery Root Pancake: Place celery root in mixing bowl, season with salt and pepper. Add chopped fresh herbs, mix well.

In separate mixing bowl, beat whole eggs until well blended. Add eggs to celery root, mix well to cover all julienne. Over medium heat, pre-heat a 6 1/2-inch teflon fry pan with 2 teaspoons of marinated olive oil. Make a thin pancake by covering entire bottom of fry pan with celery root mixture, approximately 1/8-inch thick. Using rubber spatula, smooth round edges of pancake by pushing in any stray ends. Cook first side of pancake until browned, adding more marinated olive oil as necessary. Using rubber spatula as aide, flip pancake over as 1 piece. Cook second side until browned. Using rubber spatula as aide, slice pancake into center of round dinner plate. Cook until browned.

Brush three smoked salmon slices with olive oil. Season with pepper. Form into turbans. Place in triangular pattern on top of pancake. Sprinkle plate with fava bean salad. Top with freshly ground black pepper.

4 servings

STUFFED SHRIMP WITH CHÈVRE

Zarrosta Grill
Oakbrook, Illinois
Chef Joseph Disciano

1 small onion, medium diced

3 cloves garlic, minced

1 tablespoon butter

6 plum tomatoes, peeled, seeded
    and diced

2 tablespoons chopped fresh basil

8 ounces tomato puree

1 small bay leaf

24 extra large shrimp, peeled,
    deveined and butterflied

8 ounces cream cheese

8 ounces chèvre cheese

1 bunch fresh chives, chopped
    reserving ¼ for garnish

Cracked black pepper to taste

In a large saucepan, sauté onion and garlic in butter until onion is translucent. Add tomato, basil, tomato puree and bay leaf; simmer on low heat for about 45 minutes.

In electric mixer, whip room temperature cream cheese and chèvre cheese. Mix in chives and season with black pepper.

Add cheese mixture into a piping bag and pipe onto the shrimp. Chill until mixture is slightly firm. Place shrimp on prepared pan.

Preheat oven to 400°. Lightly oil sheet pan.

Bake for 5 to 7 minutes. Pour sauce onto individual plates and place shrimp on the bed of sauce. Garnish with fresh chive sticks.

6 servings

CREAM OF HAZELNUT SOUP À LA ZARRIS

Union League Club
Chicago, Illinois

Coarsely chop:
    1 medium leek
    2 medium carrots
    2 celery ribs
    1 clove garlic

2 bay leaves

⅓ pound hazelnuts, finely chopped,
    divided

½ pound butter, divided

2 tablespoons flour

8 cups chicken-veal stock

1 cup cream

Salt and white pepper

In a large saucepan, sauté leeks, carrots, celery, garlic, bay leaves and half the amount of hazelnuts in ¼ pound butter until vegetables begin to brown on the edges. Remove from heat, blend in flour and let stand about 15 minutes.

Return to heat and add stock slowly, whisking with whip to prevent any lumps. Simmer gently for 1 hour.

Strain through cheesecloth; add remaining pound of butter, cream and remaining half of hazelnuts. Season with salt and white pepper to taste.

6 to 8 servings

OATMEAL SOUP

John Gardiner's Tennis Ranch
Carmel Valley, California
Chef Deni Curtis

½ *medium yellow onion, diced*
½ *tablespoon chopped fresh basil*
½ *tablespoon chopped fresh tarragon*
¾ *cup white wine*
½ *cup oatmeal (rolled)*
2 *cups diced tomatoes*
5 *cups chicken stock*
Salt and freshly ground pepper

Sauté onion and herbs in white wine until reduced to thin paste. Brown oatmeal lightly and add tomatoes. Cook for 10 minutes. Add chicken stock and cook for 20 minutes. Season with salt and pepper to taste.

12 to 15 servings

BLACK BEAN SOUP WITH TOMATO SALSA

Southgate Cafe
Lake Forest, Illinois
Chef Chris Mellender

½ *onion, chopped*
5 *slices bacon, chopped*
2 *jalapeño chili peppers,*
    finely chopped
3 *cups black beans*
1 *bay leaf*
3 *tablespoons cumin*
Salt to taste
Tabasco

Tomato Salsa:
6 *tomatoes, seeded and chopped*
1 *to 2 jalapeño chili peppers,*
    finely chopped
½ *onion, chopped*
½ *bunch cilantro, chopped*
Lime juice to taste
1 *ounce rice vinegar*
Salt to taste

Day before: Cover beans with water and soak overnight.
    In a large saucepan, sauté onion, bacon and peppers; add drained black beans and enough water to cover 1 inch above beans. Cook with bay leaf 1 hour or until beans are tender. Add cumin, salt and Tabasco.

    Tomato Salsa: In a bowl, mix tomatoes, peppers, onion, cilantro, lime juice and rice vinegar. Season to taste.

    Garnish soup with dollop of sour cream and chilled Tomato Salsa or red onion.

4 to 6 cups

COLD MINTED SPLIT PEA SOUP

Tallgrass Restaurant
Lockport, Illinois
Chef Bob Burcenski

2 cups dry green split peas
2 cups chopped onion
1 cup chopped celery
1 cup chopped carrots
½ cup unsalted butter
8 cups fresh chicken stock,
    preferably homemade
⅛ teaspoon ground cloves
1 bay leaf
1 cup chopped fresh mint
2 ham hocks
1 teaspoon salt
White pepper
1 cup heavy cream (cold)
Fresh mint sprigs

Wash split peas thoroughly and discard any discolored ones. In a heavy soup kettle sauté onions, celery and carrots in butter until soft. Add stock and bring to boil. Slowly add peas to stock. Add cloves, bay leaf, chopped mint and ham hocks and simmer, partially covered, for 1½ hours or until peas are very soft.

Remove hocks and bay leaf. Puree soup in food processor and strain into bowl. Season with salt and pepper to taste. Chill.

Before serving, add cream and taste again for seasoning.

Garnish with sprig of mint.

8 servings

TOMATO, BLEU CHEESE SOUP

The Greenery
Barrington, Illinois
Chef David Koelling

1 large onion, chopped
2 celery ribs, chopped
6 green onions, sliced
4 teaspoons chopped garlic
3 cups tomato juice
2 cups chicken stock
½ cup heavy whipping cream
½ cup tomato puree
¼ pound bleu cheese
¼ teaspoon dry basil
⅛ teaspoon Tabasco
Salt and freshly ground pepper

Sauté onions, celery, green onions and garlic in butter. Cover and let sweat over low heat. Add tomato juice, stock, cream and tomato puree; simmer until vegetables are very soft. Add crumbled cheese and puree in food processor. Add basil and Tabasco. Season to taste with salt and pepper.

4 servings

FINGER SALAD WITH WALNUT OIL DRESSING AND TOMATO SORBET

The Cottage
Calumet City, Illinois
Chef Carolyn Buster

Romaine, fresh inside leaves
Belgian endive

Walnut Oil Dressing:
1 cup walnut oil
1 cup salad oil
¼ cup sugar
1 clove garlic, crushed
6 tablespoons chili sauce
6 tablespoons olive paste
½ teaspoon basil
2 teaspoons freshly ground
*   black pepper*
Zest from 1 orange
1 teaspoon salt
1 cup red wine vinegar
¼ cup Dijon mustard

Tomato Sorbet:
1 cup tomato puree
½ cup tomato juice
1 egg white
Sprinkling of basil
1 teaspoon fresh lemon juice
Pinch of salt and white pepper

Wash, dry and chill romaine and Belgian endive.

Walnut Oil Dressing: Whisk oils, sugar, garlic, chili sauce, olive paste, basil, pepper, orange zest, salt, vinegar and mustard together and chill.

Tomato Sorbet: Blend tomato puree, tomato juice, egg white, basil, lemon juice, salt and pepper together and freeze in ice cream machine.

Serving suggestions: Use stemmed glass such as a bolla glass. Place approximately 2 to 3 tablespoons of dressing in bottom of glass. Stand crisp leaves in glass and place one scoop of sorbet in middle.

Guests will dip leaves into dressing and sorbet and eat with fingers!

This is a great special occasion salad.

10 to 12 servings

QUESADILLAS

Ferrée Florsheim Catering, Ltd.
Chicago, Illinois

1 large fresh tomato, chopped
1 small can mild or medium chopped
*   green chilies*
1 package soft flour tortillas
1 6-ounce package Monterey Jack
*   cheese, sliced*
1 bottle salsa sauce

Mix tomatoes and chilies together. Lay tortilla flat. Place ½ slice of cheese on 1 side of tortilla. Place 1 teaspoon of tomato and chile mixture on top of cheese. Fold tortilla shell in half.

Sauté filled tortilla in corn oil until browned and crispy. Cut into 3 triangles and serve with salsa sauce for dip.

10 servings

WHITE AND GREEN ASPARAGUS SALAD WITH SUN-DRIED TOMATO OIL

Fairmont Hotel
Chicago, Illinois
Chef John Coletta

Sun-dried Tomato Oil:
1 ounce sun-dried tomatoes
10 tablespoons olive oil
1 medium clove garlic, peeled
Juice from ½ lemon
Salt and freshly ground pepper

Salad:
32 green asparagus spears
64 mini-white asparagus spears
3 tablespoons sun-dried tomato oil
2 tablespoons olive oil

Garnish:
3 tablespoons toasted pine nuts
Fresh cracked black pepper, to taste

Sun-dried Tomato Oil: Soften sun-dried tomatoes by soaking in ample water overnight. Drain well before measuring. Combine sun-dried tomatoes, olive oil, garlic, lemon juice in blender. Let run until all ingredients are pureed. Season with salt and pepper to taste.

In boiling salted water, blanch green asparagus until tender. Stop cooking process by immersing in ice water. Drain well. In boiling salted water, blanch white asparagus until tender, immerse in ice water. Drain well. Trim off woody part of asparagus, roughly half the length. Discard stems. Brush 8 green spears and 16 white spears with olive oil.

Arrange 8 green asparagus in a fan on top half of round dinner plate, heads pointing to rim, ends in center. Arrange 16 white asparagus in smaller fan, heads covering green asparagus ends.

Using spoon, drizzle sun-dried tomato oil around edge of plate. Sprinkle with toasted pine nuts. Top with fresh cracked black pepper.

4 servings

CHICKEN POLYNESIAN

Ferrée Florsheim Catering, Ltd.
Chicago, Illinois

2 8-ounce chicken breasts, skinned
*   and boneless*
1 cup pancake batter
1 cup long thread coconut
Vegetable oil
1 jar Major Grey chutney
Melted butter to taste

Cut chicken into bite-size pieces, dip in batter. Roll in coconut, making sure all pieces are well coated.

Deep fry in vegetable oil until brown and crispy. Finely chop chutney and mix in melted butter to use as a dip.

6 servings

GRILLED PORK TENDERLOIN SALAD WITH CILANTRO CREME DRESSING

Onwentsia Club
Lake Forest, Illinois
Bennett Mulé, Chef de Cuisine

4 pork tenderloins
4 cloves garlic
Assorted fresh herbs

Cilantro Creme Dressing:
2 jalapeño chili peppers, minced
3 cloves garlic, roasted and minced
Juice from 2 limes
4 egg yolks
½ cup olive oil
1 cup vegetable oil
1 cup sour cream
Fresh cilantro, minced
Fresh parsley, minced
Salt and freshly ground pepper
2 cups vegetable oil

1 pint cherry tomatoes
1 pint yellow plum tomatoes
2 cans artichoke hearts
Mesclun lettuce for 8 salads

Marinate pork with garlic, herbs and oil in refrigerator overnight.

Cilantro Creme Dressing: Stir together jalapeños, garlic, lime juice, egg yolks and olive oil. Whisk in vegetable oil and sour cream. Stir in cilantro and parsley. Season with salt and pepper to taste. Dressing will keep up to 5 days in refrigerator.

Heat charcoal grill until very hot, remove pork from the marinade and cook approximately 15 to 20 minutes, or until juices run clear; set aside.

Toss baby lettuces and arrange them on salad plates along with the tomatoes and artichoke hearts. Slice pork tenderloins very thin and fan them over the greens. Drizzle with the cilantro creme dressing and serve.

8 servings

FISH CHOWDER

The Attic
Chicago, Illinois
Chef Stephen Mourant

2 pounds fresh codfish or haddock
¼ pound salt pork
1 large potato
4 cups half and half
½ box oyster crackers
½ cup butter
Salt and freshly ground pepper

Poach fish in 10 cups water. Strain, retaining 10 cups stock. Cut salt pork into small pieces and sauté. Peel potatoes, cube and cook. Soak crackers in half and half. Add butter. Combine all ingredients and heat while stirring. Season to taste.

10 cups

THAI SHRIMP AND PAPAYA SALAD

From Pierre Gardien, Executive Chef
George L. Jewell Catering Services, Ltd.
Chicago, Illinois

Dressing:
3 tablespoons fresh lime juice
2 tablespoons light brown sugar
2 tablespoon Thai fish sauce
½ teaspoon chili paste with garlic
2 teaspoons freshly grated
*   ginger root*
2 small green onions, minced
2 tablespoons minced fresh cilantro

1 pound large shrimp, shelled
1½ ripe papayas, peeled
1 red bell pepper
½ English cucumber
12 ounces mixed greens (arugula,
*   red leaf, bibb, mache or other*
*   unusual greens)*
¾ cup pine nuts, toasted

Dressing: Combine the ingredients for the dressing and shake vigorously in a jar.

Cook shrimp in rapidly boiling water until center appears opaque, about 2 to 3 minutes. Drain, pat dry and chill.

Seed papaya and cut into ½-inch cubes. Seed pepper and cut into ½-inch cubes. Cut cucumber in half lengthwise and remove seeds. Cut into long ¼-inch wide strips, then cut into ½-inch cubes. Chill all until ready to assemble.

Wash the lettuce and wrap in a clean towel. Chill until serving time.

Spread lettuce evenly on four plates. In a bowl, toss shrimp, papaya and vegetables with dressing. Place on top of lettuce and garnish with sprigs of fresh cilantro.

4 servings

COLD CARROT GINGER SOUP

Hyatt Regency Chicago
Chicago, Illinois
Chef Robert Lang

1 large onion, chopped
2 bay leaves
2 tablespoons fresh ginger root,
*   chopped*
1 tablespoon olive oil
6 cups chicken stock
4 large carrots, peeled and chopped
1 tablespoon sugar
Salt and freshly ground pepper
1 cup whipping cream

Sauté onion, bay leaves, and ginger in olive oil. Add chicken stock, carrots and sugar. Cook until soft and puree. Chill and add salt, pepper and heavy cream.

4 to 5 servings

ARTICHOKE-MUSHROOM FRITTATA

Avanzare
Chicago, Illinois
Chef Mark Greco

2 tablespoons carrot, julienned
4 ounces angel hair pasta
2 ounces baby or globe artichokes,
    sliced
¾ cup domestic mushrooms, sliced
½ cup Spanish onion, sliced
¼ cup Parmesan cheese
Salt
2 egg whites
1 teaspoon margarine
3 ounces favorite tomato sauce

Blanch carrot, chill. Cook pasta, chill.

Sauté, separately, in minimal amount of vegetable oil the artichokes, mushrooms, and onions. Chill. In small bowl combine pasta, vegetables, Parmesan cheese, salt, and egg white. Mix until evenly blended.

Heat 6-inch non-stick pan and add margarine. Add all ingredients, making sure they are distributed evenly. Cook approximately 1 to 2 minutes or until brown on first side. Flip and cook on other side until golden brown. Serve on top of tomato sauce.

This recipe is "heart healthy" according to guidelines set by the American Heart Association.

1 serving

VITELLO TONNATO

Judy Markey
WGN-Radio Personality, Chicago Sun Times Columnist

3½ pound rolled veal or turkey roast
1 onion, chopped
1 clove garlic, crushed
3 tablespoons vegetable oil
    (not olive oil)
1 beef bouillon cube
1 cup water
1 6½-ounce can tuna, in oil
2 to 3 tablespoons mayonnaise
2 to 3 tablespoons vinegar
2 tablespoons white wine
Fresh lemon juice
Salt and freshly ground pepper

Garnish:
Drained capers
Parsley and lemon

Brown roast, onion, and garlic in oil in a large pot. Add bouillon cube and water. Cover and simmer slowly for three hours. Remove from pot and let cool.

Puree tuna in oil with mayonnaise, vinegar and wine until the consistency of thick soup. Mix in lemon juice, salt and pepper to taste.

On an oval serving platter, spread 2 to 3 tablespoons of tuna puree. Slice roast very thin and fan out slices on top of puree. Pour remainder of puree over the sliced roast. Chill for 4 to 48 hours.

Serve garnished with capers, parsley and lemon slices.

4 to 6 servings

MALFADINE AL FUNGHI

Carlucci
Chicago, Illinois
Chef Paul LoDuca

1 ounce dried porcini mushrooms
1 cup minced onions
¾ cup pure olive oil, divided
2 cloves garlic, crushed, divided
½ cup Marsala wine
½ cup white wine
2 cups chicken stock
2 cups whipping cream
1 tablespoon cornstarch
¼ cup water
½ cup butter
1 pound Malfadine pasta
8 ounces portobello mushrooms,
*   chopped in 4 to 6 pieces*
8 ounces cremini mushrooms,
*   chopped in 4 to 6 pieces*
Salt and freshly ground pepper
1 tablespoon fresh chives, chopped
1 tablespoon tomato concasé
*   (rough chopped tomato cooked*
*   until dry)*

Soak dried porcini mushrooms in 1 cup hot water for 30 minutes. Drain thoroughly, reserving liquid.

Caramelize onions in half of olive oil with one crushed garlic clove until well browned. Deglaze with wines and strained liquid from porcini mushrooms; reduce by ⅔. Add chicken stock and porcini mushrooms. Bring to a boil and cook 10 to 15 minutes. Add cream, ½ cup at a time, reducing slightly after each addition. Mix cornstarch with water. Thicken slightly with cornstarch. Add butter, strain and keep hot.

Cook pasta until al dente.

Sauté portobello and cremini mushrooms with remaining oil, one crushed clove garlic, salt and pepper, until cooked. Add hot porcini cream sauce. Toss in pasta and heat until warm. Place on serving platter.

Garnish with chives and tomato concasé.

4 servings

SPAGHETTI SAUCE

Lynne and Paul Harvey
Nationally-known Radio Commentator

1 15-ounce can tomato paste
1 15-ounce can water
1 18-ounce can Italian tomatoes
*   (mashed)*
1 15-ounce can tomato sauce
1 large onion, cut fine
1 tablespoon sugar
Salt, pepper and oregano, to taste
1 bay leaf

Simmer ingredients for two hours, stirring frequently. If too thick, add a little water. Remove bay leaf before serving.

VERMICELLI WITH TURIDDU SAUCE

Anthony J. Terlato
Paterno Imports
Chicago, Illinois

½ cup olive oil
1 28-ounce can imported plum
    tomatoes
10-15 pitted black olives, sliced in
    half (not canned)
½ sweet red pepper, chopped
Salt and freshly ground pepper
Pinch of oregano
1 pound vermicelli
Dash extra virgin olive oil
½ cup grated fresh Parmesan cheese

Heat ½ cup olive oil in saucepan to smoking point for 1 minute. Add tomatoes, reduce heat and add olives, and red pepper. Season with salt, pepper, and oregano; stir well. Simmer until sauce thickens, approximately 15 minutes.

Cook vermicelli in salted boiling water until al dente, about 6 minutes. Drain well and toss in a bowl with a dash of olive oil.

Arrange on a serving platter and pour piping hot Turiddu sauce over the vermicelli. Add Parmesan cheese.

4 to 6 servings

PENNE ST. MARTIN

3 cloves garlic, sliced in half
1 tablespoon butter
3 tablespoons olive oil
1 32-ounce can plum tomatoes
6 ounces mushrooms, quartered
1 sprig fresh rosemary
    (about 20 fresh leaves)
5 to 6 fresh basil leaves
6 ounces peas
Pinch of ground red pepper
Salt and freshly ground pepper
¼ cup heavy whipping cream
1 pound penne (mostaccioli)
Grated fresh Parmesan cheese

In a saucepan lightly brown garlic in butter and olive oil, and then remove. Add tomatoes and simmer 8 to 10 minutes. Add mushrooms and simmer 5 minutes longer, stir.

Add rosemary, basil, peas, red pepper, salt and pepper. Simmer for 5 more minutes, add cream and stir.

Cook penne according to package directions. Drain.

Pour sauce over penne; mix well. Sprinkle with Parmesan cheese.

4 to 6 servings

PENNE PASTA

Lettuce Entertainment Enterprises, Inc.
Chicago, Illinois
Russell Bry, Executive Chef

2 tablespoons butter
¾ cup sliced mushrooms
¼ cup finely chopped shallots
1½ teaspoons mustard seed
¾ cup strong chicken broth
8 cups whipping cream
4 tablespoons Dijon mustard
6 tablespoons whole grain mustard
Salt and freshly ground pepper
2 pounds Penne Rigati noodles,
    cooked
3 ounces prosciutto, sliced thin
6 ounces cooked chicken breast,
    coarsely chopped
1 cup sliced mushrooms
1 cup broccoli florets, steamed until
    barely tender
Freshly chopped chives, parsley
    and tarragon to taste

Sauce: Melt butter in a deep stock pot and sauté sliced mushrooms, shallots, and mustard seed. Add chicken stock, and bring to a boil. Add cream, slowly, bring to a boil and reduce by approximately ¼ total volume. Stir in both mustards and season to taste with salt and pepper. Puree in blender until smooth. Return to pan.

Pasta: Bring sauce to a boil. Quickly add prosciutto, chicken, mushrooms and broccoli. Toss gently; season to taste. Adding chives, parsley and tarragon, add cooked pasta, mix well and serve.

6 servings

FAVORITE PASTA SAUCE

Steve Larmer
Chicago Blackhawk

½ cup olive oil
1 clove garlic, crushed
1 large onion, diced
1 28-ounce can crushed tomatoes
2 tablespoons oregano
1 tablespoon basil
1 teaspoon salt
1 cup clamato juice
Fresh parsley to taste

Heat olive oil and sauté garlic and onion until tender. Add remaining ingredients and simmer a minimum of one hour. More clamato juice may be add if desired.

Steve uses this pasta sauce before games for energy.

3 to 4 servings

BLACK PEPPERCORN TOMATO LINGUINI WITH BAY SCALLOPS AND ANCHO CHILI TOMATILLO SAUCE

Sandpiper
Macatawa, Michigan

1 pound linguini

1½ pounds bay scallops

Ancho Chili Tomatillo Sauce:
3 ounces ancho chilies, dried,
    cored and seeded
7 ounces tomatillos, undrained
1 cup chicken stock
1 2-ounce can green chilies,
    mild to hot, undrained
1 medium red bell pepper,
    seeded and diced
1 medium green bell pepper,
    seeded and diced
1 bunch scallions, green and
    white sliced
2 cloves garlic, minced
1 tablespoon cumin seeds, crushed
¼ cup pumpkin seeds, roasted
1 to 3 tablespoons cilantro,
    depending on taste
¼ cup cornmeal
½ pound chorizo sausage, cooked
    and drained
Salt and freshly ground pepper

Garnish:
1 medium yellow bell pepper,
    seeded and julienned
1 medium red bell pepper,
    seeded and julienned

Blanch pasta and lightly coat with oil. Chill. Select a good quality pasta. Combination of flavored pastas can vary depending on availability and taste.

Wash and drain. In a large saucepan, bring water to a boil. Place scallops in water, return to a boil, and poach for 3 minutes. Drain; set aside.

Ancho Chili Tomatillo Sauce: Reconstitute ancho chilies by simmering with chicken stock, tomatillos and green chilies for 10 minutes or until soft.

Sauté peppers and scallions with garlic and cumin in small amount of oil until tender. In food processor or blender, puree tomatillos mixture, vegetables and pumpkin seeds. Return to saucepan and simmer 10 minutes.

Add cilantro, cornmeal (used to add texture and adjust consistency of sauce) and chorizo.

Garnish: Blanch peppers in boiling water for 60 seconds.

Reheat blanched linguini in skillet or sauté pan with appropriate amount of sauce to accommodate pasta. The bell pepper garnish and bay scallops may be heated separately and placed on top of linguini or tossed into pasta and sauce mixture.

6 servings

HERB WRAPPED TENDERLOIN OF BEEF WITH MUSHROOM SAGE BUTTER

Colin Reeves Cuisine
Chicago, Illinois
Jack Campbell

Mushroom Sage Butter:
1 tablespoon butter
1 tablespoon minced shallots
¼ cup finely chopped mushrooms
2 tablespoons finely chopped
*   fresh sage (about 16 average-*
*   sized leaves)*
1 tablespoon white wine
1 cup butter, softened
1 teaspoon salt
1 teaspoon freshly ground pepper
1 teaspoon fresh lemon juice

1 cup Italian parsley, chopped
¼ cup fresh thyme, chopped
¼ cup fresh sage, chopped
1 beef tenderloin, 5-7 pounds
¼ cup vegetable oil
Salt and freshly ground pepper

Garnish:
8 large sage leaves

Mushroom Sage Butter: Sauté shallots, mushrooms and sage in 1 tablespoon butter over medium heat. When the mushrooms begin to soften and release juices (approximately 5 minutes), add the wine. Let the mixture cook approximately 10-15 minutes, until the wine reduces to almost nothing. Remove from heat and cool.

In a mixer with paddle attachment, beat 1 cup butter with salt, pepper, lemon juice and mushroom mixture until thoroughly combined.

Fit a piping bag with ½-inch star tip. Fill the bag with the butter mixture. Pipe onto a cool plate into stars ¾-inch wide and ½-inch tall. There should be enough mixture for 16 ½-ounce stars. Cover loosely and refrigerate overnight.

Remove from refrigerator 30 minutes before serving. Allow stars to come to room temperature but not any warmer as they will not come off the plate easily.

Preheat oven to 375°.

Mix the chopped herbs together. (The amount of herbs needed may vary if the tenderloin is bigger or smaller, but keep the same ratio of herbs.) Coat the tenderloin with the vegetable oil. Season with salt and pepper to taste. Coat the oiled tenderloin with the herbs, pressing them so they hold well. Place in roasting pan.

Roast about 30 minutes, or until a meat thermometer inserted in the center of the tenderloin reaches 130° for medium rare.

Remove tenderloin from oven and let rest 10 minutes. Slice the tenderloin into 16 to 20 slices (depending upon thickness) or two slices per guest.

Arrange slices on a plate, placing a mushroom sage butter star on each slice. Garnish with fresh sage leaves. Serve immediately.

8 servings

INDIAN BEEF KABOBS WITH CORN

1991 Beef Council Celebrity Cook-Off Winner
Michael Jordan
Chicago Bulls
The Michael Jordan Foundation

⅓ cup water
⅓ cup commercial mango chutney
1 teaspoon curry powder
½ teaspoon ground cardamom
½ teaspoon ground ginger
½ teaspoon ground cumin
¼ teaspoon sugar
¼ teaspoon pepper
⅛ teaspoon garlic powder

1 pound lean, boneless sirloin steak
2 large ears fresh corn, cut into
    8½-inch pieces
1 large purple onion, cut into
    8 wedges
Vegetable cooking spray

Place water, mango chutney, curry powder, cardamom, ginger, cumin, sugar, pepper and garlic powder in container of an electric blender or food processor; cover and process until smooth; set aside.

Trim fat from steak and cut steak into 24 cubes. Combine steak cubes and chutney mixture in a large zip-top plastic bag. Marinate in refrigerator for at least 2 hours.

Remove steak from bag, reserving marinade. Thread 6 steak cubes, 4 corn pieces and 2 onion wedges alternately onto each of 4 12-inch skewers.

Coat grill rack with cooking spray; place on grill over medium-hot coals. Place kabobs on rack, and cook 6 to 7 minutes on each side or to desired degree of doneness, basting with reserved marinade.

4 servings

RASPBERRY CHICKEN

Cafe Las Bellas Artes
Elmhurst, Illinois
Gloria Duarte

4 cups heavy cream
1 10-ounce package frozen
    raspberries, thawed
8 4-ounce chicken breasts, boned
    and skinned
Salt and freshly ground pepper
½ cup clarified butter

Pour cream into saucepan; add raspberries and reduce over medium high heat. Reduce by ¼ or until flavors are well incorporated; strain.

Season breasts with salt and pepper. Sauté chicken breasts in butter for 3 minutes on one side and approximately 5 minutes on the other or until done.

Arrange chicken on serving platter and cover with sauce.

4 servings

GOULASH
Sir Georg Solti
Conductor Emeritus
Chicago Symphony Orchestra

½ pound onions
2 ounces lard
2½ pound braising steak, cut
*   in ½-inch cubes*
½ pound beef heart, optional, cut
*   in ½-inch cubes*
2 cloves garlic, chopped
Pinch caraway seeds
Salt
8 cups beef stock
2 tablespoons paprika, finest quality
½ pound tomatoes
2 green peppers
1 pound potatoes

Peel and dice onions. Melt lard in heavy-bottom saucepan; add beef and heart, sauté for about 10 minutes.

Chop and crush garlic with caraway seeds and salt. Remove beef from heat and stir in paprika and garlic mixture. Add beef stock and return to heat with lid on and simmer for at least 1 to 1½ hours.

Peel and dice tomatoes, core and cut peppers into rings and add to meat; simmer for 30 minutes adding more stock if required to keep a soup-like consistency. Add potatoes (cut into ½-inch cubes) and cook until all is tender.

Serve with little dumplings.

6 servings

PORK TENDERLOIN
WITH APPLE-VANILLA RELISH
Sandpiper
Macatawa, Michigan

3 pounds pork tenderloin
Kosher salt
2 tablespoons olive oil
Ground white peppercorns
1 tablespoon minced garlic
2 bunches scallions, diced into
*   small pieces*
1 pound kielbasa, cut into ¼-inch
*   diagonal slices*
¼ vanilla bean or 1 tablespoon
*   vanilla extract*
Peel, seed and dice:
*   3 medium tomatoes*
*   3 large Washington apples*
2 tablespoons chopped fresh basil,
*   optional*
¼ to ½ cup chicken stock

Rub pork tenderloin with kosher salt, olive oil and ground white peppercorns.

Preheat grill or broiler. Cook tenderloin for 10 to 14 minutes or until medium, turning occasionally. Keep warm in a 250° oven until sauce is ready.

Meanwhile, heat oil in medium saucepan. Add garlic, scallions and sausage. Split vanilla bean and scrape inside of bean with tip of knife and add with the bean. Cook briefly over medium heat. Add tomato, apple and basil. Add chicken stock. Cook until tomato breaks down slightly. Slice pork on the diagonal and top with apple-vanilla relish.

Variation: Substitute a smoked turkey sausage product for kielbasa. Try substituting grilled chicken breast, fish fillet or steak for pork. Toss any leftover sauce with pasta. Serve cold or hot.

6 servings

THE OFFICIAL MANTEGNA GRAVY RECIPE

Joe Mantegna
Actor and Native Chicagoan

2 tablespoons olive oil
1 pound beef or pork neck or
    blade bones
1 medium onion, peeled and chopped
1 pound ground chuck
1 teaspoon salt or to taste
1 teaspoon freshly ground
    black pepper
1/2 teaspoon ground red pepper
1 28-ounce can whole plum tomatoes
    (or peeled tomatoes with basil,
    Italian style)
1 12-ounce can tomato paste
1 4-ounce can mushrooms
4 12-ounce cans water
1 teaspoon dried oregano leaves,
    crushed
1 teaspoon sugar
1/2 teaspoon dried sweet basil,
    crushed
2 cloves garlic, minced, or
    1/2 teaspoon garlic powder

Drape towel over left shoulder. Heat oil in a large pot. Brown bones, then remove. Sauté onion until tender, about 5 minutes. Add ground chuck, salt, pepper and red pepper. Brown meat, mixing with a wooden spoon. Pour off fat.

Strain tomatoes; discard seeds and juice. Chop tomatoes coarsely and add to pot along with tomato paste. Drain mushrooms; add to pot along with meaty bones. Add water. Bring to a boil.

Reduce heat to low. Add seasonings. Cook, uncovered for 1 1/2 to 2 hours, stirring occasionally. Add meatballs and simmer another 30 minutes. Remove bones from mixture, remove meat and return meat to pot. Discard bones.

Serve with cooked pasta and meatballs.

6 servings

THE OFFICIAL MEATBALL RECIPE

3/4 pound ground beef
2 tablespoons grated Romano cheese
1 tablespoon chopped parsley
1/2 teaspoon salt
1/2 teaspoon pepper
1/2 teaspoon garlic powder
1 egg
1/2 cup bread crumbs
Olive oil

Combine beef, Romano cheese, parsley, salt, pepper, garlic powder, egg and bread crumbs. Shape into meatballs.

Coat bottom of a large skillet with oil. Brown meatballs. Add to gravy.

12 meatballs

VEAL SHANKS BRAISED IN CABERNET WITH A SPOONFUL OF SUCCOTASH

Deer Valley
Deer Valley, Utah
Chef Julie Wilson, Director of Food and Beverage

4 veal shanks (8 to 10 ounces each)
3 medium carrots, diced
1 large onion, chopped
5 stalks celery, chopped
1 bunch thyme
6 bay leaves
1 clove garlic, halved
1 sprig rosemary
1/2 cup parsley stems
1 bottle Cabernet Sauvignon
1 6-ounce can tomato paste
1 tablespoon whole black pepper

Succotash:
1/3 cup fresh corn kernels
1/3 cup carrot balls
1/3 cup fresh English peas
Butter
Salt and freshly ground pepper

Place veal shanks, carrots, onion, celery, thyme, bay leaves, garlic, rosemary, parsley stems and Cabernet Sauvignon in large pan. Marinate for 24 hours.

Drain the shanks and vegetables, reserving the liquid. Heat a sauté pan and brown veal shanks on every side, sauté the vegetables as well, and mix everything together.

Mix tomato paste with reserved liquid and pour over the shanks. They should be completely covered. Braise in oven covered for about one hour and 15 minutes, or until the shanks are a little overcooked (the meat should come off the bone very easily). Carefully remove the veal shank and reduce the juice until the sauce coats the back of the spoon. Adjust the seasoning and strain sauce over the veal shank.

Succotash: Cook corn, carrot balls and peas al dente, season with butter, salt and pepper, and sprinkle vegetables around the veal shanks.

For best results, the veal shanks should be cooked the day before and reheated.

4 servings

MEAT BALLS

The Village Smithy
Glencoe, Illinois
Bill Lepman

1 1/2 pounds ground beef
1 cup fresh bread crumbs
1 cup diced onions, sautéed
1 egg, beaten
1 tablespoon pesto
1 teaspoon ground fennel
1 tablespoon salt
1/2 teaspoon freshly ground pepper
1 cup grated Romano cheese

Preheat oven to 325°.

Blend beef, bread crumbs, onions, egg, pesto, fennel, salt, pepper and Romano cheese and shape into large balls.

Bake for 20 minutes. Serve with Marinara Sauce.

THE VILLAGE SMITHY (continued)

Marinara Sauce:
¾ cup olive oil
1 pound onions, diced
¾ cups dry white wine
6⅓ cups crushed tomatoes
6⅓ cups whole tomatoes, broken
    in large pieces
1½ teaspoons finely chopped garlic
1½ teaspoons oregano
¾ teaspoon thyme
1½ teaspoons salt
¾ teaspoon freshly ground pepper

Marinara Sauce: Sauté onions in oil until translucent; add wine and reduce until almost evaporated. Add tomatoes, garlic, oregano, thyme, salt and pepper.
    Simmer over low heat for 45 minutes.

CALIFORNIA STATE COOLEST CHILI
Dr. Newt Bop
Dr. Bop and the Headliners

1 red onion, finely chopped
2 tablespoons oil
2 pounds coarsely ground lean beef
½ pound chorizo
2 tablespoons chili powder
1 tablespoon cumin
2 tablespoons mole sauce
1 teaspoon salt
1 clove garlic, minced
½ cup chopped peeled jalapeño
    chili peppers
½ teaspoon oregano
1 teaspoon coarse ground
    black pepper
1 teaspoon Worcestershire sauce
1 teaspoon Tabasco
1 cup Burgundy wine
1 30-ounce can tomato puree
1 teaspoon dried basil
1 20-ounce can tomato sauce
    with tomato bits

You will need a rather large pot and a big wooden spoon.
    Brown onion in oil. Add ground beef and chorizo and cook until browned. Add chili powder, cumin and mole. Stir. Combine salt with garlic and add to meat with jalapeños, oregano, pepper, Worcestershire and Tabasco; stir to blend. Add wine, tomato puree, basil and tomato sauce. Simmer at least 2 hours in covered pot. Stir occasionally to prevent sticking. Skim off some of the fat at the end.

For this recipe you seem to need a million ingredients. I have found you can forget the chorizo (Mexican sausage), just substitute more ground beef.

Hint: Jalapeño chili peppers are long and green. To peel them, roast them over a flame on your stove or put them in the oven. Breaks will appear in the skin and you can then peel it off. Wear plastic gloves. Throw the seeds away! Or you can use canned ones, but discard seeds.

4 quarts

CHRIS' SHREDDED BEEF SANDWICHES
Chris Chelios
Chicago Blackhawk

3 pounds chuck roast or round steak
Vegetable oil
1 cup chopped onion
½ cup chopped celery
2 cups beef broth or bouillon

Sauce:
1½ cups beef broth
1 clove garlic, minced
1 teaspoon salt
¾ cup ketchup
4 tablespoons brown sugar
2 tablespoons vinegar
1 teaspoon dry mustard
½ teaspoon chili powder
3 drops Tabasco
1 bay leaf
¼ teaspoon paprika
¼ teaspoon garlic powder
1 teaspoon Worcestershire sauce

Brown beef in hot oil on both sides, adding onion and celery at last minute. Combine beef, vegetables and broth in covered Dutch oven or crock pot. Simmer, covered for 3 to 4 hours, or until tender. Cool. Shred beef, separating into strands. Drain vegetables (reserving 1½ cups broth); combine with beef. Skim off fat from broth.

Sauce: Mix beef, vegetables, reserved broth, garlic, salt, ketchup, brown sugar, vinegar, mustard, chili powder, Tabasco, bay leaf, paprika, garlic powder and Worcestershire sauce. Simmer until heated thoroughly. Remove bay leaf. (This mixture keeps well in crock pot on low heat).

Serve with potato rolls or buns.

8 servings

SESAME HONEY CHICKEN
Linda Yu
Chicago Television Broadcaster

¼ cup honey
3 tablespoons Dijon mustard
2 tablespoons teriyaki sauce
2 tablespoons sesame oil
1 tablespoon oyster sauce
6 chicken breasts
2 cups toasted sesame seeds
1 orange, halved

Combine honey, mustard, teriyaki sauce, sesame oil and oyster sauce in bowl. Dip chicken breasts in mixture. Sprinkle sesame seeds on both sides of chicken.

Broil chicken. About half way through, squeeze one-half orange over chicken and continue to broil until done. Just before serving, squeeze the other half of the orange over chicken.

6 servings

SWEETNESS CHICKEN

Walter Payton
Former Chicago Bear

12 choice chicken pieces
    (3-3½ pounds)
1½ cups orange juice
2 teaspoons oregano leaves
½ teaspoon garlic powder
½ teaspoon ground sage
½ teaspoon dried rosemary leaves,
    crushed
½ teaspoon dried thyme, crushed
Salt and freshly ground pepper
Paprika
¼ cup orange marmalade
1 tablespoon cornstarch
2 tablespoons water
3 cups hot cooked rice

Preheat oven to 350°.

Place chicken in 9x13-inch baking dish, skin side down. Combine juice, oregano, garlic powder, sage, rosemary, thyme, salt and pepper and pour over chicken. Sprinkle with paprika. Cover.

Bake for 30 minutes. Turn chicken; sprinkle with paprika. Bake uncovered 30 to 40 minutes longer or until chicken is tender.

Pour pan juices into saucepan; skim fat. Add marmalade and cornstarch dissolved in water. Cook, stirring, until sauce is clear and thickened.

Serve chicken and sauce over bed of rice. Garnish with orange slices.

6 servings

BONELESS BREAST OF CHICKEN PARISIAN

The Arts Club of Chicago
Chicago, Illinois
Chef Josef Voelker

4 large chicken breasts, halved,
    skinned and boned
2 eggs
½ cup milk
Flour
Salt and freshly ground pepper
1 pound shiitake mushrooms
1 tablespoon butter or margarine

Preheat oven to 350°.

Place one piece of chicken, boned side up, between two pieces of waxed paper; working from center out, pound chicken lightly with meat mallet to make cutlet about ⅛-inch thick. Repeat with remaining chicken. Set aside.

Combine eggs and milk to make egg wash. Place both sides of chicken in flour and then in egg wash.

In oven-proof skillet, sauté chicken in oil until tender. Finish cooking in oven for 5 minutes.

In another skillet, sauté mushrooms in butter. Serve with chicken.

8 servings

CHICKEN CARA MIA

Lisa and Jay Hilgenberg
The Chicago Bears

1 10-ounce can tomatoes
4 large chicken breasts, boned
    and skinned
1/4 cup vegetable oil
1/2 onion, chopped
1 clove garlic, crushed
1 6-ounce jar marinated
    artichoke hearts
1 teaspoon basil
1/2 cup chopped fresh parsley, divided
Salt and freshly ground pepper

Place tomatoes in a bowl and squeeze until they are a soupy consistency; set aside.

Brown chicken breasts in oil. Remove from pan and set aside. Sauté onion and garlic in same oil. Add tomatoes and their juice, artichoke hearts (with marinade), basil, 1/4 cup parsley, salt and pepper to taste. Place chicken on top of mixture. Cover.

Simmer for 45 minutes. Sprinkle top with reserved parsley and serve with hot steamed rice or pasta.

4 servings

ROASTED/SAUTÉ SQUAB WITH CELERY PUREE

Tallgrass Restaurant
Lockport, Illinois
Chef Bob Burcenski

4 squab
1/2 cup rendered duck fat or
    vegetable oil
1 cup chopped onion
1 cup chopped celery
1 cup chopped carrots
1 bay leaf
1/2 teaspoon thyme
1/4 teaspoon rosemary
Water
6 cups coarsely chopped celery
1 cup heavy whipping cream
Butter
Rice

Preheat oven to 375°.

Remove leg and thighs from squab. Remove breast from squab, leaving skin on. Place legs and thighs in shallow roasting pan with duck fat and cover with foil. Roast 1 hour or until tender.

Place squab carcasses, chopped vegetables and herbs in stock pot and cover with water. Simmer 3 hours. Strain and add 6 cups chopped celery and cook until very tender. Remove celery and reduce liquid to 1/2 cup. Puree celery with 1/2 cup reduced liquid in food processor and strain through medium mesh strainer. Add cream and simmer until spoon is lightly covered with puree. Keep warm.

Sauté breast in butter on skin side until brown and crispy. Turn breast and briefly brown, making sure breast is pink in middle. Slice breast into thin medallions and fan out on plate with leg and thighs. Spoon puree around bird and serve with rice.

4 servings

ITALIAN PARSLEY AND ROASTED GARLIC CHICKEN WITH SHIITAKE RISOTTO AND BLACK BEAN SAUCE

From Pierre Gardien, Executive Chef
George L. Jewell Catering Services, Ltd.

24 cloves garlic

Chicken:
6 6-8 ounce boneless chicken breasts with skin
1 bunch Italian parsley
Salt and freshly ground pepper

Sauce:
1 cup black beans
1 clove garlic
Salt and freshly ground pepper
4 cups chicken stock
2 tablespoons butter

Risotto:
1 onion, finely chopped
Butter
Olive oil
3 cups arborio rice
6 to 7 cups chicken stock, divided
½ pound shiitake mushrooms
¼ cup chopped basil
Salt and freshly ground pepper

Preheat oven to 350°.

Roasted Garlic: Place garlic with the skin on in a pan with a little oil. Bake until tender and golden colored. Remove skin.

Chicken: Remove fat from chicken, but leave skin on. Lift skin, and put Italian parsley, sliced roasted garlic, salt and pepper inside. The mixture should only be between the breast and skin. Refrigerate.

Sauce: Soak black beans in cold water overnight. Cook beans until well done with water, garlic, salt and pepper. Drain beans and pulverize them in food processor. Thin beans with chicken stock and whisk in butter; set aside and keep warm.

Risotto: Sauté onions with butter and a little olive oil; add rice. Keep stirring until rice is "crackling" but before it browns. Add about 4 cups chicken stock, stirring constantly until it is almost absorbed. Keep cooking and stirring while adding broth, 1 cup at a time. Each cup of stock must be absorbed before adding the next one.

Sauté shiitake mushrooms with basil until tender, then toss them with rice. Season with salt and pepper to taste.

Preheat oven to 400°.

Heat an oven-proof frying pan with olive oil and a little butter. Sauté chicken, with skin side down first, until they are a crisp golden color. Turn breasts and place in oven.

Bake for 15 to 20 minutes.

Place risotto in middle of a plate. Slice chicken and arrange on top of rice. Spoon sauce around and serve hot.

6 servings

CHICKEN CACCIATORA - SPANISH STYLE

Jose Cardenal
Former Chicago Cub

1 3½ pound chicken, cut up, skinned
1 onion, chopped
1 green pepper, chopped
1 tablespoon olive oil
1 8-ounce can tomato sauce
1 bay leaf
3 cans beer, or 2 cups red wine
    and 2 cups water
4 potatoes, peeled and quartered

Combine onion, green pepper, olive oil and tomato sauce, pour over chicken and marinate for 20 minutes in a large pot. Add bay leaf and beer (or wine and water) and cover.

Cook over medium heat for 15 minutes. Add potatoes and cook for another 35 to 40 minutes.

4 servings

FETTUCINI DUCK
WITH CASHEW BUTTER

Rigoletto
Lake Forest, Illinois
Chef Peter DeCarl and Chef Jay Weiss

Butter:
3½ ounces cashews
14 tablespoons butter, room
    temperature
1 shallot, finely chopped
¼ teaspoon Tabasco
Italian parsley, chopped
Salt and freshly ground pepper

Duck:
½ duck
3 scallions, sliced
8 to 10 sun-dried tomatoes, julienned
2 cups whipping cream
1 pound dry pasta
¾ cup grated fresh Parmesan cheese

Preheat oven to 450°.

Butter: In food processor, grind cashews coarse. Blend together cashews, butter, shallot, Tabasco, parsley, salt and pepper.

Duck: Roast ½ duck for 30 to 45 minutes, or until skin is crisp and meat is slightly undercooked. When cool separate the meat from the bones. Cut into bite-size pieces.

Sauce: Sauté duck, scallions, and sun-dried tomatoes in butter or oil for 1 minute. Add cream to pan. As sauce comes to a boil add cashew butter and mix until smooth.

Drop pasta into pot of boiling salted water. Cook until al dente; remove, strain and add to sauce. Toss while sauce is hot and add cheese.

Serve immediately.

4 servings

SUPREME OF ILLINOIS PHEASANT WITH CHANTERELLES

Le Ciel Bleu
The Mayfair Regent
Chicago, Illinois
Executive Chef Clifford Pleau

1 Rudy's Rooster Pheasant
Bay leaf
Thyme
Peppercorns
White Wine
Consumme
Pinch Kosher salt and ground
　　white pepper
2 tablespoons corn oil
1 tablespoon finely minced shallot
1 small celery root, celeriac, peeled
　　and cut into fine slivers
12 chanterelles (small to medium
　　size, left whole)
¼ cup dry sherry
2 teaspoons soy sauce
½ cup natural pheasant jus

Remove breasts from pheasant, leaving skin on, and wing bone attached. Cut skin and meat away from wing bone. Cover and set aside.

Natural pheasant jus: Place bones and legs in a stock pot with bay leaf, thyme, peppercorn and the trimmings from the vegetables and mushrooms. Add white wine and consomme to cover. Simmer 2 hours, strain.

Preheat oven to 375°.

Season breasts with salt and pepper. Heat corn oil in a sauté pan over medium heat, place pheasant breasts, skin side down and brown. Once the skin side is brown, remove breasts. Add shallots, celeriac and chanterelles, sauté 30 seconds. Add sherry, soy and pheasant jus, bring to a simmer and return pheasant breast skin side up.

Bake 7 to 9 minutes.

Remove breasts, slice and arrange on top of a nest of celeriac. Arrange chanterelles and autumn vegetable salpicon around the nest and spoon over jus.

2 servings

AUTUMN VEGETABLE SALPICON

1 ear fresh corn
French green beans
Red sweet pepper
Chanterelles
1 teaspoon garlic, minced
1 teaspoon minced fresh tarragon
Dash sherry
2 tablespoons corn oil
Pinch Kosher salt
Freshly ground white pepper
2 tablespoons butter

Cut corn kernels from cob. Cut an equal part of beans, red pepper and chanterelles uniformly and the same size as the corn kernels.

Place vegetables in bowl and mix with garlic, tarragon, sherry, corn oil, salt and pepper.

Heat a medium sauté pan, add butter and when lightly brown add vegetable mixture. Cook 2 to 3 minutes, serve as a garnish with pheasant.

Seasonal, Simple and Natural

2 servings

ROAST BREAST OF DUCK IN RED WINE
WITH CELERY ROOT AND BUTTERNUT SQUASH

The DuPage Club
Chef Christopher Spitz

3 5-pound Long Island or Pekin ducks

Duck Stock:
1 large carrot, peeled and quartered
2 large onions, peeled and quartered
4 celery ribs, roughly cut
Thyme, bay leaf and peppercorns

Duck Sauce:
2 carrots, peeled and chopped
1 large onion, peeled and chopped
2 celery ribs, chopped
Thyme, bay leaf and peppercorns
4 cups Burgundy wine
12 cups duck stock

Potatoes of choice, cooked
1 small celery root, diced and cooked
1 small butternut squash, diced
*   and cooked*
1 large spaghetti squash, steamed
Salt and freshly ground pepper

Duck: Remove breasts and legs from ducks. Trim excess fat from duck breasts. Remove thigh bone, leaving legs whole and boneless. Reserve duck livers.

Duck Stock: Prepare duck stock by covering bones with water and adding 1 carrot, 2 onions, 4 celery ribs, thyme, bay leaf and peppercorns. Cook until you have a nice rich broth; strain. Chop and roast duck carcasses.

Duck Sauce: Heat large saucepan add small amount of oil. Brown duck legs, skin side down. Turn over and brown; remove. Sweat 2 carrots, 1 large onion, 2 celery ribs, thyme, bay leaf and peppercorns. Deglaze with wine and reduce by ½.

Add reserved duck stock and bring to slow boil. Put duck legs back in and cook very slowly until tender. Remove duck legs and cook liquid until rich, but not over reduced. Skim fat off top constantly. When sauce is cooked to taste, mince the livers and let them sit in sauce off heat. Do not boil at this point. Pass sauce through a fine strainer.

Duck: Heat another sauté pan with a small amount of oil for the duck breasts. Start skin side down, seasoning tops. The majority of cooking is done on the skin side, reducing the fat out of it. When breasts are almost cooked, flip breast over, sear briefly and remove.

Assembly: Arrange potatoes and vegetables on plates. Sauté steamed spaghetti squash in butter, salt and pepper and place in center of plate. Put a braised duck leg on top of spaghetti squash. Slice each breast very thin with a long sharp knife and lay the sliced breast over the duck leg. Warm the butternut squash and celery root, arrange on plate. Heat plates in oven. Spoon warm sauce over duck. Serve at once.

6 servings

SAUTÉED WALLEYE PIKE WITH ARTICHOKES, MUSHROOMS, WILD RICE AND HERBS

The DuPage Club
Chef Christopher Spitz

¾ cup wild rice
3 tablespoons sherry
Salt and freshly ground pepper

Garnish:
Assorted baby vegetables

2¾ pound walleye pike fillets,
    skin on
Salt and freshly ground pepper
1 11-ounce can artichokes, drained
    and quartered
8 ounces domestic mushrooms, sliced
1 ounce fresh basil
1 ounce fresh parsley
1 ounce fresh thyme
1 ounce clove garlic, minced
2 cups vegetable stock or unsalted
    chicken stock
2 tablespoons fresh lemon juice
6 tablespoons sweet butter

Vegetable Stock:
Peel and roughly cut:
    ½ large carrot
    ½ small celery root
    1 medium onion
1½ ripe tomatoes, chopped
½ large leek, rinsed between layers
    and chopped
1 shallot, peeled
½ small head of garlic, unpeeled and
    cut in half horizontally
2 parsley stems
2 cups Chablis
4 cups water
Thyme, bay leaf and peppercorns

Cook wild rice in water, sherry and seasonings.

Garnish: Blanch vegetables until cooked to taste, then season. Set six dinner plates with vegetables and wild rice.

Heat oil in a large sauté pan. Cut pike into 6 ounce pieces, season with salt and pepper and dust very lightly with flour. Sauté fish until medium, not browning too much. If pan gets too hot, remove from stove.

Arrange fish on dinner plates when cooked. Add artichokes, mushrooms, basil, parsley, thyme, and garlic to pan and sauté. Add vegetable stock and lemon juice and reduce by half.

Heat plates with vegetables and rice in oven. When stock is reduced by ⅓ or ½, whisk in butter. Remove plates from oven and sauce them evenly.

Vegetable Stock: Put thoroughly washed vegetables in a 6-quart saucepan. Cover with wine, water and herbs. Cook over low heat until reduced by ⅓. Pass through fine sieve, pressing vegetables firmly with a ladle. Cool. Freeze remaining stock for future use.

6 servings

ALSATIAN-STYLE NORWEGIAN SALMON

Crickets
Chicago, Illinois
Chef John Carey

4 small white cabbages
32 bacon strips
1 cup Alsatian Riesling, divided
8 baby carrots with tops, washed and peeled
32 baby turnips with tops, washed and peeled
32 small red potatoes, washed, do not peel
3 cups chicken stock, preferably homemade
4 7-ounce salmon fillets
Salt and freshly ground pepper

Cut cabbages in 8 equal pieces, retaining core. Wrap in bacon and skewer with toothpick.

Heat large skillet over high heat. Place cabbage in pan and brown bacon evenly on both sides. Deglaze pan with ½ cup Riesling wine. Add vegetables and potatoes, let wine reduce by half. Add chicken stock to cover. Cook vegetables until tender, keep warm.

Season salmon with salt and pepper. In a non-stick pan, cook salmon 4 minutes on each side. Deglaze pan with remaining Riesling and reduce until almost dry.

Place salmon in center of plate with juice of salmon and wine. Arrange vegetables around fish. Sprinkle with parsley. Serve immediately.

4 servings

FRESH SALMON WITH FRENCH GREEN LENTIL SAUCE SAUMON AVEC LENTILLES VERTES

Bistro Banlieue
Lombard, Illinois

Sauce:
3 finely chopped shallots
½ cup white wine
¾ cup fish stock or clam juice
¾ cup heavy whipping cream
1 tablespoon prepared horseradish

3 green onions, finely chopped
½ carrot, finely diced
1 celery rib, finely diced
¼ cup French green lentils, cooked and strained

4 6-ounce fillets salmon
¼ cup olive oil

Sauce: In a saucepan, reduce by half the shallots, wine and fish stock. Add cream and bring to a boil. Add horseradish and whisk until thick. Thicken sauce with 1 tablespoon cornstarch mixed with 2 tablespoons water.

Blanch onions, carrot and celery in boiling water and strain. Add lentils.

Salmon: Heat olive oil in large skillet until hot. Sauté salmon until brown on both sides. Serve with green lentil-horseradish sauce.

4 servings

SPICED SALMON WITH COUSCOUS

Montparnasse
Naperville, Illinois
Chef Suzy Crofton

Spiced Glaze:
1 teaspoon ground red pepper
3 tablespoons curry powder
3 tablespoons cumin
¼ cup high-quality soy sauce
¾ cup white wine
¾ cup honey

Stir-Fry Garnish:
3 small zucchini, julienned
3 small yellow squash, julienned
15 pea pods, julienned
¼ head red cabbage, julienned
1 yellow pepper, seeded and diced
1 red sweet pepper, seeded
    and diced
1 ear fresh corn (kernels only)
1 bunch broccoli separated
    into florets
2 ounces vegetable oil or
    clarified butter
Salt and freshly ground pepper

1 box couscous, cooked according to
    package directions
2 tablespoons unsalted butter

4 8-ounce salmon fillets, skinned
Salt and freshly ground pepper
¼ cup hot oil or clarified butter

Spiced Glaze: In a small saucepan over medium heat, bring red pepper, curry powder, cumin, soy sauce, white wine and honey to a boil; whisking constantly for 10 minutes, or until medium thick. Check seasoning (if too hot add extra honey and white wine), remove from heat.

Stir-Fry Garnish: Place zucchini, squash, pea pods, red cabbage, yellow and red pepper, corn and broccoli in a bowl; mix well. Reserve 2 handfuls of vegetables for couscous and finely dice.

Place vegetable oil in medium sauté pan over medium heat. When hot, add stir-fry garnish and toss continually until limp. Season to taste; set aside.

Couscous: Flake cooked couscous with fork. Place 2 tablespoons butter in medium sauté pan over medium heat. Add reserved diced vegetables, cook 5 minutes. Add 3 cups cooked couscous, mix. Season to taste; set aside.

Preheat oven to 425°.

Salmon: Season with salt and pepper, place top side down in large oven-proof sauté pan with 2 ounces hot oil or clarified butter, brown lightly over high heat for 4 to 5 minutes. Turn over and place pan in oven for about 5 minutes, or until cooked (be sure not to overcook). Brush one side of salmon with glaze.

Assembly: On each of 4 plates, spread couscous in circle leaving a border. Place glazed salmon on couscous, top with garnish, run glaze around edge of couscous. (If you like, some of the spice mixture may be added to a little beurre blanc to sauce the plates.)

4 servings

HERBED BAKED CATFISH

Catfish City Fish Market
Waukegan, Illinois

1 medium clove garlic, minced
2 tablespoons butter, melted
3/4 teaspoon paprika
1/2 teaspoon dried thyme
1/2 teaspoon dried basil
1/2 teaspoon dried oregano
1 teaspoon salt
2 pounds catfish fillets
1/2 teaspoon ground pepper
2 tablespoons fresh lemon juice
2 tablespoons chopped fresh parsley

Preheat oven to 350°. Combine garlic and melted butter and spread evenly over 9x13x2-inch baking dish.

Combine paprika, thyme, basil, oregano, salt and pepper; sprinkle on both sides of fillets. Arrange on top of butter mixture in prepared dish. Drizzle with lemon juice.

Bake for 15 to 18 minutes or until almost done. Move dish 4 to 6 inches from heat and broil 4 to 6 minutes, or until fish flakes. Remove to serving platter and pour pan juices over fish. Garnish with parsley.

6 servings

OVENFRIED CATFISH

Catfish City Fish Market
Waukegan, Illinois

1/4 cup yellow cornmeal
1/4 cup dried bread crumbs
1/2 teaspoon salt
1/2 teaspoon paprika
1/4 teaspoon freshly ground pepper
1/8 teaspoon garlic powder
4 7-ounce catfish, farm raised
    and skinned
1/2 cup skim milk
1/4 cup margarine, melted

Preheat oven to 450°. Place oven rack slightly above middle. Spray a 9x13-inch baking dish with cooking spray.

Mix corn meal, crumbs, salt, paprika, pepper and garlic in large bowl. Dip fish in milk and coat with cornmeal mixture. Arrange fish in prepared pan and drizzle with margarine.

Bake uncovered for 17 minutes, or until fish flakes very easily.

4 servings

SEAFOOD DELIGHT

Heller Catering
North Chicago, Illinois
Chef Linda Heller

½ cup butter
1 cup chopped Bermuda onion
3 cups sliced mushrooms
1 cup dry sherry
4 cups chopped green bell peppers
4 cups chopped tomatoes
1 pound salmon fillets
1 pound (20-25) shrimp
1 pound crabmeat chunks
1 pound scallops, rinsed

In a large saucepan, melt butter. Sauté onions and mushrooms until onion is yellow. Add sherry and boil until sherry is reduced by half. Add peppers and tomatoes. Bring to boil and add in order: salmon, shrimp, crab, scallops. Bring to boil and cook 5 to 10 minutes until seafood is flaky and not translucent.

Serve with wild rice.

12 servings

SEAFOOD RAGOUT

Oak Brook Hills Hotel & Resort
Oak Brook, Illinois
Waterford Chef David J. Lodygowski

Egg wash
4 puff pastry squares
Butter
1 pound (8 to a pound) scampi,
    shelled
¼ pound sea scallops
½ pound lobster tail, cut into
    1-ounce pieces
¼ cup sherry
½ cup heavy whipping cream
Salt and freshly ground pepper

Garnish:
4 tomato roses
4 whole basil leaves

Preheat oven to 350°.

Cut puff pastry into shell shapes, egg wash top and bake 10 minutes or until light brown.

In saucepan over medium heat, melt a little butter; add scampi and sauté for approximately 1 minute. Add scallops, lobster tail and sauté an additional 2 minutes. Add sherry and reduce. Add heavy cream, bring to a boil and let reduce. Season with salt and pepper to taste.

Cut puff pastry shells in half, place seafood and sauce in bottom half of shell. Replace top half and garnish with tomato roses and basil leaf.

4 servings

ORIENTAL SHRIMP WITH GARDEN ORZO

Foodstuffs
Evanston, Illinois
Executive Chef Jay Liberman

¾ cup orzo (rice shaped macaroni)
2 jalapeño chili peppers
¼ cup minced garlic
2 tablespoons chopped fresh ginger
1 medium onion, chopped
½ cup sesame oil, divided
4 cups tomato sauce
¼ cup honey
2 tomatoes, seeded and diced
14 leaves basil, cut into
    julienne strips
1 pound shrimp (21-25 count),
    cleaned and deveined
1 green bell pepper, diced
1 red bell pepper, diced
1 yellow bell pepper, diced

Bring large pot of salted water to a boil. Add orzo and cook until done, about 5 minutes. Drain and set aside to cool.

Wearing rubber or plastic gloves, seed and chop jalapeño peppers.

Sauté garlic, ginger, onion and jalapeños in ¼ cup sesame oil until translucent, about 5 minutes. Add tomato sauce and honey, cook over low heat for 10 minutes, stirring gently. Add chopped tomatoes and basil; set aside.

Sauté shrimp in remaining sesame oil until opaque. Remove shrimp from pan and add to sauce.

Sauté peppers in same pan until done, about 5 minutes. Mix peppers with orzo. Place pepper and orzo mixture in a ring around perimeter of plate. Fill center of ring with shrimp mixture and serve.

Hint: This dish is perfect for a party, as it can be kept warm in a chafing dish. It can also be reheated in a microwave.

4 servings

SMOKED SALMON PIZZA

Zarrosta Grill
Oak Brook, Illinois
Chef Joseph Discianno

1 recipe focaccia dough (page 117)
¼ cup extra virgin olive oil
6 plum tomatoes, sliced
1 small red onion, thinly sliced
½ pound smoked Norwegian salmon
8 ounces cream cheese
Fresh dill

Prepare focaccia dough according to recipe.

Preheat oven to 450°.

Roll dough to a 12-inch diameter and ⅛-inch thickness. Brush dough with olive oil. Layer with plum tomato slices and sliced red onion. Top with smoked salmon pieces, cream cheese and fresh dill.

Bake until golden brown. Top with fresh chives, if desired. Slice into desired pieces and serve.

12-inch pizza

CHEESE BREAD

Jaqua
Chicago, Illinois
Chef John Clancy

1 cup lukewarm water (110°-150°C)
1 package active dry yeast
1/2 teaspoon sugar
3 1/2 to 4 cups all-purpose flour
2 teaspoons salt
1 1/2 cups grated sharp
    cheddar cheese
3 eggs, divided
2 teaspoons unsalted butter, divided
2 tablespoons milk

Place water, yeast and sugar in small bowl. Let stand until mixture bubbles.

Combine 3 1/2 cups flour, salt, cheese and 2 eggs in large mixing bowl. Add yeast mixture. With a wooden spoon, stir mixture until flour has absorbed liquid. Gather dough into a ball and place on clean floured surface. Knead for 10 minutes. If dough sticks to your hands, dust with a few tablespoons of flour. Continue to knead until dough is smooth.

Lightly grease bowl with one teaspoon of butter. Place dough in bowl, turning so dough is lightly coated with butter. Cover with a towel and let rise until double in size. Punch dough down and let rise a second time.

Grease 9x5x3-inch loaf pan with remaining butter. When dough has risen, punch down. Shape dough into loaf pan. Beat remaining egg and milk and brush top of loaf. Let dough rise to top of pan. Gently brush again with egg wash.

Preheat oven to 375°.

Bake for 45 minutes. Remove from pan and cool on wire rack.

1 loaf

CANDIED SWEET POTATOES

Don Zimmer
Former Manager-Chicago Cubs

6 large sweet potatoes
3/4 to 1 16-ounce box dark
    brown sugar
1/2 to 1 stick margarine
1/4 cup orange juice

Preheat oven to 325°. Grease baking dish.

Boil sweet potatoes in a large pot until tender. Peel off skin. Combine brown sugar, margarine and orange juice in a saucepan. Cook until mixture starts to boil and becomes thick. Place sliced sweet potatoes in prepared baking dish and pour mixture on top.

Bake for 30 minutes. Flip potatoes over in glaze before serving.

ASPARAGUS SOUFFLÉ

Chez Paul
Chicago, Illinois

2 pounds asparagus, cleaned
3 tablespoons butter
1/3 cup flour
1 1/4 cups milk
Salt and freshly ground white pepper
Freshly grated nutmeg
4 egg yolks
6 egg whites
Breadcrumbs

Peel asparagus and cut off hard stem part. Cook in boiling salted water 20 minutes or until tender. Drain well. Remove stringy parts; puree in food processor.

Melt butter in saucepan over medium heat; add flour and combine over low heat, stirring well with a wooden spatula until mixture foams lightly. Add cold milk and whisk to combine well. Season with salt, pepper and nutmeg to taste. Gently bring to simmer, whisking continuously until mixture starts thickening. Remove from heat and cool for 5 minutes. Add yolks one by one whisking to combine. Add asparagus puree, combine well. Taste mixture and correct seasoning, if necessary.

Butter soufflé dish and coat with breadcrumbs on sides and bottom. Tap dish to remove excess crumbs.

Preheat oven to 400°.

Beat egg whites until firm peaks are formed, but do not over beat. Fold 1/3 of egg whites into asparagus mixture and combine well. Fold asparagus/egg white mixture into remaining egg whites and combine well. Fill souffle dish to the rim.

Bake for 25 to 30 minutes. Serve immediately.

Variation: Asparagus tips can be reserved and used as a garnish or folded into souffle mixture just before adding egg whites. Canned or frozen asparagus can be used, drained well and dried in a linen towel before reduced to puree.

ASPARAGUS TIMBALE
WITH SWEET RED PEPPER SAUCE
Public Landing
Lockport, Illinois
Chef Bob Burcenski

Soured cream:
2 cups heavy whipping cream
1 cup sour cream

2 pounds asparagus
2 whole eggs, beaten
2 egg yolks
Salt
White pepper

Sauce:
1 medium sweet red pepper, cored,
    seeded and pureed
1 2 ounce shallot, finely chopped
1/4 cup dry white wine
1 tablespoon fresh lemon juice
1/4 cup chicken stock
1/2 teaspoon salt
1/4 teaspoon white pepper
1/2 cup unsalted butter

Garnish:
Sweet red pepper cut in diamond
    shapes

Soured cream: Heat cream and sour cream in saucepan stirring constantly until lightly warm to the touch (110° at the most). Place in bowl and leave at room temperature over night or until very thick.

Preheat oven to 325°. Butter eight 1/2-cup ramekins.
Break off asparagus woody ends and trim asparagus tips for garnish. Cook asparagus tips in salted water until barely cooked, 3-5 minutes. Drain, set aside. Cook remaining asparagus in water for 20 minutes or until very tender. Drain, puree in food processor and strain through fine-mesh sieve into a bowl. Add eggs and egg yolks, 1 1/4 cups soured cream; mix well. Season to taste with salt and pepper. Pour asparagus mixture into ramekins and set in water bath.
Bake for about 30 to 40 minutes or until tester is placed in center comes out clean.

Sauce: In a saucepan, combine pureed pepper, shallot, white wine, lemon juice, chicken stock, salt and pepper. Reduce to 1/4 cup. Add 1/2 cup soured cream and swirl in butter. Season to taste.

To serve: Run knife around timbales and invert on warm plate. Spoon sauce around timbale and garnish with reserved asparagus tips and diamond shaped red peppers.

8 servings

CARIBBEAN SQUASH PIE

Marjorie Vincent
Miss America 1991
Oak Park, Illinois

1 12-ounce package frozen yellow
  squash, thawed
1 egg
1 tablespoon butter
1 tablespoon cornstarch
1 tablespoon vanilla extract
½ cup sugar
1 teaspoon cinnamon
1 teaspoon ginger
1 teaspoon nutmeg
½ large can evaporated milk
Juice of ½ lemon or ½ lime
1 ready-made graham cracker
  pie crust

In a large bowl, mix squash, egg, butter, cornstarch, vanilla extract, sugar, cinnamon, ginger, nutmeg, milk and lemon juice with hand-beater or whisk for 2 to 3 minutes. Pour into large saucepan. Cook over low heat, stirring constantly until thick. Pour into pie crust and refrigerate overnight.

Garnish with whipped cream and a slice of fresh fruit.

WARM ARTICHOKE BOTTOMS, STUFFED WITH WILD MUSHROOMS & SPRING HERBS

Crickets
Chicago, Illinois
Chef John Carey

4 each 24 count artichokes
Juice of 2 lemons
12 ounces wild mushrooms,
  three types
½ cup whole butter
2 each French shallots
Salt and freshly ground pepper
2 tablespoons brandy
1 ounce fresh herbs

Trim artichokes to remove spikes with scissors. Blanch in lemon and salted water approximately 30 minutes or until tender. Clean artichokes and reserve bottom and tender inside leaves.

Preheat oven to 400°.

Slice mushrooms. Sauté mushrooms in butter with shallots, salt and pepper. Flame with brandy. When tender, cool. Stuff artichoke bottoms with wild mushroom mixture.

Bake for 10 minutes, or until artichokes are hot.

Garnish plate with artichoke leaves. Place artichoke bottom in center of plate. Dust with spring herbs and serve immediately.

4 servings

OUR FAVORITE RISOTTO
Mary Ann Childers and Jay Levine
Chicago Television Broadcasters

1 medium onion, finely chopped
1/2 cup chopped prosciutto
4 tablespoons extra virgin olive oil
1/4 cup butter
1 cup arborio rice
4 to 5 cups chicken broth, divided
1/2 cup dry white wine
1/4 teaspoon Spanish saffron
    (I use a good pinch of stems)
3/4 cup freshly grated Romano cheese
Salt
Freshly ground pepper
2 tablespoons butter

Sauté onion and prosciutto in oil and butter until onion is soft and translucent. Add rice, and cook over medium heat for several minutes, stirring gently. Add 1/4 cup of simmering chicken broth, stirring constantly. As the broth is absorbed, continue to add 1/4 cup hot broth at a time as needed, stirring continually. After 20 minutes, add wine and continue stirring. Stir saffron threads into 1/4 cup hot broth and add to risotto. All broth should be absorbed and rice should be very creamy, but still firm.

Just before serving, stir in cheese and season with salt and pepper to taste. Stir in two tablespoons of butter and serve immediately on warm plates.

Variation: You can vary the amount of prosciutto to your taste.

2 servings as main dish, 4 servings as side dish

CORN FLAKE POTATOES
Kim and Mike Singletary
Chicago Bears

1 2-pound package frozen hash
    brown potatoes, thawed
1/2 medium onion, chopped
6 tablespoons margarine, divided
1 10¾-ounce can mushroom soup
1 cup sour cream
1 cup crushed corn flakes
1 cup grated cheddar cheese

Preheat oven to 350°. Grease 9x13-inch baking dish.

Layer potatoes in bottom of dish. Sauté onions in 2 tablespoons margarine. Mix in undiluted mushroom soup and sour cream. Pour over potatoes. Melt 4 tablespoons margarine and mix in crushed corn flakes. Spread over potatoes and sprinkle with cheese.

Bake for 45 minutes covered with foil, then 10 minutes to brown cheese with foil off.

8 to 10 servings

CREAM SPINACH

The Berghoff Restaruant
Chicago, Illinois
Jan C. Berghoff

1 cup whipping cream
1 cup milk
2 tablespoons cornstarch
¼ cup milk
6 tablespoons diced onion
¼ cup melted butter
1 pound spinach, ground, cooked
Nutmeg (to taste)
½ teaspoon garlic powder
½ teaspoon ground celery seed
Salt
1 teaspoon chicken base (bouillon)
1 tablespoon steak sauce
     (A-1 sauce or Maggi seasoning)

In a small saucepan, warm cream and milk. Mix cornstarch and ¼ cup milk. Add to cream and stir constantly until thickened. Strain to remove lumps

Sauté onion in butter until light brown, add spinach, nutmeg, garlic powder, celery seed, salt, chicken base and steak sauce; heat until hot.

Add cream sauce and mix well. Cook, stirring constantly, to prevent burning. Serve hot.

5 servings

BANANA BREAD

Steve and Lori Thomas
Chicago Blackhawk

2 cups all-purpose flour
1 teaspoon baking soda
½ teaspoon salt
½ teaspoon cinnamon
½ cup unsalted butter, softened
1 cup sugar
2 eggs
1 cup mashed bananas
¼ cup orange juice
1 teaspoon vanilla
1 cup chopped walnuts, optional

Preheat oven to 350°. Grease and flour a 9x5x3-inch loaf pan.

Sift flour with baking soda, salt and cinnamon. Cream butter and gradually add sugar, beating until the mixture is light and fluffy. Beat in eggs, one at a time. Add dry ingredients, alternately with bananas and orange juice, stirring only to blend. Fold in vanilla (and nuts). Pour batter into greased loaf pan.

Bake for 1 hour. Let cool 30 minutes in pan.

1 loaf

P E N A L T Y   B O X   C H E E S E C A K E

Stu and Pam Grimson
Chicago Blackhawk

Crust:
1¼ cups graham cracker crumbs
⅓ cup melted butter
¼ cup brown sugar
1 teaspoon cinnamon

Filling:
4 8-ounce packages cream cheese
1¼ cup sugar
2 tablespoons flour
4 extra large eggs
2 egg yolks
⅓ cup whipping cream
1 teaspoon vanilla

1½ cups chopped Oreo cookies

½ cup sour cream
¼ cup sugar
1 teaspoon vanilla

Swiss Fudge Glaze:
½ cup whipping cream
4 ounces semi-sweet chocolate
1 teaspoon vanilla

Garnish:
Halved Oreo cookies
Strawberries

Crust: Mix together graham cracker crumbs, butter, brown sugar and cinnamon. Press into a 10-inch springform pan. Refrigerate crust.

Preheat oven to 425°.

Filling: In a food processor, beat together cream cheese, sugar and flour. Add eggs and yolks, mix well. Add whipping cream and vanilla. Pour half of batter on crust. Sprinkle with chopped Oreo. Pour remaining batter over and smooth with a spoon.

Bake 15 minutes, then decrease to 325° and bake 45 minutes. Mix together sour cream, sugar and vanilla. Decrease oven temperature to 350°, spread top of cake with sour cream mixture and bake 7 minutes.

Refrigerate immediately overnight.

The next day: Remove sides from springform pan.

Swiss Fudge Glaze: Scald cream in pan. Add semi-sweet chocolate and vanilla. Stir 1 minute. Remove from heat and stir until chocolate is melted. Refrigerate 10 minutes.

Pour glaze over cheesecake (it is good to let some of the chocolate drip over the side and onto the edges of your cake).

Garnish: Decorate cake with halved cookies (cut in half with a sharp knife) and a large strawberry in the middle. Enjoy!

I like to offer additional sliced strawberries to my guests.

12 to 14 servings

COCONUT CAKE

Diana and Mike Ditka
Chicago Bears

1 18-ounce white cake mix
1 14-ounce can sweetened
    condensed milk
1 15-ounce can cream of coconut
1 8-ounce carton frozen whipped
    dessert topping, thawed
1 7-ounce package flaked, sweetened
    coconut

Preheat oven to 350°. Grease a 9x13-inch pan.

Prepare cake mix and bake as directed on package. Cool in pan.

When cool, poke holes in top of cake with handle of a wooden spoon. Pour condensed milk, then cream of coconut over top. Let cake stand for 2 hours.

Spread cake with dessert topping and sprinkle with coconut. Store in refrigerator.

12 servings

CHOCOLATE BUNDT CAKE

Madame Chocolate's Kitchen
Glenview, Illinois
Elaine Sherman

1 cup Dutch process cocoa
2 cups all-purpose unbleached flour
1/2 teaspoon baking powder
1/2 teaspoon salt
3 tablespoons instant coffee powder
1 1/2 cups unsalted butter,
    room temperature
3 cups sugar
2 teaspoons pure vanilla
5 large eggs
1 cup buttermilk

Glaze:
1/4 cup light corn syrup
3 tablespoons water
2 tablespoons unsalted butter
8 ounces bittersweet chocolate,
    chopped

Preheat oven to 325°. Butter and flour a 10-inch Bundt cake pan.

Sift cocoa, flour, baking powder, salt and coffee together; set aside. Cream butter until light and fluffy in large mixing bowl. Add sugar; beat until sugar is dissolved, about 5 minutes, on high speed.

Slow mixer; add vanilla. Add eggs one at a time, beating well after each addition. Add dry ingredients alternately with buttermilk, beginning and ending with dry ingredients. Pour into prepared pan.

Bake for 1 hour and 20 minutes, or until tester inserted in center of cake comes out clean. Cool cake in pan on rack for 20 minutes; turn out on rack to cool completely. Place cake on serving plate.

Glaze: Bring corn syrup, water and butter to a boil in a 1-quart saucepan over high heat. Remove from heat; add chocolate. Blend with whisk until mixture is smooth, shiny, and cool.

Spread cooled glaze on cake. Do not refrigerate cake, simply cover gently with plastic wrap or plastic dome.

12 to 16 servings

BEST EVER LEMON PIE
Ann Landers
Syndicated Columnist

1¼ cups sugar
6 tablespoons cornstarch
2 cups water
3 egg yolks
⅓ cup lemon juice
1½ teaspoons lemon extract
3 tablespoons butter
2 teaspoons vinegar
1 baked 9-inch deep pie shell

Never-Fail Meringue:
1 tablespoon cornstarch
2 tablespoons cold water
½ cup boiling water
3 egg whites
6 tablespoons sugar
1 teaspoon vanilla
Pinch of salt

Mix sugar, cornstarch together in top of double boiler. Add two cups of water. Combine egg yolks with juice and beat. Add to rest of mixture. Cook until thick over boiling water for 25 minutes. This reduces the starchy taste. Add lemon extract, butter and vinegar and stir thoroughly. Pour into pie shell and let cool.

Preheat oven to 350°.

Never-Fail Meringue: Blend cornstarch and cold water in a saucepan. Add boiling water and cook, stirring until clear and thickened. Let stand until completely cool. With electric beater at high speed, beat egg whites until foamy. Gradually add sugar and beat until stiff, but not dry. With mixer on low speed, add salt and vanilla. Gradually beat in cold cornstarch mixture. With mixer on high speed, beat well. Spread meringue over cooled pie filling.
Bake for 10 minutes, or until brown.

8 to 10 servings

DOUG'S CHOCOLATE CHIP COOKIES
Doug and Kathy Wilson
Chicago Blackhawk

1 cup shortening, not butter
½ cup granulated sugar
1 cup packed brown sugar
1 teaspoon vanilla extract
2 eggs
2 cups plus 2 tablespoons
    all-purpose flour
1 teaspoon baking soda
1 teaspoon salt
1 12-ounce package chocolate chips

Preheat oven to 375°.
Cream shortening until very light and fluffy. Continue beating while adding granulated sugar, brown sugar and vanilla. Blend in 2 eggs. Stir in flour, baking soda and salt. Mix well. Stir in chocolate chips. Drop by large tablespoonfuls onto ungreased cookie sheets.
Bake for 10 to 12 minutes.

CHOCOLATE FONDANT

Amourette French Cafe
Palatine, Illinois
Chef de Cuisine Robert Jones

1 cup butter
8-ounces semi-sweet chocolate,
    chopped
1 cup sugar
4 eggs
2 tablespoons dark rum

Preheat oven to 350°.

Combine butter, chocolate and sugar in mixing bowl. Place over double boiler. When melted, add eggs, and whisk by hand for 2 minutes with a large whip. Add rum. Pour mixture into six 4-inch baking molds and place in water bath.

Bake for 20 minutes. Turn out on serving plates while warm and refrigerate. Garnish with fresh whipped cream and fresh raspberries.

6 servings

CELESTE'S DELICE OF CHOCOLATE WITH RASPBERRY SAUCE

Carlos
Highland Park, Illinois
Chef Don Yamauchi

3½ ounces tempered dark chocolate
8 5-inch x 1½-inch strips of plastic
    (firm but bendable)

Mousse:
3½ ounces white chocolate
2 egg yolks
1 egg
⅔ cup sugar
1¼ cups whipping cream,
    whipped
¼ cup simple syrup
    (½ cup water and ¾ cup sugar)

Raspberry Sauce:
2 pints raspberries

Garnish:
¼ cup chopped hazelnuts

Melt tempered dark chocolate in top of double boiler over hot water. Run one side of plastic strip through chocolate to coat. Fold into tear drop shape, with chocolate coated side inside. Secure with paper clip. Place on cookie sheet to cool. Stand on rim, not on sides.

Mousse: Melt white chocolate in top of double boiler over hot water. Beat yolks and egg in large mixing bowl until ribbon stage. In a small saucepan, mix sugar with a small amount of water until dissolved. Heat to 120°. Slowly add sugar to egg mixture and whip until cool. Fold in white chocolate, then whipped cream.

Simple syrup: Combine water and sugar in small saucepan. Cook over low heat until clear. Raise heat and boil for 1 to 2 minutes. Cool.

Raspberry Sauce: In blender puree raspberries and simple syrup. Strain mixture.

Fill each teardrop with mousse mixture. Remove plastic forms. Spoon sauce onto the plate, place teardrop in center and garnish with chopped hazelnuts.

8 servings

SOUFFLÉ AU CHOCOLAT

Le Titi De Paris
Arlington Heights, Illinois
Chef Pierre Pollin

2 ounces bittersweet chocolate
2 tablespoons whipping cream
Zest of 1 orange
¼ cup fine granulated sugar
2 tablespoon Kahlúa
¾ cup plus 2 tablespoons egg whites
    (about 7 egg whites), at room
    temperature

Preheat oven to 350°. Butter and sugar four individual soufflé dishes.

In a double boiler over simmering water, melt chocolate with cream. Remove from heat; add orange zest and sugar and mix for 5 minutes (can use hand mixer on low). Stir in Kahlúa.

Beat egg whites with a pinch of salt until soft peaks form. Mix a few tablespoonfuls into chocolate mixture to lighten. Gently fold in remainder. Turn batter into soufflé dishes.

Bake for 12 to 15 minutes. Serve immediately with a sauce of ¾ cup crème anglaise (page 196) mixed with 2 ounces melted white chocolate.

4 servings

GRAHAM PUDDING SQUARES

Steve Konroyd
Chicago Blackhawk

1 box graham crackers
2 packages instant French vanilla
    pudding
3½ cups milk
1 9-ounce container frozen
    Cool Whip, thawed

Icing:
3 1-ounce squares bitter-sweet
    chocolate
2 teaspoons light corn syrup
1 teaspoon margarine
1½ cups powdered sugar
3 tablespoons milk

Butter a 9x13-inch pan. Line with graham crackers. Make pudding with 3½ cups milk. Mix pudding with Cool Whip. Pour half of mixture over crackers. Layer again with crackers. Top with remaining pudding.

Icing: Heat chocolate, corn syrup, margarine, powdered sugar and milk in saucepan over low heat. Add water to make spreading consistency, if needed.

10 to 12 servings

TIRAMISU
Bice Ristorante
Chicago, Illinois
Graziano Buzzi

4 cups strong coffee or espresso, cooled
1/2 cup rum
1/2 cup Kahlúa
3 cups sugar, divided
3 packages (24 each) lady fingers
4 cups whipping cream
2 pounds mascarpone cheese
1 cup sugar
Strega liqueur, to taste
1 teaspoon vanilla extract
7 eggs, well beaten

Cocoa powder
Powdered sugar
Chocolate shavings

Line bottom and long sides of 15x10-inch jelly roll pan with parchment paper or flour and butter bottom and sides of pan.

Combine coffee, rum, Kahlúa and 2 cups sugar in bowl. Dip lady fingers in coffee mixture. Cover the bottom of the pan with 36 lady fingers.

Cheese layer: Whip cream with mascarpone cheese, sugar, liqueur and vanilla. Add eggs and mix well. Spread half of the cheese mixture over the lady fingers. Dip the remaining 36 lady fingers in the coffee mixture and layer over the cheese mixture. The fourth layer is the remaining cheese mixture spread over the lady fingers. Chill.

To serve: Sift cocoa on the top, then top with powdered sugar. Cut the tiramisu in squares and serve on plate surrounded by chocolate shavings.

20 servings

PIZZELLE COOKIE WITH FRESH FRUIT
Zarrosta Grill
Oak Brook, Illinois
Chef Joseph Discianno

1/2 pint fresh berries, in season
2 whole eggs
1/3 cup sugar
1/4 cup butter, melted
1 teaspoon anise extract
3/4 cup all-purpose flour
1 teaspoon baking powder
1/4 cup chocolate sauce
3 kiwi fruit, peeled and sliced
6 strawberries, sliced
1 quart of favorite ice cream or gelato
White chocolate shavings

Clean and slice fresh fruit.

Cookies: Prepare cookie batter by beating together eggs and sugar. Add cool melted butter and anise extract. Sift together flour and baking powder and add to egg mixture. Batter will be stiff enough to be dropped by a spoon. Spoon batter onto a hot pizzelle baker and bake until golden brown.

Paint each plate with chocolate sauce and layer with pizzelle cookie, fresh fruit and top with another pizzelle cookie. Serve along with your favorite gelato and garnish with white chocolate shavings.

Try blueberries, blackberries, or raspberries for variety.

6 servings

RAINFOREST NUT BARS
Bill Curtis
Chicago Television Broadcaster

When I had completed working on a documentary film
regarding the destruction of the world's rainforests, I hosted a gathering to screen
the finished work. I decided to offer a rainforest buffet,
featuring many of the foods based on products native to the rainforest as a
demonstration of the vast plant resources that may well
be headed toward extinction. One of the items on the dessert
buffet was a variation on an old favorite of mine, Pecan Squares - only this time
we substituted nuts from the tropical rainforest for
the pecans. One of the nuts, Brazils, can only be harvested from the
forest, and cannot be successfully grown on plantations.

2/3 cup confectioners' sugar
2 cups all-purpose flour
1/2 cup sweet butter, softened

Topping:
2/3 cup (11 tablespoons) sweet butter,
*   melted*
1/2 cup honey
3 tablespoons heavy whipping cream
1/2 cup packed brown sugar
1 1/4 cup coarsely chopped
*   macadamia nuts*
1 cup coarsely chopped Brazil nuts
1 1/4 cup halved cashews

Preheat oven to 350°. Grease a 9x13-inch baking pan.
   Sift flour and sugar together. Cut in butter until fine
crumbs form. Pat crust into prepared pan.
   Bake for 20 minutes, remove from oven.

   Topping: Mix melted butter, honey, cream and brown
sugar together. Stir in nuts, coating them thoroughly. Spread
over crust.
   Bake for 25 minutes. Cool completely before cutting into
36 squares.

36 squares

HOT FUDGE
The Village Smithy
Glencoe, Illinois
Bill Lepman

5 tablespoons unsalted butter
1 cup granulated sugar
1 cup brown sugar, packed
1 1/2 cups Dutch process
*   cocoa powder*
1 cup whipping cream
Scant pinch salt

Melt butter in heavy bottom saucepan on low heat, add
sugars, cocoa powder and whipping cream and salt.
   Cook for 30 minutes, or until smooth.

MARJOLAINE WITH RUM SOAKED BANANAS

The Dupage Club
Chef Christopher Spitz

Meringue Layers:
6 tablespoons soft butter
²/₃ cup flour
4 ounces hazelnuts, toasted
8 ounces sliced almonds, toasted
1¹/₂ cup granulated sugar

8 egg whites
¹/₄ cup sugar

Praline Butter Cream:
1 pound unsalted butter
4 ounces praline paste
8 egg whites
¹/₂ cups plus 1 tablespoon sugar
1¹/₂ teaspoon cream of tartar

Chocolate Cream:
14 ounces semi-sweet chocolate,
    chopped
4 cups whipping cream

Whipped Cream Filling:
2 cups whipping cream
¹/₂ cup sour cream
3 tablespoons powdered sugar
Meringue nuts, optional

Bananas:
3 small bananas, sliced and soaked
    in 2 shots dark rum

Meringue: Preheat oven to 350°. Butter and flour two 12x16-inch sheet pans.

In food processor, or by hand, grind hazelnuts, almonds and sugar into fine crumbs. Reserve 3 tablespoons. Whip egg whites until frothy, at medium speed. Add sugar slowly; when sugar is all added, whip whites at high speed until medium peaks form. Fold in nut/sugar mixture gently. Divide evenly between baking sheets and spread evenly to ¹/₈-inch thick. Run finger along sides of sheet pans, leaving ¹/₄-inch space between meringue and edge of pans. Bake until golden brown. Remove from oven and run spatula around edges of pan. Cut lengthwise into 3 even strips very quickly as the meringue will harden as it cools. Store in a dry place.

Praline Butter Cream: Soften butter in mixing bowl with praline paste. Whip egg whites, sugar and cream of tartar using the same method as above. Meringue and the butter mixtures should be the same consistency or the butter cream will break. Fold two together gently and chill.

Chocolate Cream Filling: Melt chocolate in a double boiler and scald cream, but do not boil. Whip the two together and chill overnight.

Whipped Cream Filling: Whip cream and sour cream together until stiff. Fold in powdered sugar and a few meringue nuts.

Assembly: Whip chocolate cream until light but not broken. Soften praline butter cream slightly. Pull out whipped cream mixture and reserve ¹/₃ for frosting.

Invert a baking sheet and cover with foil wrap. Put one meringue layer on foil and pipe layer of whipped chocolate cream, then smooth out. Put a layer of meringue on top of chocolate cream and repeat with praline butter cream and with one even layer of rum soaked bananas. Repeat with whipped cream mixture. Repeat again with chocolate, then praline cream ending with last meringue on top. Frost cake with remaining whipped cream mixture. Slice while cold but serve at room temperature.

TARTA À LA VALENCIANA

Mesón Sabika
Naperville, Illinois
Chef Francois Sanchez

Dough:
2¾ cups flour
½ cup sugar
8 ounces unsalted butter,
    cut into cubes
2 egg yolks
¼ cup heavy whipping cream
2 tablespoons orange rind

Filling:
10 ounces El Caserio cream cheese
¾ cups sugar
2 eggs plus 1 yolk
¼ cup fresh orange juice
1 tablespoon grated orange rind
1 teaspoon vanilla extract

Garnish:
1½ cups water
1½ cups sugar
Thinly sliced oranges

Sauce:
Syrup from orange garnish
Juice of 1 orange
½ cup whipping cream
1 tablespoon butter

Dough: Sift flour into bowl with sugar. Toss butter cubes into flour and coat. Crumble butter into flour until it resembles cornmeal. Combine egg yolks, cream and orange rind. Pour into flour and mix with hands until it comes together in a ball. Add extra cream if necessary. Wrap in plastic and refrigerate at least 2 hours.

Preheat oven to 350°.

Roll dough to fit a 9-inch tart pan or pie plate. Line with foil and fill with pie weights or dried beans. Bake for 10 to 12 minutes. Remove foil and weights and cool.

Preheat oven to 300°.

Filling: Beat cream cheese and sugar until softened. Scrape down bowl. Add eggs. Scrape down bowl, add orange juice, rind and vanilla. Pour into pre-baked tart shell.

Bake until set. Cool. Garnish with orange slices and serve with sauce.

Garnish: Bring water and sugar to a boil. Cook until syrupy. Remove from heat. Add orange slices. Remove orange slices after about 30 seconds and let them dry on a rack. Cut orange slices in half and arrange on tart.

Sauce: Reduce the syrup from orange garnish until it begins to caramelize, or about 10 to 15 minutes, watching very closely so it does not burn. When golden brown, carefully add orange juice, cream and butter. Serve at room temperature.

RUM VANILLA CUSTARD WITH CARAMEL SAUCE

Sandpiper
Macatawa, Michigan

¼ vanilla bean or 1 tablespoon
   vanilla extract and add last
½ cup sugar
1 cup half and half
1 cup whipping cream
10 egg yolks
¼ cup dark rum
½ cup caramel fudge
1 tablespoons dark rum

Preheat oven to 300°.

In a medium saucepan, bring vanilla bean, sugar, half and half and whipping cream to a simmer.

In a stainless steel bowl combine rum and yolks. Gradually stir cream mixture into yolks and rum, being careful not to scramble yolks, stirring with a rubber spatula or large spoon. Combine caramel and rum and divide between six 8-ounce ramekins. Pour custard into ramekins. Set ramekins in a baking dish. Fill dish with hot water to half cover ramekin.

Bake for 45 minutes to 1 hour. To check, insert small knife along the inside of ramekin and carefully ease custard away from the side. If there is no liquid present, remove and cool. Refrigerate until served.

6 servings

SUE'S MOTHER'S CABINET PUDDING

Sue Phillips
Executive Director, Infant Welfare Society

3 envelopes unflavored gelatin
¾ cup cold water
12 eggs, separated
1 cup sugar
1 cup best quality bourbon, or
   1½ cups sherry
2 dozen almond macaroons,
   crumbled
1 cup maraschino cherries, drained
   and chopped
1 cup whipping cream, whipped

Soften gelatin in cold water.

In a large bowl, using an electric mixer, beat egg yolks with sugar until thick and pale. Stir in bourbon. Transfer to top of a double boiler over simmering water. Cook, stirring constantly, until very hot and thickened. Add softened gelatin and stir until dissolved. Cool.

In a clean large bowl, beat egg whites until soft peaks form. Fold in bourbon mixture.

Pour ⅓ of bourbon mixture into a mold. Sprinkle with ⅓ of macaroon crumbs and chopped cherries. Repeat twice, ending with crumbs and cherries on top. Refrigerate overnight.

Serve with whipped cream.

Hint: If you substitute sherry for bourbon, you will need more to give pudding sherry flavor.

10 to 12 servings

JOE'S CRICKET COFFEE
Crickets
Chicago, Illinois
Created by Joe the Bartender McClure

Granulated sugar
Cinnamon
Lime wedges
3 tablespoons Grand Marnier
3 tablespoons Amaretto
10 ounces hot coffee
Whipped cream

In a bowl, mix together 2 parts sugar to 1 part cinnamon. Rim two 8-ounce stemmed glasses with lime wedge and dip in sugar mixture to form a 1-inch deep sugar ring around the top of the glasses. Hold a flame close to the sugar ring, turning the glass slowly until ring is crystallized all around.

Pour 1½ tablespoons Grand Marnier in each glass. Ignite. Holding the glasses by the stems, pour flaming Grand Marnier from one glass to the other for 10 to 15 seconds, turning glasses slowly and keeping it flamed at all times. Put out the flames.

Add 1½ tablespoons Amaretto and 5 ounces hot coffee to each glass.

Top with whipped cream and serve.

2 servings

MICROWAVE POPCORN
Joan Esposito
Chicago Television Broadcaster

Dear Infant Welfare Cookbook Committee:
I haven't sent a recipe for "Sugar Snips and Asparagus Tips"
because I don't have a recipe worthy of your cookbook.
My "specialty" is microwave popcorn!
Joan Esposito

MENUS & WINE

Menus & Wines

"During the last two centuries, throughout the world,
winemaking has been modernized extensively and this certainly will
continue in the constant search to produce
wines with grace and harmony, wines with depth and complexity,
wines that are an expression of the soil and
the artist who produced it."

Anthony J. Terlato

A special thank you to noted wine authority,
Anthony J. Terlato, CEO of Paterno Imports for sharing his knowledge
of wines and choosing the wines for our menus.
Mr. Terlato is regarded as one of the nation's most celebrated
importers and distributors of premium wines.

MEXICAN BREAKFAST
FOR TWO

Chilled and frothy fruit juice

Huevos Rancheros with Salsa Verde *

Spicy Salsa * and Sour Cream

Frijoles de Olla* "Ranch Beans"

Fresh Fruit Salad of Jicama, Orange, Lime and Cilantro

Mexican Hot Chocolate *   Café con Leche *

CHICAGO JAZZ BRUNCH

Freshly squeezed orange juice

Spicy Bloody Marys *   Lemon Zinger "South Sider" *

Smoked Salmon with Bagels and Whipped Horseradish Cream *

Cucumber, Tomato and Onion Salad *

Scrambled Eggs with Asparagus and Sweet Red Pepper *
Pork Sausages grilled over hot coals

Rhubarb Bread *   Fruit Oat Bran Muffins *

Bowl of Fresh Seasonal Fruits
Wine: "J" Jordan Sparking Wine, California

Fantasy Fudge Brownie Bars *
a.k.a. Killer Brownies

Coffee

LADIES LUNCHEON

Champagne Fruit Punch *

Rich Cream of Asparagus Soup *

Mushroom Palmiers *

Saipan Chicken Salad *
Wine: Rochioli Sauvignon Blanc, California

Chilled Lemon Souffle *
Raspberry Almond Meringue Bars *

Coffee and Tea

AFTERNOON HIGH TEA

Buttermilk Scones *
with Whipped Cream, Preserves and Orange Marmalade

Tea Sandwiches
Strawberry Cream Cheese * Watercress Lemon Pinwheels *
Curry Chicken Almond *

Marbleized Tea Eggs   *Spiced Mixed Nuts

Meringues * with
Lemon Curd * and Seedless Raspberry Preserves

Flourless Chocolate Cake *

Darjeeling Tea
Milk, Sugar Cubes, Crystalized Ginger
and Thin Fresh Lemon Slices

SWEETS TABLE

Fruit Tart Parisienne "Fresh seasonal fruit tart" *

Edinburgh Currant Tarts   *Coconut Sponge Cake *
Pecan Lassies *   Chocolate Glazed Eclairs *

Almond Cheesecake with Fresh Nectarine *
Three Layer Buttercream Mocha Cake *
Strawberries Romanoff *

Wine: Gancia Asti Spumante, Italy

HALF TIME PARTY

Good beer and wine
Beer: Baderbrau Beer, Illinois
Popcorn, peanuts in the shell, and tortilla chips

Crunchy Spicy Cole Slaw *   Prairie State Corn Bread *

Beef Chili with Limes *

Swirl Sliced Honey Baked Ham
Basket of Fresh Rye Bread
Assorted Mustards
American, Coarse-grain, German, French Mustard with Tarragon

Apple Pecan Crisp * with Ice Cream,
Hot Caramel Topping and Whipped Cream

Hot Coffee

BAND SHELL PICNIC

Chilled Avocado Cucumber Soup *   Fines Herbes Toasts *

Antipasto Tortellini *
Wine: Santa Margherita Chardonnay, Italy

Superb Carrot Cake *
Basket of Fresh Fruit

Iced Sun Tea

GREEK GRILL
FOR ALL SEASONS

Greek Tzatziki Cucumbers with Yogurt *
with Crusty Greek Bread

Greek Salad *

Marinated Grilled Leg of Lamb *
Mint Pesto *

Red Pilaf *   Lemon Artichokes *

Wine: Boutari Grande Reserve, Greece

Minted Melon Balls *
Galatobouriko "Custard Pastry" *

DINNER BUFFET

Herb Cheese Stuffed Pea Pods *
Wine: Chapoutier "La Bernadine" Chateauneuf-du-Pape, France

Sun-dried Tomato Balsamic Vinaigrette with Mixed Greens *
Fresh Bread Baquettes *

Pork Tenderloin in Dijon Sauce *
Wine: Robert Modavi Chardonnay Reserve, California

Risotto alla Milanese *

Beet and Horseradish Molded Salad *
Garlic Buttermilk Dressing *

Peach Cream Pie *

Coffee and Tea

"HEALTHY HEART" GOURMET DINNER
"No Sodium, Lower Fat and Cholesterol, Reduced Sugar"

Crostini con Broccoli Italiano *

Marinated Mushroom and Artichokes   Pita Toasts *
with Mozzarella *

Paella *
Wine: Corvo (White), Duca de Salaparuta, Italy

Orange Asparagus Salad *

Delicioso Chocolate Grand Marnier Cheesecake
with Raspberry Sauce *

Decaffeinated Espresso

Recipes developed for "Healty Heart" demonstrations by
Preventive Medicine clinic of Rush Medical Center.
Demonstrated by Infant Welfare member Suzanne Maviano.

COCKTAIL PARTY

Baked Pecan Brie * with Seasonal Fruits and Crackers
Chicken Liver Pate * with French Bread, Cornichons and Dijon Mustard

Simple Elegant Artichokes *
Served in Chafing Dish with Toast Points

Salmon Tartare Pie with Cucumber Sauce

Vegetable Spinach Dip * with Crudites
Chutney Cheese Pinwheels *   Mustard-Ham Bites *

Cocktail Meatballs with Green Olives *

Pizza di Verdura *
"Individual Vegetable Pizzas"

Platter of Assorted American Cheeses:
Vermont Cheddar, Maytag Blue and California Goat Cheese

Wine: Masi Soave Classico Superiore, Italy

ELEGANT FIVE COURSE
DINNER PARTY

Marinated Dilled Shrimp in Cabbage "Mum" *   Sesame Asparagus *
Wine: Allegrini Amarone Classico Superiore, Italy

Pasta Roselline *
"Pasta Roses"

Assorted Greens with Walnut Vinaigrette *

Tenderloin Chasseur *
Wine: Markham Merlot, California

Tomatoes d'Medici *

Nut Cream Cake *

314

PASTA BAR FOR A CROWD

Antipasto Terrine *
Chilled Italian Egg Lemon Soup *

Italian Bread Salad with Dandelion and Arugula Greens *

Pasta Con Tre Fromaggi e Noce *   Linguine with Grilled Chicken,
"Three Cheese Pasta with Walnuts"   Sun-dried Tomatoes and Pesto *

Carbonara Sauce on Tortellini *

Wines: Frescobaldi, Castello de Nipozzano Chianti Rufina, Italy
Pio Cesare Chardonnay, Italy

Italia di Frutta with Orange and Lemon *
Italian cheeses: Mascarpone, Fontina, Gorgonzola
Italian Anise Bisotti

MIDNIGHT SUPPER

Shrimp Paste * in a Crock
Tasty Crackers and Long Narrow Baguettes of French Bread
Marinated Mushrooms *

Herbed Creamy Cucumber Salad *

Gingered Chicken Breasts *
Wine: Castello Gancia, Dry Sparkling Wine, Italy

Fluffy Steamed White Rice
Fresh Green Beans
Tossed with Buttery Browned Macadamia Nuts *

Glistening Strawberry Tart *
Whipped Cream

Very Dry, Light — Fresh, tart, subtle flavor. Serve with lightly flavored dishes (seafoods, light pasta, vegetables and soups). Rieslings, Italian Chardonnay and Pinot Blanc.

Dry, Full-Flavored — Fruitier with more body. Serve with full flavored, but not sweet or spicy dishes (rich fish, poultry, game, light meats and quiche). Chablis, Chardonnay, Pouilly-Fuissé, Sauvignon Blanc and white Burgundy.

Slightly Sweet, Fruity — Fresh fruit flavors. Serve with rich spicy food ingredients. Chenin Blanc, German whites, Johannisberg Riesling.

Sweet, Full Bodied Whites — Sweet, lots of flavor, not as heavy as dessert wines. Accompanies fruits and cheeses well. German Spätlese or Auslese, Sauternes, Late Harvest Riesling.

Fruit, Light Reds — Very fresh, berrylike flavors. Serve chilled with flavorful spicy foods (sausages, pasta, ham and meatballs). Beaujolais, Chianti, light Pinot Noir and red Burgundy.

Medium-Body Reds — Rich fruit flavor. Serve with poultry, soufflés, red meat and casseroles. Bordeaux, red Burgundy, Pinot Noir, Cabernet.

Full-Body, Tannic Reds — Deep red, full flavored. Serve with game roasts, barbecue meats and spicy casseroles. Cabernet Sauvignon, Chianti, Bordeaux, Côtes du Rhône and red Zinfandel.

Rosés and "Blush" — Light colored wine made from red grapes, varies from light-dry to dark-sweet, but fresh and fruity. Serve chilled at picnics or with smoked or spicy meats. Pinot Noir Blanc, White Zinfandel, Grenache.

Sparkling — Champagnes vary greatly. Serve with zesty appetizers and light desserts. California, French and Spanish champagnes, Italian Spumante.

Aperitif — Dark colored, strong flavored wines; dry-light to sweet-heavy. Famous for stimulating the appetite. Sherry, Marsala and Madeira.

Dessert — Sweet wines made from red or white grapes with strong, rich flavors; known as a sipping wine. Serve with cheese, nuts and chocolate. Madeira, Ports (Ruby is fruity, Tawny is lighter, smoother and nuttier; serve with chocolate), Sweet Muscat, Sançère and Château d'Yquem.

CONTRIBUTORS AND TESTERS

While testing a recipe, we may make a few changes. We may add an
ingredient, eliminate one, alter a measurement, adjust cooking times, and so forth,
and yet we remain faithful to the original recipe of the creator!
It is our sincere hope that no one has been inadvertently overlooked.

Woman's Auxiliary of the Infant Welfare Society of Chicago Centers

Arlington Heights	Frankfort	Lake Bluff	Palos
Barrington	Glencoe	Lake Forest	Park Forest
Beverly Hills	Glencoe Wings	Lisle	Riverside
Burr Ridge	Highland Park/Ravinia	Mount Prospect	South Shore
Chicago Woman's Club	Hinsdale	Near North	Western Springs
Clarendon Hills	Hinsdale Juniors	North Shore	Wheaton
Downers Grove	Kenilworth	Oak Brook	Wilmette
Flossmoor	Kenwood Social Club	Oak Park-River Forest	
Flossmoor Juniors	LaGrange	Palatine-Inverness	

Ann Anderson	Sandy Biel	Linda Bussey	Marjorie A. Collins
Mary Anderson	Donna Birney	Lucy Butler	Veronica Concannon
Lani Anderson	Joan Blackburn	Rebecca Busch	Christine Connolly
Wendy Anderson	Patsy Blackburn	Donna Byram	Mildred Connelly
Kaye Angel	Kathy Blakemore	Valerie Callas	Joanne Cook
Karen Anselmo	Nona Boc	Rebecca Caleel	Lynne Grady Cornell
Nancy Apmann	Mary Ann Boorazanes	June Campbell	Carolyn Crane
Mary Arbutti	Lucy Borg	Joan Carlson	Ethel Creager
Ruby Arbutti	Dawn Boroian	Ann Carpenter	Betty Cushing
Lorraine Arenberg	Araceli Bosch	Terry Carr	Suzanne Dabbert
Cynthia Armour	Nancy Bourtsos	Barbara Carroll	Laura Dalton
Linda Asper	Beverly Brand	Kathleen Casper	Mary Jo Davia
Thelma Asper	Joan Brennan	Louise Catanzaro	Sheree Davidson
Marilyn Athas	Arlene Breuder	Betty Catlin	Nancy Davis
Julie Austin	Carolyn Broion	Linda Celesia	Peggy Deaton
Elisa Bailey	Allison Brown	Mary Lou Cesca	Nancy Dee
Jean Barclay	Jackson Brown	Rachel Chan	Judy Dehr
Linda Barder	Mel Brown	Barbara Chen	Bernadette Delmonico
Linda Barnard	Susan Browne	Holly Clark	Sue Delves
Sr. Claire Basar, RSC	Joan Bruning	Donna Clay	Alison Deniston
Ann Bates	Barbara Buck	Margaret Clayton	Lori Deprizio
Lois Becker	Barbara Buikema	Joan Clifford	Anne Devine
Inez Brown Behrns	Kay Burchett	Lynn Cloud	Rosemary Dignan
Peg Bellich	Lin Burdett	JoAnn Coghill	Adele DiNatale
Patrice Bender	Bonnie Burhans	Osa Coghill	Debbie Dipert
Barbara Benezra	Roy Burlew, III	Pam Coghill	Jacquie Doerge
Doris Berghoff	Joanne Burnham	Beverly Cole	Rosemary Doherty
Gwen Bergendorf	Karen Burry	Doris Cole	Mary Beth Donnelley
Ann Bicknell	Virginia Bussell	Sandy Cole	Mildred Donnelly

Kyle Dougherty
Diane Douglas
Gloria Duarte
Lynne Duetsch
Sally Dustin
Arlene Eckmann
Susan Ehrhardt
Nancy Eichler
Fran Ekizian
Nancy Ekizian
Pat Eldon
Jan Emmert
Laura Evans
Lauren Eula
Ann Falduto
Alice Falls
Betty Farkas
Betsy Farwell
Franchesca Fauls
Karen Fawcett
Fran Ferrazzano
Dorothy Fitch
Judy Fivian
Carol Forbes
Shanna Foster
Vickie Foster
Jeanine Fowler
Judy Frame
Nancy Franks
Bonita Friedland
Karen Fritz
Cyndi Frost
Ruth Fucik
Josie Gallagher
Nancy Gallaher
Dorothy Garrity
Patricia Gee
Diane Geiger
Kathryn George
Gay Georgi
Ellen Gerken
Judy Girten
Pat Gianone
Peggy Gilluly
Jean Glasan
Ellen Gleason
Nancy Gmitro
Linda Gonnella
Jennifer Goodsmith
Suzanne Gorden
Ginny Grane

Mary Grannis
Ann Grant
Lois Grayston
Jane Greenwood
Emilie Grimm
Bee Gruber
Dian Gruber
Lillian Gustafson
Jean Guerin
Tina Haight
Marianna Hames
Mary Hanson
Lois Harb
Sandy Harden
Diane Hassenplug
Beverly Hastings
Bobbi Hauser
Priscilla Heerens
Yvonne Held
Dorothy Helland
Linda Heller
Bonnie Hendricks
Sue Hennessy
Sally Heraty
Marilyn Helfers
Mary Henderson
Judy Herman
Marjorie Hilden
Jan Hines
June Hocter
Rosalind V. Hodgkins
Richard L. Holden
Leslie Wells Holling
Virginia Horan
Chris Howard
Mary Ann Howie
Irene C. Hulse
Pat Hunding
Linda Hurney
Joan Hurst
Candy Hoyt
Sharon Jenness
Kathy John
Sue & Chuck Johnston
Carol Jones
Vivian Kaczmarek
Kathy Kahn
Alice Karaba
Diane Karzas
Kathleen Sullivan Kaska
Carolyn Kelly

Mary Beth Kennedy
Ruth Kern
Janet Kien
Mary Kimmel
Sylvia Allen Kinney
Betty Kirka
Donna Kirkgaard
Mary Glenn Kirkland
Clarie Klein
Joan Klenk
Janet Klotz
Lola Knapple
Silvia Koch
Ruth Kolosoki
Marilyn Krafthefer
Jari Kral
Dorothy Kraybill
Anne Krebs
Donna Kristensen
Betty Kroh
Mary Lou Kroll
Ruth Krome
Sally LaCrosse
Susan Lamberson
Patti Lancaster
Lori Lankes
Pam Larsen
Annette Larson
Caryl Sue Larson
Gladys Larson
Janice Latko
Joan Latta
Lynn Leader
Marylou Lenke
Pauline Leonard
Sharon Leslie
Steven Levasseur
Ellen Levy
Peggy Lincoln
Cindy Lind
Sue Lindeman
Carol Lingenfelter
Syndee Link
Pam Liska
Sharlene Lissuzzo
Valerie Litchfield
Donna Littleton
Jeanine Parkhurst
  Lopez
Bridgette Louise
Ann Lucas

Roz Ludwig
Jeanine Lukach
Judy Luken
Kristin MacRae
Natalie Machul
Lynn Magneson
Nancy Malo
Sue Manko
Rita Mann
Liz Manz
Chris Markovitz
Carol Martinez
Charlene Mathis
Jackie Mauthe
Suzanne Maviano
Marva Maxwell
Sally Mazza
Jane McCoy
Pat McDonough
Kathy McElligott
Peg McElroy
Ruth McElwain
Charlotte McGary
Joan McGill
Darlene McGurn
Elaine McIntyre
Nanci McKeon
Jeanne McKissic
Madeleine McMullan
Mary Jane McNamee
Linda Meierdierks
Dottie Mele
Gladys Memler
Dorothy Menker
Michele Meronk
RoseAnne Merrill
Jill Metcoff
Anna Marie Meyer
Renee Meyers
Ruth Meyers
Alma Miller
Susan Miller
Carrie Mitsch
Andrea Moen
Pauline Monahan
Dolores Moncada
Donna Monco
Clare Moore
Shelia Morgan
Jean Morley
Janis Morrisroe

Susan Mortenson
Lenore Mulcahy
Ginny Munson
Suzanne Murin
Karen Murray
Linda Nelson
Mary Nelson
Betsy Neri
Stella R. New
Tudy Newlin
Janice Newman
Marsha Noble
Nancy Novit
Ann O'Brien
Marge O'Farrell
Nancy O'Mara
Sally O'Neil
Chris Ogden
JoAnne Olaes
Judith Olson
Mao Oslac
Ashley Ost
Kirsten Ost
Louise Ost
Faye Osterman
Sharon Palmatier
Shelia Palmer
Gail Paris
Grace Parkhurst
Jeanine Parkhurst
Char Pankros
Carolyn Parsons
Ruthie Parsons
Nora Partenheimer
Thea Pat
Barbara Patten
Jeanne Pavlica
Catherine Payne
Donna Peake
Beverly Pearce
Tammy Pearce
Jill Peck
Joanne Peitzsch
Maria Penland
Sylvia Penn
Elsie Perez-Pelaez
Jenny Perkins
Susan Perkins
Diane Pesce
Nancy Petkunas
Judy Petrole

Carol Pettay
Leslie Petter
Teresa Pfaff
Adrienne Phelps
Sue Phillips
Josephine Picket
Alma Pinkston
Gene Pipin
Rosalie Plechaty
Ann Pleotis
Barbara Politano
Mickie Polk
Sherry Potts
Lorna Powell
Maggie Powell
Amy Proegler
Connie Prothero
Betty Puchalski
Barbara Purdy
Linda Puryear
Karen Quinn
Louise Quinn
Joann Raber
Sarah Raines
Edna Ramsey
Mary Redmond
Darleen Reig
Ann Reiland
Louise Reis
Lita Rena
Sandy Robertson
Sandy Robinson
Karen Roche
Margaret Rogers
Helen Rogus
Maria Romero
Cindy Rosman
Louise Ross
Angie Rossetti
Susie Roudebuch
Sarah Rowland
Robbie Ryden
Marlene Sanders
Minnie Sandstedt
Jean Sauer
Jacque Schafer
Ann Schenck
Randy Schorle
Carol Schuetz
Mike Schuetz
Nancy Schuetz

Dorothy Schulenberg
Helen Schultz
Leanne Schuneman
Kim Scodro
Laura Scodro
Karen Sebela
Terry Shaker
Sally Shearon
Charlotte Shestokas
Nicoline Shields
Sandra Shrear
Georgie Shubalis
Mary Sido
Kathy Siefken
Gail Simek
Marilyn Siska
Mary B. Smith
Cindy Smurda
Rosalie Snyder
Chris Socher
Nancy Soder
Sharon Sodikoff
Brenda Sollitt
Kathy Sorrell
Rose Sowsky
Helen Speir
Linda Spicer
Shar Spurgeon
Sonya Stahl
Jennifer Stambik
Grace Stearns
Lindy Steeves
Nancy Stewart
Kathy Stinnette
Mary Ann Stitak
Gene Stoerzback
Gisela Stole
Mary Stolz
Jane Stone
Joan Stone
Trish Storino
Susan Strachan
Sharon Streb
Dee Stuart
Dee Stubbs
Luella Stubbs
Christine Sullivan
Eileen Sullivan
Joan Sweenie
Cynthia Swinson
Sandra Szejner

Pat Taylor
Luella Tedtman
Vera Tell
Shari Templin
Ursula Tetreault
Ursula Thebault
Carolyn Theim
Judi Thomas
Charlene Thompson
Jann Thompson
Linda Thompson
Becky Throckmorton
Elizabeth Tipton
Gloria Tison
Michael Tison
Shannon Tridle
Cherie Troglia
Janet Tucker
Anne Turner
Janet Turzak
Liz Twede
Cathy Ugron
Debbie Upp
Maggie Van Dyk
Penny Van Horn
Andy Vaughan
Judie Wagner
Penny Wainwright
Kathy Waterloo
Wendy Watkins
Jane Weeden
Patricia B. Wehner
Peg Weis
Mary Weiss
Suzanne Weinzelbaum
Barbara Westover
Sally Whipple
Miriam Whitaker
Elizabeth White
Valerie Wiley
Mary Jo Williams
Sue Williams
Alice Wilton
Julie Wilson
Barbara Wing
Kay Wing
Dian Witt
Susan Wittmer
Gail Wolff
Anne A. Wood
Sue Yochim

Order Form

Please send _____ copies $22.95 each _____
    For books sent to Illinois
    address add 8% sales tax   1.84 each _____

    Add shipping & handling   3.00 each _____

Total   _____

Please make your check payable to:
INFANT WELFARE COOKBOOK

Please charge to: _____ Master Card   _____ VISA

Card Number:

— — — — — — — — — — — — — — — —

Expiration Date   __ __ __ __

Signature _____

Sugar Snips & Asparagus Tips
2751 N. Clybourn, Chicago, IL 60614
(312) 929-7720

Name _____
Address _____
City _____
State _____ Zip_____
Daytime Phone _____

Please allow three weeks for delivery.
If you wish cookbooks to be mailed
to other addresses, please enclose
additional names and addresses on
a separate piece of paper.

Price subject to change.

Thank you for your order.
All proceeds from the sale of
Sugar Snips & Asparagus Tips
will be used to benefit
**The Infant Welfare Society
of Chicago**

Order Form

Please send _____ copies $22.95 each _____
    For books sent to Illinois
    address add 8% sales tax   1.84 each _____

    Add shipping & handling   3.00 each _____

Total   _____

Please make your check payable to:
INFANT WELFARE COOKBOOK

Please charge to: _____ Master Card   _____ VISA

Card Number:

— — — — — — — — — — — — — — — —

Expiration Date   __ __ __ __

Signature _____

Sugar Snips & Asparagus Tips
2751 N. Clybourn, Chicago, IL 60614
(312) 929-7720

Name _____
Address _____
City _____
State _____ Zip_____
Daytime Phone _____

Please allow three weeks for delivery.
If you wish cookbooks to be mailed
to other addresses, please enclose
additional names and addresses on
a separate piece of paper.

Price subject to change.

Thank you for your order.
All proceeds from the sale of
Sugar Snips & Asparagus Tips
will be used to benefit
**The Infant Welfare Society
of Chicago**

I would like to see **Sugar Snips & Asparagus Tips** in the following stores in my area:

Store Name _____

Address _____

City_____ State_____ Zip _____

Store Name _____

Address _____

City_____ State_____ Zip _____

400001

I would like to see **Sugar Snips & Asparagus Tips** in the following stores in my area:

Store Name _____

Address _____

City_____ State_____ Zip _____

Store Name _____

Address _____

City_____ State_____ Zip _____

400001